'Billy' Hope

Psychic Photographer
"Extra"- ordinaire!

Controversy, Proof, Vindication

compiled and commented on
by
Ann E. Harrison

Published by
Saturday Night Press Publications
England

.

www.snppbooks.com
snppbooks@gmail.com

ISBN 978-1-908421-58-6

www.snppbooks.com

Cover design by Ann Harrison - Saturday Night Press Publications.

Dedication

*to all those who knew and trusted in the
work of this man,
and all those who believe in him now
I give this retrospective
that their belief can be knowledge.*

Acknowledgements

My heartfelt thanks go:

To all those unseen folks who have guided and nudged me to look here and there to find the information I needed.

To Paul J. Gaunt, Curator of Britten Museum and Library who guided me to look at books and publications I had not heard of during my research week at the Arthur Findlay College Study Week, and permission to use the excellent photograph of William Walker with the "extra" of Arthur Smedley, from the Britten Library and Museum archive.

To IAPSOP for their amazing on-line archive of publications of more than 100 years ago.

To Leslie Price for permission to quote from his letter in 'Psychic News' of 27 years ago.

To the Editor of 'Psychic News' for permission to reprint the article and portions of the letters that set me on the journey 27 years ago.

To Anabela Cardoso for permission to quote from an edition of the ITC Journal.

To Gerald O'Hara for permission to use the photographs from his book.

And finally to Lionel Owen, whom I met for the first time in the closing stages of writing. Having heard of him and his knowledge of Billy Hope for so many years, I cannot thank him enough for the conversations we have had and his insightful Foreword.

Thank you all.

Without your help I could not have achieved this investigation – verification and what I hope is a tribute to Billy Hope's work.

Contents

Appendices

Sources

Journals

Light, (many editions from 1908-1933.)
The Two Worlds (many excerpts 1915-37)
Psychic Science, (British College of Psychic Science Journal, 1922-33)
The Lyceum Banner (1916 & '33)
International Psychic Gazette (1917 & '33)
Psychic News (1995)
Journal of the Society for Psychical Research (May 22 p 271-283,   Jan 23 p4-10; July 23 p112-114 ;   Jan 24 p 190-199; Mar 24 p226-228.)
Proceedings of the Society for Psychical Research (1933)

Books

"News from the Next World" vols 1 & 2 (Rev. C.L. Tweedale, 1947)
"Man's Survival After Death"   (Rev. C.L. Tweedale, 1920)
"The Case for Spirit Photography" (Sir Arthur Conan Doyle) 1922
"Autobiography of Alfred Kitson" Alfred Kitson
"Death is her life" story of Lilian Bailey, (W.F. Neech, 1957)
"Battling Bertha, the biography of Bertha Harris" (M. Leonard, 1975)
"When an Animal Dies" (Sylvia Barbanell, 1955)
"Photographing the Invisible" (Prof. James Coates, 1911)
"Proofs of the Truths of Spiritualism" (Rev. Prof. G. Henslow, 1919)
"The Search for Truth" (Harry Price,1942)
"Spirit Photography" (Major Tom Patterson 1965)
"Dead Men's Embers" (G.O'Hara, 2006)
"Faces of the Living Dead" (Paul Miller, reprint 2010)
"Blue Island"   (Estelle Stead & Pardoe 1922)
"History of Spiritualism" vol2 (Sir Arthur Conan Doyle, 1926)
"Vital Message" (Sir Arthur Conan Doyle, 1918)
"Spiritualistic Experiences of a Lawyer" 1937/8
"Miracles in Modern Life" (Rev J. Lamond)
"Photographing the Invisible" (Permutt, 1988)
"Experiments in Psychics" (F.W. Warrick, 1939)

William "Billy" Hope 1864 – 1933

Photograph by Dora Head, Holland Park Ave. for *Psychic Science,* 1924.

Foreword

It is with much pleasure I respond to the request to write a foreword to this excellent volume about Spirit Photography in general and the mediumship of William (Billy) Hope in particular.

Billy Hope has featured in my life for many years, especially since I inherited from a much loved Aunt, many of his spirit photographs. These had been given to her by her eldest brother, Robert, who sat with the Crewe Circle on many occasions. Once these photographs came into my possession, I decided to investigate Hope's mediumship as far as I could and also to create a slide presentation using the photographs to show to as wide an audience as possible. This I have done, not only in the UK but also in countries overseas, including Japan. Interestingly the Japanese referred to such mediumship as 'thoughography' as they were convinced the images were thought forms. That some spirit photos are, seems to be confirmed by some of the experiments referred to in this book. The leading exponent of thoughtography in Japan once visited William Hope in Crewe and they had a long discussion about their respective psychic gifts.

I gave my first presentation in the United States, at the Spiritualist church in Santa Barbara. Among the audience was an excellent British medium, at that time unknown to me. This was George Daisley who had moved to live near Santa Barbara several years earlier. George was one of that select band of mediums who demonstrated their gifts at the Royal Albert Hall before hundreds of people in post war Britain. Following my lecture we became firm friends and remained so until his passing. George had known Billy Hope and he had seen so many fraudulent photographs passed off as genuine in lectures in the States, he came to my lecture to scoff but as he told me afterwards, stayed to admire.

This admirable volume by Ann Harrison is a timely addition to books on this subject. Timely because, due to the emergence of digital photography and 'Photoshop', it is a subject much neglected today. During my researches I became convinced that the relatively recent discovery of dark energy and dark matter could provide us with an explanation for the way spirit photographs are produced. Though Earthly scientists currently have no real understanding of dark matter and dark energy, they just calculate they must exist, the spirit world referred to them long before scientists even suspected their existence.

In his book '*The Lowlands of Heaven*', published in 1920 and written by spirit through automatic writing, George Vale Owen wrote the following:- "Perhaps if we endeavour to enlighten you on the chemistry of the heavenly bodies it may be both interesting and helpful to you. We do not mean the physical aspect of science, as understood by modern astronomers, but the deeper study of their constitution." He goes on to explain that in addition to the physical matter in each solar system there are particles which are between the physical and the spiritual which are too sublimated to register on any physical measuring instrument then available. Such particles, he says interestingly, may be used and acted upon by gravity in both systems (physical and spiritual). They are the means by which spirit bodies are clothed so as to be visible on the photographic plate and sometimes even to the human eye. (Materialisation). Notice that all those years ago spirit used the word particles. To me that is as clear a reference to dark energy as you can get. Furthermore, the guide of physical medium George Robertson explained in the 1920's that by an effort of will he was able to take the energy (particles?) circulating among the sitters at a seance and convert it into temporary physical form (ectoplasm). This reinforces my view that mind is probably the greatest but least understood power in the universe, that dark energy and dark matter can be manipulated by it and possibly by nothing else. An example too of Einstein's famous equation $E=MC^2$ but a reversal of the experiment that produced the atomic bomb.

I have always been convinced of the genuineness of Hope's mediumship and due to my lectures, became fairly well known as a kind of expert. So much so that when the National Museum of Photography, in Bradford, England, decided to hold an exhibition of super normal photographs, they asked me to provide some of mine for use in the exhibition. They said that before using them they would carry out tests. Subsequently they wrote to me saying whilst not agreeing they were spirit photographs, "they were satisfied all were genuine photographs and what was shown on them was what had been received through the lens of a camera. None were double exposures or had been interfered with in any way."

This book is a most valuable contribution to general understanding of a fascinating subject, giving, as it does, examples of clear photographs of people no longer living on Earth. Photographs that cannot be explained through the normal processes of photography. These photographs are accompanied by testimony from unimpeachable sources. This did not stop those who for their own reasons, tried to prove they were fraudulent. A valuable function of this book is to provide, in detail, not just these allegations but also the intelligent and detailed exposure of their scurrilous nature. It is astonishing the lengths to which some people were prepared to go to undermine this wonderful source of evidence of the continuity of life and the comfort it brought to so many sorrowing relatives and friends. It is one of the few forms of mediumship where the evidence can be taken home by the investigator.

I sincerely hope this book will encourage careful experimentation in spirit photography and scotography in future. Claims that digital photography makes such experiments worthless, is bogus in my view. Yes there are ever more sophisticated ways to alter photographs but such can be detected by equally sophisticated means. People need not be afraid to experiment but they do need to ensure such experiments are carefully conducted so as to avoid the possibility of fraud or deception.

I warmly congratulate Ann on her detailed research and for producing a fascinating and intellectually disciplined addition to the written material on this much neglected form of mediumship.

Lionel Owen.

October 2022

NOTE. – *The image of the extra imprinted within the closed slide is formed by psychic light shining, or operating, in the space between the closed shutter and the plate; and not by the said light passing through the closed shutter.*

Rev. Charles L. Tweedale
"Vindication of William Hope"

Introduction

There are very few good physical mediums — there are very few physical mediums *per se*, but each one has his/her own particular expertise in an aspect of the phenomena. Some are extremely good at materialisation, some transfiguration, some the direct voice, others independent direct voice – voices that come from the air right away from the medium – some produce voices so quiet that they need an instrument to amplify them – what is known as a trumpet.

Others, many years ago, developed the ability to influence photographic plates. It is of one of these mediums I want to write; to draw together the published writings of a hundred years ago – and more; to set straight the record which has persisted of the wonderful ability of the medium —nay—the two mediums— known as the Crewe Circle.

So let me begin.

Twenty-seven years ago when I had experienced very little psychic phenomena, I was intrigued and excited by an article in the *Psychic News*. (see overleaf)

I wanted to know more.

A few weeks later a letter appeared in the Correspondence column, vilifying the inclusion of the Easter Message plate, as "everyone" knew Hope was a fraud and it had been "proved many times." I was puzzled. If this was so, why would such a prestigious publication republish an event after 85 years if it was a fraud?

I had seen the photos of the Harrison, Besant and Hudson families with "spirit extras" taken by this photographer, and knew the history behind them; also those of the Cowell-Pughs and Battens – all well respected Middlesbrough Spiritualist families. Tom Harrison (later to be my husband) had told me how the plates would be developed in the bathroom, some even at the Hudson's house (later to be his in-laws) and held up to a gaslight to see if there was an "extra" on the glass plate before they were printed. How could they be fakes? Why would someone suggest they were?

Within a month, Tom on one of his monthly visits to see a 90-year-old spiritualist in Sheffield, borrowed a book from him, bought seventy-three years earlier. It was Sir Arthur Conan Doyle's *A Case for Spirit Photography*, written in defence of the medium following a

Spirit world delivers Easter sermon of peace

A REMARKABLE Easter sermon from the spirit world, received in a seance held by medium William Hope in 1910, was read in the parish church of a dignitary who took part in the test sitting.

The perfect script was so small that a very strong lens was needed to decipher the 84 lines which testified to the survival of the human spirit.

The Venerable Archdeacon Colley — he was Rector of Stockton, near Rugby, at the time of the seance — was a keen photographer of 50 years standing.

Colley bought a light-proof packet of photographic plates, which was then held between the hands of six Spiritualists present for just 39 seconds.

He then loaded the plates into his own camera — which he set up and focused in the rain outside the medium's house — and Hope then merely pressed the bulb.

When the plates were developed — again, by Colley himself — one was found to contain 1,710 words written in perfect copperplate script by an unknown spirit entity.

Colley was so delighted with the result of the experiment that he had the plate reproduced for distribution, entitling the script: "Spiritual resurrection: Being a sermon for Easter, written by no mortal fingers."

The script's words are as pertinent today as they were over 80 years ago.

"Everlasting life," it assures us, "pulsates in every faculty. There is, therefore, a spirit life."

In the eyes of God, the communicator points out, "there are no dead; all who have been still are, their spirits have not been spent as a lightning flash, they are still living, loving, conscious and still active."

It goes on to explain the wonderful reunion that takes place when a soul eventually meets loved ones in the spirit world

"We tell you that neither life, nor death, nor principalities, nor powers, nor height, nor depth, nor anything else shall separate you from the love of God and your loved ones," the messenger from the Other Side assures us.

William Hope — he passed in 1933 — was one of the greatest spirit photographers of all time.

The Crewe-based medium and carpenter discovered his unique psychic ability by accident in 1905.

He and a friend had been photographing one another on a Saturday afternoon. When one plate was developed, though, an extra figure could be seen, that of a transparent woman, behind whom the brick wall was clearly visible. This was the first of many such photographs upon which spirit extras appeared.

A circle was formed together with six friends in order to develop his gift, which he refused to commercialise in any way.

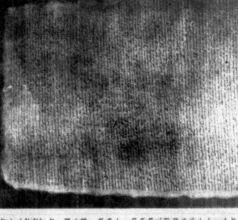

ABOVE can be seen a replica of the script inscribed on photographic plate during a 1910 seance held by medium William Hope.

P.N. 15/4/95.

Psychic News. Published by Psychic Press Ltd at 2 Tavistock Chambers, Bloomsbury Way, London WC1A 2SE. Tel: 071-405 3340 and 3345. Origination by Psychic Press Ltd at our Tavistock Chambers address. Printed by the Chiltern Press, Reans Road, Amersham, Bucks. Post production by Genesis, 71-79 Waterside, Chesham. Psychic News is obtainable from newsagents. Annual postal subscription: inland £26.00, overseas £32.00/US $66.00. Payment may be made by sterling or US dollar cheque, by international money order, to Post Office Giro account no 548 9052, or Access and Barclaycard. Advertisements appearing in Psychic News do not necessarily reflect editorial policy. No responsibility can be accepted for unsolicited manuscripts, articles, photographs, cassettes, etc. ©Psychic Press Ltd.

ISSN 0033-2801
15

charge of fraud by Harry Price and the Society for Psychical Research (S.P.R.).

This was a door to another world. I devoured the words and began to understand how despite hundreds of people confirming the appearance on photographic plates of images of deceased loved ones just ONE person could cry 'FRAUD' and it was believed and accepted above all others. And 70+ years later some still believed it, despite the many positive responses from known and unknown sitters, researchers and experimenters.

As it approached 100 years from the original outcry, I decided to try to solve the puzzle. I was given the opportunity of delving into the archives of publications of the time at the Arthur Findlay College. I spent many hours searching others preserved in the IAPSOP site on the 'net', as well finding detailed records in the books lining the shelves in my small study, to bring you "watertight" and moving accounts from the ten years following Price's "exposure" – as well as those from the years before William Hope was well known. It has not been an easy journey and I have to say there is more to the Price-Hope controversy than I first thought. Unravelling it has been a challenge – and there were others.

Was William Hope a true medium with a rare and particular gift — or a trickster as some believed?

Even as I compile this book, the *Daily Mail-on-line* recently published this article:

"The first 'ghosts' caught on camera: How these 'spirit photographs' had the world captivated in the 1920s... but all wasn't as it seems..."

The reporter has obviously not done a thorough search but is maintaining the fable of "proved fraud", and has derived his 'copy' from many previous pieces, and in using the resources of the National Media Museum inadvertently given us valuable photos. One of which I have been able to be add to Chapter 21.

I have placed events in chronological order as far as possible and added some as Appendices for further "back up" reading. I decided that the best way to give you a more balanced view of the action was to compile verbatim accounts, letters and editorials of the time, rather than transpose them into my words, in the hope I can present a reasonably balanced case – though having worked through all the records I do believe he had a genuine gift and fervent wish to bring comfort to the bereaved.

For you to differentiate between the reports and my comments I have chosen to use two different fonts. This one I'm using for the Introduction and comments etc. and this – the other font for the reports and quotations which tell the story. Only a little difference but in a parapgraph it is clearly seen. By doing this I hope that you are able to follow the flow.

I make no apology for the quality of the images. I have given you a as wide a selection as possible from as many sources as possible and have only changed them from sepia to grayscale and lightened or darkened as needed with Photoshop. No other changes have been made. Unfortunately those 'lifted' from *The Two Worlds* are very 'grainy' However, I felt they were important to give you an over-all view of the evidence of the time.

There is a great deal of talk of Hope having used pre-prepared plates on which were "ghostly" faces draped in a fine substance. These plates were then substituted for the sitters own plates to provide a psychic "extra". In an attempt to resolve the anomaly of the ghostly "extra" on a prepared plate I turned to the internet and to my niece who is a photographer. This was the response from www.techradar.com

> **"The first exposure or layer of the image serves as the <u>base layer</u> upon which elements of the second frame will blend into. The second layer is just as important as your base, and it can be the hardest layer to shoot. For double exposures that show ghostly apparitions, you're more likely to use the same scene for both layers. The only difference is, when shooting the second layer, you'll have your subject move out the frame or to a different position to get that translucent, ghost-like appearance."**

My niece confirmed this – the first exposure is behind the second.

So, the use of a 'prepared plate' would mean the "extra" appeared *behind* the sitter!

Most of the photographic examples in this book show the fine energy or drapery *in front of the sitters* and were taken under strictly observed conditions so could not be from a previously prepared plate.

Some extras have no drapery and, if small and round, it was suggested that they were produced by using a small Flashlight device to imprint them on to the plate. There are several of these – but is it not possible the spirit teams were also experimenting with different forms depending on the sympathetic energy available?

See what you make of it.

Ann Ellis Harrison
    October 2022

Hope of Crewe–a Brief History

As the Rev. Charles Tweedale wrote in his chapter 'Hope of Crewe'[1] so do I —"In his birth certificate, which lies before me as I write, his full Christian name is given as William. He was born at Moor Side, Worsley, near Swinton, in the Manchester district, on December 10th, 1864."

He was the son of Thomas and Jane Hope and his father is described as a carpenter.

Felicia Scatcherd wrote this account of his early life, in Conan Doyle's *The Case for Spirit Photography*:

"His first memory [of seeing spirit] is of having scarlet fever when he was four years old. During the fever he used to see all sorts of faces peering at him through the doorway and became so frightened that he screamed for his father to come and send them away. Now that he knows about clairvoyance, he thinks otherwise of those visions. He lost his mother when he was nine and remembers little about her. When asked did he grieve much for his mother's death, he replied that he was brought up in a religious family, his father being a local preacher. ... Mr. Hope was well cared for by his mother as long as he had her, and afterwards by his stepmother. "She was a good woman: and I had an aunt of a religious frame of mind who also kept an eye on me."

By the time William was sixteen the family was living on Chorley Road, Worsley and his father, now remarried, is described as a joiner /draper; while William was now an Apprentice Plumber.

As to how his life developed thereafter there are varying accounts and this report gives us some clue.

Rev. Tweedale writes:

"Growing up to manhood he obtained employment in Liverpool, and remained there until the works closed down. Then he opened a drapery business near Blackpool, but trade was not to be his forte, and returning to the Manchester district he was employed in a dye works near Pendleton."

In 1886 he married Mary Atherton. They had two children, Jane and Harold, born in the Swinton-Pendleton area in the next three years. Was it in these years, before moving to Cheshire, his interest in

---

1. *'News from the Other Side'* p219

photography blossomed? Rev. Tweedale tells us that Hope's youngest son, Arthur, told him:

"at this time amateur photography coming to the fore, he was keenly interested, and he made a camera out of an old box and began to study the art."

In the 1880s glass 'Dry' plates had only just come in and one report[2] suggests it may even have been a "tin-type" plate he used for the first experiments. In fact the following article implies it was a normal glass plate which needed developing and printing.

In 1914 Glasgow Association of Spiritualists invited Mr. W.J. West the photographic expert to attend "a series of séances to be given by Wm. Hope of Crewe". This was the first visit and as they said they did not wish to be "hoaxed". An account in *The Two Worlds* in 1937 of an address he gave to the Leeds S.P.R , Mr West says:

"Interrogating him in my Glasgow office, he said to me:

"The first spirit photograph that I took came about in this way. I should say it was about thirty years ago, I was employed in a bleach works, near Manchester. I had become a bit interested in photography, in an amateur way, and one day in the dinner hour I put a workmate of mine against a wall to have his photograph taken. When I began to develop the plate, I thought the whole thing was spoiled. There was what looked like a blur on the plate, but in making a print I saw it was no blur at all, but a woman's face.

How it came there I did not know but thinking the plate must somehow or other have been exposed before, I handed the photograph to my workmate. His face went as white as a sheet. 'That face!' he gasped 'It's the face of my dead sister!'

I was as much staggered as he was. I had never seen his sister and did not even know she was dead. The whole thing was a mystery to me until one of the men at the works came along. He had been interested in Spiritualism and told me it was a 'spirit-photograph'. Eventually—though a Salvationist—I became deeply interested in Spiritualism and began to develop my gifts as a psychic photographer, with the result that I have been able to take hundreds of such photographs of the departed. How the spirit comes to be photographed is about as much a mystery to me as it is to you."

If this interview was in 1914 then we must assume that these first spirit photographs must have been in the late 1880s while he was still in Lancashire.[3]

By 1891 the Hope family were living in Wharton Bridge Works, Cheshire, where he is described in the Census return as a painter.

---

2. '*Photographing the Spirit World*', by Cyril Permutt.
3. See also *Light* p.222; April 2nd 1921

From this entry it looks as though he took what work he could. The family grew again with another daughter, Annie, born in 1892.

Ten years later, having returned for a short time to Swinton in Lancashire, where their third daughter, Florence, was born, they were back in Cheshire, in Winsford. Jane, the eldest daughter had left home and was working as a servant in Winsford. On the Census for 1901 he is now registered as 'John', a 'Photographer on his own account' working from home. All other family members are as previously entered and tie in with later entries too. So why the change of name?

It must have been better than working at the saltworks or a dye factory and he saw an opportunity[4]. Did spirit images appear on some of the photos?

There is no record of that happening but William, or as he was generally known, 'Billy,' found that, although a Salvationist, he needed to know more about Spiritualism and in 1905, about a year after they had moved to Crewe, he visited the Spiritualist Church in Crewe. It happened that on that evening a visiting medium told a woman in the audience that she had a potential for mediumship and after the meeting he approached the woman and her husband, who had been playing the organ, and told them of his photographs. They agreed to form a circle for the development of this gift, and with three other sitters their adventure began.

He lived at 50, Oakley Street for the rest of his life. Their family was not without sorrow as their daughter, Jane, died in 1908 and their son Harold died just two years later in 1910 aged 22. However, there was another addition to the family in the form of Arthur born in 1909.

The Buxtons who lived a few doors down the street later moved a few streets away to a larger house at 144 Market Street where the sittings for psychic photographs were later held.

In an interview for *Light* in 1921 it is revealed that:

"Mr. Hope has laboured in his little workshop at Crewe making picture frames, and at the same time supervising a drapery business[5]. This is his sole means of earning a livelihood, for he emphatically denies that he has ever accepted fees for his services as a psychic photographer."

In the census returns for 1911 and 1921 he returns to being William but still describes himself as a photographer – adding in 1921 "in a small way" which is then crossed out by the Recorder to read "on own account."

---

4. As my great-grandfather did. He moved his family to the North-East around Newcastle and set up a 'Photographic Studio' to provide opportunities for the residents of the area to have their images immortalised.

5. "supervising a drapery business" possibly refers to Annie's occupation as a Dressmaker (1911) and Florence in the 1921 census as a "Machinist on own account" –and in particular – "Pinafores"

One of only two references to him being a photographer was made by William Walker in a letter to Dr A. Wallace in a letter in *Light,* August 30th 1913 – "*The fact of the medium being a photographer* does not shut my eyes nor yet prevent me exercising vigilance at the séance." (The other reference is on page 56.)

In some of the accounts in the following chapters, the style of Hope's handwriting comes up when sceptics have challenged the veracity of the copperplate writing received in psychographs. It has been suggested that he could have faked them. Before 1911 the census forms were completed by an official but subsequently the main occupant had to complete and sign. Here on the census form is an example of his writing and also his signature .

Extract from the Census for 1921 (Crewe, 50 Oakley Street)

Signature from the Census for 1921

That is the historical side of the background to our story but what of William Hope himself? How did others see him over the years?

Sir Arthur Conan Doyle wrote in 1922:

"Hope is a man who gives the impression of being between fifty and sixty years of age, with the manner and appearance of an intelligent working-man. His forehead is high and indicates a good, if untrained, brain beneath it. The general effect of his face is aquiline with large, well-opened, honest blue eyes, and a moustache which is shading from yellow to grey. His voice is pleasant, with a North Country accent which becomes very pronounced when he is excited. His hands with their worn nails and square-ended fingers are those of the worker, and the least adapted to sleight-of-hand tricks of any that I have seen.

He gives an impression of honesty and frankness, which increases as one comes to know him more closely, who seemed to me from manner and appearance to be less likely to be in a conspiracy [together with Mrs Buxton] to deceive the public.

Hope is not in a strict sense a professional medium. I have never met anyone who seemed to me less venal than he. He charges the ridiculous sum of 4s. 6d. per dozen for prints from the negatives obtained. This sum is calculated upon the average time expended at the rate of his own trade earnings."

Ernest Oaten said of him:

"Mr. Hope was a man of no education, but he had an alert and quick mind. Conjurors and researchers have gone to the most absurd lengths to lay definite traps for him, but his quick mindedness and psychic sensitiveness generally made it easy for him to see through them.

I knew him personally and spent many hours with him in other pursuits and conversations than that of Spirit photography and will always cherish the memory of a simple, kindly, erratic man, slovenly in his photographic work, variable in his temperament, but a man who could be a true friend."

James McKenzie, wrote in 1922;

"I can only say that I have never found Mr. Hope, during the few years I have known him, show the least inclination to act otherwise than as a most honest and straightforward man. I have, during the past two years, had very close relations with him at the College, and have always found him straight. No complaint of fraud has been made during this time, and many have been greatly cheered and comforted by remarkable results obtained through his mediumship."

Bernard Munns, the artist, having worked with him in 1919 wrote:

"My experience of him was that he knew very little of the technical side of photography and that duplicity was absent from his character." (see Ch 11.)

James Norbury, Editor of the *Lyceum Banner*[6] writing in 1933 says:

"I do not know quite what I expected when I arrived at Crewe but I certainly did not expect a funny little man, in a dirty old cap, with a face wreathed in smiles, and a welcome in every word, to open the door to me at

---

6. The *Lyceum Banner* is the journal of the educational sector of the Spiritualist Movement founded back in 1890.

144, Market St. With Billy Hope one glimpsed a faith so sublime, a surety in the guiding hand of God so certain, that one's own halting acceptance gained new re-assurance, a vitality that was stronger than anything one could build into one's philosophy of life from reading tomes or burning the midnight oil for years."

James Coates, the photographer wrote in 1921:

"Take Mr. William Hope, possibly now the greatest living psychic photographer. I know him to be positive, lacking in tact, careless to a degree, and not always too thoughtful about those little niceties of care, give and take, in his relation to others or his patrons as he might be. But I have no doubt whatever of the genuineness of his mediumship. A man of integrity, with a character of unusual Christian sweetness. His simplicity, nay, even inefficiency in matters photographic, was only equalled by his sincerity and impulsive warmheartedness."

Mr G.H. Lethem J.P. Editor of *Light* wrote in the *London Magazine:*

"All those who knew Mr Hope know that he is no magician,but just a simple, earnest, God-fearing man."[7]

Mr. James Douglas, Editor of the *Sunday Express*, wrote of Hope, with whom he had experimented:

"He is uneducated. He is homely. He is humorous. He is simple. He is religious. He seems quite artless and sincere. Altogether he is an amazing character." [8].

Lady Glenconner said in *Light* 1919:

"I have known Mr Hope for close on three years, and I have pleasure in introducing him to you as my friend, and a man of integrity and the utmost honesty of purpose.

See more of these 'Observations' on "Billy" Hope in Chapter 24.

From here on I shall call him William, for that is how the writers of the time addressed him.

7. *Light,* 1920 (p133) (Quotation from Warrick *Experiments in Psychics*)
8. *Daily Express,* 9th Dec., 1921. (Quotation from Warrick *Experiments in Psychics*)

People you will meet along the Way

Having spent more than three years working through 100 year old journals, magazines, and books to me these people are as familiar as old friends, but their backgrounds and status may be unknown to you. To give you some perspective of their 'standing' in the accounts that follow I introduce them here. They are presented, as near as possible, in order of appearance, as are the characters in a play.

Felicia Scatcherd (1862 -1927) a member of the S.P.R., a researcher a Journalist and a Spiritualist. She helped W. T. Stead found Julia's Bureau. She was associated with the study of psychic photography from the very early days of the century with some study being undertaken in France. She worked with William Hope from 1909, becoming a good friend and champion and careful scrutineer until her passing in 1927.

Rev. Charles. L. Tweedale, Vicar of Weston Church. He was educated at Durham University, England. Having worked in slums, and suburbia he later moved to the country parish of Weston, near Otley, in Yorkshire. A talented and versatile man, he was an astronomer, a musician, a maker of violins and an inventor. He published books on astronomy and discovered a comet. His wife was a good clairvoyant and trance medium and they had their own home circle with their daughter.

In the early 1920s, he founded the Society of Communion for spiritualist members of the Church of England. The society "insisted on the acceptance of the doctrine of the divinity of Christ" and existed mainly to encourage psychic study among Anglicans. He was a close friend of psychic photographer William Hope, whom he defended against hostile criticism. He published the following books on Spiritualism: *Man's Survival After Death* (1909, 1920, 1925, 1931); *Present Day Spirit Phenomena and the Churches* (1917); The *Vindication of William Hope* (1933); *News From the Next World* (1940). He died June 29, 1944.

Mr. W. J. West, the managing director of Kodak's manufacturing arm in Scotland, an expert photographer and interested in Spiritualism. He was invited to be present at sittings with the Crewe Circle in their first excursion to Glasgow in 1914 and he interviewed Hope as to his beginnings in his office (see Chapter 1). Later he often sat with Mrs Perriman in Direct Voice séances.

Mr. William Walker (1849-1915) An ex-Railway employee, he was a man of many activities and interests, a bee-keeper, geologist, botanist and a love of painting in both water colours and oils. He had a keen inquisitive mind. His connection with Spiritualism commenced in the early 1880s. In 1884 he left the Church of England and commenced "sitting" at home with a few friends. The outcome of this circle was the Cromford and High Peak Society. The meetings were held in his house. He became a well-developed trance speaker, always in demand among Societies in Derbyshire and the neighbouring counties. A former President of Buxton Photographic Society) and lecturer on Psychic Photography, illustrated with Lantern slides, many taken by Wm. Hope when Walker was present. He first sat with the circle in 1910, and became a close friend of Hope and the Circle until his passing in 1915.

Sir Arthur Conan Doyle (1859 – 1930) physician, author, spiritualist, lecturer. Member of the S.P.R. from 1890s. He had memorable conclusive sittings with the circle and sprang to their defence in 1922 with *The Case for Spirit Photography*. He travelled widely promoting spiritualism and wrote – *The New Revelation, The Vital Message* and *The History of Spiritualism* on the subject as well as his better known Sherlock Holmes stories.

Mr. James Coates: A highly regarded photographic expert, investigator and author of *Photographing the Invisible* (1911). Host to sittings at Rothesay on the circle's first visit to Scotland in 1914. A member of the S.S.S.P, he sat privately a number of times with the Crewe circle with excellent results.

Mr Ernest Oaten (1875 – 52), A good medium, he edited the journal *The Two Worlds* (1919-1945). He became president of the International Federation of Spiritualists and the Spiritualists' National Union (1915-20, 22-23). In his role as chairman of the Parliamentary Committee of the Spiritualists National Union, he pressed for reform of the Witchcraft and Vagrancy Acts. He worked closely with Sir Arthur Conan Doyle, fighting for the rights of spiritualist mediums.

In 1934, Oaten made history by becoming the first person to speak about Spiritualism and mediumship on a live radio broadcast of the BBC. He was convinced that the spirit world exists around us like the atmosphere. He said that death is similar to a railroad terminal where we change trains to move on to the next world. "Hence, let me say categorically and emphatically – I know that there is a life beyond this, for I have talked with the people who live in it."

Oaten published *Some Problems Concerning the Next State of Life* in 1915, *The Relation of Modern Spiritualism to Christianity* in 1924 and *That Reminds Me* in 1938.

Ven. Archdeacon Thomas Colley Rector of Stockton (Warks) (1839-1912) Some called him eccentric – he was certainly 'colourful'. The title Archdeacon came from his time in Natal. For more detail see Chapter 5. He worked extensively with the Crewe Circle in the early years, producing many psychographs as well as photographs. He introduced Felicia Scatcherd and Professor Henslow to the Crewe Circle (see Chapters 4-6).

Rev. Prof. George Henslow. The Rev. Professor George Henslow was another eminent scholar who took an interest in Hope's work through his friendship with Archdeacon Colley, and his book *"Proofs of the Truths of Spiritualism"*, published in 1919, has been a treasure chest of records on the early work of the circle. After achieving an M.A. degree at Cambridge he went into the church. He later became the Headmaster of two Grammar schools, Lecturer in Botany at St Bartholomew's Hospital and Queen's College. He then returned to the Curacies of churches in London while pursuing his interest in Botany. He became Honorary Professor of the

Royal Horticultural Society and he was a prolific author and speaker on botanical subjects. Around 1904 he moved to Leamington and later to Bournemouth where he died on 30 December 1925.

Mr. Alfred Kitson A well-known and well-loved figure in Spiritualist Lyceum Circles (the Educational arm of the Movement). Growing up in a mining family in West Yorkshire, he was 'down the pit' by the age of nine with just two afternoons a week allowance to attend a local school. (1864). He then educated himself and grew to lead Spiritualist Lyceums and write pieces for the early Lyceum Manuals, guided many times, by his hero Andrew Jackson Davis, the American seer.

Mr. Stanley De Brath (1854-1937) A frequent contributor to the journal *Psychic Science,* published by the British College of Psychic Science, from 1922 and to *Light.* He was a psychical researcher, author, and translator. He trained as a civil engineer and spent 20 years in government service in India before becoming headmaster of a preparatory school in England. In 1890 he attended a séance by Cecil Husk and thereafter became intensely interested in psychical research and Spiritualism. His own contributions centred upon his writing, editing, and translating work. His early books include *Psychic Philosophy* (under the pseudonym "C. Desertis", 1909), *The Mysteries of Life* (1915), and *The Science of Peace* (1916). In 1918 he began spending time in Paris, collaborating with the French researcher Gustave Geley at the Institut Métapsychique International. He was responsible for the English translation of Geley's *From the Unconscious to the Conscious* (1920). He died December 20, 1937, at Kew, London.

Sir William Barrett, (1844-1925) One of the distinguished early psychical researchers, a principal founder in 1882 of the Society for Psychical Research in England. Born in Jamaica, educated at Old Trafford Grammar School, Manchester, England. He became a science master, physics lecturer, and, from 1873 to 1910, professor of physics at the Royal College of Science, Dublin, Ireland. A fellow of the Royal

Society, the Philosophical Society, and the Royal Society of Literature and a member of the Institute of Electrical Engineers and the Royal Irish Academy. He was a highly respected scientist, responsible for important developments in the fields of metal alloys and vision.

James Hewat McKenzie and his wife, Barbara were founders of the British College of Psychic Studies in 1920. Mr McKenzie was a British parapsychologist. He studied and investigated it for many years and presented a series of lectures in London, Edinburgh and Glasgow in 1915. The following year he published *Spirit Intercourse: Its Theory and Practice* and the pamphlet *If a Soldier Dies*, which received very wide circulation.

McKenzie toured America in 1917 and again in 1920, searching for good mediums. In 1920, he founded the British College of Psychic Science, funding it himself. Sir Arthur Conan Doyle commented, "the Psychic College, an institution founded by the self-sacrificing work of Mr. and Mrs. Hewat McKenzie, has amply shown that a stern regard for truth and for the necessary evidential requirements are not incompatible with a human treatment of mediums, and a generally sympathetic attitude towards the Spiritualistic point of view."

Psychic Science, the college quarterly magazine, began in 1922. That same year McKenzie and his wife visited Germany, Poland, and Austria, investigating mediums and psychics along the way. He was especially interested in physical mediumship. They had regular sittings in their special 'quiet room' for meditation. Barbara was the medium, "and as she sat she became aware of various new influences operating on her receptive mind, which seemed distinct from her ordinary thoughts of which she had full control. Various personalities 'spoke' through her, giving evidence regarding matters of which she had no knowledge, but, illustrating the influence of the mind, they would very often answer questions on which her husband had been pondering, arising out of his intensive reading".[1]

On his death in 1929, his wife took over the presidency of the college. She was then succeeded in 1930 by Mrs. Champion de Crespigny. The Crewe Circle were held in such esteem that they were "part of the fabric" from the first months of its being.

---

1. Source of quote: Hankey, *"J. Hewat McKenzie: Pioneer of Psychical Research"* from http://www.survivalafterdeath.info/articles/mckenzie-barbara/harris.htm

Mr. William Jeffrey a prosperous Glasgow merchant, a man of singularly keen and incisive intellect, and one of the finest amateur conjurors in this country, and possibly a former chairman of the "Magic Circle" in Scotland. Mr. Jeffrey went into the movement with the idea that in the course of a month or two he could show the whole thing to be a fraud. "But within the course of a month or two he came to a very different conclusion, with the result that he is one of the most trenchant, powerful and unflinching advocates of the spiritualistic cause," (Dr. Ellis Powell, chair, Queens Hall April '21 the Third Arthur Conan Doyle lecture). He was present at the first visit of the Crewe Circle to Glasgow. He became a member of the S.S.S.P. and a good friend of the Circle. In 1920 George Lethem said of him in *Light*, June 1920: "he is as keen a conjuror as ever, but he is ready to tell all and sundry that the Crewe Circle spirit photography is beyond a conjuror's art." (See photos of opening veil drapery in Chpt 10.)

Estelle Stead. (1880-1966) Daughter and co-worker of W.T. Stead. After his passing on the 'Titanic' she continued his work at Julia's Bureau and worked with Pardoe Woodman to receive writings from her father producing *The Blue Island* and other writings tranmitted by her father. She supported the work of Mrs. Deane in the cenotaph pictures which caused so much controversy in the early 1920 but was backed by information from her father in the Spirit World. (see Appendix 11)

Mr. Wm. Cowell Pugh Born in Shrewsbury in 1870, he sought work in various towns till he arrived in Middlesbrough in 1894. He soon became an active member of the Lyceum there. He met his wife at the Lyceum and later became Secretary of the Lyceum District council while he was a Postmaster by day and host to the Crewe Mediums on their visits there. His wife was a powerful medium herself. He passed in January 1925.

Mr. Henry Blackwell A Vice-President of the S.S.S.P. – he had wide experience of spirit photography from the early days of Mr Boursnell. with whom he had many sittings. He sat with Mr. Hope and Mrs. Deane, also with mediums for photography in Canada and the United States, and had a collection of some two thousand Extras obtained at his own sittings, including deceased relatives, the faces of a great number of well-known statesmen, writers, politicians; also fairies, flowers, etc. He was a convinced spiritualist and his long-continued practical experiments confirmed him in his conviction. He regarded the photographic extras as the work of the departed in the spirit world; and his experience with mediums, photographic and other, was so vast that his interpretation of the phenomena he witnessed must carry much weight. He defended Hope in the Oliver Lodge controversy in 1909.

Mr. A.W. Orr. Director of *The Two Worlds* Publishing Company a well-known figure in the early Spiritualist movement; he was instrumental in setting up the Britten Memorial Trust shortly after the death of Emma Hardinge Britten in 1899 with co-workers Mr. J. Burchell, Mr. J. J. Morse, Mr. S. Butterworth, Mr. S. S. Chiswell, and Mr. J. Venables. Mr. A. W. Orr was Hon. Sec, a position he held for over twenty years. He had many experiences of good genuine psychic photographs with the Crewe Circle for himself, and friends he introduced. Orr died on August 31st 1937.

Mr. W.G. Mitchell. A Vice-President of the S.S.S.P., and President of the Darlington Photographic Society. President of the Darlington Spiritualist Society. He was a photographer and investigator of considerable previous experience.

Mr. Baguley, President of Crewe Spiritualist Society who defended Hope over the Oliver Lodge psychograph dispute in 1909. He knew the members of the circle well as they attended his Society's meetings in Crewe.

Lady Glenconner She had many experiments at Crewe. Most notable for receiving photo of McKenzie's son but not her own and identifying their unrecognised extra. She did eventually get one of her son in 1919 at her home, with Mr Colledge and Mr Munn also there to verify there was no fraud.

Mr. Colledge, professional photographer living in Innerleithin, Scotland, used a stereoscopic camera alongside William Hope in sittings at "Glen" in 1919. (see Chapter 12)

Mr. Bernard Munns, professional artist commissioned to paint a portrait of the Glenconners' son; witness to the Colledge-Hope sittings in 1919. (see Chapter 12)

Mr. Harry Price (1881 – 1948) a British psychic researcher and author, who gained public prominence for his investigations into psychical phenomena and his exposing of fraudulent spiritualist mediums. Although Price claimed his people were from Shropshire, he was actually born in London in Red Lion Square, in Holborn. Price later became an expert amateur conjurer, joined the Magic Circle in 1922 and maintained a lifelong interest in stage magic and conjuring. His expertise in sleight-of-hand and magic tricks stood him in good stead for what would become his all-consuming passion, the investigation of paranormal phenomena. He became a member of the S.P.R. in 1922 but formed an organisation in 1925 called the National Laboratory of Psychical Research as a rival to the S.P.R.. In a letter to *Psychic News* Leslie Price[2] reports that Dr Trevor Hall (*Search for Harry Price*) wrote in a letter to him " ... his first publicity in psychical research in the 1920s came from his exposure of Hope, the spirit photographer of the Crewe Circle."

Mr. James Seymour, a conjuror linked to the Magic Circle, colluded with Price in a "Test" sitting on Hope in February 1922 at the suggestion of Eric Dingwall, research officer of the S.P.R.

Mr. Eric Dingwall, (1890-1986), psychical investigator, anthropologist, author and librarian, was born in Sri Lanka. He studied at Cambridge. He spent a year in America working for the American Society for Psychical Research before joining the Society for Psychical Research (S.P.R.) in 1920, becoming its Research Officer two years later. He was noted for a robustly critical approach that often brought him into conflict with colleagues. He was a leading member of the Magic Circle.

2. Letter in *Psychic News* June 1995. Leslie Price's letter continues– "The point here is that in psychical research there are three ways to become famous: to report positive results, to expose someone, to get into the media. Harry Price did all three regularly, but nothing may be what it seems, starting with a fictitious early life documented in Dr Hall's book."

Mr. Fred Barlow. A paranormal photographer from Birmingham, described by James Coates as "the energetic secretary of the S.S.S.P." (The Society for the Study of Supernormal Pictures) and said to be one of the leading authorities on Supernormal Photography. He was Honorary Secretary of the Birmingham and Midland Society for Psychical Research (S.P.R.). He wrote the Preface and Chapter 8 of Arthur Conan Doyle's book *The Case for Spirit Photography.*

He states in 1921 "I got results, using cameras of my own: plates loaded in dark slides, exposed and developed entirely by myself. Mr. Hope not even being in the dark room either for loading or development. I have obtained supernormal results with Mr. Hope in my own home under the most stringent conditions. In fact, in something like a score of experiments conducted during the last few years Mr. Hope has simply had no opportunity whatever of tricking, even if he had wanted to do so."

After years of vigorously testing and defending William Hope, in 1932 he did a volte-face, and with Major Rampling-Rose accused Hope of producing fraudulent pictures by the use of a miniature flashlight instrument. (see Chpt. 22).

Major Rampling-Rose was a commercial photographer with "the usual professional bias against psychic photography. He deals with numberless films every year. He is naturally impressed by the fact that he never comes across psychic photographs and concludes therefrom that when others do they are not sufficiently expert or sharp not to be taken in by photographic freaks or fraud. The fact is that the persons who claim to, or are thought to produce psychic photographs are extremely rare."[3]

F.W. Warrick adds "Many professional photographers possessing assuredly as much knowledge of photography have made careful and prolonged study of the very exceptional persons by the influence of whom Extras appear and have come to a different opinion on the matter."

---

3. Quotation from F.W. Warrick in *Experimemts in Psychics* (1939).

Quotes from Observers

"Psychic photography is a fact, but its phenomena are varied. Fraud there may have been, on occasions, mistakes of observation also, but there is now a vast body of evidence which can no longer be ignored or denied, establishing the fact that it is possible to obtain original photographs of those who have "departed this life."

(*Psychic Photography,* by Rev. C.L. Tweedale, in *Light* March 1918)

"Many storms have broken over the Crewe Circle, but the cause of them has usually been the limited knowledge of the strange possibilities of psychic photography on the part of the sitters and of the public and ... 'the critics' ignorance'. Hope himself was as much interested as anyone in the problem as to how the effects were produced, and had often discussed the matter, although, of course, he was satisfied that they were due to spirit agency."

(*The Problems of Psychic Photography,* a lecture by F. R. Scatcherd, Feb 1921)

Mr. East, a miner, of 36, New Street, Port Talbot, after a sitting in 1920 reported: "When I asked what their charges were, Mr. Hope replied: 'Four and sixpence a dozen. For the sitting, nothing. This is a gift from God, and we dare not charge for what is freely given us. Our pay is often the wonder and joy depicted on the faces of those, like yourselves, who have found that their loved ones are not entirely lost to them. We get all kinds and classes of people here. Some even are threadbare and too poor to pay train-fare, but we treat them all alike, as we recognise in each a brother or sister.'"

(*The Case for Spirit Photography,* Sir Arthur Conan Doyle 1922).

"It is advisable to mention at the outset that I am fully alive to the possibility of fraud and trickery and that they constitute the great difficulty in experimentation in the field of psychics, and that trickery is (however respectable the medium or subject) ten thousand times more probable than supernormal occurrences. At the same time, I would point out that trickery in the taking of photographs under reasonably strict conditions is by no means as easy as is stated in some quarters, and such continuous trickery over a period of twenty-seven years (as in the case of Mr. Hope) without detection in the very act is unthinkable."

(*Experiments in Psychics*, F.W. Warrick , 1939).

The Work Begins – 1908-09

In Conan Doyle's book, *A Case for Spirit Photography*, Felicia Scatcherd tells us that:

'the circle sat every Wednesday from eight until nine, securing a picture on an average of one a month at the outset. One of the circle was a non-Spiritualist but was later converted when a picture of his father and mother were obtained.'

She continues:

"A strange thing is that when all were anxiously desiring a picture, a message appeared on the first plate exposed. This message promised a picture next time and stated that it would be for the master of the house. The promise was kept several sittings later, when the picture of Mr. Buxton's mother and of Mrs. Buxton's sister came on the plate. Mr. Buxton was of the opinion that this was given to do away with the idea of thought photography. They were all thinking of a picture and never dreamed that such a thing as a written message would be given."

As they persevered with their sittings Hope's own mediumship developed. From various reports we know that he was clairvoyant, occasionally giving a description, (before a sitting), of the spirit person who was close by, and later he was known to be in a light trance, under the control of a spirit "Master of Ceremonies" who in more than one report is named as "Massa". This trance state may have accounted for his distracted behaviour, frequently commented on in reports, when taking the photographs.

Even here at the beginning of his development the first controversy begins. Felicia Scatcherd records in Conan Doyle's book:

"Many storms have broken over the Crewe Circle, but the cause of them has usually been the limited knowledge of the strange possibilities of psychic photography on the part of the sitters and of the public. One of the most notorious of these so-called "exposures" (which really were exposures of the critics' ignorance) was in 1908 and arose out of Archdeacon Colley's first sitting. He had heard that the Crewe Circle were simple-looking folk, and this attracted him, so he broke his journey at Crewe and [in early March,1908] called upon Mr. and Mrs. Hope, who had just lost their eldest daughter. The Archdeacon apologised for having come at such a time, but Mr. Hope sent him on to Mr. and Mrs. Buxton, where he was shown the photos and asked to see the negatives. He was shocked when he heard that they had all been destroyed, and from that time kept all negatives he was able to get hold of."

Shortly after this Archdeacon Colley arranged to have photographs taken with his own camera and Rev. Professor Henslow in his book *Proofs of the Truths of Spiritualism* gives us Colley's verbatim account of the appearance of his own mother and father:

"One wet afternoon, one of the three members of the Crewe circle[1] staying with me at Stockton Rectory wished me to take a photo of the group. Not knowing why, I did so in the open. The portrait of my mother, whom I nor anyone else had ever taken when she was on earth, nearly obliterated the heads and bodies of the two sitters, while my father appeared over myself.

The clairvoyante member of the circle exclaimed 'That is the Archdeacon's mother, and she has on the brooch she wore.' I asked what she meant, and she replied that my mother had appeared to her on the previous day and said she would be with my own portrait. That was why she asked me to photograph them. The clairvoyante added that my mother appeared to her in white, and of an 'angelic form' but would be as I knew her of old. Such was the case. My mother had never been photographed in earth-life."

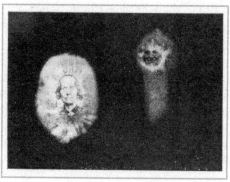

Left: The psychic photo of Rev. Colley's parents. (March 1908) Above: Life photo of Rev. Colley's father taken in 1888.

Henslow continues:

"In a second photograph (not here presented) taken immediately after the first, barely half a minute intervening, the spirit parents have altered their position, relatively to their son. The father's face is, in the first photograph, above the head of Archdeacon Colley (erased from the plate shown) while in the second he appears at his right hand where the mother stands, while she has moved to where the father stood."

As soon as the photographs were taken Archdeacon Colley himself developed them.

---

1. I assume here he refers to Mr. Hope and Mr. & Mrs. Buxton

A few days later, having seen the prints, Hope noticed the likeness between "Mrs. Colley" and a picture he had (as a working photographer) copied about two years before. When he realised the similarity between the two women, he cycled to Nantwich, around twenty miles away, to see Mrs Spencer and check with her as to the identity of the woman in the photograph. She immediately identified it as her grandmother, and cried out, "Oh, if this had only come with us how pleased we should have been!"

Hope then wrote to Archdeacon Colley telling him it could not be his mother, as it had been recognised at Nantwich. The Archdeacon said it was madness to think a man did not know his own mother, and advertised in the Leamington paper, asking all who remembered his mother to meet him at the Rectory, when eighteen persons selected the photograph from several others and testified in writing that the picture was a portrait of the late Mrs. Colley, who had never been photographed.

He would hardly have done that double checking if he had attempted a fraud on the Archdeacon and then brought it to the attention of the Archdeacon himself. This was the action of an honest man, not a trickster —as some later labelled him.

Colley himself sent the photographs to the journal *Light* in June 1908 which they published in an article about 'Psychic Photography':

"The photograph was taken on one of the Archdeacon's own diamond-marked quarter-plates, in his own photographic slide, and with his own camera, on Monday afternoon, March 16th, 1908, out of doors in a shower of rain. The spirits who appear are both recognised. The lady is said to be the Archdeacon's mother, who departed this life on August 8th, 1858, aged forty-three years, the gentleman being his father, who passed away on June 13th 1891, aged eighty-one. The face of the father may be compared with the photograph of him, which was taken by Archdeacon Colley himself on August 25th, 1888.

Archdeacon Colley states that no photograph of his mother was ever taken during her earth-life, but the spirit photograph of her has been recognised by many persons now living in Leamington and elsewhere. The attestations (eighteen in number) under their own signatures, of those who recognise her face may be seen at this office...."

It was six years before this question over the photograph of the Archdeacon's mother again reared its head – some eighteen months after the demise of the Archdeacon – in a series of letters to *Light*.[2]

---

2. *Light,* The trail of letters begins on Feb 14th 1914 and continues until July that year.

It seems that Hope had revealed to Mrs Spencer that the photo was purported to be Mrs Colley. For some reason she later told a friend of this, who wrote to *Light* and a suspicion of fraud was born.

In a letter Hope wrote to an acquaintance[3] at that time he said:

". . . When he (the Archdeacon) sent us a copy ... I noticed it was just like Mrs. Spencer's grandmother. ... I pointed it out to our circle, and took it on my cycle to show it to the Spencers at Nantwich. . . . Now, I did not go straight out and say to Mrs. Spencer, 'Here is your grandmother, whom the Archdeacon claims as his mother.' I should have been a fool to do that. No, I thought I would see if she could recognise it so I showed it to her, and she claimed it at once, and I did say more, 'Nay, it's the Archdeacon's mother.' but I said it only it to get a more definite statement from her."

The well-experienced investigator Henry Blackwell, of whom James Coates says "a gentleman of whom it may be said that few men have had such experiences—at home or abroad—with photographic mediums"[4], put forward this explanation:

"Some spirit people find it very difficult to remember how they looked on earth, and refresh their memory by referring to a photograph or portrait. ... I have had the privilege of photographing some partially materialised spirits in my own home. They were clearly visible to the visitors and myself. *Yet, two of these forms are exactly like their last photograph, except that they are now surrounded by spirit drapery.*" (The italics are Mr. Blackwell's).

If this is the case – and as Mrs. Colley had never had a portrait/photograph taken in her lifetime – maybe she found one as near as she could, so as not to disappoint her son. She had been 'dead' fifty years! Can you remember exactly what you looked like 10-20 years ago never mind fifty?

Around this time Archdeacon Colley tried relentlessly to interest Sir Oliver Lodge in the 'reality' of psychic photography, in particular psychographs, and this again led to a dispute which featured large in the psychic press.

The tests with Sir Oliver Lodge started in late 1908 but with mixed results. We learn from Mr. Orr that on one occasion, in response to a remark by one of the circle that putting the packet into water would not affect the plates, this was done. They were afterwards put before the fire to dry, with the result that the lead melted and consequently they were spoiled.

On January 7th, 1909, Hope himself travelled to Birmingham to deliver the latest of the six tests to Sir Oliver. However, Lodge was too

---

3. *Light,* July 24th 1914. Letter from W Gregory reporting on letter from Hope.
4. *Light,* Dec 26th 1921 in James Coates on 'Practical and Theological Aspects of "Supernormal" Pictures'

occupied to see "this person from Crewe"[5] and the following controversy arose in *Light* more than two months later.

Asserted Supernormal Photography. (*Light* Mar 20th 1909)

"Sir, The Rector of Stockton, near Rugby, better known as Archdeacon Colley, has taken a good deal of trouble to try and convince me of the reality of supernormal photography to the extent of obtaining an impression on unwrapped and unexposed plates by the imposition of hands, without a camera.

I have accordingly had certain plates wrapped up in a carefully noted manner, and handed to him from time to time, to deal with, by deputy or otherwise, as he thought proper.

Most of the plates duly returned by him have been quite honestly dealt with, and have no impression upon them. But the plates last received back, which have been in the custody of some people at Crewe, have some faint writing showing upon them—the writing being such as would be produced by writing upon lamp-blacked glass, and then throwing the shadow of this writing, as by a printing process, upon the pair of sensitive plates still face to face, without separating their film-touching surfaces.

The envelopes, which were cut open in my laboratory in a responsible manner, were immediately removed by the person from Crewe who brought them; but Archdeacon Colley has now succeeded in getting them returned to me. I find that they show distinct and unmistakable signs of having been tampered with, carefully opened, and re-sealed; so that I am absolutely convinced, whatever may happen in other cases, that in this case the impression was produced by the most commonplace and normal means.

In order to prevent the good-nature of the Rector of Stockton and some of his friends from being imposed upon, I have therefore sent a certificate to him, of which the enclosed is a copy:

Certificate.

"In the matter of the envelopes which enclosed a pair of plates which had been in the hands of certain people at Crewe, and which were returned with some obscure writing upon them—this is to testify that these envelopes, when returned to me, showed distinct signs of having been tampered with and opened, probably by steam.

The indelible pencil marks, which were scored over certain flaps, have lost their glaze locally, precisely as they do when slightly moistened; and moreover, certain gum streaks which had been originally on the envelope, and purposely left there, had been cleaned off.

5.This appears dismissive but identities were concealed at that time as the members of the Crewe Circle had their working lives to consider.

Comparing this set of envelopes with another duplicate set, which had also at one time been in your hands for experimenting, but on which the plates had received no impression—the contrast was very marked. This duplicate set had not been tampered with. But I have not the smallest doubt that the envelopes enclosing the plates which had received an impression had been opened, in ways that can be assigned."

Yours, &c.,

Oliver Lodge."

In *Light,* Mar 27th there came a reply:

Asserted Supernormal Photography.

"Sir,—With reference to Sir Oliver Lodge's 'Certificate' to Archdeacon Colley regarding 'Asserted Supernormal Photography', in *Light,* I beg in fairness and justice to the circle at Crewe, who apparently have been giving their time to carry out certain experiments in psychic photography. ...

Sir Oliver Lodge says: 'The envelopes, which were cut open in my laboratory in a responsible manner, were immediately removed by the person from Crewe who brought them.'

Surely if they were opened 'in a responsible manner' it means that the packet was most carefully checked over in every detail to see that the seals were intact. On the other hand, if they were not in order, why in the name of Psychical Research was a protest not made at once. ... As to any suspicious markings found on them some days afterwards: after an unnecessary journey to Crewe and back, any paper covering would, naturally, get rubbed and soiled. It would have made the record of the case more complete had the wording of the message or writing been given, and also whether it appeared as a negative or a positive. Both kinds have been obtained at various times during the past twenty years.

Remembering the many and various forms of manifestation adopted by the unseen workers, the investigator should patiently study each particular form of manifestation in all its phases, and also see that proper and suitable conditions are given, as in many cases it has been proved that want of knowledge and hasty assumption have led to grievous injustice being done."—

Yours, &c.,

H. Blackwell.

Letters went back and forth in *Light* between Oliver Lodge and Henry Blackwell until on April 17th this letter from Mr. Baguley of Crewe gave details of the affair:

A Vindication.

"Sir,—In *Light* of March 20th I was astonished to read the statement and certificate to Archdeacon Colley from Sir Oliver Lodge. Knowing how unjust the statement was, I have been eagerly expecting to see some reply from the persons implicated, but as no answer has appeared in *Light* perhaps you will allow me a few words upon this subject, since Sir Oliver Lodge has made the matter public property by taking your readers into his confidence, and by virtually asking them to accept his deductions.

No thoughtful reader of *Light* I feel sure, would be so unfair as to accept Sir Oliver's conclusions in the absence of any explanation from the persons charged. Nor does there appear to the present writer sufficient evidence to warrant Sir Oliver in bringing forward a charge of fraud against unknown persons in a responsible public journal, more especially as this charge was preferred without the least inquiry from such persons.

Having a knowledge of the circumstances of this case, having known each individual member of the circle for some years, and having been associated with them in society work, I, for one, cannot allow this charge to be brought without making a protest, and the following statement of facts:

1. It is a fact that the packet was intact when received from the person from Crewe, hereafter known as Mr. Hope.

2. It is a fact that Sir Oliver wired his permission that Mr. Hope, who insisted upon it, should be allowed to see the plates developed in a responsible manner.

3. It is a fact that Sir Oliver's representative did so develop them in a responsible manner, and gave Mr. Hope a written and signed declaration to that effect.

4. It is a fact that Sir Oliver wired his permission that Mr. Hope, who again insisted upon it, should be allowed to take the outward wrappings with him. This permission, it appears, was given under protest. Why did Mr. Hope insist upon bringing back the envelopes? Simply because he had been asked to do so by the members of the circle who, naturally, were curious to verify the statements of the 'control' or 'guide', who had previously told them how the packet was made up.

5. It is a fact that the same control or guide, through Mr. Hope, asked that the packet should be plunged into water so that the magnetism, or psychic force, could pass through the lead foil.

6. It is a fact that this circle has never received any remuneration for the time, trouble and patience they have given to the subject.

The above are facts which I believe cannot be disproved. As regards the marks on the envelopes, is it not obvious that these would get rubbed and lose their glaze by being handled by the members of the circle!

Granted that it would have been better had the envelopes not been brought away, this does not affect the fact that the test was successful throughout."

—   Yours, &c

G. H, Baguley,

Ex-President, Crewe Spiritualists' Society.

This was joined, in the same issue, by a further letter from Mr. H. Blackwell with the certificate of affirmation from January 7th, given by Lodge's assistant Mr. Robinson.

"Sir,—The circle at Crewe, who kindly gave their services during six sittings in order that the spirit workers should be able to give a test to Sir Oliver Lodge, desire me, on their behalf, to protest strongly against the charge which has been made against them, and to deny emphatically that any of the envelopes containing the plates were opened or tampered with before they were returned. The outer envelope was fastened with gum. Unquestionably this should have been sealed with wax, suitably impressed, seeing that the parcel had to pass through many hands, but of course the circle had to deal with it as received. The 'guides' informed them as to the contents of the packet, and so anxious were the members to verify the statement and see the result of the experiment, that they each made a contribution towards the expenses of one of their number, who, losing a day's work, took the package back to Sir Oliver's laboratory in Birmingham.

This was on January 7th, and the envelopes were 'responsibly' examined, and the plates developed on that day. Ten weeks later, on March 27th, there appeared in your columns Sir Oliver Lodge's letter, but in it there is a most significant and unjust omission as to certain facts which occurred on January 7th.

When the messenger (Mr. H.) arrived, he was received by Sir Oliver's assistant, Mr. E. E. Robinson. This gentleman, having done up the package, was specially authorised by his principal to check and open the same and develop the plates. Before this was done Mr. H. stipulated that he should be given a certificate if the guides had correctly described the contents, which proved to be very carefully protected in four separate envelopes by tissue paper, lead foil, &c. It was also agreed that Mr. H. should be allowed to take the envelopes back to Crewe to show them to the circle. Mr. Robinson then critically and methodically examined each cover. Finding them intact and in good order, the following certificate was then given:

"This is to say that the guides are quite right in saying that the packet contains two or three or more envelopes, lead foil strips and tissue paper and two plates face to face."

Edward E. Robinson.

January 7th, 1909.

On the plates being developed by Mr. Robinson in the presence of Mr H. and two others, there appeared a long message on each plate. It consisted of twenty-one lines, which being compressed into a very small space only two inches by two and a half, is somewhat difficult to read, but it gives sound advice as to the best way of carrying out psychic experiments. (The message has since been repeated but more distinctly).

Mr Robinson was so thoroughly satisfied as to the supernormal result of the test thus completed that he accompanied Mr H. to the railway station, and actually wrote and paid for two telegrams, one to the circle at Crewe:

'Successful, your friend started back. Robinson',

(and the other to Archdeacon Colley.)

Mr H. was heartily welcomed by his friends on his return, for their labours had been requited by success, and their faithful guides had indeed proved true.

The envelopes were, of course, handed round to a great many curious inquirers, and afterwards sent on to the Archdeacon, who, I understand, had them photographed and then took them to London, where they were again handled and examined by a number of persons.

Sir Oliver Lodge then sees them for the first time, and very naturally finds that they have been 'tampered with'. He then most unfortunately concludes that his assistant and accredited agent must have been deceived when he so carefully tested and opened the fresh envelopes some time previously.

Without even asking for a second test Sir Oliver then still more unfortunately publicly charges someone with having opened the envelopes and produced the impression on the plates 'by the most commonplace and normal means.'

A great reputation carries with it a great responsibility, and this most unfounded accusation has no doubt been eagerly reproduced by newspapers, who will take no notice of the vindication. Those working people at Crewe, however, feel the slur which has been so undeservedly and unkindly cast upon them just as keenly as Sir Oliver would feel a reflection upon his own honour.—   Yours, &c."

April 12th.   H. Blackwell.

The Crewe Circle and its mediumship were, hereby, seen as honest and no more was heard on this matter.

Six months later Rev. Professor Henslow carried out a remote test with the Circle, giving it a separate chapter in his book titled:

"A MESSAGE ON THE THIRD OF AN UNOPENED PACKET OF TWELVE PHOTOGRAPHIC PLATES (OCTOBER 1st 1909).

"This came through Mr. Hope as the medium. Not being able to attend the séance at Crewe, I sent the packet just as it was bought, but with tape wrapped round it, and sealed on the ends and sides. After a week Mr. Hope returned it intact for I found it exactly as I had sent it. There was not the slightest indication of the seals having been tampered with, etc. I at once took it to a professional photographer and asked him if the packet had been opened. He was good enough to write me the following certificate. "I am quite satisfied that these plates had not been opened or tampered within any way. — H.L.Y."

(This was subsequently corroborated by the manager of a leading firm of photographers in London). He allowed me to accompany him to his dark chamber, and I there informed him all about it. He procured fresh materials for development. I cut the cover across the middle and so could remove the two ends.

Taking out the first parcel of four slides, I developed the third plate only. The message was on it."

With the returned package was a letter from Mr. W. Hope, as follows:

"Dear Sir— We are sending you the packet and hope there is something on the plates, although we have to chance it. Please send word as soon as you can, as we are anxious about it.

Our guide says they have tried to impress the third plate from the top. Please see the plates developed yourself. All we ask is fair play and fair dealing which we know we shall get at your hands and as soon as the development is completed, we should be greatly obliged if you would send word as to the results, as we are in great expectation. If the third plate has failed, develop the first half-dozen; but if the third has been written upon, there will be no need to develop more.

Yours respectfully,

W. Hope, 50 Oakley Street, Crewe."

So anxious were the Crewe circle about the plates that Mr. Hope also wrote to the Archdeacon, hoping he would be present when the plates were developed, stressing the importance of the timing:

"... don't miss developing on Tuesday, as we shall send all our sympathy and get the Professor to see them opened and watch development and do impress the photographer to be careful and please let us know results as soon as it is over. Don't wait until Wednesday, but send word at once, as we are all eagerly awaiting results. On our part we can safely say we have dealt honestly with them (the guides); and if they fail us now after promising faithfully, I shall be inclined to throw it over. On the other hand, if they keep to their word, I shall be more than ever attached to them; so see they (the plates) are done on Tuesday, and let us know as soon as possible. I am writing to the Professor.

Yours respectfully, W. Hope."

Note the stress in the letter above of the day they must be developed. This is because in some cases when developing was delayed, the image placed by the spirit team had degraded and sometimes vanished completely.

Prof. Henslow continues: "As soon as I could, I wired to Mr. Hope at Crewe, to tell him that the message had come on the third plate just as the controls had arranged that it should. I received the following reply from Mr. Buxton, both he and his wife being members of the Crewe 'circle'.

"Dear Sir, —Yours to hand, we were very pleased to hear from you, as we have been greatly excited as to the development of the plates. About the information you are seeking, Mrs. Buxton had gone to lie down, but suddenly called out 'Success! Success!' and when spoken to she woke up. I was sent for at once and went from the workshop into the house. Mr. Hope had just called in. Then she told us she had got 'Success, victory has crowned your efforts.' (That was before they had received the telegram).

When the wire arrived and proved my wife to have been correct, we were not half so excited. Mr. Hope sends his thanks for the wire, and is very pleased to hear that the plate has given you satisfaction.

Yours truly, A. Buxton."

"When I later asked Mrs. Buxton how she came to realize the success. She said it was not a 'voice' but by 'sensing it'. This is the usual expression of psychic people."

The psychograph is as follows:

"Friend Henslow, The message is just the same as before. Be quite sure that you are satisfied as regards our work. Then, if you find it true, stand side by side with our friends and push forward this grand work and may God bless the Archdeacon, he has suffered much, but great shall be his reward. Now, we think we have given you proof enough. Give our respects to the Lady, Miss S. , and our love to all our friends. God bless you."

Professor Henslow added this comment:

"Mr. Britton Harvey mentions in his *Science and the Soul*, that on the authority of Dr. Pio Foa, Professor of Pathological Anatomy in the University of Turin, that able conjurers had admitted that these phenomena could not be explained by trickery.

Such, too, was my experience, with regard to the third plate of my unopened packet. Both Mr. Marryat and Mr. Maskelyne[6] informed me that it could not be done, as well as Sir W. Crookes."

---

6. Marryat and Maskelyne were well-Known 'magicians' of the time (see Wikipedia)

A message to Professor Henslow on the third plate of an unopened packet of twelve; with a private message (below) to the Archdeacon.

As a final example of the work being achieved in those early years I include this unusual photograph of the Archdeacon accompanied by a "floral psychograph".

Prof. Henslow tells us:

"The remarkable photograph, representing 'Archdeacon Colley surrounded by Lilies', was given to me by the Archdeacon adding: 'This slide was in an unopened packet brought by myself to Hope's home at Crewe. It was taken by myself, in my own camera and Mr. Hope (the medium) had nothing to do with it.'

The Archdeacon's late wife was named 'Lily', and whenever written communications came from her, she always drew a small lily in place of her name.

On the back of the photograph is written in the Archdeacon's handwriting – 'Psychic photograph taken on Wednesday afternoon (4 p.m.) December 22, 1909.

This quarter plate slide was bought at Lancaster and Sons, Birmingham. I counted 75 mentally, for daylight was waning. I then at once developed the plate to find that my late wife, Lily, had thus again been invisibly present

'Archdeacon Colley surrounded by Lilies'.
Psychic photograph taken at Crewe on December 22, 1909.

with me, as in the drawing of a lily in my psychograph, which I developed on March 9th, 1909, so making this the second symbol of her botanical name[7], by which she was known and last called by me in Natal over thirty years ago.' "

In appreciation of the work Hope and the Crewe Circle were doing Archdeacon Colley gave him one of his cameras – a Lancaster 1/4-plate model, similar to the one shown here below.

Hope was extremely proud of this camera and used it for many years. The old tripod became rickety and the lens cap was lost but amazing results were still achieved.

Right: A dark slide. The plates would be placed either side of a light tight centre divison and the whole device slotted into the back of the camera.

7. Reference to a psychograph from Dr. Monck through Dr. d'Aute-Hooper, the medium).
Image in *Proofs of the Truths of Spiritualism* facing p 195.

Archdeacon Thomas Colley

Archdeacon Thomas Colley was to become the moving force in William Hope's mediumship and the 'Crewe Circle' as it became known.

Born in 1839, the son of a painter, he was educated at Oxford and in the 1870s travelled to South Africa as an Archdeacon for Natal for some years before returning to England.

Alan Griffin's account of him from the *Our Warwickshire* website recounts that:

"Archdeacon Colley was rector of Stockton from 1901-1912 and a splendid eccentric... Locals mention that Rectory Close used to be called 'The Radical' after him and that he founded allotments in the village for the benefit of local residents. ...

Rev. Archdeacon T. Colley

On at least one occasion he is said to have secreted a wind-up gramophone behind his prayer desk on which he would play, without announcement, a negro spiritual or some other sacred song to the utter astonishment of the congregation gathered for the service. He frequently rendered a baritone solo from the pulpit and doubtless also entertained the bemused Stockton worshippers with recitals on the bugle. Colley was a spiritualist, a 'high' churchman and was a friend of Sir Arthur Conan Doyle, a fellow spiritualist.

He claimed to have taken many 'spirit photographs' during prayer meetings in the Rectory and also to have foreseen the death on the 'Titanic' in 1912 of his close friend, the journalist, W.T. Stead." [1]

---

1. The Archdeacon printed a pamphlet entitled *The Fore Ordained Wreck of the Titanic*. The forecast of the disaster was sent to Mr W. T. Stead and his reply was as follows: "Dear Sir, Thank you very much for your kind letter, which reaches me just as I am starting for America. I sincerely hope that none of the misfortunes, which you seem to think may happen , will happen; but I will keep your letter and will write to you when I come back. Yours truly, W. T. STEAD." (From Henslow's *Proofs of the Truths of Spiritualism*)

The most detailed, true description of him is found in his friend, Professor Henslow's, book *Proofs of the Truths of Spiritualism*.

"I have great pleasure in introducing the name of Ven. Archdeacon Colley the great spiritualist for forty or more years but it is curious how non-believers show their mind at once on hearing of him, for one will burst out laughing; another puts on a supercilious smile, saying 'Oh! he was a man who did a variety of things', as if one who has versatile abilities must necessarily be a crank.[2] With regard to his many sidedness, besides having been Archdeacon of Natal and Rector of Stockton, he was a musician, having an organ in his rooms in Leamington; in addition, he was a composer. I have in my charge some 30 'blocks' of the music and words, being either 'arrangements' or compositions of his own for chants, etc. used in his own church. He has been a photographer for some half-a-century and lastly a conjurer, having learnt from the same teacher as Mr. Maskelyne.

I knew him for several years and had frequent conversations with him. I attended the séances held in his own private rooms in Leamington and helped him in developing plates, etc. I saw much to admire in him, and greatly appreciated his friendship.

His procedure was always on the strictest and most scientific lines to guard against any tampering. His invariable rule was to buy a packet of quarter plates, and never allow then to go out of his possession, as when the psychograph was being impressed within his hands or if the photographic plate was put into the camera, or taken out, he always did it himself and he had no assistance when they were developed in his own laboratory. He was not at all psychic himself; so that the reader may rest assured that all the spirit-photographs and psychographs in this book are perfectly genuine, including others besides his.

If the communication (or faces) is not received as a spirit-photograph and not taken by a camera – it is impressed on some one or more selected plates in an unopened packet of twelve. The Archdeacon would hold the packet in his left hand, placing the right hand over it, then each member of the 'circle' present would do the same and lastly the 'Control' places the medium's hands one above and one below. In about thirty seconds, when the control removes his hands, all do the same. The Archdeacon would then put his packet in his pocket and develop it at home. It is customary for the 'Control' to say on which plate or plates out of the twelve the communications will be found. So only those particular ones need be developed. He may also add 'You will find a message or faces,' as the case may be.

---

2. Henslow wrote as a footnote – "If this book will, in any way, lead people to think differently about him and, at least, respect his memory as a pioneer of the great and solemn truth of spiritualism it will not have been written in vain."

As this fact seemed to me to be an important one for the proof of spirit-work, I asked Sir William Crookes if he knew of any force, e.g., X-rays, radium, or other, by which a particular plate could be impressed in an unopened pack. His reply was that it was impossible; the whole pack can be affected, less and less from top to bottom, but not otherwise.

I asked Mr. Marriot, who wrote in *Pearson's Magazine* of exposing fraudulent methods of so-called mediums; but he said it could not be done. Mr. Maskelyne corroborated this fact, i.e., without substituting one plate for another; but, of course, the packet must be opened to do this."

Miss Scatcherd tells us that:

"Archdeacon Colley had a prejudice against the psychic cloud that showed, as a rule, round the spirit "extras." In a photograph of himself and a friend taken for ordinary purposes, such a cloud appeared round the Archdeacon's own head, much to his astonishment. I asked, him of what he was thinking at the time, and after a little hesitation, he confessed that he was in great distress for a friend who was in terrible trouble, and that while being photographed he prayed very earnestly that this friend would receive help. "Now you see," said I "what an extraordinary value that photograph has; for saints are seen with halos."

As already recorded, Archdeacon Colley sought out the Crewe Circle in March 1908, having heard of the phenomena that was developing within their circle, and thus began a fruitful collaboration in the following four years – but it was not without its challenges.

He attended the Church's conference in late 1910, together with Felicia Scatcherd to promote their Spirit findings. *Light* in a brief report on this event said:

"nothing very exciting appears to have occurred ... About the only cleric present [ref. to Colley] that would have helped them on their way had no lot or part in the official proceedings,"

— and added this comment sent in by a 'friendly correspondent':

"When in Cambridge last week during the congress I saw both the Rev. Archdeacon Colley and Miss Felicia Scatcherd of the MSR, Lond., and of the Institute of Psychology, Paris, who were working in the endeavour to rouse the interest of the teachers and leaders of the Established Church by way of a very fine collection of psychographs and the distribution of large

3. F. Scatcherd on Problems of Psychic Photograpy, *Light*, Feb 1921

quantities of literature. The room taken by the Archdeacon was well attended by enquirers, and Miss Scatcherd's testimony was much appreciated as being corroborative of the experiments of the Archdeacon."

In February 1912 he resigned from the position of rector at Stockton and during a visit to Middlesbrough in late September 1912 he passed away, as described in *The Two Worlds* on Oct 11th of that year:

"A correspondent,who is an active supporter of our Cause in Middlesbrough,[4] sends the following account, for which he has our thanks. He says: "Archdeacon Colley arrived in Middlesbrough on Sept. 30th at 5.05 pm., very weak. I at once got him into a cab and took him to a friend's home in Grange Road, near the church.

Having had some tea, he felt better. I stayed with him until nearly seven o'clock. After that time he grew rapidly weaker and a doctor was brought, but he passed away at 10 p.m. While I was with him, he told me what he intended doing during the Congress, and what a help Miss Scatcherd would be to him, and that she was a member of the London Spiritual Alliance and of The Society for Psychical Research, London and would arrive at 10.30pm. He asked me to meet her, but not to bring her to see him that night as it would upset her, as she was a fine psychic. He asked me if I would have him carried to the hall if he was unable to walk.

I promised, and he then said that should he be unable to go at all Miss Scatcherd would manage. On my way down to the station our treasurer (Mr. Watts) met me and informed me that the Archdeacon had passed on at 10 p.m. and I was wanted. Mr. Watts was alone with the Archdeacon when he passed on, as Mr. Roeder had stepped out to send a telegram to Captain Colley, his son. I met Miss Scatcherd at 10.30, and we went to the Archdeacon's lodgings in Grange-Road.

Captain Colley arrived on October 1st, and was pleased we had carried out his father's wish of continuing the exhibition.

He was with us on October 2nd at our hall and gave us valuable information about spirit photographs.

Every evening our hall was crowded, and the exhibition has been a great success. The Archdeacon's body left Middlesbrough on Thursday Oct 3rd for Birmingham, according to the terms of his Will.

Though the presence of the Archdeacon in Middlesbrough was well known to scores of the visiting clergymen, not one evinced the slightest interest in his transition nor made any inquiry whether any service could be rendered. What did Thomas Hood say about Christian charity?"

---

4. See Chpt 11 in 'A Middlesbrough Connection' re Archdeacon's writing on psychic photograph.

An Abundance of Psychographs

Throughout those early years Archdeacon Colley continued his work with the Crewe circle, and they produced many detailed psychographs – that is, the plates are not placed within the camera but held between the hands of the investigators and the mediums (Mr. Hope and Mrs. Buxton), usually in unopened, sealed boxes containing several plates. The sitters often specified on which plate they wished an image to appear, but sometimes the spirit control would say on which plate it would be found.

Felicia Scatcherd, was introduced to the work of the circle when she received a telegram from Archdeacon Colley to go to his home at Leamington. There on July 16th 1909 she met Rev. Professor Henslow and two members of the Crewe Circle who were on a visit to the Archdeacon.

This is her report of the occasion from Henslow's book:

"A séance for spirit photography was held. It was disappointing in one sense. Prof. Henslow was told that he would find impressions on certain plates in a sealed packet on the table which was not to be opened for a fortnight.

I prepared to say good-bye, when Mr. Hope said he would like to do something for 'the visitor from London'. "The friends say that if the lady can remain the night, they will give her a test." I replied that the only test of interest to me was one that would convince my fellow-members of the Society for Psychical Research. The mediums insisted, but I refused to stay unless Prof. Henslow also remained and took charge of the proceedings.

"Sir, do stay!" pleaded Mr. Hope, "There are five of us—you (Henslow), the Archdeacon, Mrs. Buxton, Miss Scatcherd and myself. You must buy five plates from your own photographer. Each plate must be put into a light-tight envelope and worn by the sitter, with the sensitised surface next to the person, until the séance. It will not take long to fetch the plates and bring them back to us. Thus, we shall have an hour to wear them before the séance this evening. It is the only way to get them magnetised so as to have immediate results. You can each develop your own plate to-night and then Miss Scatcherd will know whether the friends have kept their word."

Prof. Henslow good-naturedly agreed and drove off with the Archdeacon to purchase the plates. I remained with Mrs. Buxton and Mr. Hope. Within an hour the Archdeacon returned with four plates put up as directed. Prof. Henslow had gone home to dinner wearing his plate in a wood slide contrived by Archdeacon Colley. Mrs. Buxton and I tucked ours inside our blouses and Mr. Hope placed his in that trouser pocket – which has aroused such evil suspicions in the minds of investigators. We remained together until Prof. Henslow joined us. It was full daylight. We sat round the table when Mr. Hope asked:

"What do you want, Miss Scatcherd? A face? A message? What shall it be?"

"You forget my conditions; Prof. Henslow must decide. Let him choose," I replied.

Prof. Henslow said he did not care what came so long as the same thing appeared on all the plates.

It was a remark worthy of the speaker, conveying, as it did, a most crucial test, in view of the fact that he had never let his plate out of his own keeping. The usual séance was held.

Prof. Henslow developed his plate first. I developed mine under Archdeacon Colley's supervision, then Mrs. Buxton and Mr. Hope developed theirs.

The results are of interest. The Archdeacon did not wear a plate so as to leave "more power for the others."

Mr. Hope's plate was blurred.

The tablet on Prof. Henslow's was identical in outline with Mrs. Buxton's and mine, both of which were sharp and clear, but Mrs. Buxton's was the best.

Mrs. Buxton had been with me the whole time, and her six-months-old baby had never left her arms.

The message addressed to Prof. Henslow was appropriate, but the writing was so microscopically fine that we could not read it that night. Mr. Hope was very disappointed.

"Never mind," he said, "when we get home, we will ask the guides to give it us again!" He and Mrs. Buxton were leaving by the early morning train. The Archdeacon had charge of the negatives and had promised to let us know as soon as he had deciphered the message. The mediums did not like their lodgings, so slept at my hotel. I saw them off in the morning, before any of us knew what the message was.

A day or two later I received from the mediums a duplicate of the message not yet known to them or to myself. But this time the writing was large enough to be read by the naked eye. As Prof. Henslow had requested, the same thing had come on all the plates in differing degrees of distinctness.

This was my first experience of a Crewe 'skotograph' [1] and it was decisive.

---

1. 'Skotograph' was a word proposed by Miss Scatcherd from the Greek meaning "dark writing" for psychographs ie. spirit writing on photographic plates in unopened packets.

As I wrote in the *Psychic Gazette* from notes submitted to Archdeacon Colley at the time, and afterwards read by Prof. Henslow when published, no suspicions could fall either on the mediums, Archdeacon Colley or myself, as not one of us had had the chance of tampering with Prof. Henslow's plate, nor could Prof. Henslow and his photographer have prepared a series of plates for an occasion on which they had no reason to have reckoned... This incident is recorded thus by Prof. Henslow:[2]

"At 8 pm. the message came as promised. It was identically the same on all the plates. The writing is microscopically small and written as given below. It consists of sixteen lines, the upper four and the five lower most are horizontal, the latter being upside down but the other intermediate seven lines are oblique so that the whole takes the form of a Z."

Unfortunately the plate itself was not able to be published, so it was illustrated thus in his book.

Professor Henslow frequently took part in sittings at Crewe, and he recorded this about some of the longer psychographs:

"It will be noticed that the words are written on what looks like a rough-edged oblong piece of glass, held by a hand. It would seem to be good proof that the long messages so often received in a few seconds, are all written out before-hand on tablets; then being held up, are precipitated on to the photographic plate. ...

If the tablet be transposed, then the writing would presumably be reversed if held before the medium the wrong way."

226   THE TRUTHS OF SPIRITUALISM

The following is the message sent. The last five lines were written upside down. It is all as stated in microscopically small letters.

To the Rev. Professor,
    Friends,
        We are doing this to show you that it is possible to speak with you by this means ; and now that you have seen for yourself

We want and ask you with all earnestness We can, to stand by the Archdeacon, as he is worthy of your best. He has worked hard for the cause he holds so dear. Remember there are more for you than all that are against you.

Give us the conditions and we will give you the proof you require. Be generous friends to our friends and we will work together for the good of all. Good Night.

(Nos 47, 48.)

Illustration of the 'Z' psychograph.

2. *Proofs of the Truths of Spiritualism.* pp. 224-7.

To test the supernormal origin of the psychographs the Archdeacon sometimes requested that the messages be in two, three or more languages. Henslow tells us:

"This Message was written in Latin (September 16th,1910), under the Archdeacon's hands (without a camera), being also immediately developed by him. He made a sudden request that any writing vouchsafed might partly be negative and partly positive, the whole being written in some twenty or thirty seconds. Hence in the following transcript of the original, three English words, viz., and, so, and—are positive; while the 24 words in Latin, with the English word friends are negative.

"*Friends*

"Certain pete finem, *and* confide recte agens; Fortuna favet fortibus. *so* principisis obsta. Esto quod videris. *And* de mortuis nil nisi bonum magna est veritas et praevalebit."

The following is spirit's own translation of the Latin message sent to Mr. Hope and Mr. and Mrs. Buxton. As they knew no Latin spirit gave them the translation in the same manner as the original message came with the Archdeacon Colley.

"*Friends*, aim at a sure end *and* fear not while acting justly. Fortune favours the bold, *so* oppose the first appearance of evil. Be what you seem to be. *And* let nothing be said of the dead but what is favourable. The truth is powerful and will ultimately prevail."

On another occasion a psychograph in French, English and Latin came in reply to a request made by Archdeacon Colley, containing Latin, French and English words. Professor Henslow shows how the words were spaced on the plate:

"*Nisi Dominus frustra. Cette fois*
We content ourselves with saying
Dilige amicos
And in   near   your wishes
the   future
shall be favoured"

A free translation is:

'Unless God be with you, all will be in vain. This time we content ourselves with saying, love your friends, and in the near future your wishes shall be favoured......' ."

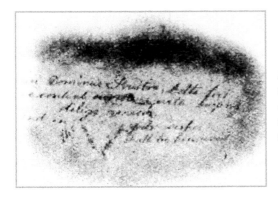

Psychograph of the lower text on the page facing. Note the word 'the' is written obliquely and 'near' and 'future' form a V shape.

Archdeacon Colley wrote this of another successful experiment:

"This psychograph came in a very informal way, yesterday evening at our devotions of prayer and praise, the four of us[3] together. As we are all singers and love singing, the power unseen about us was very strong and this is the secret of the success of our friends at Crewe.

"It is the *Salvation Army spirit* they have, that seems to work so potently with them. For all day here (at Stockton Rectory, to which he had invited the Crewe circle) as my guests, they go about the garden singing for the very love of it, and I am told that from time to time their unseen helpers are (clairaudiently) heard by them joining in with them in their melodies and long drawn-out harmonies delighting me to hear."

The writing, in three languages, runs both ways in a spiral, with the centre filled with a message in archaic Greek characters.

'Friends all, we greet you in the name of our Father, and we will use our powers, *ne plus ultra*, to provide you with a little food for thought and, *autre fois pourvu que autre* conditions are favourable; and by virtue of faith we may be enabled to grant or help you to get your desires in regard   to a lady, *videlicet.* ... that confidence, friendship and support, materially and spiritually, may be extended to all who are doing their best to bridge over gulfs between the two worlds.   God bless you.'

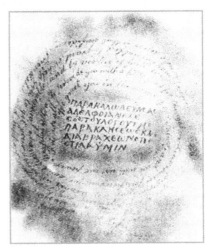

Message in four languages

---

3. 'The four of us would be' – Archdeacon Colley, Mr. Hope & Mr. & Mrs. Buxton.

The Archdeacon was able to decipher the Greek to read:

"By means of excellent proofs,
Brothers, bear up
Against the crowd of howlers.
Exhort, (as by heralds)
With the arm (?'uplifted) in a way
Well known to you.."

Communications were often suddenly stopped, so some circular psychographs were unfinished – being hollow in the centre because the writer was called away to some important work he had been appointed to do.

On one occasion two psychographs were received by a visitor to the Crewe circle. They were precisely the same, but one was larger and the reverse of the other.

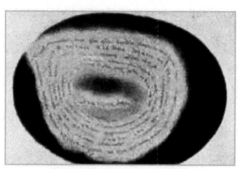

The writing was written spirally as usual and the larger had the sitter's face in the middle. The control said that the reason why the central part of the image was not filled up as usual was because the 'scribe' was called from the work of writing.

The uncompleted psychograph received by a visitor to the Crewe Circle

The following example of a foreign language psychograph was sent to Henslow by a member of the circle at Crewe. There is no date given but it must have been about 1909. It was given in the home circle without the Archdeacon present. He writes:

"I am a member of the circle composed of six sitters, who have been meeting weekly for three years. Our purpose is spirit photography. After about two years, each member had obtained some evidence of this particular phenomenon, except myself. My turn having come, we sat for a photograph of my mother. None of the sitters had seen a photograph of her taken in earth-life. The day and hour were fixed, and arrangements made for myself with the photographer[4] to bring the plates. In consequence of some misunderstanding we missed each other, with the result that while I was

---

4. The writer is referring to Hope, a photographer as well as the developing medium at that stage. The sittings were always held at the Buxton's house and not at Hope's own home.

waiting in the house he was waiting in the street. Unable to wait longer he purchased the plates himself.

After explanations, we began the sitting. In spite of my experience hitherto, this initial blunder, as trivial as it may appear, produced in my mind a sense of disappointment and dissatisfaction. The control, reading this condition, met it by commenting upon it, and offering to produce a Greek message for my own special satisfaction in addition to mother's photo, stating that I could choose the number of the plate and it should appear upon it. The message being in Greek we should not be able to read it, so would require an interpreter; but it could be found in the 17th chapter of St. Luke's Gospel, the 4th and 5th verses.

Choosing the fifth plate, we immediately held them between our hands in the customary way, not having been unpacked, but just as they came from the chemist. In a few seconds the control declared it done.

Acting under the instruction of the photographer, who did not touch them, I then unpacked the plates, developed the fifth myself, with the result here shown.

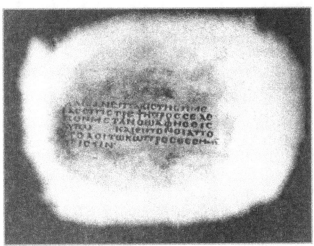

Psychograph of the Greek Text received

It has been submitted to a number of interpreters and all verify the truth of the control's statement. While in the dark room, I myself put one of the plates of the same packet into the slide and immediately we went to sit in broad daylight in the open air for mother's photo. This also was successful, being a photo of mother just as she lay in her coffin.

It was acknowledged by her eldest daughter, who is a Wesleyan Methodist and entirely opposed to spiritualism." (Signed M.V.)

58

Professor Henslow tells us:

"The psychograph was at once seen to be exactly like, as far as the letters were concerned, to the Codex Alexandrinas, the very one given to Charles I in 1628. On going to search for it in the British Museum, I found it to be in a glass case, as stated by the spirit control, but inaccessible to a near approach, as it was railed round. As the keeper of the MSS. possesses in the library in his office a photographic facsimile, Archdeacon Colley was enabled to take a photograph of it as well as of the psychograph.

The original Alexandrinas Greek Text

On comparing the two it will be at once seen that the psychograph was not a facsimile, but a copy; the differences being as follows. In the Alexandrine, the lines were evidently ruled as the letters are strictly parallel and all the strokes full length and perpendicular.

In the psychograph, though the words of each line begin and end as in the original, they are not accurately parallel, nor are the strokes of full length or perpendicular. It may be described, therefore, as a neat copy, but inexact in the formation of the letters and facsimile. A comparison of the corresponding letters shows numerous differences.

In the psychograph, as in the Alexandrine M.S.[5] , it is as follows 'And if seven times in the day, he turn again to thee saying I repent thou shalt forgive him. And the Apostles said unto the Lord, 'Increase our faith.' "

---

5. In other Manuscripts there is an extra line [Hamarte eis se, kai heptakis tes hemeras] which was somehow omitted in the Alexandrinus and all later copies. The verses in the King James version of th NT. reads "And if *he trespass against thee seven times* in a day and seven times turn again to thee saying I repent; thou shalt forgive him."

Continuing with the biblical theme, in 1910 *The Two Worlds* published the following under the heading:

Remarkable Spirit-Photography at Crewe!

A Poser

We have for a considerable length of time heard privately of remarkable photographic phenomena taking place at the Crewe circle, with which Archdeacon Colley has had much experience. A friend recently calling upon us narrated the substance of the following communication, which he sent us at our request. We give the account exactly as it reached us:

"Several interested Spiritualists at Crewe have been sitting for a considerable period for the purpose of obtaining spirit photographs, and they have been favoured with a large measure of success, both with the camera and without it. The following recent incident is a remarkable one, as showing how the spirit-friends overcame a sceptic, who, like many others, considered the spirit-photographs obtained were not genuine. The gentleman concerned sent a packet of photographic plates, as purchased from the dealer, after taking precaution to seal the same, as an extra safeguard. Later on, he was allowed to be present when the circle sat, so that he could witness the whole procedure. After the meeting was opened with singing and invocation, during which time the packet of photographic plates lay upon the table, the controlling spirit asked the sceptic to say upon which plate he desired a message, and he said, 'On No. 5 from the top.'

At the close of the meeting, the plate was taken from the packet and developed in his presence, when it was found to have on it the following: 'See Luke, chapter 10, verses 3, 23, and 24.'

On referring to the passage the sceptic was so well satisfied of the genuine result that he wrote a letter to the circle certifying his conviction of the truth. The remarkable point herein is that the message will be found [to be] one full of meaning so aptly suitable for the circumstance. Also, for other sceptics, it may be remarked that the other plates in the said packet were entirely unaffected by the chemical action or actinic force by which the message on the plate was produced. It would be a service to our cause if all friends would report such remarkable instances of spirit power. "Truly it is a poser. Here is a chance for the Marriotts of the conjuring world to whet their wits."

The verses written were:

Luke Ch 10 v3: Go your ways: behold I send you forth as lambs among wolves.

v23: And he turned him unto his disciples and said privately, Blessed are the eyes which see the things that ye see:

v24: For I tell you that many prophets and kings have desired to see those things which ye see, and have not seen them; and to hear those things which ye hear, and have not heard them[6]."

A Prophetic sign of things to come??

The psychographs continued to appear and this one from July 1912 must have been one of the last obtained by the Archdeacon before his passing two months later.

It is a composite message in Greek, Latin and English. This is the Archdeacon' s account of it:

"This psychograph was given us in the picture-room of Stockton Rectory (Rugby) as we sat round the fire singing hymns and holding for a few seconds between our hands an unopened packet of Sovereign quarter-plates, on Wednesday evening, July 3, 1912.

I immediately developed the photo plate as suggested by 'Massa' (one of the controls), *viz.*, the fourth from the top of the unopened packet of twelve plates, which I bought last week. I found the following communication upon it. This was in the presence of Mr. Hope (the medium) and two members of the Crewe circle. The writing was beautiful and clear, like copperplate engraving. Here is line for line the message as I developed it."

'Friends,

Deo favente, we will try to prove to you

That there is a power

beyond that of man, which, as you see by——'

There followed six lines in Greek similar to those in a subsequent communication but the film has become crumpled up since it was taken, and so made it illegible.

However it said:

'Your getting, and our giving you, this message in this manner shows you that it is genuine. Our advice to you is 'Esto quod videris, (Be as you are seen) and hold fast to the truth, for Magna est veritas et praevalebit (the truth is great and will prevail). Unite yourselves together in brotherly and sisterly love; for then, and not till then, shall a second Pentecost be given unto you.

God bless you.'

---

6. See the King James Version of the *New Testament* for the wording.

An Easter Message

Before some of the psychographs in the previous chapter there had been one to outshine all others – the one that had intrigued me in the *Psychic News* article in 1995.

Six months after it had been received by the Archdeacon and the Crewe Circle he sent it to *The Two Worlds,* and they gave it to the world on September 2nd 1910, introducing it by this note in their 'Current Topics'.

A Remarkable Phenomenon

"Archdeacon Colley's contribution in this issue of *The Two Worlds* is in many particulars a notable one. We are privately informed as to the medium concerned and the Circle in which the results were obtained, while the name of Archdeacon Colley is a quite acceptable guarantee for the guarantee of the *bona fides* of the manifestation. The diagram accompanying the sermon shows the sizes of the photographic plate and the actual area covered by the writing.

A photographic print from the negative is before us, and shows the accuracy of the outlines of the spaces concerned. The printing follows the original exactly, line by line. As to the context of the sermon, that is a matter for each reader to decide upon as he may.

The one point to bear in mind is the circumstances under which the message was produced. It equals anything we have seen as the product of the mediumship of Mrs Everitt, of London, though in former years, the spirit friends of her band produced some very wonderful "direct" writings upon cards and paper, while equally as wonderful were the many of the direct writings obtained by David Duguid.

The Archdeacon will be at the forthcoming Church Congress, and is having the article reprinted for distribution at the meetings. With commendable persistency he continuously addresses himself to his clerical brethren, and we have reason to believe, not without effect."

Imprinted on a glass half-plate (4¾x 6½ inches – 120x165mm) but only occupying the space of roughly a quarter-plate image, there were 84 lines, with 1,710 words, written in perfect copperplate script by an unknown spirit entity.

Under the Archdeacon's heading of SPIRITUAL RESURRECTION, *The Two Worlds* journal reproduced his diagram of the dimensions within the half-plate negative.

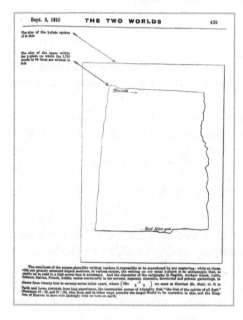

Archdeacon Colley's diagram of the position on the plate of the psychograph received.
The upper writing reads:
The size of the ½ -plate spoken of is this.
Below this it reads : The size of the space within the plate on which the 1,710 words in 84 lines are written is this-

The lines below the sketch read:

"The smallness of the copper-plate-like writing renders it impossible to be reproduced by any engraving; while at times, our greatly esteemed unpaid mediums, in various circles, the writing on our usual ¼ plates is so microscopic that, to enable us to read it, a high-power lens is necessary. And the character of the caligraphy in English, Archaic Greek, Latin, Hebrew, Italian, French, Arabic, varies continually in our several, separate domestic, devotional and private gatherings, in places from twenty-four to seventy-seven miles apart, where we meet as directed (St. Matt. vi. 6) in and Love, KNOWING, from long experience, the inscrutable power of Almighty God, "the God of the spirits of all flesh" Numbers .16: 22; and 27: 16), who, thus, and in other ways, permits the Angel-World to be operative in this, and the Kingdom of Heaven to have rule abidingly with us here on earth."

When the Archdeacon had this copied into type for a Broadsheet, he made sure the lines followed those of the original psychograph.

Now using modern technology I have reduced this typed version of the message, with no other changes, into a <u>true size</u> replica of the original so you might see how amazing this was.

The outer line, opposite, is the size of the half-plate negative. The inner shaped line is that of the <u>actual size</u> of the received psychograph.

God bless you

This is the actual size of the message received by the circle on March 6th 1910, on a 'half-plate' sealed up from all access of light, and held between the twelve hands of six Christian Spiritualists for thirty-nine seconds. (T. Colley).

(The outer 'box' is the actual size of the half plate used.)

Too small to be engraved on to the plate by a human hand but when examined under a microscope this is what was imparted:

"Friends

At present we would like to speak to you on the subject of the spirit-world and the destiny of man.

The thought of a future state in relationship to man has in some form or other ever been opposed and frowned upon by men of sceptical minds. To go no further back than the days of the great teacher, Jesus, we find there existed a Sadducean class, who denied all future existence to man. They said there were no spirits either of angels or men; and therefore, regarded the stupendous doctrine of the resurrection of humanity as a fanciful thing, and denounced it as such.

In these modern times infidelity has become more rampant and positive, and has endeavoured, to the very utmost, to confirm and establish its most repulsive and cheerless theories by deductions of science. Not a single science has ever been found out that has not been eagerly sought after by the enemies of our common immortality to help their godless theories, which are fully bent, if possible, on despoiling your spiritualism of her brightest ornament, which is proving the lofty and glorious truths of God's revelation, which proclaims with great power the deathlessness of man. But we are glad to say that every science, like an advancing tide, has thrown back upon them their own baseless thoughts, and rolled onward. Bearing on its bosom its mighty and resistless testimony of the truth of God and the Immortality of man.

The last form of argument which has assailed the future existence of humanity is the materialistic theory or doctrine of homogeneousness. Its advocates have asserted that man has but one identical nature, that he is altogether earthly and earth born, that his intelligent mind is nothing more than the delicate offspring of matter. Their favourite argument is that the mind grows and dies with the body; that it is infantile with the infant body, and perfect in the adult; and therefore, it must perish with the body at death. Now, if man be nothing more than simple matter, if the mighty spirit corresponds exactly in all cases to the size of the human body, then there is a strong presumption that the dissolution of the physical organisation is the utter extinction of the entire man; but such conclusions are repugnant to reason and fact. It is readily granted that the soul manifests greater power as the body ripens to maturity, and that when the body yields to the withering touch of time the soul often seems to yield too; but this is not because it either grows or declines, but because the body as a habitation is too weak and frail for other than a limited and gradual development of its great powers.

How often has some unexpected news so excited the immortal spirit that its very emotional workings have proved too powerful for its frail tenement, and the body has given way under the strain. It is the body, therefore, that is infantile and weak and not the soul. Such being the nature of the spirit in man, the death of the body can no more affect its existence than the mere throwing off of a garment can annihilate the person of its wearer. Everlasting life pulsates in every faculty. There is, therefore, a spirit life. When the world's Creator breathed into man's nostrils the breath of life, He beheld in him the image of His own great self; He saw divinity assuming humanity, and humanity becoming immortal. In the eyes of God there are no dead; all who have been, still are; their spirits have not been spent as a lightning flash, they are still living, loving, conscious, and still active. We would remind you or a verse from your hymn book, "Life is real, life is earnest, and the grave is not its goal. Dust thou art, to dust returnest, was not spoken of the soul.

The spirits' after-condition is a theme which touches you all. Many who were dear to you have passed over; they have thrown off their mortal coil and taken on the immortal, firmly trusting in God's love and mercy; and fondly hoping to behold His glory the very moment they put off the mortal. Are you to regard them as deaf, speechless, and blind? And will such be your destiny when you make the grand transition? Is the power of hope to be blasted when in fullest bloom? Will the river of life be checked when its flow towards the eternal ocean is the greatest? Is it all a mockery or a delusion? True it is that in the Bible death is depicted under the beautiful and peaceful image of sleep; but such representation invariably refers to the body, and not to the soul. The moment death's shadow falls upon the entrance of the gateway of life, and in the twinkling of an eye the disembodied spirit is receiving the reward of its works while in the body; just as the arctic sun dips into the ocean, it hastens again on its glorious career up the sky; so the instant the natural eye is eclipsed in death, the spiritual eye opens in eternity. One step, and the soul is on the spirit-side of life. A troop of angelic beings, unseen, crowd the chamber of death, and are ready with outstretched arms to welcome and bear the spirit to its home immediately on its emancipation. What a moment of wonders: one moment surrounded by weeping friends and bleeding hearts, and taking the last fond embrace this side the grave; the next, a companion of happy spirits, leaving their friends wondering why this should be. But here we would say, they know only in part, they see as through a glass darkly. The greatest efforts of your greatest men are as the opinions of children, and in the words of your Bible we say, "Eye hath not seen, nor ear heard, neither hath it entered into the heart of man the things which God hath prepared for them that love Him."

Yet, though the eye and the ear and the mind of men are inadequate to the giant task of grasping this, when Christian people say they have communion with the saints, they gladly avow their firm belief of being able to speak with their loved ones.

No, friends, death has not really separated us from you. Of course, as far as the mere physical relationship is concerned, it has; but there are spiritual, holy affinities which it cannot sever. The mortal flesh becomes pulseless clay under its cold, withering touch; the compound unity of man's disembodied person is dissolved by it into the distinctive principles of flesh and spirit.

Yet, while the flesh perishes and becomes food for worms, the spirit lives on, defying its power, and laughs at the corruption of the grave. Therefore, along with us, you can rejoice together and say in very truth, "O grave, where is thy Victory; O death, where is thy sting?" For, friends, we tell you that neither life, nor death, nor principalities, nor powers, nor height, nor depth, nor anything else shall separate you from the love of God and your loved ones. With what a lot of love and kindly affection you look forward to a reunion with your dear ones! Their forms, faces, and smiles are constantly floating before you; their voices sound sweetly on your ears; their well-remembered names are as pouring oil on troubled waters. You love them still; you cannot forget your sainted dead. No, you have known them too well for that; you have wandered hand in hand with them through the tangled woods of life; you have seen them wrestle and strive with circumstances in that life, and, at last, you have seen them place their foot on the boundary land of another world; you have seen the heavens open and the angels descending, and they have been born away from your sight.

How, then, can you cease to remember them? But no sooner are they lost to your sight than questions such as these come to you: "Shall we meet them? Shall we love and be loved by them again?" To answer these, we will turn first of all to the Bible for support. Turning to the second book of Kings, the sixth chapter, the sixteenth and seventeenth verses, you will find these words: "And he answered, Fear not, for they that be with as are more than they that be with them. And Elisha prayed and said, Lord, I pray thee open his eyes, that he may see. And the Lord opened the eyes of the young man, and he saw; and behold, the mountain was full of horses and chariots of fire round about Elisha." Then, again, the eighth chapter of Ezekiel, third verse; there you will find how a spirit-hand lifted him up. There again, Moses appeared in visible form at the transfiguration of Jesus on Tabor, while his body was still lying in a valley in the land of Moab. Again, there is Samuel, who, hearing a voice, said: "Speak, Lord, for Thy servant heareth." All these, and many more we could mention, give proof of a continued existence. And here are a few thoughts from your modern great men on the same subject. We think we have seen our loved one die, but if our eyes could be opened, if only for one moment, we should see that life was uninterrupted: this from one of the ministry of the Church of England. And now, friends, we bring this little message to a close, but would like to remind you once again that you stand at the vestibule of an eternal world, so make the best use of your time here; sow to the spirit, place God first in all you do; then, when you have finished your work in the body, you will be able to say with the apostle: "I have fought a good fight, I have finished my course, I have kept the faith; henceforth there is laid up for me a crown of righteousness"

May the peace and joy which passeth all human understanding be yours.

God bless you."

The copy in *The Two Worlds* finished with the Archdeacon's footnote to the broadsheet:

Printed for private circulation., Easter-Day, March 27th, 1910, and sent to all the bishops of the Church of England by ARCHDEACON COLLEY, Stockton Rectory, Rugby, who in writing to their Lordships says: "In the interests of the church, it is from reports reaching me from all over the world relative to psychic matters, of urgency that I should be quickly examined by a committee of the Bishops, including those of their Lordships who are members of the Society for Psychical Research."

Archdeacon Colley used it as his sermon at Stockton that Easter Day and later distributed it at the church's conference in Cambridge.

I hope that you have read it through—or will take time to read it—as the message is as appropriate and meaningful now as 112 years ago.

SPIRITUAL RESURRECTION.

BEING A SERMON FOR EASTER WRITTEN BY NO MORTAL FINGERS

The Archdeacon's print of the message as a 'Broadsheet' was included in 'The Two Worlds' report.

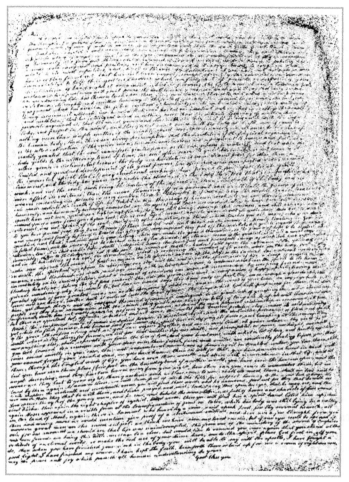

*Above: Copy of the original psychograph (actual size)
from Prof. Henslow's book
'Proofs of the Truths of Spiritualism'.*

*Right: A small enlarged
portion of the psychograph
to show the copperplate
writing of the message
received.*

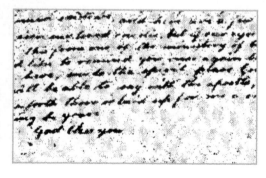

William Walker, W.T. Stead & the Spirit of the Archdeacon

Following the publication of the Archdeacon's photographs in *Light* in June 1910 and the 'Spiritual Resurrection' psychograph in *The Two Worlds* in the September, news of the happenings at Crewe started to spread, and in late 1910 William Walker of Buxton in Derbyshire started to take an interest in the photographic results that were being achieved.

"He was an ardent photographer with over 40 years' experience and had gone through the trials of the wet plate process, and thus developed the patience and carefulness which stood him in such good stead with the dry plates. He won many prizes with his photos at various exhibitions. He made an especial study of colour photography.

His connection with "psychic" photography dated from November 7th, 1910, when he had his first sitting with Mr. and Mrs. Buxton and Mr. Hope – the Crewe Circle – and as a keen photographer he entered into the study of the various stages of their photography closely. He tested the mediums and spirits in many ways, achieving by careful process what he termed psychic photography with absolute proof. Those who accompanied him through the various processes know he was justified in this. The photographs and messages obtained were many and wonderful."[1]

James Coates published Walker's first experiences in detail in his book *Photographing the Invisible* in 1911.

The Testimony of Mr. Walker

Mr. Walker says:

"On November 7th, 1910, I sat with the Crewe Circle, and was photographed by the camerist of the Circle. Two plates were exposed on me – time, 15 seconds each, the day being dull. On one plate, in addition to other "extras", is the portrait of my friend Mr. Alfred Smedley, late of Park Mount, Belper, so well-known years ago in spiritualism. On the second plate Mr. Smedley appears again, but on the opposite side of me, with another "extra", said to be that of the spirit responsible for the phenomena produced at this Circle. The background used was the grey side of an American cloth table-cover

---

1. *The Two Worlds,* August 6th 1915; Wm Walker Obituary

In-life photo of Mr. Alfred Smedley taken from his book "Reminiscences".

Mr. Wm. Walker with pschic 'extra' of Mr. Alfred Smedley, his life-long friend, taken by the Crewe Circle, 7th November 1910.. (Photo courtesy of the Britten Library & Museum.)

I purchased the plates, which no one handled after the maker packed them save myself. In the dark-room I cut open the box and, after carefully examining the dark slide, I inserted two plates. The remaining ten plates in the box were carried in my pocket.

I purchased the plates, which no one handled after the maker packed them save myself. In the dark-room I cut open the box and, after carefully examining the dark slide, I inserted two plates. The remaining ten plates in the box were carried in my pocket.

The camera, which I examined, was empty and the lens clean. I inserted the dark slide. After exposure, I took it, with plates, into the dark-room and developed the latter, with results which I have already sent to *The Two Worlds*. ... The camerist with-drew the shutters and made the exposure, but neither he nor anyone else touched the plates."

James Coates continues:

"Apart from the signed certificate obtained from all present as to the facts recorded, my confidence in Mr. Walker's skill and honesty is unbounded, and his evidence is sufficient. Mr. Alfred Smedley and Mr. W. Walker were life-long friends, and there can be no doubt as to identification. But since receiving the foregoing account, I have obtained the following:

Derby Road, Belper,

April 8th, 1911.

Certificate.

I have much pleasure in certifying that the spirit photographs taken with Mr. Walker at Crewe in November last, are of my father, the ascended Alfred Smedley, and also that the portraits are identified by the undersigned, whose names are appended to this certificate.

Lilian R. Smedley.

Thomas F. Smedley, Derby Road, Belper.

Geo. Wheeldon, Joseph Street, Belper.

Hy. Wigley, Bridge Street, Belper."

* * * * *

The Spirits had promised Mr. Walker a message in three languages if he sat the next day, and this is Coates' account of this sitting:

"For this purpose Mr. Walker brought his own plates, and these (wrapped in light-proof paper) were not out of his possession, save for a quarter of a minute, while being impressed between the lady medium's hands. Even then the packet was never out of his sight. He developed the plate.

The original writing can only be read through a magnifying glass. At my request he was good enough to enlarge the photograph for these pages.

"Dear Friends, – The following are a few words intended to prove an Intelligence at work far beyond the capabilities of the sitters. It is a *le chef d'oeuvre* as far as they are concerned. Our advice to you at present is to *audi alteram partem de crainte que* you may make a mistake and be misjudged. *Cedant arma toga* and *adfinem asto fidel*s and in all you do *cedo Deo*."

. . .the following is a rough translation of the French and Latin:

"Dear Friends, – The following are a few words intended to prove an Intelligence at work far beyond the capabilities of the sitters. It is a *masterpiece* as far as they are concerned. Our advice to you at present is to *hear both sides lest* you may make a mistake and be misjudged. *Let the opponent give way* to the law, and *be faithful to the end*, and in all you do *walk with God*."

William Walker concludes with this:

"None of the sitters could have produced the message; even if they had the opportunity, which was non-existent. The message can only be read from the film side, as if taken by camera; the latter being out of the question."

Coates continues:

"I have taken special pains since the Lodge-Colley controversy to acquaint myself with the *bona-fides* of the Crewe Circle, and of the mediumship of three of its members, and the excellent character which all bear. I have therefore all the more pleasure in giving the above case reported by Mr. Walker. Since the foregoing psychograph was sent me, the meaning of which at the time was not clear to Mr. W. Walker, ... I obtained the following on 15th January 1911:

"Dear Mr Coates, – When I last wrote I said: "At present it is cryptic to me." Now the part of the message, "Our advice to you at present is to hear both sides lest you make a mistake and be misjudged. Let the opponent give way to the law and be faithful to the end," has become clearer to me. A question concerning a boundary fence to property had been put into my hands to see it through. I had the matter in correspondence at the time the message was given to me. However, the owner, who is a very old person, having been annoyed by trespass, ordered a fence to be put up, and it was completed. I was not made aware of this until notice had been given to the adjoining owners to remove a portion of the fence, which is said to be on their land. On my visiting the site, I found it necessary to see the other side and to hear their version, as directed in the message. After fully considering the various points raised, it was decided to take this fence down and "give way to the law". This I consider has a just bearing upon the case. It shows the spirit friends who gave me the message knew of the case, and knew how it stood, as well as knowing what would follow, of which I at the time was not only ignorant, but our friends at Crewe could not have known."

Yours faithfully, W. Walker.

Buxton.

James Coates added:

"I have seen an enlargement of the original psychograph which contained the sermon.... It was certainly a remarkable psychograph. Many – almost as phenomenal – psychographs have been and are obtained through the psychics of the Crewe Circle. I am of the opinion this received by William Walker was another of them."

* * * * *

William Walker continued with the experiments with the Crewe circle and later sent the following to *Light*:

"I would very much like to give one striking case to set aside the erroneous idea of it being 'thought' photography.

On April 5th, 1911, we sat in our usual way at Crewe, myself and daughter-in-law as sitters to the camera.

When I had developed the plate after exposure through the camera, I found a message around the sitters which could only be partially read. "One of your friends" could be deciphered. At right angles to the sitters, near their elbows, appeared a psychic head and face, well formed, the head covered with a Tam-o'-Shanter.

We did not discover its meaning, and although I made enlargements from the negative, it did not assist us. On May 15th, 1911, we sat again. On the first plate the same form appeared with that of a child. On the second plate the same form again appeared, and also, against my head, the face of a lady.

Hundreds of people have looked through my album in different towns visited by me, but I could find no owner for the forms appearing on those plates. However, in the early part of this year, I was showing the book to a very old friend of mine at his home. When he turned over the leaf bearing the print of the message with the head and face, I noticed that he was much affected, and with tears in his eyes, be said, "That is a photograph of our son." The mother and daughter confirmed it; also gave me the name of the lady whose form appeared as above stated. The child was also owned as being the form of a daughter of another son. None of these three psychic forms were known by the sitters [in the circle], yet the photographs had been obtained several months prior to the forms being identified.

Unto all I would say, investigate with an open mind, an honest desire and intention. Then the spirit-friends will do their best so far as the medium's power will admit."

Walker's enthusiasm for securing images of the 'dead' in this way led him to contact William Stead shortly before the tragic journey of the 'Titanic' in which William Stead drowned.

In a letter to *Light* on May 25th 1912 he gave the background to his contact with Mr. Stead.

"On September 21st, 1911, I called by appointment at Mr. W. T. Stead's office to show him my album of psychic photographs, my wife being with me during the interview. Mr. Stead took great interest in the photographs and thanked us for calling. He expressed his sense of the 'great value which psychic photography gave to Spiritualism,' and said that as I had been so successful he hoped I would 'follow it up.' As we were separating, he took my hand in his and said, 'Do go on with the good work you have in hand, and will you kindly keep me posted!'

I thanked him and promised that I would keep him posted.

My next visit to Crewe was on October 16th, 1911, when two plates were exposed through the camera, with me as the sitter. On one plate appeared two psychic forms, and on the other a message. The letters are around me on a white ground, in an irregular form; also, they are positive (so that the ordinary laws of photography were set aside; as a positive and negative, my portrait, appeared on one plate). The message is to the point, and to those concerned clearly shows that the spirit friends have regard for those who assist them in these demonstrations. It was as follows:

'Tell A. *cura ut valeas* and we will help him, also great care is required in things generally. Do this and all shall be well. Let there also be perfect unity.'

As none of us are Latin scholars we had to look up what *'cura ut valeas'* meant, and found that it could be translated to read 'take care that you keep strong,' or 'well'. The advice was appropriate to A.'s then condition.

Knowing Mr. Stead to be a very busy man and seeing in the daily papers what was passing about that time, I did not forward to him copies from the negatives referred to above, and, owing to causes not under my control, my visits to Crewe had to be suspended until the present month.

When the news of the sad calamity and loss of Mr. W. T. Stead appeared in the newspapers, my wife said, 'You promised to keep Mr. Stead posted, but now it is too late.' I felt very sad at the loss of so many lives, and at the thought that among the victims should be Mr. Stead, a champion of all that was good and true, and in reply to my wife I said, 'Possibly he will comprehend why I did not write to him and send him copies as I promised, but he will perhaps try to keep me posted.'"

This is how he recorded what followed Stead's passing:

W. T. Stead's Signed Message through the Camera.

"Sir, On May 6th, as I was sitting with my friends at Crewe for psychic photography, we received a signed message from Mr. W. T. Stead through the camera. My own plates were used, and the whole of the handling of the plates, developing, &c., was performed by myself. There was thus no opportunity for the substitution of plates or for faking a message or otherwise tampering with the plates used (even if that had been attempted, which it was not, as the friends sitting in circle are as honest in their intention and desire as myself).

For my visit on the 6th May, I put, as is my usual practice, the sensitive plates – Rapid Brand – in my pocket, so that they could become magnetised, and carried them about with me for several days. The package was placed on the table at Crewe. Ten minutes or so were spent in singing, and after a few words of prayer a 'control' manifested. He told us to use the camera and to give a long exposure to one plate and a very short one to the other. As is my method, and by willing consent of my friends, the lens, camera, and slide were examined and found in order and clean.

I adjourned to the temporary dark-room, put the two plates in the slide, and carried the slide to the room where the exposures were made. The first plate had fifteen seconds exposure and the second one-twenty-fifth of a second, so that the difference in the exposure was three hundred and seventy-five times greater for No.1 than for No.2 plate.

Pyro. soda tabloids were used. I mixed the developer, and used the same developer, undiluted, for both the plates. No. 2 gives a good negative and does not show under exposure. That being so, No.1 should have flashed up and gone past any reasonable use, but as that was not so, some control over the actinic power during the exposure would appear to have taken place. The following message appears on both plates:

"Dear Mr. Walker,– I will try to keep you posted. – W. T. STEAD."

On No.1 plate the message is positive, and not very clear on the print, but easy to read on the negative. On No.2 plate it is negative, and comes out on the print clear and readable.

What could be more to the point than this message, in response to my words spoken to my wife, as before stated, in our home on the day we read of the 'Titanic' disaster? To those unacquainted, and who prefer to theorise rather than investigate, the idea 'thought photography' occurs quite naturally; but I am informed by one who for years was in close touch with him, that the 'handwriting perfectly resembles Mr. Stead's.' That being so, as we who sat for the psychic photos were not cognisant of the character of his handwriting, thought transference from us to the sensitive plates does not fit. I thank Mr. Stead for his message, and hope for more."

Yours, &c.,

W. Walker.

Buxton, May 16th 1912.

In his letter to *Light* he also included these details of sittings at Crewe:

"I may mention that we sit to offer the spirit friends every opportunity to guide us, by their advice, how we may best obtain with their help messages or portraits. Even medical prescriptions have been given, the names of drugs, with the weight of each drug, being shown in a proper manner. Such prescriptions have been presented at the chemist's and the medicine supplied. In all such cases the patient has derived much benefit by taking the medicine.

Photograph of William Walker with the message in the handwriting of Mr. W.T. Stead. The message on this plate appeared as "mirror writing'" so the print is shown here 'flipped' to enable the message to be read.

I refer to this only to show my readers that we have confidence in our spirit friends, and they reciprocate it. So far, I have never sat for a psychic photograph, with or without the use of the camera, without obtaining good results."

In September of 1912 the culminating point of the experiments at Crewe came when one afternoon two photographs were obtained in direct colours by the Paget[2] process. To achieve this, very careful preparations were required for many weeks both on the part of the spirit friends and the mediums.

2. See Appendix 2 for more information

It was not long before lantern slides of photographs obtained under strict test conditions at the Crewe Circle found their way into William Walker's popular lectures and in March 1913, at the close of one of his lectures, he made this request:

"Someday our National Union may purchase a lantern outfit and permit societies to hire it at a small cost, plus the carriage. I shall be willing to assist towards defraying the cost, by giving a lecture on 'Psychic Photography; or Can the Dead be Photographed?' in any town that may be selected, for out-of-pocket expenses. Then the public may see what spirit photographs are like. I have now over seventy slides, and as our esteemed friend W. T. Stead (who has given me his psychic portrait since he left the body) said to me, 'Do go on with this good work'; it is my sincere intention to do so, and I know that my friends of the circle, who devote freely and willingly their time to this work, will assist me to obtain even greater results."

Even at this stage the names of the mediums were not being released in the press to preserve the anonymity of this circle, for as James Coates rightly said, − "its members had to earn their living at their daily employment and were unable to give sittings to all and sundry, which further publicity would have brought to them."

Early in February 1913 Walker took two acquaintances, Mr. Brittain of Hanley and Mr. Jno. Williams of Rhyl, to Crewe for the purpose of sitting to obtain, if possible, psychic photographs. Mr. Brittain, president of the Hanley Spiritualist Society 'understands photography and can produce a good photograph. Mr. Williams, a professional photographer and a gold medallist (London), is an interested investigator.' William Walker sent the following to *Light* under the heading of '*Absolute Proof.*' [3]

"When the medium arrived, he said that the Crewe circle had been prevented from holding their usual mid-weekly meetings, and he feared we should not get any result. As I have never yet come away empty-handed, it was pleasant for me to remind him of that fact to clear away his pessimism. He then said, 'We shall want a packet of plates.' I replied that we had already purchased a packet. However, he desired that another packet should be purchased, and he and Mr. Williams left the room to buy the plates. It appeared to me at the time to be strange that the medium should insist upon a second packet of plates being purchased; later on it was obvious that he did it under the influence of the spirit friends.

We sat round the table, on the top of which were placed the two unopened packets of plates, also the plates which my friends had carried with them.

---

3. *Light*, March 29th, 1913

When the medium was under influence, he gathered up the packet *last purchased* and requested the lady sitter[4] (who is highly mediumistic) to hold it between her hands. He then placed one hand over and the other hand under her hands, directing me to do the same, and the other two gentlemen followed suit. Almost immediately our hands had settled a sudden throb took place through the medium and we were directed to use the *fourth* plate from the top as a psychograph. I was given the plates to take care of until required for the developing. [All italics are **Mr Walker's**.]

The other packet of plates (purchased on the way to the meeting) was treated in a similar way, and we were instructed to expose the *two* top plates through the camera. This packet was given to Mr. Brittain to take care of while arrangements were made for the sitting.

While the temporary background and chairs were being arranged, I put the dark room in order, with water supply, etc. Mr. Williams had brought with him a supply of hypo., also of pyro. ammonia developer. We entered the dark room together, and Mr. Williams, after examining the dark slide, the only one in use, transferred two plates from the packet of plates last mentioned to the slide. We three visitors were the sitters as directed by the spirit friends. After the two plates had been exposed, Mr. Williams developed them in our presence.

With regard to the above-mentioned fourth plate, which up to this time was in my pocket, I gave the unopened packet in which it was to Mr. Williams, and again in our presence he took out the fourth plate from the top; also, at my request, he developed the third plate from the top, which had lain film to film with the fourth plate. Now for the results:

(a) *Through the camera.* One plate shows the psychic form of a lady with abundant dark hair and a beautiful figure, not yet identified. The other plate shows the psychic form of an Indian, whose face partly covers my face, and whose feathers adorn me after the manner of Indians.

(b) *Without the use of a camera,* and *out of the packet direct as purchased, without any action of actinic rays of light as we understand them,* the results were: Fourth plate from the top. In the middle of plate an ellipse and in it a message which reads:

'My dear friends, do let unity prevail; we want it, we are anxiously awaiting it.—T. Colley.' – in the usual form of the Archdeacon's well-known handwriting. ...

On the third plate, which, as previously stated, was film to film with the fourth plate, nothing is shown."

---

4. Mrs. Buxton

Mr. Williams, returned to sit with the Crewe Circle several times. Described as the Photographic Expert of the Portland Studio, Rhyl, he sent a short report for publication in *The Case for Spirit Photography* in 1922.

"It is with the greatest pleasure that I add my testimony to the truthfulness and absolute sincerity of Mr. Hope and Mrs. Buxton.

They have been known to me for several years; altogether no less than six times I have had sittings with them. In every case they have allowed me every facility to eliminate any possible fraud, which as a photographer of nearly fifty years' experience, I was eager to discover.

One experience with the Crewe Circle was this: ... On the fourth plate was a message from the late Archdeacon Colley. This negative I have by me and anyone wishing to see same can do so with pleasure. No one could wish for a better test than this: no one but myself touched the plates at any time during the sitting."

(signed) Jno. Williams,
Portland Studio;
Rhyl.

A Lace Coat, A 'Second Thomas' and Alfred Kitson's Experiences

Despite William Walker's statement of the experiment with his friends being *'Absolute Proof'*, a declaration of fraud concerning the Stead message was made at the end of Felicia Scatcherd's first address in London in May 1913[1].

Miss Scatcherd described her researches into the phenomena from as early as 1903, and commented on her beliefs that:

"Physical phenomena, must be dealt with by specialists and experts. Amateurs could but bring ridicule upon themselves and the objects of their studies by claiming the slightest authority to speak on these matters, or even to describe happenings witnessed by themselves. When Sir Oliver Lodge finds the Crewe mediums unworthy of patient and prolonged investigation, and his views are published while their explanations are withheld, one naturally forms an opinion adverse to their claim. But if one stumbles upon such persons 'by chance', and find reason to believe that an error of judgment has been committed, it is one's duty to point out that error, even at the risk of being regarded as a foolish, meddlesome person."

Her talk closed with a description of the unexpected result of her visit to the Archdeacon's Rectory at Stockton in July 1910. Disguising Hope as 'Mr Faith' she told the assembled audience:

"On July 5th, 1910, in reply to an urgent summons, I had rushed off to Stockton, Rugby, meaning to return that same evening. A storm was threatening. I had not waited to get into travelling clothes, but had slipped on a thin dark rain-coat over my white indoor dress. I could not get back as there was no train available, so slept the night at the Rectory. In the morning the Archdeacon suggested that I should be photographed in the garden before leaving. He put a plate in his camera and focussed it and called to me to come. I replied, 'If you let me miss my train, I will never come to see you again.'

'Here, Mr. 'Faith', you take Miss Scatcherd's picture while I run over to the "Barley Mow" to hurry the cab. Do not touch the camera. It is focussed all right, just press the bulb when she is seated in the chair.'

Mr. 'Faith' was on a visit to the Rectory and was amusing himself in gardening. As he crossed the lawn to press the bulb, the thought flashed across me as to my erratic action in running off without a coat, and I said to

---

1. *Light*, 19th July 1913, 'Psychophasms and Skotographs'

myself, 'Even had you had your little lace coat you would look less ridiculous than you do now.' If the housekeeper had been there I might have said what I thought. It was the merest passing idea, and I inwardly laughed at myself for tearing off a hundred miles in such a fashion.

A few days later the Archdeacon sent me the result. He had not intended anything but just to take my photo, and was delighted with a psychophasm[2] which Countess 'Blank' had recognised as the late Canon 'Someone's' self or brother. People see resemblances as one sees faces in the fire. What filled me with amazement was the attempt on the plate to reproduce the coveted lace coat, at that same moment reposing in my wardrobe in London.

I used the word 'attempt' advisedly. The lace pattern does not show, but a thin transparent coat is seen, and I was wearing only a blouse. That it was a hit at that identical jacket is proved by the corners being rounded off. All my other coats had square corners.

Image taken in the garden at Stockton showing the lace coat and an "extra" (to her left).

It's a mad world, but while that is so and all things improbable may still be possible, yet here was an incident that set them all at naught.

The 'ghostly form' might have been already on the plate. The seemingly innocent person tidying the garden and singing salvation songs over his work may have substituted a prepared plate for the one the Archdeacon had just put in the slide, but neither hypothesis explains the appearance on the negative of the sensible image of the thought that arose just as Mr. 'Faith' pressed the bulb.

I found the dress I wore that day which I had thrown aside to be sent with other things to the country, and tumbled as it was, put it on to see if it contained a seam or wrinkle, anything that could suggest the lace jacket, and had myself photographed in it—as I knew already, there was nothing of the kind."

Loud applause from her audience was followed by comments from the floor by Mr. A.W. Orr and Dr. Abraham Wallace.

---

2. This was a term she applied to the appearances of "extras" on the plates.

Mr. A.W. Orr told the assembly of an incident which had convinced a very sceptical photographer friend of his, a professional photographer in Manchester, who had seen many negatives of spirit photographs, and with whom he had often discussed the subject of psychic pictures, but without convincing him of the possibility of discarnate people impressing sensitised plates. At Orr's request and in his presence the friend marked a plate and placed it in two Tylar's light-proof envelopes, both of which he sealed and secured so that they could not be opened without detection. Mr. Orr continued:

"I took the packet from him, and a few days later, with Mr. Walker, attended a sitting with the Crewe mediums. The 'control' desired that I should place the packet in the hands of the medium, the other three sitters, viz. Mrs. B., Mr. Walker, and myself, placing their hands on those of the medium. The control, after a few seconds, said that as the person who had sent the plate was a great doubter, he had imprinted the words 'Second Thomas' on the plate. This was on Friday, March 14th.(1913)

On the following Monday I took the packet to my sceptical friend and told him what had taken place. He examined the packet carefully and expressed himself satisfied that the envelopes had not been tampered with. We then repaired to his dark room, where he opened the packet and developed the plate, on which appear the words 'Second Thomas' as stated by the control, and also the signature my friend had first written upon it. Another point that should be mentioned is that Mr. Ward (my friend), after sealing up the inner envelope, wrote on the outside of it the words 'Film up' and these can be seen on the print, only reversed. Mr. Ward was surprised at the result, but at once admitted that he was satisfied it was beyond the power of ordinary photographic science to explain how it was produced.

... This must be admitted as absolute proof of spirit energy and intelligence, because no other person touched the plate than my (then) very sceptical friend, Mr. E. Ward, Oxford-road, Manchester, as he is prepared to certify. What is of not less importance, it incidentally proves the *bona fides* of the medium, who has not escaped undeserved aspersion of his mediumship, which is a matter of great satisfaction to all who have had the privilege of a sitting with him and are thus able to testify to his perfectly straightforward conduct in connection with these experiments."

Dr. Abraham Wallace followed this by saying that he was, as was known, much interested in psychical research, but he must have a large amount of evidence before he could accept these things. It was so easy to produce faked pictures. He had two photographs produced in the Crewe Circle and they were very evidently faked.

He was referring to Stead's writing around William Walker, as negative and positive, which had recently been published in *Light*.

There was no follow up that evening to the statement concerning the supposedly "faked" Stead plates but, in the following weeks, a vigorous correspondence began in *Light* between William Walker and Dr. Wallace about the veracity of the psychic photos obtained by Mr. Walker with W.T. Stead's message to him.

During this dialogue Wallace stated:

"there are distinct indications of the super-imposing of a picture containing an alleged message from Mr. Stead in the midst of some flocculent material, probably cotton wool, on a plate containing the figure of a gentleman. ....."

To which William Walker responded through the columns of *Light:*

"The Doctor is at a disadvantage, inasmuch as he was not present when the two psychic photographs in question were obtained. ... I took up this case in defence of my Crewe friends, but now I must defend myself against the possible effect of the Doctor's imagination.

At the close of one of my lectures on psychic photography in December last, a gentleman asked if he might see the slide, made by contact with No. 2 plate, on the screen again, and the lanternist put it in position, showing a picture about six feet square. Other slides having similar aura were also repeated by request. The gentleman then came forward and closely scrutinised the effect of the aura as it appeared on the screen.

After doing so, he turned to my audience, and said: 'I am a photographer, and assure you that I am not acquainted with any material substance that Mr. Walker or anyone could use to produce such a delicate network effect as shown by these photographs on the screen.'

My readers may perhaps take that as being better evidence, coming as it did from a professional photographer after seeing the pictures in question so much enlarged, than Dr. Wallace's remarks about faking with 'flocculent material, probably cotton wool.' Does the Doctor wish to dictate to the spirit friends the manner in which they are to give us these psychic photographs, seeing that we know nothing whatever about the difficulties in the way of their doing such work?"

Dr. Wallace declined Mr. Walker's invitation to view his collection of 'spirit' photographs and psychcographs, deeming it a waste of his time and Mr Walker's.

* * * * *

Late in 1913 Alfred Kitson made his way to Crewe. With the help of William Walker and his family he was able to sit with the Crewe Circle. He purchased a packet of "Imperial Sovereign" dry plates from the Taylor Drug Stores in Batley, (Yorkshire) and kept them close by him to "guard them from being tampered with in any way."

As many have already expressed in these pages, care was taken that no fraud could take place, and he did likewise on that Saturday:

"The method of procedure was to hold a spirit circle round the kitchen table. Singing took place, and prayer for God's blessing on the object that had drawn us together was offered. Then Mr. Hope was controlled and directed the operations; gave instructions who were to pose before the camera, in what order, and the number of photographs to be taken. Then each member of the circle—which was composed of the following persons: Mr. Hope, Mrs. Buxton (the two mediums), Mr. and Mrs. Walker (senior), from Buxton, Mr. and Mrs. Harry Walker (junior), of Crewe, and myself— were requested to place one hand under the unopened packet of plates, and the other hand on the top; the hands of Mr. Hope being the last.

Then a spasmodic thrill seemed to run through the medium's body, down his arms, into his hands, which appeared to be for the purpose of imparting a psychic charge of power to the photo plates. The plates were then taken into the dark room, the seal of the packet broken, two plates were taken out by me and placed in the carrier which was afterwards closed. The camera was then examined for signs of any secret springs, slides, screens, etc., spoken of by the professional photographer as being the secret means whereby spirit photographs are faked. But I failed to find any evidence of trickery.

After the plates were exposed in the ordinary way I went back to the dark room, removed the plates from the carrier and placed them in the developing dish, and carefully watched them develop, to make sure of the genuineness of any results that might appear. I found Mr. Hope and all the other members of the circle very obliging and assisting in every way to give satisfaction.

I have given the above detailed description of the *modus operandi* in order to satisfy the reader that every precaution against fraud was taken."

Of the four plates exposed on that occasion three had results. On the first, was an image of Andrew Jackson Davis, the well-known American seer, who appeared as a positive on the plate which resulted in the face being in the negative on the print. Kitson was intrigued as to why this should have occurred and during a sitting in the Home Circle later he asked his spirit guide Zela. She explained:

"Brother Davis was desirous of giving you evidence of his presence, for which purpose he had carefully built up a good presentation of himself by your side as so to appear full of vigour. But unfortunately, some disturbance, in your mental conditions, destroyed the result of his labours just as the plate was about to be exposed, and in order to prevent a failure he instantly brought all his will-power to the task of building up a 'thought picture' of himself, with the result as shown on the photo."

An incident on the train just 3 hours before the sitting had annoyed Kitson and although he thought he had put it out of his mind it obviously affected the sitting.

Plate 1. Andrew Jackson Davis in negative on the print. Sitter Alfred Kitson (obscured).

Plate 2. A Greek Greeting. Sitters Wm. Walker, Alf. Kitson, Mrs. Hry. Walker & Mrs. Wm. Walker

The second plate showed a greeting in Greek, and it was several years before Dr. Ellis T. Powell, the eminent Greek scholar, was contacted to translate it. It read 'These things are so,' – with a strong accent on the word 'are' .... Dr. Powell added:

"I should take them to mean that the manifesting intelligence wished emphatically to affirm that the principles which the sitters accepted were veritably true. Certainly, it is a most interesting manifestation and whenever you are having another copy taken from the same negative I should very much like to possess one."

The third had two faces. One of which resembled his sister Alice but was recognised by his clairvoyant eldest sister (Mrs Thomas) as their

Kitson's sister Ada who died at 11 months old and their Great-Grandfather who had raised their mother.

youngest sister, Ada, who had passed forty-six years earlier at the age of 11 months in 1867. She had grown to womanhood in spirit, and this was how she showed herself, to her sister (clairvoyantly).

The gentleman in the picture is said to be his mother's grandfather, with whom she was reared from being two weeks old, her mother having died, giving birth to her – her first child.

Alfred Kitson continued to visit Crewe over the next seven years and had numerous other psychic results; this next confirmed by the spirit himself in a home circle in Runcorn.

"Being engaged to serve the Longton Spiritualists' Society on October 26th, 1919, I decided to pay another visit to Crewe, on my return journey on the Monday; I arranged with Mr. Hope accordingly, stating I should not trouble to bring my own plates, but trust him to supply what were necessary.

I arrived at Crewe at 11-02 a.m., and had to leave by the 12-32. I hurriedly explained this on reaching Mr. Buxton's. Mr. Hope did not think results could be obtained under such conditions but promised to try. Two plates were exposed, on one of them appeared an "extra" which, seen in the negative, appeared like the face of a female, which, however, turned out to be an unknown youth. (See image opposite).

I sent copies of it to friends at Longton, Runcorn, and Middlesbrough, in the hope that some of them would be able to recognise the spirit, but all failed.

Mr. G. A. Mack, of Runcorn, showed it to the members of their Home Circle. When Mr. R. Bostock, the medium, saw it, he at once exclaimed, "Good heavens! It's ar' Jack!"

It appears that Mr. Bostock lost his brother about seventeen years before; and since then he had been instrumental in bringing Mr. Bostock into Spiritualism; and had often controlled him at the Home Circle.

Taken at Crewe, October 27th '19 and recognised in Runcorn as "Ar Jack."

Two weeks previously, when visiting Runcorn, I was privileged to attend Mr. Mack's Home Circle, where I made the acquaintance of "Jack", whose voice and manner was more like that of a young lady than of a young man. He made the enigmatical remark, "I am going to Crewe, to Yorkshire, and then coming home."

All present thought that he intended to pay visits to Crewe, Yorkshire, and then return to them. Later when the members of the Circle complimented him on the surprise he had given them in appearing as an "extra" on my photo, he smilingly remarked, "I told you I was going to Crewe, to Yorkshire, and then coming home!"

Alfred Kitson[3] never did get one of his spirit friend, Zela, for which he longed. On a visit to Middlesbrough in 1921 at a 'table sitting', by which messages were spelled out through the alphabet on a table, he learned it would never be possible as "she is too etherial."

It seems no photo was possible of a more evolved spirit, but he had been able to received one photo of spirit, his sister Ada, who had remained closer to the earth vibration after her death, even though there was no earthly image of her in existence.

---

3. T here are many more experiences in his book, *The Autobiography of Alfred Kitson.*

The Circle's Fame Spreads

The next few years became very busy ones as anonymity was dropped. Invitations came in from all over England and Scotland with requests for sittings in Crewe and to visit spiritualist societies and psychic investigators across the land.

In January 1914 Mr. Walter Howell secured a sitting with the Circle at Crewe and went with Mrs. Henry Walker (daughter-in-law of Mr. Wm. Walker.) This is the report appeared in *The Two Worlds* in May 1914 and I include it in full so you, the reader, may understand the care sitters took to ensure a genuine result.

"I may say, in commencing, that I have for over thirty years suspended judgement concerning psychic extras.

I have had some experiences in the attempt to obtain spirit-photographs, and until now have been unconvinced from personal experience, but I have admitted the possibility of such phenomena on the weighty evidence of Traill Taylor and others, who had a right to give a verdict.

On January 23rd, 1914, I visited Crewe for the purpose of making investigation into the claims there made. I purchased quarter-size sovereign Imperial Company's dry plates at a chemist's in Birmingham. These I carried about my person, as suggested by the Crewe friends, to magnetise them. On this particular date, at 2.30pm in company with my hostess, Mrs. Henry Walker, I went to the residence of Mr. and Mrs. Buxton, where the sitting was to be held. Shortly after our arrival Mr Hope came in. We immediately formed ourselves into a circle, placing the unpacked plates in the centre of the table. After singing and prayer. Mr. Hope passed under control and spoke of spirit-friends who were near us and asked the object we had in view. On being told by myself that I wanted to obtain evidence of psychic extras under the most favourable test conditions, the control said that the spirit-friends would do their best for me.

We then held the packet of plates between our hands—the right hands on the top of the plates and the left supporting the underside. We remained thus for two or three seconds. I was then as asked to accompany the medium into the dark room, carrying with me my packet of plates. I was permitted with my own hands to unpack the plates and place two of them, films outermost, with a carbon sheet between the two plates, in the dark slide. Not being accustomed to manipulating the dark slide, I could not fasten it easily, whereupon Mr. Hope offered to do so for me, so the dark slide containing the plates was out of my hands only for a few seconds.

The critic has a right to take note of the absence of the plates for those seconds. (I mention the fact, as I wish to be very accurate as to detail.) I am morally certain there was no change of dark slide during those few moments.

The dark slide was then given to me to convey to the operating room, where the exposures were to be made. Here I examined the camera and found it to all appearances as innocent as any amateur's camera could be.

Knowing what is said to be possible by an obscuration of figures on a screen, I examined the improvised background, and found it only a brown woollen blanket, quite guiltless of such artifice. When Mr. Hope had focussed the sitters (Mrs. Walker and myself), I handed him the dark slide. Presently the exposure was made – I should think for about 30 seconds – then Mrs. Walker was requested to move from the field of vision, and I was left to sit alone for another exposure. For this Mrs. Buxton manipulated the shutter, and again the exposure would be of similar duration.

I then received the dark slide from the camera, conveyed it in my pocket to the dark room. There I withdrew the plates from the dark slide and deposited them in the bath for development. Mr. Hope poured the 'developing' liquid on to the plates in the bath. I oscillated the bath in my hands until Mr. Hope said that they were sufficiently developed, Then I poured the developer from the bath, and Mr Hope poured on the 'fixing' liquid. When the negatives were fixed, we carried them into the light. And on the negative first exposed we found a message in the 'positive' form so as if is printed we have to hold it to a mirror to read.

The message is: '*Bon jour. Ad finem esto fidelis.*' The interpretation of which is: 'Good day. To the end be faithful.' I can fully appreciate that message, for it has considerable significance in a way I need not here relate. The second exposure reveals a plainly defined figure, with two other forms silhouetted at the side. I am unable definitely to recognise who these forms are but am waiting further investigation as to identity.

We took the plates from the house and printed from them at the residence of my host and hostess, Mr. and Mrs. Walker, so that the mediums appear to me to be only psychic accessories. Although the French and Latin in the message may be regarded as common-place phrases, if I may make the suggestion without any reflection on either Mrs. Buxton or Mr. Hope, I do not think them sufficiently well-educated to produce even this slight knowledge of French and Latin, much less what I shall hereafter record."

"On March 13th, 1914, Mrs. Howell and myself had an appointment with the Crewe circle for further experimentation. Mrs. Walker again accompanied my wife and self to the residence of the Buxtons. It was about 3 p.m. Mr. Hope presently joined us, and, as before, I took with me plates from Birmingham, same size and manufacture. As before, we commenced our circle with singing and prayer, and again the packet of plates was held between the hands. I informed the control that I wanted intellectual certainty regarding these phenomena, and that I wished to protect the plates from possible substitution by others, and they quite acquiesced in my suggestions. My wife and I both entered the dark room. and I unpacked the plates, and in the case of two that were exposed on my wife, I placed our initials on the corner of the plates with indelible pencil. I had the manipulation of plates in relation to dark slide as before but found no difficulty in fastening the dark slide when the plates were inside. As before, I retained the dark slide until wanted for use in the camera. At this sitting four exposures were made in all.

I superintended the 'developing' and 'fixing' process, and when we exposed the negatives to the light, we found that three out of the four exposures proved successful as regards psychic 'extras'. On one we have a message of considerable length, which I am not able to give a complete interpretation of here, until I have the services of an academic friend for the purpose of translating the Greek portion of the message. The message contains English, French, Latin and Greek. Now, is it reasonable to suppose that these uncultured people could produce a message of this kind, even if so disposed? I may say that I know sufficient of this message to recognise its personal significance to myself.

The other two exposures reproduce apparently in different positions the 'form' of the 'friend' who manifested at the first séance, so that, whoever she is, she is persistent in trying to make herself known.

It will, I think, be admitted, after so long a suspense of judgment as before referred to, it cannot be said that I have rushed in 'where angels fear to tread'. I wish to acknowledge my indebtedness to the Crewe friends for giving me these opportunities of research. It should be said in their favour, I think, they do not commercialise their gifts."

*****

Here we have further positive results and an excellent description of the care taken to prevent interference with the plates.

However, in February that year a letter was published in *Light* which revived the controversy of that original photo of the Archdeacon's mother. Admiral Usbourne Moore[1] involved himself in the controversy – voicing his opinion during a lecture in London.

The Admiral declared: "Nothing is so easy as fraud in spirit photography.

---

1. Author /Investigator. Wrote *The Voices* and *Glimpses of the Next State*

This particular deception is one of the most vulgar and contemptible kind. I resent it, because I know that to obtain photos and simulacra of people who have once lived on this earth is possible, and therefore a counterfeit is to me abominable."

But he did not have the facts correct, and did not make an opportunity to test the work of the Crewe Circle for himself.

Others were more persistent in their desire to experience the work of the circle and after much persuasion Mr. Hope and Mr. and Mrs. Buxton travelled to Glasgow to demonstrate for the good people of that city.

This is the report from Peter Galloway, President of the Glasgow Spiritualist Association, published in *The Two Worlds*, June 31st 1914.

<u>Crewe Circle in Glasgow, June 26th 1914</u>

"Sir, Like many others. I have followed with deep interest the controversy regarding the above subject, but although I have seen a good deal of phenomena in my time, up till last week I had no personal experience of psychic photography.

Some time ago I wrote to Mr. Buxton, one of the members of the now famous Crewe circle, asking if he would come to Glasgow, also their terms, etc. After several communications had passed between us, I got them to promise to come, provided we paid their train fares and put them up. They wrote however that they would accept no fee, and I think it is only fair to them to state these facts.

Well, they came to Glasgow on Saturday, June 26th, and on Sunday morning they held their first séance.

First let me state the conditions:

The circle consisted of Mr. W.[2] manager of one of the largest depots in Scotland for cameras, photographer's supplies, etc.; Mr. D.L.W. , a press photographer, and nine others.

Mr. D.L.W.[3] is not a spiritualist, but he was recommended to me as being a capable man, and our meetings were held in his studio in West Regent-Street. He provided the screens, developers, etc. The medium had never been in this studio before. Our first concern was to examine the camera, lens and slides with which we were thoroughly satisfied, and the circle was then formed in the usual way by sitting around a table and opening with prayer, after which we sang hymns while the medium was being controlled.

---

2. Mr. West, managing director of Kodak's manufacturing arm in Scotland, an expert photographer and interested in Spiritualism.
3. Mr. David L. Wilson was the manager of the Scottish Press Photo. Agency, of 65, West Regent-street, Glasgow, whose studio was used.

Mr. W. had his own plates, which the medium magnetised by holding one of his hands over and the other under the hands of Mr. W. and the other sitters, but at no time did the medium touch the packet himself.

He then asked Mr. W. to go into the dark room with him, which was well lit up by an incandescent gas light burning in the studio and shining through the ruby glass. There was sufficient light to show all the movements of the medium.

The medium then held out the slides, and Mr. W. opened his packet and placed his plates in position, but Mr. Hope never put a hand on them.

They immediately came out and exposed the plates by photographing the group, and the same two gentlemen (Mr. W. and Mr. D.L.W.) at once took the slides and again went into the dark-room and developed the plates. On examination one of them was seen to have on it a face, and on a print being taken it was clearly recognised as that of our late President, James Robertson.

There can be no doubt on this point, because I have shown it to many of his personal friends, members of our Association, his sons and one of his daughters. Without exception they are all agreed about the undoubted resemblance to Mr. Robertson's face, and the sons mentioned that there is no photograph of him similar to this, so that it could not be copied.

If this matter is of interest to your readers, I have a number of excellent spirit photos taken by Mr. Hope in the same studio and under similar conditions, where recognition is undoubted.

Now, if there is any weak spot in the conditions I have stated, will some of your readers who are experts in photography come forward and state how it was possible for Mr. Hope to give us such excellent results, and at the same time deceive us, bamboozle us, or hypnotise us in broad daylight?

I look upon him as being an excellent medium and a very worthy man, but if he is able to produce "faked" photos under the above-mentioned conditions, he is a much smarter man than I presently gave him credit for."

Yours, etc.,   Peter Galloway,
Glasgow.

As well as the 'extra' of former Psychic Society President, James Robertson, there were a number of other successes.

A sitting for Mr. Wm. Jeffrey, President of the Scottish Society of Magicians, and his daughter, provided an insight to the process of psychic (spirit) photography. Here is a man who is 'the last person to be deceived by any sort of trick.'[4] The first plate exposed 'was partly covered with auric drapery' or as Arthur Conan Doyle puts it —"the ectoplasm bag is exposed in its complete form" — as though the plate

---

4. Conan Doyle in *The Case for Spirit Photography*, p32

had been exposed too soon – and the second plate had a clear psychic portrait of his wife, Mrs. Jeffery within the gossamer fine drapery now covering the sitters, as if she had opened out the veiling.

The first plate exposed shows Mr. Jeffrey and his daughter with a drape of fine "ectoplasm" in front of them.

A few seconds later the second plate was 'exposed and the veil 'opened' to show Mrs. Jeffrey, his late wife.

In a letter from Mr. Jeffrey to the Rev. Chas Tweedale[5] we learn:

"During that first visit of Mr. Hope to Glasgow, Mr. Peter Galloway, of 58 Argyle Street, a well-known business man, had a photo taken of himself and wife by Mr. Hope. On this is a perfectly clear and distinct picture of their little daughter, exactly as she was in the earth life, and which they clearly and distinctly recognise. She never had her photograph taken while in the mortal body, nor was any sketch or drawing ever made of her. At the time the photograph was taken both of them were thinking of their deceased son, and hoping they would get his picture. Instead of the son's picture they got the daughter's, proving once again that those pictures are not thought forms.

A number of other spirit forms were obtained at Glasgow, including message in English, French and Greek which appeared on the sensitive plate in front of Mr. and Mrs. Sloan."[6]

5. Excerpt from Tweedale's book *Man's Survival after Death*, 2nd Ed. 1920
6. 4 years later, in 1918 Arthur Findlay started to sit with John Sloan in his home which resulted in the book *On the Edge of the Etheric*.

A Commemorative Photo taken by the Glasgow Association, June 1914.
Bottom Row, left to right: Mr. William Hope. the photographic medium,
and Mrs. Buxton, a remarkable sensitive: Mr. Buxton, in whose home in
Crewe the bulk of the psychic pictures and 'writing' has been obtained. Mr.
William Jeffrey, member of the S.S.S.P; Mrs. Sloan, a sensitive; Mr.------.
a reporter; Mrs. Galloway, Mr. Charles Kerr, and Mrs, Birrell.
Back Row: Mr Peter Galloway. President of The Glasgow Association,
member of S.S.S.P., and Mr. Sloan, a gifted psychic in private life.
(Photograph and detail provided by Mr. James Coates, 'Light', Dec 11th 1921).

James Coates, recorded the details of the visit of the Crewe Circle to his home at Glenbeg, Rothsay following the weekend in Glasgow[:7].

"On June 30th, Mr. Wm. Jeffrey, of Glasgow, telegraphed me to the effect that he was bringing the Crewe Circle to Rothesay for a sail, and would call that day. On receipt of the news, I went into town and purchased two packets of quarter plates Imperial Rapid—and had one sealed up by the vendor, Mr. William Meldrum, chemist. Returning home, I notified Mr. and Mrs. McAllister, visitors to Rothesay—residing in a villa adjacent, of the coming of the Crewe Circle. Mr. David McAllister, who holds an important position in the Egyptian and Cairo Railway Company was on holiday, and I knew of his interest in Spiritualism and, his scepticism about psychic photography, and that his good lady was an enthusiastic amateur photographer, I felt that I would like to have them with us.

When Mr. Jeffrey and his guests arrived, Mrs. Coates, in her genial way, entertained them. After lunch I proposed a sitting. The two packets were placed on a little table, the unsealed packet being held in the hands of Mrs. Coates, the Crewe Circle. Mr. Jeffrey and myself. Mr. Hope, under control,

---

7. *Light*, Jan 1st 1921. 'Practical and Theological Aspects of " Supernormal Pictures."Part 5.'

described my father and Mrs. Coates' son, David, and intimated that there was a "Methodist lady present who had come down on the steamer with them." I could not make out who it could be and determined to wait.

The Crewe Circle had been favourably reported to me, yet this was the first time I had the pleasure of meeting Mr. and Mrs. Buxton and Mr. William Hope. I determined that in experimentation nothing should be left to chance. A large piece of dark cloth used for a cabinet was suspended between the gaselier and dining press door, for a back-screen. The quarter plate camera, presented to Mr. Hope by his old patron the late Archdeacon Colley, was examined. I took the unsealed packet of plates from the table and with Mr. Hope entered the dark-room and I loaded the carrier. After exposure I took the carrier away, developed the plates, and [Plates] 1. and 2. were the result.

Plate 1. at Rothesay *Plate 2. at Rothesay*

Taking the packet of plates out of my pocket, I put two others in the carrier, and Mrs. Coates and I sat again. Upon development of these two plates, one had a high light over Mrs. Coates, and the fourth plate, nothing in addition to ourselves. During my absence in the dark-room Mr. Wm. Jeffrey, Mr. and Mrs. McAllister and Mrs. Coates remained in the dining-room and testified that neither Mr. and Mrs. Buxton nor anyone else touched the camera. While Mr. Wm. Hope operated the camera—with Mrs. Buxton in proximity, Mrs. McAllister also took our portraits with her camera. On development of her plates there were no other results on them save that of the visible sitters. This is a summary of proceedings as far as the photographs (1) and (2) are concerned."

He adds: "When the party left—with our hearty good wishes —Mr. Hope took the balance of the un-used plates to use on the trip. There were no fees offered or paid."

Mr. David McAllister, being so pleased with what took place on the 30th of June, determined on the first opportunity to visit Crewe. He did so, and in his letter from the Crewe Arms Hotel, dated July 13th, 1914. said:

"I am very pleased to tell you I had a sitting with our friends. Mr. Buxton was not able, owing to pressure of work (Mr. Buxton is a wood-worker), but Mrs. Buxton and Mr. Hope very kindly sat for me. Two out of the four exposed have psychic results on them. One shows a face which I cannot as yet recognise. The other has a written message round and round my image (see Fig. 3). It is clearly and finely written, and speaks for itself as follows:

"'Dear Friend, We are very glad you are here, for the lady who manifested at our friend's house at Rothesay is here again with you and is most anxious that she should be known. She gives her name as Lydia Haigh. She was on

holiday and left the body at Rothesay on the 13th of September, 1906. We give this as a proof of spirit presence. Please ask our dear friend Coates to enquire about this, then when he has proved this statement, let him convey her undying affection to those she left behind and you friend, speak of our mediums and their work just as you find them.'

What do you think of that for a message? I think it is wonderful, and I hope you will try to find out about it.

Kind regards to Mrs. Coates and self.   Yours very sincerely,"

The spirit message written round the portrait of Mr. David McAllister.

D. McAllister.

This gave the first hint of the identity of psychic portrait on Plate1, and Coates notes that the writing produced on Mr. McAllister's plate 'suggested that it came from someone with more culture than possessed by the psychics. Mr. Hope's calligraphy is totally different and inferior to that of the psychograph.'

He sent this information to Mr. Jeffrey asking him to get confirmation of this date of death from the Registrar in Rothesay. A copy of Registrar's Certificate revealed the facts related of the lady's death were substantiated, and they now had the name and address of the lady's husband. Coates wrote to Mr. Haigh giving an account of the occasion together with his wife's message, and the photographs figs 1. and 2.

In his reply Mr. Haigh said:

Crown Cottage, Ryhill.
October 10th, 1914.

"Dear Sir,—I duly received your letter of the 6th inst., also the photographs referred to.

I have no difficulty in recognising the photo of my dear wife in the one marked (1). I have a photo very similar which was taken of her in life, and it is also similar to one which was published in the "P.M. Magazine" in 1907.

I do not know much about the psychic. But if there are any further particulars you would like to know which would be of interest, I should be glad to let you have them. —I am,

-Yours sincerely,"   Wm. C. Haigh.

Coates continues:

"On the receipt of this letter my feelings were mixed, with satisfaction that the psychic picture (1) was recognised, but with a shade of disappointment that a similar picture had appeared in a publication. This notwithstanding the fact of the impossibility of substituting plates for mine in Rothesay, I asked permission to have, for inspection, the cabinet photograph[8] and the "Aldergate Primitive Methodist Magazine." Upon examination of the photograph and the faithful semi-tone in the magazine, I was struck with the remarkable similarity of the three, i.e., the two normal and the supernormal pictures.

"I experimented with the photograph and the reproduction in the "P.M. Magazine," and failed to obtain a photograph identical to the psychic picture. Failing, I sent the Budget to Mr. Wm. Jeffrey to get expert advice. He consulted Mr. W. J. West, managing director in Scotland to Kodak, Limited. In his, Mr. West's report. No. 6840, dated at Glasgow, October 22ml, 1914, he says:

"Dear Mr. Coates,—I have had an opportunity of inspecting the photographs, which you sent to Mr. Jeffrey. In my opinion the psychic photo, the portrait in the Magazine, and the photo on the cabinet card, are of one and the same person, and that the psychic photo could not have been copied

---

8. A cabinet photograph was a style widely used for photographic portraiture after 1870. Intended for display it consisted of a thin photograph mounted on a card typically measuring 108 by 165 mm (4¼ by 6½ inches). Also known as a 'Cabinet Card'.

from either of the other two. The expression and likeness in the psychic photo is almost identical with the other two, but the 'tout ensemble' is slightly different."

This is conclusive, but if not, Mr. Hope had never seen the cabinet photo, and the psychic photo is without the stipple-marks of a semi-tone cut. This is not all, no photograph or portrait of the original of (2) ever existed."

At the end of October he felt it was important to send Mr. Haigh a complete statement of what had passed in Rothesay, with Mr. West's report, when returning his lady's photograph and the Magazine. To which he obtained the following reply:

31st October, 1914.

"Dear Sir,—I am duly in receipt of the 'P. M. Magazine' for June, 1907, together with my wife's photograph, also, the two psychic photographs (1 and 2) for which I thank you, also the report contained in your letter of the 29th inst:, which is interesting. I hope to reply further in due course.—I am,

Yours sincerely,

Wm. C. Haigh.

Some months later Mr. Jeffrey, while in Yorkshire on business, (Brown & Co., Ltd., saw millers, wood-workers and timber merchants in Glasgow), took the opportunity to call on Mr. Haigh. Mr. Jeffrey here learned the name of the lady in psychic photograph (2). The lady was an aunt of Mr. Haigh and passed away after their visit to Rothesay (in 1906). The photograph faithfully portrayed the lady and her general attitude when sitting.

Following this, Mr. Wright, a friend of Mr. Wm. Jeffrey, visited Crewe and obtained a remarkably clear psychograph of a lily, in a sealed packet of plates and another psychograph with words to the following effect:

"Dear Friends,—There is a lady here who wishes you to push forward her request, named Lydia Haigh."

When Mr. Jeffrey was told of this he sent the details to Mr Haigh.

So not only was the identity of the unknown originals of the psychic portraits 1 and 2 thoroughly established, but the fact of psychic photography placed beyond dispute.

Coates closes his report with this:

"Mr. Haigh is neither a Spiritualist—his whole outlook in life being indifferent rather than antagonistic—nor is he acquainted with photography or photographic procedure. He cannot conceive how these photographs were obtained, but it is due to his valuable assistance that the identity of the psychic portraits has been established."

* * * * *

In the introduction to a lecture for the LSA. in London in 1915 William Walker said:

"Spirit photography is regulated by natural law and by a type of mediumship which at present we do not fully understand. With a suitable medium present and with harmonious sitters, it is possible to obtain psychic photographs. So far, I have never yet made a journey to the Crewe circle without obtaining some results in psychic photography, either when alone or when I have been permitted to take visitors. We cannot command these results. We can, however, do our best to fulfil the laws of health and to maintain a pure and holy aspiration, as like attracts like in occult experiments as elsewhere."

During the evening he recounted many of the instances already recorded in these chapters and also gave details of the processes involved in obtaining the first colour photographs, explaining briefly the Paget method of obtaining direct colour photography and exhibited a few slides to show the effects of natural colours when photographed by that process.

At the close of the evening Sir William Vavasour, presiding, said that it was only about a year before that he had made Mr. Walker's acquaintance. At that time he had supposed that Mr. Walker was simply a collector of psychic pictures, but .... they would all agree that Mr. Walker was a scientist in the phase of psychic phenomena.

LONDON SPIRITUALIST ALLIANCE.

Meetings of the Members and Associates of the Alliance will be held in the SALON OF THE ROYAL SOCIETY OF BRITISH ARTISTS, Suffolk-street, Pall Mall East, S.W. (near the National Gallery), on

THURSDAY EVENING, JANUARY 14TH, WHEN AN ADDRESS WILL BE GIVEN BY

MR. W. WALKER
(Ex-President of the Buxton Photographic Society)

ON

"THE PUZZLE OF SPIRIT PHOTOGRAPHY"
(WITH LANTERN ILLUSTRATIONS).

The doors will be opened at 7 o'clock, and the meeting will commence punctually at 7.30.

Admission by ticket only. Two tickets are sent to each Member, and one to each Associate. Other friends desiring to attend can obtain tickets by applying to Mr. F. W. South, 11 St. Martin's-lane, W.C., accompanying the application by a remittance of 1s. for each ticket.

Dr. Abraham Wallace was also present and commented that he had, that night, been presented with a great number of puzzles. He had inspected Mr. Walker's photographs some time before and had arranged with him that he should one day pay a visit to the Crewe circle. Owing to his professional engagements, however, he had not yet been able to do so... He hoped that he might yet be able from personal knowledge to endorse the genuineness of all the photographs Mr. Walker had shown them.

This was quite a step forward for only sixteen months earlier Wallace had been declaring that the photographs of Stead's writing were faked — "distinct indications of the super-imposing of a picture containing an alleged message from Mr. Stead in the midst of some flocculent material, probably cotton wool, on a plate containing the figure of a gentleman." ... and he had at that time declined to waste time on meeting Mr. Walker.

Unfortunately, William Walker passed away suddenly in July 1915 and the reports from the circle's supporter, recorder and broad-caster of the contact being made by the spirit world, were cut short.

However, it was not long before he made himself known to family and friends from the world of spirit. In February 1916 the family obtained this photograph at Crewe.

In this photograph *(left)* the sitters are Mr. & Mrs. Henry Walker (left) and two friends.

Mr. Walker Snr. looks considerably younger than in his previous 'in-life' photos.

Note the fine veiling in front of the sitters.

More Successful Visitors and Visits

Estelle Stead

It appears that their first visit to Glasgow was not the last for the Crewe Circle for they soon returned, as Estelle Stead, the daughter of W.T. Stead, writes in her Preface to *The Blue Island*:

"The photograph given as frontispiece to this volume was taken by the Crewe Circle at Crewe in the autumn of 1915. In the spring of that year, I had met Mr. Hope and Mrs. Buxton at the house of a mutual friend in Glasgow, and they very kindly invited me to call and see them in Crewe, if I should ever have an opportunity to do so. Soon after my return to London, father asked me to arrange to go to Crewe as he said he wanted to try and give me his picture on the same plate with mine. Accordingly, I arranged to spend a week-end with some friends at Crewe and have some sittings with Mr. Hope and Mrs. Buxton.

I bought a box of plates in London and took them with me, and I can truthfully say that that box of plates never left my sight or my possession all the time I was there. I even slept with the box clasped tightly in my hands. We had our first sitting on the Saturday, when I obtained two extras, neither resembling my father. One was of interest because it was the picture of a lady who had appeared on a plate with my father when he was experimenting with Mr. Boursnell in the 'nineties'.

I took my box containing the rest of the plates away with me after the sitting; bought another box of plates in Crewe and took both boxes with me to the sitting on the Sunday. We did not use my first box at all at this sitting, and I kept it all the while just inside my dress. We sat around the table, putting our hands over and under the second box for a few minutes; I then held the box for a minute against Mrs. Buxton's forehead.

After this I was instructed by Mr. Hope's guide to take the box myself into the dark room (note, the box had not been unsealed or the plates exposed to the light). When in the dark room, I was to unseal the box and take out the two bottom plates, taking particular care to note which was the bottom plate, and then to develop both plates. Mr. Hope was to come in with me, but not to touch the box or plates. I carried out the instructions. I found the bottom plate not even fogged, and on the other plate two messages, one from Archdeacon Colley, deploring father's inability to write; one from Mr.

Walker, the father of my host, and in one corner of the plate a faint outline of my father's face. When I got back to my friend's that evening, we had a sitting at which father expressed his keen disappointment at his failure to give his picture. "It is all my fault," he said "I am so excited at the idea of getting my picture beside yours after I have been so called 'dead' for so many years that I break the conditions; however, many have promised to help me tomorrow, and if I fail again we have something else prepared to slip on so that you will not be quite so disappointed."

The following morning she went for a further sitting with the circle. Using her own plates these two images were obtained. On both, there were pictures of her father. Neither Miss Stead nor those who knew Mr. W. T. Stead intimately ever saw similar portraits of her father.[1]

In writing to James Coates she commented:

"The photos of my father are splendid. Don't you think so? If anyone can give me faked photographs of my father – under the same conditions as those were produced—I shall be pleased to give them the opportunity."[2]

This excellent likeness is used as a frontispiece for 'The Blue Island'. *This large less distinct image shows W.T.Stead almost obscuring Estelle.*

Miss Stead was soon to return to Crewe for another sitting:

---

1. See Tweedale's comments in Appendix 3
2. *Light,* Dec 18th 1920; James Coates on " Supernormal Pictures."

"A short time before I went to Crewe. I was sitting alone one evening in my office, after the rest had left. I suddenly felt my brother present. I asked him mentally if he would come to Crewe and be photographed. I explained to him, I felt that would be a greater proof to some than obtaining one of my father, who is so well known. I received the impression that he would be there. I kept this to myself. My Friend, Miss Scatcherd thought I was anxious to get a photograph or a message from my father.

The photograph produced is the fulfilment of the psychological interview. I may add, while thoroughly identified, it is not either the same or similar to any photograph taken of Mr. William Stead in his lifetime. The portrait—psychically produced bears its own testimony to the fact."

Sitters: Miss Estelle Stead and Miss F. R. Scatcherd. The psychic extra is Mr. William Stead, Miss Stead's brother.

James Coates writes:

"Mr. William Stead's portrait was obtained in Crewe, October 21st, 1916 – about nine years subsequent to his transition in December 1907.

Miss Stead purchased a packet of quarter plates in London. Arriving in Crewe, she entered the dark room, unwrapped the packet and placed the signed plates in the dark slide; afterwards carried the slide into the operating room. There she carefully examined the camera, and handed the slide to Mr. Hope, whom she carefully watched. After exposure Miss Stead rose, took the slide out, and entered the dark room, where she developed the plates, on one of which came up the negative picture of her brother. Not till after development did Mr. Hope touch the plates. The illustration produced is from a print untouched, taken from the untouched negative."

* * * * *

Another visitor sent the following to the *Lyceum Banner:*

Spirit Photo of Clarence W. G. Pears,
who entered the Higher Life, February 27th, 1915,
aged 13 years.

" His is the gentle voice we hear
   Soft as the breath of ev'n,
That checks each fault and calms each fear,
   And speaks of heaven."

———

" The above photo was taken at Crewe on July
11th, 1916. The plates were bought at Coventry, and
never left my possession until the picture was produced," (that is, until she handed them to Mr. Hope
for production of photo). My aim in putting photo
in the LYCEUM BANNER is in Loving Memory of my
dear, dear Sonny; also in grateful thanks to God for
the abundant proofs I have received that my dear
ones still live and love. Trusting it may bring comfort and help to all the bereaved children of earth
with whom it may come in contact is the earnest
prayer of A. A. PEARS.

Sir William Crookes

In May 1916 Lady Ellen Crookes passed over and in the November Sir William Crookes paid a visit to the circle with Miss Scatcherd and another friend, having been intrigued sitting by this result in his own home earlier in the year.

Sir William Crookes and his first recognised psychic "extra"

A luminous patch had appeared on the plate above Sir William's head. When he intensified it and found there was a face there. This discovery, so interested him that he went to Crewe.[3]

In an interview for the *International Psychic Gazette* in 1917 Sir William Crookes wrote:

"I went down to Crewe and had my photograph taken by the psychics known as "The Crewe Circle". My portrait was a very good one, and on the same negative was a good, recognisable portrait of my departed wife, just by the side of me.

I had taken the packet of plates with me from London in my pocket. I bought them in this neighbourhood, and took the packet down unopened just as I had received it. And when I got to Mr. Hope's (the photographer) I went into his dark room with him; he was quite willing. I then opened the packet of plates myself and took out one of them, which I marked with my initials. I wrapped up the remaining eleven plates in the paper they came in. Then I put my marked plate in the dark slide and put it in my pocket. We next went out into the room where Mr. Hope takes his photographs.

I sat down in a chair, and when all was ready for him to photograph me, I handed the dark slide to the lady who was with me, from London, and she handed it to him. Mr. Hope simply put the slide into the camera, opened it, took my photograph, shut it up again, took the slide out of the camera, and handed it back to the lady, who gave it to me. Thereupon I took it into the dark room and developed the plate myself. I may say I am an experienced photographer. Mr. Hope did not touch the plate until after it was fixed. I brought it home here and printed from it.

Now that, I think, is a very good test. I had only the one photograph taken.

3. F.R. Scatcherd on 'Problems of Psychic Photography', *Light* Feb 12th 1921.'

There was no one visible by my side, and the lady who accompanied me from London saw nothing there. I will show you the picture. Everybody who has seen it who knew my wife –not simply our relations and family – recognises it as her portrait. It is not like any other portrait I have. The expression is similar to that she wore during the weakness of her last illness." [4]

The Editor of the *International Psychic Gazette* added: "One such testimony from such a man sweeps away like so much chaff the opposition of those who, never having made an honest and patient investigation and devoid of practical experience, endeavour to discredit a subject of which they know nothing."

James Coates wrote, "In a private letter which I have seen, Sir William, writing on December 14th 1916, shortly after the incident, says:

'The photograph is easily recognised by all to whom I have shown it. I find that it is very similar in likeness to one I took

Sir William Crookes and the psychic "extra" he recognised as his wife.

about ten years ago, although by no means a facsimile reproduction. This makes it all the more satisfactory to me.' "

In *The Life of Sir William Crookes*. E. E. Fournier d'Albe wrote of these photographs:

"The negatives according to Mr. Gardner (his secretary) showed clear signs of double exposure, but Crookes clung to the conviction that this was a real 'spirit' photograph of his dead wife, and treasured it accordingly. Sir William wrote, after the experiment to his best friend: 'I look upon the picture as a sacred trust, and do not like it to be shown to anyone as a curiosity'."

In a review of the above book in *Psychic Science*, April. 1924, we read: "The marks of double exposure[5] are very well known to Mr. Hope and to all who have investigated this matter under the most rigid conditions, and remain one of the problems of psychic photography, which is a physical phenomenon.

---

4. Note:The drapery is in front of the sitter so not a double exposure from a prepared plate.
5. Rev. Chas Tweedale wrote on this anomaly. See his article of Jan 1921 in Appendix 3

Something in the nature of a psychic film of matter of a fineness unknown to us may be produced in the process, and deposited on the ordinary photographic film, at some unknown moment of the experiment. But these are matters in which we need the brains and intuition of another Crookes to help us."

On one of the psychic pictures obtained by Sir William at Crewe, Archdeacon Colley wrote:

"*I most earnestly ask you, Sir William, to tell Sir Oliver that when* ..."

Here the writing stopped, and they could get nothing further. Sir William left, taking the plates with him. A fortnight later a friend of his was photographed and the following was received:

"*... he is ready, the invisible helpers, with the Christian circle at Crewe, will do all that we can for dear Harum-Scarum.—T. Colley.*"

On comparing notes Miss Scatcherd found that the message completed the broken one to Sir William Crookes. It was signed by Archdeacon Colley, who shortly before his death declared he would never cease, in this world or the next, to endeavour to convince Sir Oliver Lodge of the truth of the Crewe phenomena.[6]

"Harum-Scarum" was a playful name applied to Miss Scatcherd by the Archdeacon.

The purport of the message was that as soon as Sir Oliver Lodge was convinced the Archdeacon would give Miss Scatcherd the crowning evidence that would finally convince her. This message from the Archdeacon is explained by the fact that he was grieved that during his earth life he had not succeeded in convincing Sir Oliver Lodge of the truth of spirit photography.

Sir William Crookes died in 1919.

* * * * *

Mr. W. G. Mitchell of Darlington

Mr. W.G. Mitchell of Darlington, an experienced photographer and investigator became a moving force in the formation of the Society for the Study of Supernormal Pictures in 1916. As President of the Darlington Photographic Society and the local Spiritualist Society, he had persuaded William Walker to give his lecture there in 1914 and to visit other interested bodies in the area. He had 'sat' with Mr. Wyllie in Ireland some years earlier and he knew what to look out for in the ways of trickery in psychic photographs.

---

6. F.R. Scatcherd lecture at the MSA, on 'Problems of Psychic Photography,' *Light* - February 1921

This is the report that he sent to Sir Arthur Conan Doyle in 1922:

" .... I had arranged with a friend who was at that time editor-manager of an important Northern newspaper to visit Crewe for the purpose of meeting The Crewe Circle. As brother members of a psychical research society, we desired to add to our experiences. Having taken the precaution of purchasing plates locally and following the usual recommendation of carrying them in close proximity to the body, we looked forward to our journey.

The appointed day arrived, but no day in modern history could have been more unsuitable or less conducive to good results. It was December 16th, 1914, and the news tapped out over the 'private wire' was most disquieting; the Huns were shelling Scarborough and West Hartlepool. My friend realised that it was impossible for him to desert his editorial chair, and he hurriedly gave me his box of plates.

I met Mr. William Walker, of Buxton, en route, and together we journeyed to Crewe. A short devotional service was held in the kitchen of Mrs. Buxton's home, during which I was informed that only one box of plates could be dealt with. I selected the box purchased by my absent friend and expressed a desire that some result should be given that would give him satisfaction and conviction: I was instructed that four plates would be dealt with and that I could select any particular four I desired from the box. I named the third and fourth, ninth and tenth. This selection secured two pairs of plates that would be packed film to film, and would probably be hinged together with emulsion.

The box, unsealed, was then placed on the centre of the table and as it bore a rubber stamp impression of the firm from which it was purchased, I am quite satisfied that there was no substitution of boxes. Mr. Hope then insisted that I should dismantle his camera. This I did most thoroughly, giving special attention to the dark slides, lens and shutter. Having placed the dark slides in my pocket, we entered the dark room, where I unpacked the box, selecting the particular plates decided upon, wrote my initials across the corner of each, placed them in the two double back dark slides and placed the remainder of the plates together with the dark slides in my pocket. We adjourned to the studio, where Hope allowed me to choose my position in relation to the background. Mr. Walker sat in the chair, I focussed the portrait on the focussing screen of the camera, placed the dark slide in position and left all ready for making the exposure. I then went and took a seat beside Mr. Walker. Mr. Hope manipulated the lens cap with one hand and with his other clasped Mrs. Buxton's, thus forming an arc over the bellows of the camera. After the first plate was exposed, I went to the camera, closed the dark slide and reversed it, then sat for the second exposure.

The third plate was next used. Mrs. Buxton asked me to place the dark slide containing the only unexposed plate on her forehead, this I did for about ten seconds.

I then retired with Mr. Hope to the dark room, where I personally developed the four plates. On three out of the four supernormal effects flashed up, and after fixing in the hypo-bath we brought them out to the light for examination.

Plate No. 1, in addition to the normal image, showed a lengthy message of exceedingly minute copperplate writing, too small to read without the aid of the magnifying glass. I could just discern that there were Greek characters intermingled with other languages, including English.

No. 2 plate bore only the normal image.

No. 3 plate showed the supernormal figure of a lady draped in some material of fine texture, standing by my side.

No. 4 plate, the one held on Mrs. B.'s forehead, showed a well-defined face of a lady.

The long message on No.1 contained 145 words, and was written in a jumble of languages, English, Greek, French, and Latin, and concluded thus:

"And now, friends, we have given you this advice in mixed languages, so that it will help to support the claim that the unlearned of to-day possess the same powers as the humble fishermen of biblical history. We thank you for the common-sense way in which you have met us ..."

It was quite two years before I was able to get the Greek portion translated. I eventually met a young Greek, a student of Armstrong College, Newcastle, who told me that it was a very ancient style of Greek. The message, when translated, was quite intelligible to me.

No. 3 plate, with supernormal portrait, proved to be undeniably the portrait of the deceased mother of the wife of my friend. On comparing it with a life portrait, it left no doubt in the mind of any reasonable person.

The portrait on No.4 plate I cannot recognise.

I have a profound conviction that Mr. Hope is a genuine medium, honest and straightforward, and it would take a great deal to shake my confidence in his integrity. I have followed his operations for years and find them a fruitful source of instruction.

It is only those who have experimented in "fake" effects who can realise the difficulties, and with a knowledge of photography I challenge any professional or amateur photographer to produce anything approaching the same effects under any conditions. They find it absolutely impossible under the same conditions.

It is unthinkable that Mr. and Mrs. Buxton would cooperate, aid and abet in a continuous fraud on the widowed wife, the sorrowing parent."

(Signed) W. G. MITCHELL."
3, Harewood Terrace,
Darlington.

A Middlesbrough Connection

The friends in Middlesbrough to whom Mr. Mitchell refers to would have been Mr. & Mrs. Cowell Pugh, officers in the Middlesbrough Spiritualist Church. They were well known to my husband, Tom Harrison, and his family. In fact, Tom remembered as a young boy he used to count the stamps in the Post Office when his mother worked for Mr. Cowell Pugh in the 1920s. Tom inherited from her a collection of the psychic photographs taken in those early years.

It is not known when the Pughs first sat with the Crewe circle but it must have been before 1915 as William Walker included the following in his lecture in London in January of that year:[7]

"A spirit message to Mr. and Mrs. Cowell Pugh from the Venerable Archdeacon Colley, in the Archdeacon's unmistakable handwriting with his signature attached, was shown. It had reference to his passing on to the higher life when at Middlesbrough attending the Church Congress, and read as follows:

"Dear Friends,—I thank you for the help you gave to our dear friend Miss Scatcherd at Church Congress. I try to be with you in spirit—Faithfully yours, T. Colley."

This message was obtained on a plate exposed in the camera with Mr. and Mrs. Cowell Pugh as sitters, and the spirit message was in front of the sitters. In order to be read it had to be reversed and the sitters shown in negative. It offered many puzzling points. An important feature of the message was that it referred to an event which took place after the Archdeacon's demise in 1912—there could be no room for any suggestion that the photograph was something written by the Archdeacon before his transition."

It seems from this that the Crewe Circle had visited the North-East of England in 1914, as well as Glasgow. There is other evidence that the Crewe Circle were in Middlesbrough in 1914 and again in 1918 in these next photographs from Tom's collection.

The Pugh's son John was born in 1904, and would be about 10-11 years of age in the photograph above left placing it about 1914. The "extra" was recognised but the record of identity has not survived.

---

7. From the Report in *Light* Jan 30th 1915. p56

Left: Mr. and Mrs. Pugh with their son John, probably 1914.

Below: Mr. and Mrs. Bob Abbott with his first wife as the 'extra'.

This one (*right*) is another from those early years showing sitters Bob and Agnes Abbott with the 'extra' being his first wife – clearly recognised. Note the signature at the top of the plate to prevent substitution.

Agnes Abbott was the sister of the two ladies in the next photograph. She was a gifted trance medium, passing in 1942 and thereafter became the main communicator in Minnie Harrison's home circle in the 1940s-50s.[8]

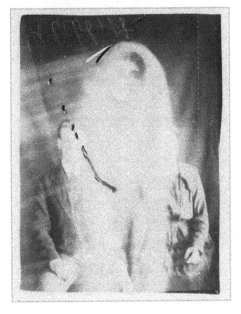

The Crewe Circle returned to the Middlesbrough area many times, possibly annually, – 'on holiday' – as indicated by Mr. Mitchell and Mr. Pugh and I think the following shows they were there in the summer of 1918. This next can definitely be placed in 1918.

8. See detail of Agnes Abbott in *Life After Death: Living Proof* by Tom Harrison (SNPPbooks.com)

The photo (*right*) is of Mary Gregory (*seated left*) and her sister Minnie Harrison on the right. Minnie appears to be heavily pregnant and in August of that year gave birth to her only child, Thomas, – placing this summer visit of the Crewe Circle quite decisively.

The "extra" in the photo is Mary's son, who had died fourteen years before, at 2½ months old. Hope given her the name 'Albert Ernest' before the photograph was taken – that was the name of her son who now showed himself as he had grown in spirit life.[9]

The identity of the "extras", in the photo, left, taken of Mr. and Mrs. Pugh on the same "hot" summer visit in 1918, has not been recorded but here we can see two different forms of the "drapery" around the "extras" faces, the 'cotton wool' for the man– which aroused so much suspicion in researchers and sceptics – and the 'veil' for the lady.

Note that the "extras" are in front of the sitters, Mrs. Pugh being almost obscured by the psychic energy withdrawn from her.

This final photograph is of Mr. Pugh almost obsured by a beautiful young girl (identity and date unrecorded).

9. Tom Harrison had the foresight to gather details of his mother's family, the Bessants, etc. from his Aunt Mary before she passed in 1965.

Rev. Charles Tweedale

In September 1918, having made one incognito visit to Crewe three years earlier, he took his wife with him for the second visit, with a view to obtaining further psychic photographs. In *Light* he writes:[10]

"I had furnished myself with a new and unbroken packet of quarter plates which I also carefully sealed with my private seal.

"At the little sitting which always precedes the photography, the small table at which we sat begun to sway to-and-fro and last beat time forcibly to a hymn which we sang. When I saw this I knew we were about to get something good in the way of results, as this is a phenomenon that we often get through my wife's psychic powers. Mr. Hope and Mrs. Buxton were surprised at this manifestation and said that they had not previously experienced it at their sittings. Taking the packet of plates and most carefully examining the seals, which I found perfect and unbroken. I proceeded to the dark room where I thoroughly examined the slide, which I then loaded with plates myself, not permitting Mr. Hope to touch them, and carefully replacing the unused plates in my pocket each time the slide was charged.

I made a thorough examination of the camera and immediately after each pair of plates was exposed jointly by Mr. Hope and Mrs. Buxton I took away the slide and developed the plates at once, not allowing Mr. Hope to touch them until the plates were fixed. Each plate was signed by me and carefully examined for the signature before and after development. Forms and faces extra to myself and my wife appear on five plates out of the six exposed, I purpose in this article to deal with one of them, which is reproduced herewith. This Crewe photo shows myself and my wife seated, and between us stands the form of my wife's father.[11] Mr. Frank Burnett, (who died in 1913). It is a splendid likeness of him, recognised instantly by us all, beyond any possibility of doubt. There is no photograph in existence showing him with a beard but without a hat, as this does [and there is a smile in his eyes too]. In the only photograph showing him bearded he is wearing a hat. There was no copy of that photo within sixty miles of Crewe when the psychic photo was taken, and we obtained the result, within half-an-hour of entering the psychics' house. This is a true psychic portrait of one who has departed this life.

That the psychics of the Crewe Circle have the power to obtain supernormal portraits of the departed is proved up to the hilt by the experiences of myself and of many others. That such psychic portraits of the "dead" can be obtained and have been obtained is scientifically proved, and any further evidence can only confirm this fact.

---

10. *Light,* December 11, 1920: "Psychic photography and the Crewe Circle."
11. Photographs overleaf, copied from *News from the Next World* by Rev. C. Tweedale.

Above: Mr Frank Burnett in life – hatted, bearded and sombre.

Left: Rev. and Mrs Tweedale with the psychic "extra" of her father, now in spirit, hatless and looking much happier.

I have sent many bereaved ones and many seekers of the truth of spirit return and human survival to the Crewe psychics and had the great pleasure of seeing these people come to my Vicarage exhibiting the photographic evidences of the survival of their dear ones, and filled with joy unspeakable.

Persons who have had no experience of their powers and who have made no investigation worthy of the name say that the "extras" are printed in [by the photographer] after the photographs are taken. This shallow and absurd theory, together with many similar, is blown to the winds by the following facts.

1. That, as in the case of Sir William Crookes, the plate has been immediately taken away from the psychics' house and printed off by the sitter.

2. That in scores of cases all the details of the psychic "extra" have been carefully noted immediately after development.

3. That recognised portraits of deceased persons have been produced by the Crewe Circle in cases where no photo, painting, drawing, or any other representation of the deceased has ever been made during the mortal life. I possess such photos.

4. That I have, by means of gas-light photo-paper, taken a print from the negative immediately after development before the negative has dried by squeegeeing the paper down on to the wet gelatine surface and so getting a print before the negative has left my hands.

The fact that supernormal pictures of the departed "dead" can be obtained is now completely proved."

Sir Arthur Conan Doyle

It wasn't until 1919 that Sir Arthur Conan Doyle made his first visit to Crewe[12] as he writes:

"I bought my plates in Manchester and then travelled over to keep the appointment which had been made a week before. Arriving at Crewe, I went down to the little house in Market Street, which is so modest and humble that it furnishes an argument in itself against any undue cupidity on the part of its tenant. Two spiritualistic friends, Mr. Oaten, editor of *The Two Worlds*, and Mr. [Henry] Walker, were my companions.

Mr. Hope and Mrs. Buxton were waiting for us, and, after a short religious service, Mr. Hope and I went into the dark room. There I opened the packet of plates, put two into the carrier and marked them then and there. The carrier was then taken into the room and Mr. Hope inserted it into the camera. We three spiritualists sat in front with a rug, or blanket, as a background. The exposure having been made, the carrier was taken back into the dark room where, with my own hands, I took out the plates, developed them and fixed them. So far as I could judge, there was at no stage any possibility of changing the plates.

But this question does not really arise. No changing of plates would account for the effect actually produced in fig.1. There is a hazy cloud covering us of what I will describe as ectoplasm, though my critics are very welcome to call it cotton-wool, if it eases their feelings to do so. In one corner appears a partial materialisation of what seems to be the hair and forehead of a young man. Across the plate is scrawled,

"Well done, Friend Doyle, I welcome you to Crewe. Greetings to all. T. COLLEY."

How can we determine that the message was really from Archdeacon Colley? The obvious way would be to get a sample of his writing in life and to compare it with that upon the plate. This I have done, as shown in fig. 2. Can anyone deny that the handwriting is the same in both instances, or can anyone suppose that the rough script of Hope could possibly be modified into the scholarly handwriting of the Archdeacon?

Whence, then did this message come? Does anyone imagine that a private forger is retained by Hope and lurks somewhere in that humble abode?

It may be remarked incidentally that my own strong desire was to obtain some sign from my son who had passed away the year before. The result seemed to show that our personal wishes do not affect the outcome.

Having failed to get what I desired, I remained at Crewe for the night, and next morning went down to Market Street again. On this occasion I used

---

12. *The Case for Spirit Photography* (1922) pps18-19

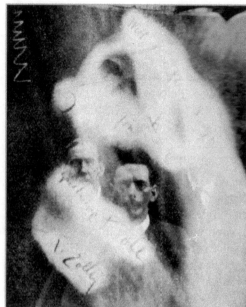

Left: Fig.1. Conan Doyle's first psychic photograph at Crewe, with a written message from Archdeacon Colley almost obscuring the sitters.

Below: Fig. 2. An example of Archdeacon' Colley's writing in his lifetime, for comparison.

Hope's own plates, having left mine at the hotel.

He gave me the choice of several packets. The result obtained under all the precautions which I could adopt (it would only weary the reader if I gave every point of detail) was a photograph of the face of a young man beside my own. It was not a good likeness of my son, though it resembled him as he was some eight years before his death. Of the three results which I obtained at Crewe it was the one which impressed me least.

On examination with a lens, it was noticeable that the countenance was pitted with fine dots, as in the case of process printing. This is to be noticed in a certain proportion, possibly one in ten, of Hope's results, and occurs in the case of persons whose faces could by no possibility have appeared in newspapers. One can only suppose that it is in some way connected with the psychic process, and some have imagined a reticulated screen upon which the image is built up.

I am content to note the fact without attempting to explain it. I have observed the same effect in other psychic photographs.

The third result was the most remarkable of any. I had read that Hope can get images without the use of the camera, but the statement sounded incredible. He now asked me to mark a plate and put it in a carrier, which I did. We then placed our hands on either side of the carrier, Mrs. Buxton and her sister joining in. At the end of about a minute Hope gave a sort of shudder, and intimated that he thought a result had been obtained. On putting the plate into the solution, a disc, the size of a shilling, perfectly black, sprang up in the centre of it. On development this resolved itself into a luminous circle with the face of a female delicately outlined within it. Under the chin is a disc of white, and two fingers which are pointing to it. The disc is evidently a brooch, and the pointing seemed to indicate that it was meant to be evidential.

The face bore a strong resemblance to that of my elder sister, who died some thirty years ago. Upon sending the print to my other sisters they not only confirmed this, but they reminded me that my sister had a very remarkable ivory brooch in her lifetime and that it was just the one object which might best have been chosen as a test. I regret that this picture is so delicate that it will not bear reproduction.

Such were my three results at Crewe.

Their full significance was not realised until I had made enquiries, but after that time I felt it impossible to doubt the supernormal nature of the powers which had produced such effects."

Mr. & Mrs. James Hewat McKenzie

Having heard of the death of their son, Second Lieutenant William McKenzie (2nd Battalion London Scottish), in Jerusalem, on June 12th of 1918, his parents longed to make that contact they knew was possible.

On November 22nd, 1918 Mr. McKenzie made an appointment for a sitting with Mr. Hope, of Crewe, hoping to be successful in obtaining a portrait of their son.

Mrs. Barbara McKenzie wrote this account[13] some time later:

"My son, Lieut. W. McKenzie, was wounded in Palestine in the spring of 1918, and "passed on" in Jerusalem six weeks later. Within a month we had news from him through Mrs. Osborne Leonard, Miss Naomi Bacon, and other mediums.

In the autumn my husband, on his way to Scotland, visited the Crewe Circle and sat for a psychic photograph, hoping that my son might be able to manifest. But it was the face of an unknown youngish man, with a moustache, which appeared as an "extra".

On his return from the journey, he had another sitting with Mrs. Leonard,

13. A condensed version had been published in *Light* Nov. 6th 1920, under 'Unseen Presences' for 'Armistice Day'.

and when my son communicated, expressed his disappointment at the Crewe result. Our son replied that he had produced an "extra" of himself at Crewe with "Bim's" mother. (We knew that "Bim" was the son of Lady Glenconner, and that he had been killed early in the war.) We were acquainted with Lady Glenconner through our mutual interest in psychic studies, but we were not always in touch, and I did not know that she had been at Crewe.

With the Crewe Circle, Mr. Hope and Mrs. Buxton, we had only a casual acquaintance at the time, through one previous interview, when I obtained an excellent "extra" of my mother. At this period, 1918, the British College had not been begun, and our close acquaintance with Hope was in the future.

He had never seen any of my family. "Feda", Mrs. Leonard's guide, described my son's "extra" carefully. It was not as good as he had hoped, but his mother would recognise it.

It was veiled on one side of the face; there was a mark on the temple indicating the wound which caused his death.

Almost unbelieving, Mr. McKenzie reported this to me. I found an ordinary photograph of my son and enclosed it to Lady Glenconner, telling her the story and asking whether she had been to Crewe and had received any unrecognised "extra". By next post came a reply enclosing an "extra", saying that she had been trying to get him placed among her own friends but without success, and that both she and Lord Glenconner saw at once from the photograph I had sent that it was my son. She had never seen any of my family. On examination, the "extra" confirmed all that had been given by "Feda".

The face was emaciated, the result of six weeks when little food could be taken, as verified to me later by the chaplain at Jerusalem, who visited me in London, but I had no difficulty, nor had any of the family, in at once recognising it. I had seen my son two years before in an English hospital, emaciated by a previous wound and subsequent dysentery.

The face was veiled on one side, and the temple had the mark of the wound. The latter, the cause of death, was known only to a few of the family circle. The "extra" was closely examined by a sculptor and by a miniature artist, by measurements, etc., and independent corroboration received in every detail. The "extra" was surrounded by two veils, an inner drapery, and a second arch, beautifully woven, which I have only seen in a few of Hope's early "extras".

Here was repeated confirmation that an attempt had been made and succeeded, and of which we might have remained in ignorance but for the Mrs. Leonard sitting. A sitter, associated sympathetically with us, had been made use of. We had other evidence that "Bim" and other young men had joined in achieving his result, although, curiously, Lady Glenconner herself never had the satisfaction of getting a good "extra" of her son, whose picture had often appeared in public journals while that of my son had not.

A curious sequel followed. I did not see Lady Glenconner personally for several months as I was not in London, but in the beginning of 1919 we met, and she showed me her various "extras". Returning home, I had a strong impression to send her a copy of the unrecognised "extra" of the young man with the moustache which Mr. McKenzie had secured at Crewe. The reply

Sitter, Lady Glennconner with the psychic "extra"
later recognised as Lt. W. McKenzie
(from "News from the Next World" by Rev. Tweedale)

came that it had gained her own and her husband's immediate recognition as an excellent likeness of Lord Elcho, her nephew killed in the war, and that she had sent it to his mother, then attending the Versailles Conference. He had worn such a moustache previous to the war period. I had a letter from Paris from his mother, confirming this, and saying that the "extra" had been clearly recognised by Lord Balfour and other friends in Paris.

Later it was sent to his wife who had gone to India, but I had no further news about it. We did not know that such a person as Lord Elcho existed.

Here was an attempt at cross-correspondence in psychic "extras" indicating the work of a group on the other side who were aware of the mutual interest between Lady Glenconner and ourselves, and that anything that was sent through might have a chance of being traced. We had once been the means of introducing Lady Glenconner to a medium from abroad who had provided remarkable evidence of "Bim's" survival, so that we have the element of gratitude in this almost unique example of cross-correspondence in psychic photography.

Mrs. Hewat McKenzie

Here is a wonderful example of "side-stepping" to rule out the possibility of 'thought transference' of desired effects in psychic photography.

Sir Oliver Lodge thus writes "Evidence is cumulative; it is on the strength of a mass of experience that an induction is ultimately made, and a conclusion provisionally arrived at.
If we can establish the survival of any single, ordinary individual, we have established it for all."

Prof. Henslow quoting Lodge in 'Proofs of the Truths of Spiritualism'

A Professional Photographer tests William Hope

Lady Glenconner did eventually get a picture of her son Edward when William Hope and Mrs. Buxton visited 'Glen', near Innerleithen (Peebleshire) in September of 1919. The local professional photographer, Mr T.H.M. Colledge was invited to be present and work with Hope to make sure everything was as it should be. It so happened that Bernard Munn, the artist, was also at 'Glen', having been commissioned to do a portrait of their son from sketches and photographs. Lieut Hon. E.W.Tennant, affectionately known as 'Bim', was only 19 when he died 'on the Somme' as mentioned in the previous chapter. Lady Glenconner asked Munn to sit in on the séances and—as a stranger and as an artist—'find out if there was anything of a fraudulent nature about them.'

Mr. Munn wrote an article to *Light* confirming Mr Colledge's report and giving more detail of the "extras" that appeared than Colledge had. No identification was given but it is highly likely some were of 'Bim' and some his friends who helped in getting their images through. It follows Mr Colledge's report, which contains important details of the test, as this is the first time there is a reference to William Hope working with a stereoscopic camera—and under close supervision, with images appearing on the plates. Unfortunately, there are no copies of the photographs taken at Glen.[1]

For those readers not familiar with stereoscopic photographs I include this example, unfortunately without an "extra". Although this is not connected with the experiences described here, as it is the only illustrated reference to the use of a stereoscopic camera, I judged it worth including.

Fred Barlow, in *Light*, Jan,1921, writes of his experiments with Mrs. Deane:[2]

"The two halves of the plate in a stereoscopic camera were void of any supernormal result (see Fig.i.), whilst the plate in the camera next to it, exposed simultaneously with the plate in the stereo camera, showed clear supernormal images (see Fig.ii.). This experiment was repeated several times.

---

1. *Light,* January 30th 1933 "A Professional Photographer tests William Hope."
2. James Coates' 'Practical and Scientific Aspects of " Supernormal Pictures." Part 8.

122

Above: Mr Barlow's Fig.i.
Right: Mr Barlow's Fig.ii.

*Above: Fig.i. print separated along
'division line' as when mounted for
viewing*

*The finished print of a
photograph taken through
a stereoscopic camera
would be viewed through
a binocular viewer such
as this:*

Mr. Colledge's Report

"On Tuesday, Sept. 23rd, 1919, previous to the séances to which I refer, I went to 'Glen' and arranged a room to be used as a darkroom for photographic purposes.

I took with me on this occasion my own stereoscopic camera; also three double dark slides, along with lenses, together with several other articles all packed in one case.

The double dark slides were filled by myself in my own studio dark room on Sept. 23rd with Imperial special sensitive half-plates, and were not marked in any way. This camera can be used either as a half-plate, or a stereoscopic camera by special adjustments.

On the 26th, I was asked to set up the camera in the room used for the séance. Before sitting for the séance, I took one of the dark slides from the case and placed it on the table without any cover. Sitting round the table for the séance were Lady Glenconner, Mrs. Beadon, Mrs. Platt, Mr. B. Munns, two members of the Crewe Circle (viz. Mr. Hope and Mrs. Buxton), and myself. The time was about 11.30 a.m., and the room was well lit and flooded with sunshine. During the séance, Mr. Hope indicated that a group would be taken of her Ladyship, Mrs. Beadon, Mrs. Platt and Mr. Munn; also a single sitting of Lady Glenconner.

As customary at Mr. Hope's séances, the slide was lifted from the table by Mr. Hope, who places his hand underneath it and the other hand on the top of it, the whole hand fully extended, the person sitting on his right places his or her hand over the hand of Mr. Hope, then the next on the right, and so on till the various sitters pile their hands top and bottom of the slide simultaneously ; and I invariably noticed that Mr. Hope's arms after a little time gave a sudden jerk, and then he remarked "that will do." This finished the sitting.

I then went and arranged my stereo camera and focussed the group. I used the slide which had been on the table during the séance, and which I had taken possession of at once after the sitting was over. I was satisfied that it was my own slide. I placed it in position in the camera; as I was using a double shutter for the twin lenses, I set this, and Mr. Hope asked if he might be allowed to press the bulb and make the exposure. I consented. Mr. Hope took the bulb in his left hand and held his right hand over the camera from the left side of the camera. The clasped hands (of Mr. Hope and Mrs. Buxton) were held at least six to eight inches high above the camera, immediately over the centre and at no time during exposure did they ever touch the: camera, as I stood within a yard of them behind and watched the proceedings very closely. I judged the exposure to be about ten seconds.

I removed the slide from the camera myself, and laid it on a chair behind me, and no one approached the slide or touched it while I arranged the camera for the single sitting of Lady Glenconner. I placed the slide, after focussing, and set the shutter. Mr. Hope and Mrs. Buxton joined hands over the camera as for the previous exposure, he holding the bulb in his left hand, and they stood in exactly the same way as while exposing the group—I standing closely behind them, noting every movement they made, but they never at any time touched the camera either with their hands or bodies.

The exposure was similar to the exposure for the group, and at its conclusion, I myself removed the slide and at once went to the. dark room and developed it.

There could be no question as to the substitution of another slide as I never allowed the slide out of my sight, and no one handled it except during the séance when the various persons present placed their hands on top and bottom of it.

After developing and fixing the two plates from the slide I found on examination a stereoscopic negative of the group with no psychic result on No.1 plate. On No. 2 plate was a stereoscopic negative of Lady Glenconner, also a psychic impression of considerable interest.

In order to understand how I arrived at my conclusions in regard to this psychic impression, I may take the liberty of briefly explaining a stereoscopic camera and the result obtained by its use. The stereo camera is in reality two cameras in one, and gives two negatives on the same plate though taken at slightly different angles, and this gives solidity and relief to a stereoscopic print when properly mounted and viewed through a stereoscope, which relief is wanting in any ordinary photograph.

On examining plate No. 2 from the slide, I found the stereoscopic effect correct, so far as Lady Glenconner's negative was concerned; and *I also found an impression of a young man's head on the left division of the plate four times impressed, without similar impressions on the right division where it was plainly impressed three times and twice by blurred movements—but of the same face.*

But in no respect were these stereoscopic impressions, as the position of the head measures from a given centre does not compare or agree in either of the two divisions of the plate. (italics are mine-A.H.)

I concluded, from this examination of the plate and the nature of the movement, that the impression had been made without the aid of the camera, and probably during the time of the séance.

I explained this to Mr. Hope and asked if he would consent to give another sitting in order to try and get a result without the aid of the camera. He very willingly consented, and in order that there could be no mistake about the plates, or any other circumstance I could foresee, I opened a new box of plates, the seal of which was intact as it left the the factory and put two plates into the same slide, Nos. 1 and 2.

At Mr. Hope's request, I was to allow no one to touch the slide but myself; and, in order to safeguard it, I buttoned it under my jacket during the passage from the dark room to the sitting room. When the others were seated, I laid it on the centre of the table where it lay openly in view of all of us during the séance.

On this occasion, Mr. Hope did not lift up the slide and put his hands on top and bottom nor did any of the others. During the séance, Mr. Hope told me take the slide away and develop it at once – he seemed at that moment to be coming out of a trance.

I took the slide to the dark room at once and developing both plates, found one blank but normal, the other had the impression of the same face on it, not moved as on the stereoscopic plate. I was satisfied from this result that impressions may be obtained without the use of the camera.

On Saturday, Sept. 27th, I again attended a séance at 'Glen' in the forenoon. The conditions were the same as on the previous day, and the same persons were present,

Mr. Hope again allowed me to use my own stereoscopic camera. I put a slide on the table containing two plates Nos. 1 and 2, and these were newly filled by myself from my own box of plates.

When I laid the slide on the table, I suggested to Mr. Hope that he might try putting the hands on top of the slide without moving it, in order to avoid blurring the impression on the plates if made at that particular moment. He said it was unusual, but consented to try this method.

Consequently, at the time of taking the slide into the hands of the sitters at the séance, the hands were laid on it as requested. Mr. Hope put his right hand on the slide, then Lady Glenconner put her right hand on his Mr. Hope putting his left over her ladyship's, then put her left hand on top of his, and the next all in the same order—or as nearly as I can remember. Mr. Hope, during this séance, said that the two plates should be exposed on a group of the same party as on the previous day. I used my stereo camera, doing everything myself, but on developing the plates found no psychic results.

When I told Mr. Hope this, he suggested that we try and obtain a result by simply holding a slide in contact with Mrs. Buxton's forehead.

I had two extra slides in my case, each containing two plates. I took one out of the case and gave it to Lady Glenconner, who took it in her left band and pressed it against Mrs. Buxton's forehead, at the same time placing her right hand behind her head in order to maintain the slide in position. During the period the slide was held to her forehead, Mrs. Buxton gave several spasmodic jerks. The slide was under my supervision the whole time, and I am certain it was my own slide, as I could identify it at a glance from its make and special markings upon it.

I took the slide from her ladyship and developed the two plates simultaneously. I found one blank but normal; and on the other a well-defined face, three times impressed. Two were side by side and well-defined from the brow to the mouth. The third impression masked the lower portion of the faces by being impressed almost between them, the upper portion of the brow being immediately below the mouth of the higher impressions, thus masking the lower portion of the faces, so far as I can remember, as I have not a print to refer to.

The chin was not very well defined in the lower impression either.

I could almost account for the three impressions on this plate of a similar face, in concluding that, if at the moment that the impression was being made, Mrs. Buxton gave her spasmodic jerks, the slide in contact with her forehead moved in sympathy with her bodily movement.

Apart from the primary question: How is it possible to obtain photographs of an "astral body", which you cannot see, there arise the further questions in regard to the phenomenon of obtaining results without the aid of the camera, such as: How are the faces focussed on the plate? How do they penetrate the wooden slide? And, what rays do they use for that purpose? How are the exposures so well timed on various speeds of plates to give such good results?"

T. H. M. Colledge

Bernard Munn writes:

". . . I had been invited to 'Glen' to paint a portrait of the Hon. E. W. Tennant, who had lost his life in the war, and had been there only a day or two when I was asked if I would attend a séance for obtaining psychic photographs, in order that I might watch the proceedings as a stranger and as an artist, to find out if there was anything of a fraudulent nature about them. This I willingly did, as I had never had any experience of Spiritualism and looked upon the photographic side of it as being pure trickery. I felt confident that if there was a weak spot I should be able to discover it. ....

As soon as I had become sufficiently friendly with him [Hope] to ask to be allowed to make one or two tests, I decided on a process of elimination.

In studying the photographic "extras" I found that they appeared at any angle on the plate, and of any size, which seemed to indicate that they could not be photographs of spirits in the surrounding space, as sometimes thought, capable of being registered by the photographic lens but not by the human eye. I therefore hit upon the idea of the stereoscopic camera as being likely to prove which it might be. Thereupon, Lady Glenconner sent me down to Mr. Colledge to see if he had one – it was on this occasion that he returned with me, with all his apparatus.

Throughout the tests he describes, we were in collaboration; and it is on the [stereo] one in which Lady Glenconner was the sitter that I should like to add one or two remarks from my own observations. I have the actual photograph in front of me.

The first impression of the young man's face starts on the left division of the plate at right angles to the sitter, and is quite sharp except for the mouth and chin. Then there are two or three blurred impressions of his face – blurred partly through movement and partly through superimposing. On each side of the division between the two pictures are some more or less sharp impressions overlapping. Towards the head of Lady Glenconner, in the right-hand picture, the face becomes vertical, but upside down, and immediately over her head it is still inverted and at an angle of 45 degrees.

Both these are larger than the other impressions and the last one shows the mouth and chin quite sharp so that the whole character of the face is clearly visible.

I mention these details because I am convinced that it would be almost impossible to obtain such a result by faking; and if it were, it would need elaborate apparatus to do it— which Mr. Hope certainly did not possess. My experience of him was that he knew very little of the technical side of photography and that duplicity was absent from his character. (italics in original.)

In a séance that Lord and Lady Glenconner had at the time, a head of their son was obtained which was a good likeness, yet it did not resemble any of the existing pictures or photographs which had been placed in my hands to assist me in painting. the portrait. The impression it gave me was of a face without light and shade—being unlike either a drawing or a photograph. This is sometimes the case with "extras", though they more often resemble the photographic print and never, in my experience a drawing by hand, unless they do so intentionally, reproducing an existing drawing or picture."

Bernard Munn
Edgbaston, Birmingham[3]

---

3. *Light,* February 1933, 'Mr. Bernard Munns Corroborates Mr. Colledge's Report.'

Special Note on Later Experiments

From the British College *Psychic Science* "Transactions" (October 1924) the editor reports:

"Mr. Chas. Lyle allows me to report that in July at the College he made an exposure in his stereoscopic camera in the presence of the Crewe Circle. An "extra" appeared—the same face on both plates, but in different positions on the two plates.

As in previous experiments neither Mr. Hope nor Mrs. Buxton ever saw the plates, which were loaded into the slides at Mr. Lyle's house and taken away after the experiment and developed by him.

On a marked plate exposed in Mr. Hope's camera, a few seconds before, a different "extra" appeared.

On other occasions, the same face as an "extra" has appeared on the plate exposed in Mr. Hope's camera, and on Mr. Lyle's stereoscopic plates."

* * * * *

"Photographic evidence of the supernormal on its own is only valuable if the details of the circumstances under which the photographs were produced are known.."

Cyril Permutt - 'Photographing the Invisible'

A New Venue and Unusual Results

In April 1920, following many years of research, James Hewat McKenzie and his wife Barbara founded the British College for Psychic Science at 57 Holland Park in London W11, a property he owned, and it quickly became a Mecca for "Instruction, Demonstration and Research in all that relates to the great subject of Psychic Science." As well as hosting events and providing sittings with the best of British Mediums they travelled through Europe and America seeking out and inviting good foreign mediums to visit England. One of the earliest mediums invited to demonstrate at the College was William Hope working with Mrs Buxton— as the Crewe Circle for when working together it was seen that the results were enhanced.

Just one month after its formation the College hosted the annual gathering of the 'Society for the Study of Supernormal Pictures' (SSSP).

It is not known whether Dr Abraham Wallace ever made that journey to Crewe to pursue his own research but in 1916 the Society for the Study of Supernormal Pictures was founded[1] and he became its President, as Fred Barlow writes in an article in *Light* in January 1921:

"The Society for the Study originated from a small group of photographers who had corresponded with one another in regard to Psychic Photography. The present Secretary of the S.S.S.P.[2] endeavoured to link up these investigators with each other by circulating amongst them copies of all letters addressed to him on the subject. This circle rapidly widened, and in 1916 the S.S.S.P. was founded for the scientific study and investigation of supernormal pictures. Dr Abraham Wallace was elected the first president, and Mr. Wm. G. Mitchell [of Darlington], who had started the ball rolling, was elected the first vice-president. Although the Society was strictly private in its investigations and reports, its membership rapidly increased, and now includes such well-known workers us Major R.E.E. Spencer, Miss F. R. Scatcherd, Mrs. Leila Boustead, Messrs. James Coates, William Jeffrey, H. Blackwell, and many other investigators."

---

1. The Society ceased in 1923.
2. The Secretary was Fred Barlow.

In *The Case for Spirit Photography* Conan Doyle tells us:

"At the annual meeting of the Society for the Study of Supernormal Pictures, I being present, a photograph of the members was taken in the normal way as a souvenir. As Hope was present, it was suggested that a second photograph be taken by him in the hope that we might get some psychic effect. The plate was taken from an unopened packet in the pocket of the secretary, and some fifteen of us were witnesses of the whole transaction. Hope had no warning at all and could have made no preparation.

The plate was at once developed by one of our own members, and a well-marked extra, amid a cloud of ectoplasm, appeared upon the picture. This extra was claimed by one of our members as a good likeness of his dead father. This result, which is illustrated [below] was obtained before an audience of experts—if any men in this world have a right to call themselves experts upon this subject.

Group taken by William Hope, of the members of the Society for the Study of Supernormal Pictures during Conference held in May 1920, at the British College of Psychic Science, London.

Members: Bottom row - Mrs. McKenzie and Mr. McKenzie (Hon. Principal B.C.P. Science), Mr. Arno S. Pearse (Hon Foreign Secretary), Mr Fred Barlow (Hon. Secretary), and Mr. R.P. Spencer.

Second row - Sir Arthur Conan Doyle, Dr. Abraham Wallace (President), Mr. William Jeffrey, Miss F.R. Scatcherd, Col. Baddeley C.B. C.M.G., Major R.E.E. Spencer.

Back row: Lt.-Col. E.R. Johnson, Lady Conan Doyle, Mr. Colin Keay, Mr. Jas. Coates, Mrs. A. S. Pears, Mr. H. Blackwell, and Mr. H. J. Osborn.

How can it be explained by fraud and how can such a case be lightly set aside? Granting for argument's sake that the sitter may have been mistaken in the recognition, how can the actual psychic effect be accounted for?"

In the centre superimposed on Mr. Wm. Jeffrey, is a portrait of his father, which can be seen by rotating the page to the left and viewing the group sideways.

In James Coates' series of articles in *Light*, Dec 1920-Feb '21 this important note is added by the Editor, David Gow.

<u>Special Note on Illustration</u>. (Editor of *Light*)

"While it is of value and interest to present here a group of representative men and women who have investigated and know psychic or supernormal photography to be a fact, my main object here is to call attention to a comparatively recent photograph taken under rigid test conditions.

Mr. Fred Barlow, Hon, Secretary of the S.S.S.P., in his report, summarised by me, says:

"The result was obtained on a marked plate supplied and placed in the dark slide, and removed from the same and developed by myself. The sensitive [Mr William Hope] did not touch the plate until after the image had developed up."

"The foregoing was substantiated afterwards in a communication sent to me by Mr. Barlow on a slide for lectures. On learning that the psychic face partly shown in the centre of the photograph, was recognised by Mr. Jeffrey as that of his father, long deceased, I called upon him (at his residence, 15, India-street, Charing Cross. Glasgow on Friday, November 19th, 1920) and asked about this psychic picture. He stated that he was fully convinced that it was an excellent likeness of his father, and showed me two photographs, one of his father in life and the other of a nephew. On examining these and comparing them with the psychic production. I was impressed with the physiognomic resemblance which seems to justify Mr Jeffrey's conviction.

In conclusion, it must be remembered that, apart from the scientific value of the photograph which holds good whether the recognition is undoubted or not – neither of the psychics, Mr. Wm. Hope and Mrs. Buxton could have met the original in the body, nor have seen his photograph, which is not identical with the psychic picture."

At the close of the S.S.S.P. Conference that year this 'resolution' was adopted:

"The members of the Society for the Study of Supernormal Pictures present at this meeting, desire to place on record the fact that, after many tests and the examination of thousands of pictures, they are unanimously of the opinion that results have been supernormally obtained on sensitive photographic plates, under reliable test conditions. At present the members do not undertake to explain how the results are obtained, but they assert that they have undoubtedly been secured under conditions excluding any possibility of fraud."

James Coates felt that this resolution was:

"... conclusive enough of the fact of supernormal photography; and the term "Supernormal" embraces enough to cover every phase."[3]

In an article by Barbara McKenzie in *Light* we learn of another experiment carried out at the College during that week in May.[4]

"Last May, Sir Arthur and Lady Conan Doyle made an experiment with the Crewe Circle. The "extra", a man's face, was not recognised by either, but a week later a message reached me that there was a clue to it as resembling an acquaintance of Sir Arthur's: would I send a print to a certain address? This was recognised by the widow as certainly her husband, who had died a month previously, but of whose death Sir Arthur had not been aware at the time of the experiment, as the announcement had been made in the *Morning Post* instead of *The Times* and had not been seen. The sequel came a few weeks ago, when this widow called and reminded me of the incident and told me that her husband had been a convinced Spiritualist and had even made investigations in psychic photography with the late Mr. Boursnell, but that she had always avoided the subject. Here was an effort, strengthened no doubt by knowledge and will, to bring assurance to her – and other evidence has since been added."

Mrs McKenzie also tells us –having had this experience herself – "that only a small proportion the – "extras", the "spirit" faces – obtained by means of psychic photography, are recognised by those with whom they appear. But that these may yet be of the utmost value, if only the right link is obtained, is quite evident from numerous instances of recognition by others than those who made the experiment. ...

Recently a mother who had lost an only son in the war made an experiment at the College. A clear face appeared near her, but instead of being her own son, it was recognised as the son of a friend whom she had comforted, and to whom she had taught something of the facts and philosophy of Spiritualism.

In October two visitors from Canada experimented, but to their disappointment, the face appearing, though remarkably clear, was quite unknown. They dined some weeks later with a relation whom they had not

---

3. Practical and Theological Aspects of "Supernormal" Pictures. (*Light* 4th Dec 1921)
4. "The Unknown Face." By Barbara McKenzie (*light* Dec 4th 1920)

seen for several years. An inspection of various ordinary photographs was made, and the psychic "result" was casually handed out with others. A change passed over the face of the relative, and she demanded where the "extra" had been obtained, as it certainly was the face of her husband, unknown to the experimenters.

The wife of Major Spencer, of Walbottle, had a similar experience recently. A visit to Crewe resulted in a lad's face unrecognised by her. On her showing it to some friends on her return north, it was claimed by a neighbour in the village as her son, whom Mrs. Spencer did not know, but to whom she had sent parcels during the war. She had also brought his mother into a knowledge of the subject."

Mrs. McKenzie goes on to add:

"I have a large number of unrecognised photographs and there are many others about. In the New Year I purpose having these on view at the British College of Psychic Science, and if anyone would care to trust me with any such photographs, I should be only too glad to show them and to think that even two or three might carry their messages to the right hearts."

The Neighbour's son

This "side-stepping" is a valuable piece of evidence in appearance of "extras" as it has been shown that mortal thoughts could influence the mediums and therefore the plates themselves.

To have the appearance of a face – unknown but having a link to someone "known" and placeable is spirits' aim to show their existence and, as Mrs McKenzie says, – the "will, purposeful and courageous, beyond the barriers of death, of love, constant and untiring—love, which finds a way to its object."

As the College came up to its first Anniversary, Mrs. St. Clair Stobart had a sitting there, in March 1921, and sent this report to *Light*:

"Herewith I send a brief record of a sitting with Mr. Hope and Mrs. Buxton at the College, on March 11, 1921. I obtained the plates from the Kodak Co., in Regent Street. ... as I wanted the sitting to be a test sitting, I had told the Manager of the Kodak Co, and the Chief Assistant, the use to which the plates were to be put. I asked them to place upon the plates some private mark, without showing it to me, in order that the plates might later be identified by them. This they did. I need not go into all the details of the taking of the photographs by Mr. Hope and Mrs. Buxton, and of the preliminary prayers and hymns sung and said by these sincere and simple folk they are well known to all your readers.

Four photos were taken of myself and my husband, "J." sitting together with our backs against a blank wall, upon which no shadows were reflected. Upon two of these there were "extras". In one case a full-length figure of a woman clothed in the usual filmy drapery – is it ectoplasmic? – bending over, between the two of us; and in the other, a head only, projecting from the side of my arm.

From start to finish, neither Mr. Hope nor Mrs. Buxton handled the plates at all, and from start to finish, neither of them was left alone with either the plates or the camera. Mr. Hope never handled the plates at all. He stood by me just telling me what to do.

But what about the private marks of the Kodak Co?

I borrowed the negatives from the College and took them to the Kodak Co., to the Manager and the Chief Assistant. "Are these the plates you marked?" "Can you see the marks?" I asked.

"Oh! Yes!" they replied, "look, here they are, a tiny circle enclosing a cross in the top left-hand corner, and a circle with a right-angled mark in the top middle. And for the first time I saw the marks which they had put.

It is difficult to see how, under these circumstances, there was any loophole for fraud or trickery.

The positive identification of the full length "extra", is difficult, because the person whom it resembles passed over thirty years ago, and although the features show a strong resemblance it would be necessary for complete identification that the hair and the manner of wearing it should be shown, and this is hidden by the drapery.

Yours sincerely,

M.A. St. Clair Stobart.[5]

Some months later, at a sitting with Mrs. Cooper, she was given information which enabled her to recognise the "extra" as a relation whom she had never seen, but of whom she managed to secure a photograph for comparison.

* * * * *

---

5. Mabel Annie St Clair Stobart a British suffragist and aid-worker, commanded all-women medical units to serve in the First World War. She was the first woman to attain the rank of Major in any national army. Author of several books and articles; Chair of the British College of Psychic Science, in 1924, she founded and became Chairman of the Spiritualist Community and fellow spiritualist Arthur Conan Doyle served as President until his death in July 1930. Stobart served as the chair of the Spiritualist Community Council from 1924-1941 and joined the council of the World Congress of Faiths.

At the same time as Mrs Stobart was having her sitting this 'Remarkable' report appeared in *Light:*

The Remarkable Locket Case

"There are now far too many of these "spirit photographs," taken under the strictest test conditions, and presenting deep problems, to be dismissed casually. Instead of a matter inviting ridicule and disdain, as this class of photograph has so often done in the past, there really seems here the most fascinating investigation that has ever been presented to mankind to undertake. ....

It appears from the signed testimony before us that a Mr. West and a Mr. Goodwin journeyed from Hyde to Crewe in August last, to visit Mr. Hope and Mrs. Buxton, who are so widely known as the mediums in hundreds of cases of Psychic Photography. During the visit a photograph was taken by Mr. Hope with the help of Mrs. Buxton. A spirit "extra" appeared on the plate, and was eventually identified as Mr. West's brother-in-law, by the widow, the brother-in-law having died some six years previously.

The Locket (1¼ inch long) with the photo of Mr. West's brother-in-law.

Again, in October. Mr. West and Mr. Goodwin paid a surprise visit to the Crewe mediums, Mr. West taking with him a locket containing the portrait of his deceased brother-in-law, for the purpose of showing it to Mr. Hope to prove the likeness between the portrait and the spirit extra they obtained on their visit in August. Mr. West had placed this locket in a wallet which he carried in his hip-pocket for safety. Hoping to get another sitting with the Crewe mediums a packet of plates was bought in Hyde by Mr, Goodwin before starting for Crewe with his friend.

On their arrival at Crewe, Mr. Hope at once consented to give the gentlemen a sitting, and immediately before the short service that always precedes the taking of photographs, and whilst they were seated round the little table, Mr. West showed to Mr. Hope and Mrs. Buxton the locket, which he took out of his wallet for the purpose. Both the mediums agreed that the portrait in the locket showed a close resemblance to the spirit "extra" that had appeared on the photograph taken in the previous August. Mr. West then carefully replaced the locket in his wallet, which he put in his hip-pocket, and the séance commenced.

The small packet of plates that they had brought lay unopened on the little table around which they all sat. A few minutes later Mr. West retired to the dark room with Mr. Hope; the packet of plates was opened by Mr. West, he personally placing them in the slide, and at the same time signing the two plates with his initials. He carried the slide into the little green-house which is used at Crewe as a studio, and placed the slides in the camera. The photograph was then taken by Mr. Hope, Mrs. Buxton standing close to him while he made the exposure. Mr. West then retired with Mr. Hope and developed the negatives, and it must be particularly pointed. out that at no part of the proceedings did either Mr. Hope or Mrs. Buxton at any time touch the plates. Mr. West conducting the whole of the development himself. We have the gentlemen's signed testimony to this effect.

On bringing one of the negatives into the daylight, to the amazement of everyone there appeared a reproduction of the locket four times its actual size, super-imposed on the portraits of Mr. West and Mr. Goodwin. Every detail of the locket was shown with amazing exactness. How did it get there?

The only explanation that has yet been offered by others, outside Spiritualistic circles, is that it is a thought-projection on the part of one or all of those present. At the same time, it is not unreasonable to assume that a group of spirit operators may have produced this phenomenon, and in doing so proved once again that the spirit hypothesis is after all, the simple solution of the problem of Spirit Photography. We invite our renders to study this case very carefully; the true facts are before them, and we shall welcome their opinion."

Locket and photo are superimposed on the sitters.

H.W.Engholm.
(Mng.Editor, *Light.*)

This was not the only case of a portrait in a locket being reproduced on a plate. One year before, Mr and Mrs Hobbs had visited Crewe in the hope of obtaining a photo showing their son killed in 1918 in the war.

James Coates writes in his articles in *Light,* December 1920:

"In the remarkable supernormal photograph of Mr. A. W. Hobbs ...we have not only the recognisable features of the young man, but part of the frame of the locket, in which his treasured portrait was carried on his mother's breast. The psychics, Mrs. Buxton and Mr, Hope, had never seen that locket. ... It is conceivable that the intense thoughts of the parents—especially the mother found a resting place in the subconscious stratum of either Mrs. Buxton or Mr Hope, or of both. Their guides, operating in their aura, became aware of what was sought and produced or precipitated, or otherwise deposited the picture of the departed on the plate. ... Part of the frame of the locket was reproduced also. I had no difficulty—even if the psychics had seen the locket— in assuring Mr Hobbs that the psychic production was genuine.

Fig.1. An 'In-life' photograph of A.W. Hobbs taken in France.

Fig.2. Mr. & Mrs. Hobbs with a psychic image of the painting of their son and part of the locket frame.

The intelligences operating had succeeded in obtaining an identifiable portrait from that locket. It was not a photograph of a spirit, but a portrait produced by spirit power."

Mr Hobbs later wrote:

"Did I tell you that about six weeks after I obtained the first excellent result at Crewe, I asked Mr. Hope for a still further test of the reality of the phenomenon? To this Mr. Hope consented. Under strict tests – which I need not detail – I again got my boy's picture on my own selected plate. It is not a duplicate of the former one (Fig. 2). and differs especially in the drapery effect, and the absence of the miniature frame."

Coates tells us, unfortunately, the second psychic photograph was "too delicate to reproduce" in the magazine.

Note: In both cases the drapery and the faces are in front of the sitters. Indicating the "locket" effect was added after the exposure on the sitters. So not a 'pre-prepared' plate. As the sitters have recorded in the first 'Locket' case the locket was shown to Hope as they sat down to have the séance – so no time to prepare a duplicate. In the second case Hope did not know the locket and its painting existed – again he had no time to have prepared a copy, as the sceptics maintain.

Here are genuine portraits produced by spirit power, and distinctly different from the originals, in spirit.

They are "on the spot" reproductions by a skilled team in spirit, to join the sitters and the remembrances they had of their "dead ones".

> "When evaluating supernormal photography people will often suggest that fraud or trickery of one sort or another is involved but to suggest that, for instance, William Hope practised such fraud continuously for nearly 30 years really shows the absurdity of the suggestion."
>
> *Cyril Permutt - 'Photographing the Invisible'*

"Spirit Photography Exposed"

In March 1921 the Managing Editor of *Light*, Mr. H.W. Engholm, unfolded to the readers the following case – "in the hope that they may solve the problem we are about to set forth, we are confronted at the outset with a difficulty, as Mr. Bush, one of the principals of this case has already prejudged it."

He wrote:

"Our attention was first called to this problem through a pamphlet published by a Mr. Edward Bush, who is a member of the S.P.R., entitled *Spirit Photography Exposed*. This pamphlet of some forty pages has been widely sold at the price of 1/6, and it contains an advertisement offering the public a complete outfit for producing "extras" and "psychographs" at the price of 21/-

.

From time to time we have of course seen many pamphlets of this character, but the fact that Mr. Bush was a member of the S.P.R. qualified him at once as an investigator into psychical research, and therefore claimed our serious attention. Some correspondence has already passed between us and Mr. Bush, who has courageously offered us every facility for laying his case before our readers.

The reproductions of photographs that we will give in the course of this article are in each case from the originals, which have not been retouched or amplified by us in any way in the process of block-making or otherwise.

We will now endeavour to give the facts of the case and in the first place we will deal with the viewpoint and statements from Mr. Bush.

'I may say that I visited Mr. Hope with the strong desire that I might meet genuine phenomena, and as a sensitive Mr. Hope must have felt that I was an honest seeker for truth.'

The above statement from Mr. Bush we must ask our readers to bear in mind throughout their perusal of this interesting case. We now give the following series of incidents which we have taken word for word from Mr. Bush's pamphlet *Spirit Photography Exposed*."

'I wrote Mr. Hope of Crewe, on February 21st 1920, asking for a sitting for Spirit photography.

I enclosed with the letter a little photo of Mr. Vaudreuil, my son-in-law,

The photograph sent to Mr Hope

who was staying with us at Wakefield. The following words were written on the back of the photo:

"Tell Dad if anything happens to me, I will try and let him have a Spirit Photo. Tell him to shout up to let me know where he goes to.

John Ackroyd."

Instead of signing my own name at the end of my letter to Mr. Hope, I signed the assumed name of D. Wood.'

For some reason, which Mr. Bush has not made clear, he adopted the *nom de plume* of "D. Wood" and at the same time sent Mr. Hope a photograph with a statement written on the back of it that would lead everyone to suppose that the portrait was that of someone who had passed 'beyond the veil'.

Mr. Hope on returning the photograph to Mr. Bush, replied as follows:
"Dear Mr. Wood

In answer to your letter, we are quite willing to give you a sitting and to do what we can for you.

You even ask what our fees are and say you don't want to pay an exorbitant fee. As a matter of fact, we have no fees and never have had: we never charged one penny in our lives for any sitting. We do this sort of thing because we have work and want to make our living with it. Now I'm sorry you sent along a photo of the one you could like to get an "extra" of, because if that happens to come on the plate, the people would think it had been copied but still if you wish to come and try you may do so, and also you may bring your own plates, but if you do, we stipulate that they must be brought in an unopened packet just as bought from the shop. We use ¼ plate Sovereign or Imperial brand.

Now as to time we have the 5th of March at half past two, we can offer you.

Kindly let us know if coming as early as possible.

Yours respectfully,

W. Hope."

Mr Bush continues the story as written in the pamphlet:

"Being unavailable to visit Crewe on March 5th I did so on March 27th. Notwithstanding the ugly fact that the "spirit guides" had failed to inform the circle of my real name, the name of Mr. Vaudreuil, and the fact that he was still in the flesh, and the ruse which I had adopted for the purpose of arriving at the truth, I still hoped that our four famous witnesses might prove correct and that I might have a rude but withal joyous awakening when I arrived at Crewe.

I got to 144 Market Street about 3.30pm. Mrs. Buxton informed me that Mr. Hope was engaged with other sitters. After waiting a while, I was introduced to Mr. Hope as Mr. Wood from Wakefield.

The two mediums made a good impression upon me, and the thermometer of my expectations went up several degrees. An arrangement was made for a séance at six o'clock.

Mr. Hope asked me to procure a box of quarter-dry plates which I did and we met for the sitting at six o'clock.

This was preceded by a short séance. Mrs. Buxton, Mr. Hope and myself sat around a small table, in the centre of which I placed the packet of plates, we linked or touched hands—forming thus a closed circuit. A hymn was sung and a prayer was offered by Mr. Hope who then went under control and instructed me how to manipulate the plates. I was to take the top four from my box. Nos 1 and 4 were for exposures while Nos 2 and 3 were reserved for psychographs. The séance lasted about fifteen minutes. Mr. Hope and I then entered the dark room. My hour had now come...

Well, I was not very critical with the medium, but allowed him plenty of rope. When about to mark the plates for identification I fumbled in my pocket for my pencil. Mr. Hope instantly gave me his. The light is necessarily poor when rapid plates are used, but the shelf upon which the ruby light stood was inconveniently small and high and while, under these conditions I was inscribing the plates, Mr. Hope offered his assistance—just to steady the plate—and suiting the action to his word placed his hand, for perhaps three seconds, upon the plate. There were four plates to mark, and it was only in the case of one of them that he offered his assistance. I carried the slide out of the dark room.

Exposure was made by magnesium ribbon.

On returning to develop the four plates it was found that no extras were on the two plates exposed in the camera so we discarded them. On one of the plates reserved for psychographs we got results for there came up a clear finely written message as follows:

"Dear Friend Wood—We shall do our best to gratify your wishes, but we cannot promise results, but we want you to just speak as you find both of the mediums and their work, for at the presant time (sic) there are many who profess to know and understand, but it is less than little they know of the Law of force. God bless you."

Psychograph received by 'Mr Wood'

The writing being very small I had some difficulty in reading it. Mrs. Buxton came to my relief and read it straight off. When she had done so she remarked that I might regard myself lucky to get a message, a few were highly favoured. "They must know you, Mr. Wood," said she, "for they have got your name right."

I made no reply. The unfortunate two words "Friend Wood" seemed to stick in my throat."

It will be seen that on this copy of the psychograph Mr. Bush had signed the plate with the name "David Wood", and so by that name he is addressed in the message on the psychograph. This apparent 'mistake' on the part of Mr. Hope's "spirit guides" immediately aroused a grave suspicion in the mind of Mr. Bush.

Assuming that the spirit people were indeed responsible for the message – as Bush asserts in his pamphlet – the beings beyond the veil ought to have immediately seen through his deception and addressed him with his real name.

The message is on what resembles a piece of rope. Is it – "enough rope to hang himself"? For as many know Spirit have a wonderful, if 'wicked', sense of humour.

Mr Engholm commented:

"Dismissing the suggestion of fraud on the part of the Crewe Circle, there are two possible methods by which this name was obtained and so presented on the plate:

1. Through the mentalities of Mr. Hope and Mrs. Buxton.

2. Through Mr. Bush himself, who may have exerted a strong mental influence to get it there. – But by his comment it seems unlikely.

3. Unseen intelligences, we will assume, picked up the name, relying on the Crewe Circle and Mr. Bush for its correctness. The name "Wood" was in the air, so to speak, and the name "Wood" was returned on the plate."

Or maybe the spirit 'scribes' just played along with him – if he wanted to use that name they would give it to him!

The pamphlet continues:

"My second séance took place on Saturday, March 26th, 1920, at 11 a.m. It was preceded by the same blasphemy of hymns and prayer. Mr. Hope once more, in an apparently careless manner, touched one of the plates when pointing out to me the exact place at which to make identifying marks.

Exposure was in the wash-house, by daylight. When the plates were developed, there came out on one of them, in addition to a portrait of myself—the sitter—a distinct "extra".

We carried it to the light when fixed and examined it. A portion of the face seemed very clear and distinct, but the Spirit robe obscured so much of it that I suggested it was the photo of a lady.

"Oh no," said Mrs. Buxton, "it is that of a young man."

Mr. Bush (alias Wood) with the spirit "extra"
obtained at Crewe, March 26th 1920.

I asked Mr. Hope to print a dozen each of the "psychograph" and "extra", and post them on to me. I signed the form which had been obtained to give legal protection to the Crewe Circle.

My mission to Crewe was over.

After about ten days the cards[1] came to hand. The verdict was that the so-called Spirit beside me on the photograph was no other than my living son-in-law. Mr. David Vaudreuil. He himself identified it. I sent one of the cards to a friend who knows Mr. Vaudreuil well, and he said, "It's David."

I then cut out the spirit face from one of the cards but allowed the shroud of cloud to remain. Behind the opening in the card I placed the corresponding part of the original photograph which I had sent to Mr. Hope. There could now be no two opinions as to whose face was on the "extra" and whence it had been obtained."

Mr. Engholm now continues the report:

"Without referring any further to his pamphlet or stating his conclusions therein, we prefer to give his later and probably more mature opinion of the whole matter which is conveyed in two letters he [Bush] favoured us with in answer to our inquiries respecting this case.

In the first letter, dated February 2nd, 1921, he wrote as follows:

'There were not less than three junctures in my case at which the trick could be perpetrated. (I take it for granted, here, that a trick was performed.)

First, while the plates were being marked. Secondly, (during a space of some thirty seconds) when Mr. Hope went into the kitchen for water or developer, having in his possession the dark slide. Third, at the time of development, Mr. Hope held in his hand a half plate developing dish, he asked me to tumble the two plates from dark slide into it, which I did, at this point he held the dish for about thirty seconds below the light line, while I got from my pocket the box containing the two plates reserved for skotos.

He then placed a second half plate dish upon the first and I placed in this dish two plates for skotos. While I prepared the developer, Hope held both dishes below the light line, quite advisedly, for say another thirty seconds which gave him ample time to place a skoto on the plate. But while there were all these loopholes for fraud, I maintain that he performed the trick in my case, while the plates were being marked for identification. I do so because he deliberately placed his hand upon the plates, when or after I had told him I could manage without his help.

On the Saturday morning, after he had, as no doubt he thought, successfully negotiated his last trick, he told me to watch his hands. "They say," said he,

---

1. It was usual to print the photographs on to Postcard bases. See Chpt 10.

"that I have radium or something on my fingers." Hope admitted to me in writing that he could not produce the phenomena if his hand were controlled. He admitted also that he could not produce them in a hand or magazine camera, either on plates or films.

I am sorry for this dirty work. I love *Light*. I was for many years a personal friend of Mr. Wallis, its late editor.'

When asked for the original photo which he had sent to Hope, Mr Bush replied that it unfortunately had been damaged and the negative mislaid but he had sent this damaged photograph to Mrs. Salter, Editor of the Society for Psychical Research. Mrs. Salter eventually sent it to *Light*.

Whether it was damaged, as shown, when it was sent to Hope we shall never know.

In his letter to *Light,* Mr. Bush, in granting permission for *Light* to reproduce this original photograph, laid down the stipulation to the effect that they were to reproduce side by side **three** photographs: First, the photograph showing the "extra"; Second, the photo of Mr. Vaudreuil sent to Mr. Hope, and third, the photograph of Mr. Vaudreuil printed on page 27 of the pamphlet, *Spirit Photography Exposed,* which was the only photograph of Mr. Vaudreuil reproduced by Mr. Bush in the pamphlet for comparison with the "spirit extra".

Mr Engholm continued:

"In the pamphlet, *Spirit Photography Exposed*, Mr. Bush made many comments on what he considered the *modus operandi* of Mr. Hope and Mrs. Buxton in producing these "alleged fraudulent spirit extras". In reference to the remark made by Mrs. Buxton, "It is that of a young man", Mr. Bush observes, "It struck me that she ought to know, for most likely her own hand had painted in that lovely spirit robe. Oh, how these textureless robes have taxed 'scientists'."

As to the "spirit extra", Mr. Bush suggests that Mr. Hope's part of the operation consists of imprinting the face required by means of a tablet, apparently concealed in his hand, during the moments in the dark occupied in transferring the negative from the packet of plates to the camera slide. Between them, Mrs. Buxton and Mr. Hope, Mr. Bush asserts, manage by this simple means to palm off on an unsuspecting sitter these "wonderful spirit extras."

"Mr. Bush and friends being absolutely convinced that Mr. Hope and Mrs. Buxton produced the psychograph and the spirit "extra" by trickery and fraud, and that neither Mr. Hope nor Mrs. Buxton is a medium at all, at any rate in connection with psychic photography, commented that for years apparently people of all classes including: 'Sir Arthur Conan Doyle. Sir Oliver Lodge,

Lady Glenconner, the Rev. Professor G. Henslow, the Rev. Walter Wynn, Miss K R. Scatcherd. and a number of other psychical researchers,[2] not to mention the Editor of *Light*, have been the dupes of the Crewe Circle.' "

He then added: "Let me tell Mr. Hope that it is useless for him to try to practise such "tomfoolery" on me."

When William Hope read the pamphlet Bush had published he sent the following letter to Mr Bush:[3]

"Mr. Wood, or Bush, or whatever you may call yourself, just a word in protest in regard to your small booklet which you have put before the public. When you came to see us we accepted you, thinking you were what you pretended to be, an honest investigator. We treated you with all the kindness we possibly could. Let us see now we have been repaid. Now you say there were four plates to be marked with your name on, and you say I only offered assistance on one. You know perfectly well that when I offered my assistance it was to steady the slide, for I thought at the time you were very clumsy, but I see now why you acted so, just to influence my actions. Then again, you tell the people nothing was obtained on the ones exposed through the camera, so therefore you got a genuine psychograph, and as to its reading "Friend Wood," it's only natural to expect it to do so, as that was the name you were known by to both me and the invisible ones.

Then, again, when you sent the photo of your living son-in-law, I sent it straight back, and I was really sorry you had sent it, for it just happened as I told you in my letter, I was afraid it might.

And when you have studied the subject a little more you may find, as we have done in more than one case, that a man still in the body has been obtained as an extra under strict test conditions, and with people that understood the work much better than I find you do; in fact, to be candid, in my opinion you know very little more about this subject than a pig knows about astronomy; then, again, why have you raked up the past affairs? They were settled long ago in our favour.[4]

To sum up, you must admit you have made a dirty piece of business of it, for it contains very little more than dirty suggestions, such as the following: You say it is most likely Mrs. Buxton's own hand had painted in that lovely spirit robe. This is one of the most filthy, damnable suggestions you could have made. If you were half as pure in thought and actions as she is, you would not be able to stoop to such meanness you have shown yourself capable of,

---

2. This list of names is taken from Mr. Bush's pamphlet, and indignantly Sir Oliver Lodge wrote to *Light* stating he had never met Mr. Hope.
3. Published in *Light* April 2nd 1921 but written some months earlier.
4. Bush had referred to the 1909 Lodge account of "the unopened package" examined by his assistant (see Chpt 3)

but, believe me, I could express myself better on this point were I face to face with you than I can on paper.

Then, again, you turn and show your hypocrisy by saying you love us. If the teachings of the Bible are right Judas said the same, and to show how much he loved Jesus, he even kissed him, but as following events proved, he did this for one purpose only, which you know—he sold a better man than himself for money—and I guess your blacking box inventions at £1 1s. are on the same lines.

Now you say you will give £100 for a genuine spirit photo.[5] £5 is to me, I daresay, as much value as £100 to you, but if you will produce for me what we produced for you, and under the same conditions, I will give you £5 and meet you anywhere or any time you wish, and you may use any invention you have ever made. I'll go farther; I'll lend you the very camera we used upon you; do this, and I'll not only give you £5, but I'll give you my word I'll never take another psychic picture as long as I live.

Yours respectfully,

W. Hope."

On February 15th, 1921, in reply to the above letter, Mr. Bush wrote this very strange letter to Hope:

"My Dear Friend Hope,

I have been ill in bed or would have written you before.

Your letter indicates that you are much hurt by my exposure, and I knew it would be so. That's why I hate to be compelled to lay bare these sad things in Spiritualism. Unfortunately, I cannot hit the fraud without hurting the perpetrator, but the day will soon dawn when you will grip my hand as one of your best friends, and look me in the eyes and tell me I did the right thing; nay, the only thing an honest man could do.

I was lecturing in the city of Bradford on these questions. Next day a medium called to see me privately; he told me that for many years he had practised fraud as a medium and had resolved to quit the whole thing and take his stand by my side for truth and God. He delivered up to me several books on conjuring which are now before me. Ten years have passed, but he is delighted that he got clear of the "fowler's net," although he was receiving from businessmen ten shillings per sitting.

Well, now I suppose you will call together a few friends and will give them a test seance, and every one of them will sign a declaration that there was no trick in your work. Well, if they do, God and you will know that it is a lie, and as you get older you will find lies won't make a comfortable pillow.

---

5. "I will pay any medium £100 if he can produce an "extra" in a hand camera charged in my dark room with twelve plates for exposure." —-*Spirit Photography Exposed.*

I would ask you to come on to my side and let us, together with the help of Mrs. Buxton, give this hydra-headed delusion a hard knock all over England, Scotland, Canada, and the States. I believe the world is hungering for the bread of life and truth.

In my case I have resolved on such a fight and shall do the spirit photography upon the public platform. I expect I shall bungle at first: you could beat me hollow, but I must do my best to undeceive the people.

Let not the mere financial aspect of the question trouble you. God will see to it that you are well paid for speaking the truth.

Of course you must know that I could easily accept your challenge, but the real thing is for you to accept mine as offered in the book.

I am sorry if I have imputed to Mrs. Buxton the painting of the spirit robe if she did not do it. She may, for aught I know, have clean hands in the whole matter.

What you wrote fraudulently upon my skotograph I can write from the deepest feeling of my heart, "God bless you both."

Don't be afraid to write me a line. Hit me hard if I am guilty of wrong.

Yours only for the Truth,"

(Signed) E. Bush

In response to reading the reports of the Bush case in *Light*, Sir Arthur Conan Doyle wrote as follows:

"To the Editor of Light.

Sir,—It may throw some light upon Mr. Bush and his methods if I say that about May, 1920 I received a letter signed "D. Wood," from Wakefield. In this letter I was appealed to by one who appeared to be a bereaved mourner, saying that he had had some remarkable evidence at Crewe, and that he was anxious for more. He therefore asked for the address of Mr. Evan Powell, whose mediumship I had quoted. He enclosed copies of two photographs taken at Crewe, which he allowed me to infer had satisfied him. I sent him a note of sympathy (I do not see how spirits either in the body or out of it are to recognise a tissue of lies). I said that as he had already, by my own account, received such consoling evidences, he would act well if he did not trouble Mr. Powell, but I none the less sent the address. Mr. Bush (alias Wood) then wrote telling the same story to Mr. Powell and enclosing these photographs as a proof of *bona fides*. Mr. Powell, however, was unable to meet him, and so the matter ended.

I do not think there are many psychical researchers who would descend to such dirty work as this. If an investigation begins by such methods one can have little confidence in its end.

Yours faithfully,

April 8th.   Arthur Conan Doyle."

Following the receipt of this letter at *Light* they then received a letter from Mr. Evan Powell, of Merthyr, with the two photographs that Mr. Bush first sent to Sir Arthur, and then to Mr. Powell. They are copies of the photographs showing the Psychograph and the spirit "extra". On the back of each we find in Mr. Bush's handwriting the date when the photos were taken at Crewe, his address in Wakefield, and each photograph is signed "D. Wood."

Mr. Powell, wrote that he could not understand why "this Mr. Wood" having apparently had such splendid evidence, wished to have a sitting with him. The result – he did not grant the writer a sitting.

On April 23rd Mr. Engholm again wrote in *Light*:

"The Bush case is drawing to a close. Since last week, from every part of the United Kingdom have letters come to us. For the most part they have contained detailed statements of visits paid to Crewe and the results. In every case the evidence is in favour of the honesty and integrity of Mr. Hope and Mrs. Buxton, and the conclusive proof set forth of their gift of mediumship under water-tight test conditions. Up to the time of going to press we have not received a single letter in favour of Mr. Bush's accusation that the Crewe Circle are fraudulent. At the moment he stands alone as the accuser.

So large is the correspondence that were *Light* ten times the size we could then only give a portion of the letters we have received. ...

In our endeavour to discover if Mr. Hope and Mrs. Buxton are to be relied on, we have selected a few from the great number of cases which we have recently received dealing with the Crewe Circle, giving instances where persons who have conducted their experiments, not only under the strictest test conditions, but unbiased by the prejudices so apparent in Mr Bush."

From Mr. S. Whittaker, Manchester.

"I have been very interested in the correspondence in *Light* respecting the Crewe Circle. I went to see Mr. Hope on the same day that Mr. Wood (now Bush) attended, and having to wait some little time, went into the town to get tea. I had met Mr. Bush at Mr. Hope's place and he, being the next in turn to myself, had also to wait. I met him again at the tea room, and we got into conversation, and he asked me if I would communicate to him any result I might obtain from my sitting, and he would do the same.

I sent on to him a photo with the extra on, as per enclosed enlargement, (the top right hand corner is that of my boy at the age of 12, he passed on in his 16th year), and this photo was taken immediately afterwards. I am satisfied that it is my boy, and my intimate friends to whom I have shown it, are also convinced. I never met Mr. Hope or Mrs. Buxton before, and I would like to say that I found them to be perfectly frank and honest, and fraud was conspicuous by its absence. It gives me pleasure to speak of them as I found them.

In my opinion the fraud complained of by Mr. Bush exists in his brain only."

Mr. Whittaker with the spirit
"extra" of his young son, taken the
same day as Mr. Bush.

Mrs. Sutcliffe with the spirit
"extra" of her husband, recognised
by more than 100 people.

From Mrs. C. Sutcliffe, Slaithwaite (Yorkshire):

"On February 21st I visited the Crewe Circle, taking with me a sealed packet of plates. I was successful in getting an extremely good psychic extra of my husband on my plate. I unsealed them myself, and they were not touched in any way either by Mr. Hope or Mrs. Buxton until after I had developed and recognised the psychic extra. Since receiving the photo from Mr. Hope I have shown it to many people and without one exception, immediately on seeing it they have declared it to be an excellent likeness of my husband. . .

I have over 100 signatures of persons of various denominations who have recognised the extra. Previous to his passing into spirit life he promised to show himself at the Crewe Circle when I went. This promise I mentioned to no one, and I am glad he has fulfilled it. I have visited the Crewe Circle several times, and have received other proofs of the genuineness of spirit photography.

I have always found both Mr. Hope and Mrs. Buxton honest and straightforward persons to deal with."

From J. W. Macdonald, solicitor (North Shields):

"I have read the articles in *Light* dealing with the Crewe Circle and Mr. Bush.

As to Mr. Hope perpetrating a trick in the dark room and producing an extra on the plate, I maintain that this is childish—he simply couldn't do it. I have had several sittings with the Crewe Circle, and have always been struck with their *bona fides*. The first time I had four exposures which showed nothing on the plates. A fifth exposure took place. The plate was developed in the dark room, and brought out into the light. Mr. Hope looked at it and in disappointment said there was nothing on it, and laid it on the table, in my presence. Mrs. Buxton took it up and inspected it. and remarked, "Yes, there is," and on my inspecting it, I saw there; was an extra on it—which was afterwards printed and for me it forms a most interesting photo, one face in miniature is inset in the chin of a larger one and it is the smaller face which for me has the greatest interest. The larger face is of a spirit guide with whom I had a conversation last year at a sitting with Mrs. Wriedt, who afterwards told me that he had appeared on the photograph. I would remind Mr. Bush of the saying, that when you go to look for the truth, you must take the truth with you."

From Mr. Royan Middleton, of Aberdeen:

"I have read the case Bush versus Crewe Circle with very great interest. I am, like Mr. Bush or, rather, as Mr. Bush gives us to understand he is a sincere investigator trying to get at the truth, yet my sense of justice cannot allow me to agree that the test made by Mr. Bush was fair. It seems to me that Mr. Bush's "trap" was so palpably simple that no "crook" could have been taken in by it. To my mind the whole thing only seems to show up how sincere and unsuspecting Mr. Hope is and how sophisticated and intriguing Mr. Bush is.

I consider my own case records a much fairer test. Briefly, it is this. I attended in this city (Aberdeen) an illustrated lecture on spirit photography by Mr. Galloway, of Glasgow. After the meeting, without saying who I was, I casually asked him for Mr. Hope's address. I had never met Mr. Galloway before, nor have I seen him since. Some months afterwards, when returning from London, I broke my journey at Crewe. I had not sent any warning. I had simply mentioned to my wife before leaving for London that I might visit Crewe if time permitted. I did not definitely make up my mind to do so until I was actually on the return journey from London. I arrived in Crewe about 11.30 a.m, walked to 144, Market-street, and saw Mrs. Buxton, who told me I could not have a sitting till 1.30 p.m. I said I might stay on, but was not sure. Enquiring at the station. I found that if I stayed on for the sitting I couldn't get away from Crewe till 1.30 a.m. next morning.

However, being on the spot, I decided to risk it, I bought a packet of plates at Boot's and duly presented myself again at 144, Market-street. After the usual preliminaries I had my photo taken three times in the back yard, in the open air. I was seated against the end of the house. I handled the plates myself throughout, and when they were developed, I could clearly discern on one, besides myself, the image of one very near and dear to me who had passed over three years before. On another plate there was a light and two indistinct faces. On the third myself only. The "extra" referred to was very clear and distinct, and I recognised the likeness immediately. Up to this point I had given no name and address. Mr. Hope and Mrs. Buxton could not have known me from Adam. On ordering one dozen prints from the negative I gave name and address to post to. When received, the prints fully justified my first impression, and the "extra" has been recognised by numerous relatives and friends."

Mr. Royan Middleton, with a spirit "extra" of one 'very near and dear'.

* * * * *

The following two readers sent letters analysing the features of the faces in the photographs.

Major R. E. E. Spencer, of Newburn-on-Tyne:

"Having very carefully studied the evidence for both sides of this case, I beg to record my decision.

The Crewe people are innocent of having used fraudulent means in the production of the supernormal results that appear upon Mr. Bush's plates.

Reasons.

1. If Mr. Bush's statements are worthy of credence, he would have taken immediate action to secure the apparatus he indicates at the moment of its use.

2. The entire absence of any evidence on the part of the many skilful observers who have experimented with the Crewe people during years, as to the use of any such apparatus as is described by Mr. Bush.

3. The certain recognition of faces developed upon plates above any suspicion.

4. The fact that many of these faces are those of absolutely private people.

5. The weakness of Mr. Bush's statement as to the identity of the face on the plate with the photograph sent by him to Crewe.

(a) The line of the hair is quite different; it is straight and inclined down to the left in the normal photograph. — It is curved in the centre upwards and downwards in the plate.

(b) The areas of the two foreheads are quite different,

(c) The mouth in the normal photograph is large, with full lips and rather upturned ends. — That in the face on the plate is small, finely cut, with rather compressed lips.

(d) The nose and nostrils in the normal photograph are heavy, the nostrils not being clearly seen. — The nose and nostrils seen on the plate are very clearly and finely cut. The latter are very pronounced.

6. Suspicion attaches to all Mr. Bush's statements, as it is obvious that he went to Crewe having already decided in his mind as to the methods followed by Hope and Mrs. Buxton. Further, because at the outset he adopted a line of deceit.

Again, because questions of financial profit arise, as is seen by the advertisements in his pamphlet.

7. Mr. Bush has produced no evidence whatever as to what results can be obtained by his process, for comparative purposes.

8. Mr. Bush has not produced the original negative for comparative purposes.

9. Mr. Bush has not given us the date upon which he received back his son-in-law's photograph from Crewe. This is obviously of considerable importance. Yet other dates and times are given, but this particular one is omitted.

10, I have purposely, when experimenting with Hope, watched with the greatest care for any fraudulent practice. I have never found any, though I have sat with him and Mrs. Buxton many times. At all these sittings I have supplied my own plates, have marked them, and filled the slides and developed and fixed the plates myself. To my certain knowledge the plates have not been touched by Mr. Hope.

I have obtained recognised faces in two instances, and in two other cases faces that I think are those of people I have known.

I have a practical knowledge of photography and microscopy."

* * * * *

From Mr. H. Kenneth, Enfield:

"Whether the alleged psychic "extra" is a fake or not, I know quite certainly it could not have been done from any copy of the actual photograph printed alongside it.

In the latter there is a strong shadow on the left side of the nose (as it faces you), caused by the light on the opposite side of the face. The psychic picture shows no such shadow, but rather the reverso of shadow. This alone is absolutely conclusive as far as that photograph is concerned.

Why did Mr. Bush press for the reproduction in *Light* of another photograph of the same subject which had never been in Mr. Hope's hands?"

* * * * *

Mr. Engholm writes: (*Light*, April 16th 1921)

"One may now consider the possible motives that might have induced Mr. Hope and Mrs. Buxton to perpetrate the trick of the "spirit extra" that Mr. Bush, of Wakefield, asserts they did when he visited them in the assumed character of a bereaved man seeking for proof of human survival after death. Four motives at once suggest themselves.

The first and most common motive is that of money —

The Crewe Circle cannot by the greatest stretch of imagination be accused of making a good thing out of psychic photography. They charge no fees.

The second motive, notoriety, may for the moment be seriously considered.

— If notoriety was the motive, the Crewe Circle would hardly take the actual photograph sent to them, make a copy of it, and hand it back to their sitter superimposed on the sitter's photograph as a "spirit extra". Their name and fame would be destroyed in a moment.

A third motive suggests itself — Are they, after all, a pair of fanatics who have so immersed themselves in the belief of Spiritualism that they would seek any means to an end to uphold their cause?

A fourth motive might, possibly, be at the bottom of the whole problem — that the Crewe Circle, touched to the heart by the desire of bereaved persons to see the faces of their loved ones again, resort to a trick to bring momentary comfort to the sitters.

We trust everyone will consider these motives and if they do not believe it possible or reasonable that any one of the four motives could have influenced the Crewe Circle, then we come back to the original possibility that may suggest itself on a close examination of the Vaudreuil photograph and the spirit extra, namely, is the spirit extra a copy of the Vaudreuil photograph after all?"

Presumably Mr Bush did not think so because in his pamphlet he published a different one of his son-in-law—or at least not the picture he originally sent to Mr. Hope, and he doubtless selected it for the obvious reason that it did bear a slight resemblance to the spirit "extra". Was it a different version? – The white crease marks across the face are virtually the same, the black spots on his forehead are the same and his tie is at the same skewed angle? So has there been some 'trickery' by a photographer to produce the stretched one from the squashed one, or vice-versa?

Original image sent to Mr Hope. "Extra" received on the plate by Mr. Bush Life-image published in the pamphlet.

On this point Mr Engholm wrote:

"With regard to the suggested similarity ... – one must confess that after a very careful examination it is still a moot point whether they really bear such a close resemblance to each other that a first glance suggests.

In our opinion there are many points of dissimilarity. The hair, the shadows, the high lights, the general expression of the face in the "extra" are not the same as disclosed in the Vaudreuil photograph, It is certainly not a copy such as the ordinary photographer, skilled at "faking", could have produced.

If Mr. Hope and Mrs. Buxton, by their mediumship, are able, in ninety-nine, cases out of a hundred, to obtain a supernormal photograph, why should they suddenly abandon the assistance of supernormal methods and attempt a very bad "fake"?

Until it is proved beyond question to be otherwise, we hold by our own opinion that the spirit extra which appeared on Mr. Bush's negative was a phenomenon produced by some supernormal process yet to be brought within the purview of science."

And with this I totally agree. It is certainly not a copy of the original photograph sent to Mr Hope. Would that the software of forensic scientists was openly available now to check the facial measurements of the features, as it was in the analysis by the Italian experts of an ITC photograph for a Spanish case a few years ago.[6]

"But what of Mr. Bush / Woods?" writes Engholm:

"Does his method of approach to the Crewe Circle suggest the actions of a man qualified at all to make this investigation? To the honest investigator and the true psychical researcher he shows at the outset an entire lack of knowledge of these things. ...another motive on the part of Mr. Bush that may have influenced his desire to establish, at any cost, a case against the Crewe Circle. He announced the forthcoming publication of five booklets entitled respectively, *Direct Spirit Painting, Direct Spirit Voices, Direct Spirit Slate Writing, Dr. Crawford and Miss Goligher, Spirit Materialisation,* all to be written in a similar fashion to *Spirit Photography Exposed.* At the same time, he offers to the public a complete outfit for producing extras and psychographs at the price of 21/-.

Here is apparently the nucleus of a very lucrative business, but apart from such a sordid motive, there is underlying all a suggestion of an even greater incentive—that of notoriety.

Is it not just possible that Mr. Bush had an ulterior motive when he set out to Crewe, not as a seeker after truth, but as one already biased in the subject? Pre-judgment and bias are unfortunately not unknown even amongst psychical investigators."

In a letter to the Editor of *Light* dated March 1st, 1921. Mr. Bush, after attacking all forms of Spiritualism, concluded as follows:

'I hold that all phenomena is fraudulent, including the latest, Eva C. and Miss Goligher. I have waded through these experiments. Genuine phenomena, trance, telepathy, telesthesia, automatism, are all the result of these inherent powers which produce multiple personality, etc., etc. I believe Spiritualism is the most cruel delusion that has ever afflicted the race, and I shall, by God's help, expose its weakness as long as I live.'

Again, in his pamphlet, *Spirit Photography Exposed,* on page 10. he states:

'Now I hold that spirit photos, extras, psychographs, etc., are not produced by discarnate spirits, good, bad, or indifferent; but are deliberately produced by the mediums, whatever their names, or in whatever country they practise.'

Mr Engholm writes:

"This is a very sweeping condemnation, and we must assume that Mr. Bush, in face of any evidence to the contrary, is in every way qualified to make this pronouncement.

---

6. See *ITC Journal No.29* August 2007 (http://www.itcjournal.org) "With sophisticated image identification it is now possible to analyse supposedly anomalous photographic images in order to assess their possible paranormality, and to do so with a high level of accuracy.

Does his method of approach to the Crewe Circle suggest the actions of a man qualified at all to make this investigation?

In many ways we are indebted to him for the opportunity he has unwittingly given us of proving beyond all shadow of doubt the honesty and integrity of Mr. Hope and Mrs. Buxton. These truly wonderful mediums can now rest assured that they have behind them a vast army of friends, and the mist of suspicion that was raised by an untrained investigator has been dispersed by a perfect gale of evidence in their favour. ..."

To bring this hotch-potch of a challenge to a close there are two more outstanding cases in defence of the Crewe Circle.

In October 1921 Mr. R. S. Hipwood, of Sunderland, wrote to *Light* with his story. He described how distressed they were by the attacks on Mr. Hope, and wished to be numbered publicly amongst his defenders.

To the Editor of *Light*.

"This photograph has attracted so much attention both in our local circles, and also far and wide, and is such a splendid result that I wish you to insert it in your valuable paper. ...

We lost our only son in France, August 27th, 1918, and began to ask ourselves: "Is there really a life beyond?" Our minister could not tell us anything definite, beyond so joyful resurrection in ages to come—perhaps. My wife was invited to go with a friend to the Spiritualists' meeting at Sunderland, but it was some time before she persuaded me to go. I have all my life been a true Churchman, and entirely opposed to Spiritualism in general, and spirit photographs in particular.

However, my wife and I went to the meeting, and we soon saw that this matter was no sham—that the Spiritualists are not mad: we soon learned that there is no death. Various mediums described to us a form which we recognised as our son.

Being a good amateur photographer, having it for years as a hobby, I was curious about the picture had been taken at the Crewe circle. We secured an appointment and went there on June 24th. We took our own plates with us, and I put the plate in the dark slide myself, with my name on it. We exposed two plates in the camera with only a partial success the first time, but on this second plate being exposed we got the splendid result which I am sending you to insert in your paper.

It is a very well-recognised photograph. Even my nine-year-old grandson could tell who the extra was without anyone saying anything him. I took the photo to have it enlarged; the lady manager at shop said, 'The central figure has moved.' I said, 'All the better for me, it must have been alive then.'

Having a thorough knowledge of photography, I can vouch for the veracity of the photograph in every particular. I claim the print which I send you to be an ordinary photo of myself and Mrs. Hipwood, with the extra of my son, R.W. Hipwood, 13th Welsh Regiment, killed in France in the great advance in August, 1918.

I tender our friends at Crewe our unbounded confidence in their work in proving to broken-hearted ones in such a tangible way that there is no death in God's wide world. I may say my son was always a splendid character in earth-life, a fine promising organist, with a soul and spirit full of music. He obeyed the call to duty and made the great sacrifice.

Mr. and Mrs. Hipwood with the spirit "extra" of their son killed in France.

Yours faithfully,
R. S. Hipwood.
Cleveland Road, Sunderland.

* * * * *

And finally, Mr. J. H. D. Miller, of Belfast, sent this "outstanding instance of a complete verification of the identity of the spirit extra."

"You solicit an expression of opinion upon the merits of the controversy between Messrs. Bush and Hope, from those who have had experience of the Crewe Circle. As one such I beg to submit my case.

My son was killed in France in 1918. Neither he nor I took any interest in Spiritualism before his death. Some months after his passing on, a little girl of ten or eleven years, who was entirely unknown to my family, began to write automatically sentences to this effect:

"I am Hardy Miller. Tell my daddy and mother about me." Our address was given. Writing of this description was taking place daily, and so persistent were the entreaties to tell us that after some weeks' time the guardian of the child met my wife coming out of church, asked her if she had a son killed in the war called Hardy Miller, and being assured of the fact, then told of the communications. Upon bearing this I laughed incredulously, being a matter-of-fact, hard-headed and orthodox Presbyterian. However, after much serious thinking. I decided to put the subject to a test: The lady and her little niece came to our house and what took place that evening set me thinking more seriously than ever. Incident after incident of my son's earthly life was rapidly recorded by the hand of this little stranger. Each visit brought additional and overwhelming evidence of my son's identity. A trance medium, also an entire stranger to us, was invited to come so that I could investigate the subject in a different manner. At the first sitting my mother, brother and my son were described, their names given and each furnished evidence of his or her identity, which was absolutely convincing.

During the third sitting my son took control, spoke naturally and recounted incidents in his Army life with his brother, who was a private in his company.

From this moment my prejudice was gone. My son now controls at every meeting, makes much natural fun. and gives some wonderful descriptions and explanations of the life beyond the veil.

In the Spring of 1920, I had occasion to go to Paris on business. I told my son I was going to call at Crewe to obtain, if possible, a spirit photograph of him. He had never heard of such photographs and so asked leave to withdraw for a minute to make enquiries from those who could tell him. On his return he told us there was no doubt about it, that he had been informed by those on his side who knew all about it, and that he was promised the necessary assistance to procure for me a good likeness of himself. When the time came to go, I bought the plates in Belfast and carried them in my pocket. I called on Mr Hope and had a sitting with him, Mrs. Boston, and a Miss Scatcherd who happened to be there when I called.

We all sat round a table, the plates unopened, were placed in the centre and our hands rested on the top of each other with the packet below them. After the singing of a hymn and the offering of a prayer I put the packet in my pocket and followed Mr Hope. Being an amateur photographer, I put the plates into the slides myself, wrote my name on them and. closed them up. We then went into the adjoining glass-house and here I reached them to Mr. Hope to place in the camera, after I had thoroughly examined it. I sat down in the usual way to have my photo taken. Mr. Hope and Mrs. Buxton stood on either side of the camera. Mr. Hope and Mrs. Buxton joined hands over the camera, and with his left hand Mr. Hope removed the cap for the exposure. This was repeated for the second plate. The slides were then given into my possession.

In the dark room I opened them and put the plates into the dishes, the only part Mr. Hope played was pouring on the developer. The rest was done by me exclusively. On one of the plates I saw an "extra" coming up and watched it carefully. Once when lifting the plate, my fingers slipped and a nail slightly tore the film, fortunately below the features. Having satisfied myself that it was properly cleared. I carried it to the water tap, washed it, and on holding it up to the light, my practised eye told me immediately the "extra" was a splendid likeness of my son. What delight! I told Mr. Hope I had got what I wanted, and paid him for two dozen prints.

Now, Mr. Hope never saw a photo of my son. I gave him no nformation. How then, could he have produced the desired extra? If Mr. Bush is convinced that Mr. Hope is a fraud, I am a thousand times more convinced that Mr. Hope and Mr. Buxton are genuine.

At a sitting held on my return home my son explained how the photo was taken, stating that the seeming drapery around him constituted the substance out of which he partially materialised.

Mr. Miller with an "extra" of his son; with, inset, a photograph of Hardy Miller, taken shortly before he was killed in the Great War.

I enclose you a photo of our son when in the body, and also the one taken at Crewe. *(shown right)* I might add that I have taken shorthand reports of the proceedings of my investigation of Spiritualism.

These are now in script form. I submitted this volume to Sir Arthur Conan Doyle, and in a letter from him he has favoured me with the following comments:

'As to your special case, I consider it about the most complete and convincing of any which have reached me. . . For continuity of communication, yours is wonderful. The Crewe photograph, the facsimile signature, the fact that the original communications came from a child, the continuation of them through an unpaid medium, the consistency of it all and the many evidences, make it quite overwhelming.'

Yours faithfully"

April 25th, 1921   J. H. D. Miller

In his address at the Queen's Hall in London, April 12th 1921, Sir Arthur Conan Doyle described this case as "quite overwhelming" and recounted it in detail from Mr. Miller's own account:

"In the month of February his wife met a lady belonging to the same Church, she asked his wife if she had a boy killed in the war. Mrs. Miller said she had, and then the lady explained that her little child, aged twelve, had put her hand on a planchette, and that it always wrote that it had got messages from Hardy Miller. They did not know there was such a person, so they came and asked Mrs. Miller. Mrs. Miller went home and told her Husband. He was a staunch Presbyterian and knew nothing about Spiritualism. They brought the girl round. She had never been in the house before and was only a child. She put her hand on the board and the following was the dialogue:

"Who is working this planchette?—Hardy. Mother and Daddy, I am your darling son. Do you believe it is I?

I do not know.—You will know. Do not grieve for me. I am very happy. Mother, if you could only see me! Let in Fluffy. Perhaps she will see me. Dogs are often clairvoyant. . . .

(Fluffy was a little Pomeranian. It was barking furiously in the yard. It was let in and I watched carefully. – It looked into the air and made a peculiar whining noise. The planchette wrote: 'Fluffy sees me.'

Do you know Fluffy's mother is dead?—Yes. Judy is lying on the rug as she used to do. (Judy was the correct name.)

Who allows you to come?—Daddy, dear Daddy, God does. I live in a beautiful home and I will wait until you all come over: Christ's statement about mansions is quite true. Daddy I am not really dead. I am only gone before you all to a better and a beautiful place. Daddy, do believe it is your darling son. I should be quite happy if you would not grieve for me. I am in the fourth plane.

How many planes?—Seven.

Will you rise higher?—Yes. Daddy, pray for me.

What shall I say?—God, help my son Hardy to work out his own salvation.

Then there is progress after death?—Yes.

Have you seen Christ yet?—No. Only a most beautiful light.

Can you see it now ?—No, Daddy. Not from the earth plane, but I can from the fourth plane, where my home is.

Is this all true?—Yes. It is the power of God. We do not tell lies.

Do you sing songs over there?—Yes. If they are good.

What form is your spiritual body?—The same as the Material.

Have you work to do?—Yes, Daddy. I preach to the soldiers in the lower spheres and I help them.

Would you come back?—No, Daddy: this is a beautiful place. If you could come and see it you would all wish to come on.

Does God answer prayer?—Yes. Daddy, if you pray for good, and hard enough, you will receive the answer.

Then the poor mother said: Hardy, if you had not joined up you would be alive now.

Hardy said: Mother. I only did my duty. If I had my life to live over again I would do the same thing. Death is nothing but the beginning of real life."

Conan Doyle added:

"... this is an impressive document, and I think it bears the impression of solemn truth. ... the way in which it was taken from the hand of a little child should convince even the most sceptical!"

* * * * *

In summing up this account I can do no better than add the following as they express my thoughts precisely:

From Viscountess Molesworth :

"H.W.E, has put the Bush Case before your readers in a wry, impartial manner, and asks for their opinions. After reading the case carefully, it appears to me that Mr. Bush does not "seek the truth" in the way that an honest investigator should. It is one thing to have an anonymous sitting and quite another to give a false name. Assuming that the many honest and impartial witnesses are correct in their estimate of the *bona fides* of the Crewe Circle, it seems to me that Mr. Bush obtained exactly what he asked for. The spirit helpers did not stoop to consider what name he chose to adopt (apparently it did not matter!) but they gave him the picture of his son-in-law. To them he is a spirit, whether incarnate or discarnate. Therefore, where does the fraud come in?

If it is possible, as Mr. Bush avers, for Mr. Hope to have super-imposed a print on the plate in a few seconds (it sounds like magic), why did Mr. Bush give him that opportunity. Very few investigators would be so confiding as to send a photo at all. It sounds like a trap. I suggest that if Mr. Bush really wants to prove himself an "honest seeker after truth", that he should adopt different methods, and give psychic photography a fair chance, otherwise he leaves it to those who have followed the case to infer that he is posing as an enemy to a subject he clearly knows very little about (perhaps for his own ends) and his manner or doing so lays him open to the suspicion of humbug and hypocrisy."

And Mr H.W.Engholm:

"Our correspondence has been almost overwhelming. Of the multitude or letters we have received there is not a single one that raises a doubt as to the honesty and integrity of Mr. Hope and Mrs. Buxton; all without exception proclaim in the strongest terms the fact that the Crewe Circle are not only above suspicion, but possess the gift of mediumship to a remarkable degree.

As to Mr. Bush's action, we have never yet come across a more clumsy attempt to vilify and destroy the honour and good name of two genuine mediums. We are sincerely glad that the attempt has utterly failed.

In reply to our questions as to his possession of any technical knowledge of photography, Mr. Hope stated he had none. He could take a photograph and develop it, and that was all."

"We chose these photographs from a large number offered us by Mr. Hope, selecting those, of course, that would reproduce in our journal. This page of illustrations, Mr. Hope declares is his reply to the charges made against him and Mrs. Buxton by Mr. Bush."

MR. HOPE'S ANSWER TO MR. E. BUSH.

1. A Yorkshire lady with Extra her son (plus life photo); 2. A Son at once recognised (with life photo); 3. A Sitter from Sheffield with her Mother as Extra (Life photo compare); 4. A great sceptic before he got this Extra of his mother (Life photo to compare); 5. A Glasgow lady, Extra her mother; 6. Extra recognised at once as son; 7. A Coventry couple, Extra their son; 8. Liverpool people who at once recognised their little one; 9. Macclesfield lady, with a message from Extra their son; 10. A professional photographer and his wife with their son as Extra — very good portrait.

Visitors from Overseas

In *Light* on 29th April 1922, Felicia Scatcherd published this account of succesful sittings for friends of hers from abroad. She prefaced it with these quotes:

"Fraud can do many things, conjurors can deceive the eye of the most vigilant observer, but there are limits to fraud and conjuring, and this limit is reached when a photographer is confronted without notice by a sitter, who asks him to take a photograph and produce a portrait of a deceased friend or relative on the same plate. The photographer has no means of knowing whether the relative desired is a man or a woman, adult or child. If in these circumstances the photographer can then and there produce an authentic portrait of the spirit form of the deceased friend or relative of his unknown sitter, then I say that such occurrence cannot be explained by any conceivable hypothesis of fraud or conjuring" —

W.T. Stead in *Photographing the Invisible*

"I see no reason for believing that any spirit photographs are, or have been due to any cause other than fraud."

Whately Smith in *The Case against Spirit Photography*.[1]

Sir Oliver Lodge, writing on "Psychic science", for *Outline of Science* tells us that physical phenomena are among things that psychical science is required to investigate and that "one of the commonest forms at the present time is psychic photography."

In the latter statement, Sir Oliver lodge has fallen into the error of confusing multiple reproduction with the original result. A psychic photograph, once obtained can be reproduced by the thousand, as has been the case with the much disputed "fairy" photos, but the Yorkshire instance is as yet unique. ....

Prof Barrett in his latest edition of *On the Threshold of the Unseen* quotes Mrs. Sidgwick's conclusion as to the fraudulent origin of all spirit photographs with seeming approval, and but for the courage of the present Editors of *Light* in drawing attention to the phenomena associated with photographic sensitives, after they had satisfied themselves as to the good faith of the Crewe

---

1. A paper published in *Psychic Science* in which he relies heavily on Bush's pamphlet for evidence. It was reviewed by Engholm in *Light* May 14th, 1921 (p319).

Circle, Sir Oliver Lodge and others would not have fallen into the error of supposing psychic photography to be one of the "commonest forms of physical phenomena." Its rarity would justify denial of its existence on all but those whose duty is to inform themselves of the facts.

These few words are by the way. I only wish to draw the attention of our psychical research comrades to the experience that occurred last January.

On Thursday, January 12th two ladies called at Park Square, leaving letters of introduction from --- of Paris. On Friday I returned their visit. They are staying at the Hotel Cecil, and, at their request I telegraphed to Crewe and received a reply saying Mr. Hope would be glad to see me on Saturday. We then bought packets of plates from the photographer at 86 ---- and Madame Breffaud took charge of one while Baroness Mattos de Vieira, of South America, took possession of the other.

We went to Crewe the next day, and arranged for two séances, one before tea another after tea, as the ladies were compelled to return to London that evening in order to catch the Sunday morning train to Paris. Baroness Vieira, understanding photography took charge of the proceedings, and you see her initials on plates two and three. Two plates were exposed at each séance. The first plate shows Madame Breffaud as sitter . The "extra" is her late husband, who died many years ago. This picture has been recognised by the whole family. The plate, marked 2 is the Baroness de Vieira with an "extra" of which I have not received definite details.

Left - Plate 1   *Right - Plate 2*

After tea we sat again, and this time the box of plates carried by Madame Breffaud was used. At first when they looked at the negative before a print had been made of it we thought the extra might be the father of Madame de Vieira.

As usual Mr Hope was slow in forwarding the prints, but on March 8th, Madame de Vieira wrote,

" La dernière photo n'est pas celui de mon Père mais une autre curieuse, et d'une identité indiscutable dont je ne pas envoyer un specimen, mais que vous aurez tous, l'——— de verifier ici." (The last photo is not that of my father but of

another, most curious, the identity of whom is indisputable. I cannot send you a specimen but you will all have an opportunity to verify this for yourselves when you come to see me.")

To sum up: here were four exposures on two strangers with three results, two of which cannot be disputed with representations of persons known only to the two sitters. I am giving this account because it fulfils the conditions laid down by others as well as the late Mr Stead, whose words head these remarks, as to what they would deem irrefutable proof of supernormally produced pictures.

Plate 3

After the séances the ladies took away with them the rest of their plates and developed them without exposure in a camera. They were anxious to obtain a skotograph. One plate was affected, but I have not yet received my promised copy of the result, nor have I yet had Dr Geley's report of the affair. I have just sent him the original negatives which the Crewe friends were kind enough to let me have.

> "You cannot produce from thought what it does not contain."
>
> *William Walker, lecture at the LSA Jan 14th 1915.*

A Testing Puzzle

It is thought that the decision by members of the S.P.R. to test William Hope's ability to produce genuine "spirit" photographs was down to Col. Baddeley's remark in a letter published in the S.P.R. *Journal* in April 1922 that "he has never been 'caught out,' in spite of innumerable tests with persons who were good amateur conjurers and expert photographers."[1] However, the officers of the Society had – "for some considerable time been endeavouring to persuade Mr. Hope to allow his mediumship to be tested by a competent committee. The present Research Officer [Eric Dingwall] has done his utmost since his appointment to persuade Mr. Hope and his advisers to allow him to have some sittings under almost any conditions, but without avail."[2]

Harry Price, the inveterate psychic investigator and scourge of mediums, had been applying to the Crewe Circle for a sitting with William Hope since about 1915 but had received no replies to his requests. On March 10, 1921, he had applied again, but this had met with a similar result.

However, on November 11th, 1921 he called at the British College of Psychic Science, with a letter of introduction from the Librarian of the London Spiritualist Alliance (of which organisation he was a member). He there saw the Hon. Secretary, Mrs. B. McKenzie, to whom he was a stranger, who promised to try to arrange a sitting. [3]

On January 12, 1922, he received the following letter from the College:

"Dear Mr. Price,

I enclose particulars of an experiment offered you with the "Crewe Circle."

If you decide to take this, kindly confirm as soon as possible. The fee for non-members is £2 2s. 0d.[4], to be paid on confirmation. You should provide a half-dozen packet of plates for the experiment, Imperial, or Wellington Wards are considered preferable.

---

1. *Journal of S.P.R.* Vol 22 1921-22 April 1922 p259
2. *Journal of S.P.R.* Vol 22 1921-22 May p 271
3. *Journal of S.P.R.* Vol 22 1921-22 May p 271
4. NB. the charge of £2.2.0 (2 guineas) was the fee charged by the College, <u>not the mediums.</u> The college paid all the expenses of the mediums and it included the cost of two prints from the sittings, as well as helping with the upkeep on the College itself which ran at a loss many years. No fee was paid to Mr. Hope and Mrs. Buxton.

Mr. Hope gives every opportunity to the sitter during the experiment, but he will not undertake tests and will use his own camera.

Nothing is guaranteed but good results can be assisted by sitters keeping the plates in their environment for a few days.

If you wish you are at liberty to bring a friend to share the sitting if they are sympathetic, for the one fee.

E. Ford,

Ass. Secy.   Appointment.

Friday, Jan. 27th, 10.30 a.m."

The year 1922 had started badly for members of the Crewe Circle. Following the visit of Miss Scatcherd with her friends from overseas, they succumbed to recurring bouts of influenza which had been so fatally present over the previous few years. Thus, on January 21, 1922, Harry Price received a letter from the British College delaying his sitting, saying that owing to illness the Crewe Circle would have to transfer the appointment to February 3rd. This was later cancelled in favour of February 24th, at 10.30 a.m.

Meanwhile Mr Price had been considering what steps to take in order to make sure that any results would be genuine. This was to be a covert scientific test sitting under the auspices of the S.P.R.. On January 25th, he went to the Imperial Dry Plate Co., works at Cricklewood, and later discussed the whole matter with Miss Newton, the Secretary of the SPR. In writing to her the same night, he says:

"I have spent the morning at the works of the Imperial Dry Plate Co., Ltd., Cricklewood, discussing and trying out various tests by which we can invisibly mark the plates which will be handed to Hope. We have decided as the best method that the plates shall be exposed to the X-rays, with a leaden figure of a lion rampant (the trademark of the Imperial Co.) intervening. The centres of each set of four plates will be treated, so that when the plates are placed in their proper order, the full design will be seen. This is to safeguard against the allegation that some of the plates may have been missed in the marking. Any plate developed will reveal a quarter of the design, besides any photograph or "extra" that may be on the plate. This will show us absolutely whether the plates have been substituted. I am also thinking out other safeguards that may help us."

Six of these plates were then packed by the company and sent to Mr. Price in Pulborough Sussex, where he "immediately handed them to his neighbour, Mr. H.J. Moger, in their original postal packings." Mr. Moger, then, at some point, placed the package in another envelope, sealed it with hot wax, and wrapping it in a further layer,

Sketch of the X-ray imprint on the plates.

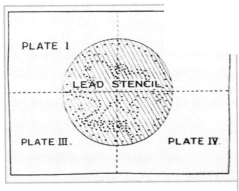

Two sheets of glass, coated with sensitised emulsion, were used. In the centre of each sheet of glass a lead disc stencil was laid. The X-Ray was then applied, and each sheet of glass afterwards cut into four plates. A corner of each plate, therefore, contains a portion of the stencil design marked by X-Rays. Mr. Price was sent six plates, three from each sheet of glass, the company retaining one plate from each sheet of glass for comparison after the Test.

sent it to the Secretary of the S.P.R., for safe keeping (apparently a locked drawer in her desk!). In this condition, we are told, they were kept until handed to Hope in the séance room at the British College of Psychic Science.

On the suggestion of Mr. Dingwall – newly appointed as Research Officer to the S.P.R.– James Seymour accompanied Price[5] to the college that morning, being as the report says; "a gentleman, by a happy concatenation of circumstances, combining precisely that knowledge of photography and trickery so essential for an experiment of this kind".[6]

The whole of this "experiment" was recorded in the *Journal* of the S.P.R. for May 1922:

"On the morning fixed for the sitting the Research Officer met Mr. Price and his companion at Holland Park Station and handed over the sealed packet of plates for use in the experiment. After it was over, both investigators immediately proceeded to the Rooms of the S.P.R., where a report of the sitting was dictated to a stenographer, in the presence of both the Secretary and the Research Officer."

It is important to our narrative that the whole of Mr. Price's Report is included here. It is, the S.P.R. report tells us, "derived entirely from the verbatim dictated report (taken down within forty-five minutes from the conclusion of the sitting" – including the comments by Mr. Seymour who had accompanied him). It was not, however, made public knowledge – even to those involved at the College – until three months later, when the May edition of the *Journal* was published.

---

5. See Chpt 2 for the background of these 3 researchers. From *Light* 1922.
6. *Journal of S.P.R.* Vol 22 1921-22 May pps 274.

Mr. Price's Report of His Sitting.

"We got to the B.C.P.S. at 10.25 a.m., and the door was opened by a clerk. We took off our coats and walked into the reception room where Mrs. McKenzie was waiting for us. We had a very pleasant conversation with her, and we were very cheerful and did all we could to impress her with the fact that we had come to Mr. Hope in a friendly manner and would put no obstacle in his way. We were escorted up to the top floor, and walked into the well-lighted studio, when Mrs. Buxton came in and was introduced by Mrs. McKenzie I made myself extremely pleasant; said how sorry I was that they had been ill with influenza, and asked after the Crewe Circle, saying that my people were natives of Shropshire. I ingratiated myself with them in every way.

Just at that period Mrs. McKenzie left us, and Mr. Hope walked in from the room outside on the left. I repeated my solicitations after his health and made myself extremely affable to him. He also seemed very pleasant and friendly. He asked me whether I had ever done any photography. I said I used to do quite a lot some years ago, as I did. The plates had been on the table during the whole of the conversation and were in the original Imperial postal wrappers as sent to me at Pulborough."

Mr. Hope then asked us to sit round the table. We sat at a small table, Mrs. Buxton facing me, Mr. Seymour on my right, and Mr. Hope on my left. I noticed Mrs. Buxton eyeing the packet with the outer wrappers very considerably, because apparently she was not used to having plates brought like that. Mr. Hope then asked me to undo the postal packet, which I did, and I cut the string in two places, and threw the postal wrappers on the floor, placing the unopened packet of plates on the table. Mr. Hope then picked up the packet of plates and started examining them. Then Mrs. Buxton said, 'They are flash-light.'

I said, 'I told the Imperial people that they were for portraiture inside a London room, and they suggested flash-light.' Then Mr. Hope examined the packet and he then handed it to Mrs. Buxton, who again examined the packet very minutely I could see her eyeing the packet. In my opinion, at that juncture they came to the conclusion that the packet had not been tampered with, because at that moment Mrs. Buxton asked me whether the packet had been opened. I said, 'It is exactly as I got it from the makers, outer wrapper and all.' I was careful to say that.

Mrs. Buxton then examined it to find the speed number, as Mr. Hope apparently could not see it. Suddenly Mrs. Buxton said, 'Here is the speed number, it is 400 on the packet,' and Mr. Hope said, 'Oh, yes, that will be all right.'

[Mr. Seymour here interpolated: "Mr. Hope said he had not worked with flash-light plates before and thought they would be quite all right and not hamper the experiment. They were thoroughly *taken in* by the packet and were not suspicious of it."]

Mr. Hope then pushed the plates into the middle of the table, and said, 'We will have a hymn,' and asked me whether I had any particular choice of hymns. I said, 'I know all the old ones. I should like *Onward Christian Soldiers*.'

Mr. Hope looked at Mrs. Buxton and said, 'Could you manage *Onward Christian Soldiers*?' She hesitated, and so, as I saw the hesitation, I said, 'Any familiar hymn will do.' So Mr. Hope then said, 'How about *Nearer my God to Thee*?'

I then placed my hands flat on the table; Mr. Hope's right hand was on my left, and my other hand was over Mr. Seymour's on my right, and Mr. Seymour's other hand was on Mrs. Buxton's we were simply linked up. Mr. Hope and Mrs. Buxton's hands were not linked during the whole of the time. Mrs. Buxton then sang several verses, six or seven of *Nearer my God to Thee*, in a tune with which I was unfamiliar and did not recognise. I did, however, join in where and how I could.

After the hymn Mr. Hope gave a long impromptu prayer, in which he thanked God for all our many mercies and hoped He would continue His blessings up to the present moment. He also craved blessings on our fellow-creatures and friends on the other side, and asked assistance in the attempt to link up with them, etc. etc. Then Mrs. Buxton sang another hymn, and then Mr. Hope picked up the packet of plates from the centre of the table and put them between Mrs. Buxton's hands; then he put his hands on hers, I put my hands on his and Mr. Seymour came last of all, making a pile of hands with the packet of plates in the centre. Then we had another short impromptu prayer by Mrs. Buxton. Then the *Lord's Prayer* was sung, and a short hymn concluded the service.

Mr. Hope now asked me whether I would like to sit by myself, or whether I would like Mr. Seymour to sit with me. Of course, I said I would like to sit by myself, and Mr. Seymour made the remark that as it was my sitting, he would prefer that I should sit by myself.

[Mr. Seymour here interpolated: "It would not have helped me to sit with him, and to be alone gave me freer movement."]

Then the plates were left on the table; I stood up, and Mr. Hope went into the dark-room, and brought his dark-slide to the door to show me. He opened it out, saying, 'These shutters pull out like this, etc.' (it was an ordinary double dark-slide), and said, 'This piece of black card in between is to separate the plates.' He handed the dark-slide to me to examine, and I marked it indelibly twice on both sides (twelve marks in all), and then I handed it back to Mr. Hope. He said, 'You see there is no film in here; some people think

I put films in and do the trick that way,' and I said, 'However could they think such a thing, it is absurd!' He then came into the room, picked up the packet of plates, which were then on the table, and invited me to go with him into the dark-room. I was about to ask that Mr. Seymour should come with me, when he took the words out of my mouth by asking Mr. Seymour to sit down at the table with Mrs. Buxton, and keep his hands on it all the time, so as to 'maintain the influence'. After the sitting was over, he said to Mr. Seymour, 'You could have come in the dark-room, if you had liked.'

At the entrance to the door he asked me whether I would open the packet of plates. While I was feeling for my knife, he pulled out a knife and opened the packet himself. He then made a remark to Mrs. Buxton to look after Mr. Seymour, while we were in the dark-room, after which he closed the dark-room door. He then handed me the dark-slide again, and also handed me the opened packet of plates. He then said, 'I will not touch the plates, as I don't want you to think there is any trickery. Do exactly as I tell you, I will not put a finger on the plates.' He then said, 'Now which two will you have, some take one and two, some one and three, some three and four. Will you take the 1st and 3rd?'

I said, 'I will take the 1st and 2nd.'

He said, 'All right, it does not matter; some have one and some have the other.'

I then opened the packet of plates in the dark-room, and I took the first two out of the original wrapper. They had not left my hands, but he touched my hand and turned it to a certain angle, saying, 'I must see that they go in the right side up.' (which was quite a natural proceeding). The box containing the other plates were in my hand the whole time. He said, 'Now do exactly as I tell you. Take the first plate and put it in this recess.' He said, 'Now I will put the black paper card over it,' which he had retained the whole time.

'Now will you put the next one on top, exactly coinciding with the other one?'

We had some trouble in closing the dark-slide; at last, with his nail, he moved the plate a fraction and so closed the slide, which I took. All this was done under the red window, which I noticed, directly I stepped into the room, was a graduated light, darker at the top. We were close up under that window. He then took the dark slide from me, saying at the same time, 'Will you do up the packet of plates again, as we may want them later?'

I said, 'Yes, I will,' and did so ; but my eyes never left that dark-slide or his hands, although I was doing up the packet, and I saw him—as he backed, giving a half turn, two or three paces from the light—put the dark-slide to his left breast pocket, and take it out again (another one?), without any —

"talking" or "knocking"[7]. He said, 'Have you finished?' I said, 'Yes.' He then said, 'Will you put the packet of plates into your pocket so as I cannot touch them.' I said, 'Yes.' We got to the door; he was just going to open it, when he said: 'Would you like to mark the plates and write your initials on them?' I said, 'I don't think it matters; would you advise it?' and he said, 'Oh, well, some do it; some do not.' I said, 'I don't think I will in this case,' and he said, 'All right, if you are satisfied, I am.' He then handed me back the dark-slide, after I said I would not write my initials on the plates, and we walked into the studio.

[Mr. Seymour said he was doing nothing at all the while waiting with Mrs. Buxton.]

Directly we entered the studio, I, thinking he would want the slide at once, pulled it out of my pocket. The excuse I made was that I thought he wanted the slide, but in reality it was to see whether my marks were on it. They were not.

But Mr. Hope said, 'Put them (the plates) back in your pocket, as there is such a bright light in here, it will fog the plates.' He then asked me to sit down on the chair. He then said, 'This is an old Lancaster camera, given to me by Archdeacon Colley,' and I remarked, 'It must be a curio.' He started focussing the camera, and asked Mr. Seymour to come over and focus it too.

Mrs. Buxton then asked me to get into position and keep still. Mrs. Buxton then came over and asked for the dark-slide and handed it to Hope. He then drew the shutter of the dark-slide, and threw the focussing cloth over it and the lens of the camera, making a cap of it. He said, 'Please be still.' I was looking full at the camera. Mr. Hope then pulled up the dark cloth from off the lens, and during the exposure he gave I counted in my mind, '1 and 2 and 3 and. etc.,' and counted in that way up to nineteen (seconds). It was an abnormally long exposure for plates of 400 H. and D[8]. He then threw the dark cloth over the lens again, and Mrs. Buxton said to Mr. Hope, 'Is that No. 1 or No. 2?' He said, 'That is No. 1.'

Mrs. Buxton then said to me, 'Will you kindly take a slightly different position for No. 2?' and I turned my head to the right, evidently too far round

7. "talking" or "knocking" - inadvertent noises made by the props which can give away the trick, i.e. two wooden slides touching each other within a small space!.

8. "Mr. Hope has always found it necessary in his psychic experiments to give the plates a much longer exposure than is required in ordinary photography, as he finds that only in this way can he secure satisfactory psychic "extras". He follows this procedure purely from impression, and it has often been a matter of the great surprise to experienced photographers, experimenting with him, that he paid no attention to the ordinary photographic laws governing exposures. They have been equally surprised to find that results have been achieved by him in spite of this seemingly erratic exposure.There is no doubt that to build up the psychic "extra" a considerable length of time is required to materialise a structure sufficiently dense to affect the plate. and that this will vary considerably according to the condition provided by the medium and the sitters." (*Psychic Science* Oct 1922)

for their idea, and they told me to turn it to the left a little, and would I look at Mrs. Buxton. This I did.

They changed the dark-slide round and withdrew the second shutter and exposed another plate, and gave as long an exposure as before. I counted up to '18 and...' While the exposures were going on, Mrs. Buxton and Mr. Hope buried their heads in the sides of the focussing cloth, as though in prayer, and kept contact with the camera.

They then closed the dark slide up and took it out of the camera, and immediately handed it to me again. I then put it in my pocket. Mr. Hope turned to Mr. Seymour and said, 'You understand photography?'

Mr. Seymour said, 'Yes.' Then he turned to me and said, 'You can develop it if you like (referring to both of us), and I said, 'I will develop it.' We three then went into the dark-room with the slide in my pocket.

Mr. Hope then started mixing some developer into a glass measure; brought me a rather dirty (stained with silver stains at the bottom) porcelain dish which just held the two quarter-plates, which were developed together. Mr. Hope took the dark-slideout of my hand and opened it. He then said, 'Hold out your hands and I will tip the plates on to your hands so that I do not touch them.' He did so. I then put the plates in the porcelain dish myself, and Mr. Hope poured the developer over them, and to my surprise, instead of the plates flashing up black at once, as it seemed they ought to have done had they been those I brought with me, the plates developed slowly (as ordinary slow plates would do).

During the period the plates were developing, we were talking upon various subjects, about photos Hope had taken; and he told us that last week he had to take ten plates before he got an "extra" on one. Naturally, I was very anxious, and I kept on looking to see the Imperial Co.'s trademark come up at the corner of the plates; not a sign of it. On the other hand, I noticed that there was an "extra" forming on one of the negatives. I then took the dish and examined the plates more closely at the red electric light, and he said, 'Don't put it too near or you will fog them, as I did so last week,' and he said he had spoken to Mr. McKenzie about this light, and he (Mr. McKenzie) had not done anything yet. I then looked at the plates again, and I saw that the trademark of the Imperial Plate Co. was not coming up on the plates, and that there was an "extra" on No. 2 negative. I cried out, 'I am so glad we have an 'extra' on here, thank you very much indeed.' I then asked him whether they were done, and he then had a look.

We waited a few minutes longer and he said, 'Take them out of the developer. Mind the step, and put them in the large dish of hypo, which is up there, and do not put them on top of each other.' I took them out of the developer and put them in the hypo. We then went into the studio again where Mrs. Buxton was awaiting us. I told Mrs. Buxton that what I had come for had been very successful and thanked her very much for her help and that of Mr. Hope.

Mr. Hope went out of the room for a few minutes, and I then asked Mrs. Buxton whether I could take the other negative away with me, as I fancied it was a good portrait of me. Mrs. Buxton thought they had no objection at all. She said, 'What will you put it in? I will try and find a box when Mr. Hope comes in.' Mrs. Buxton then went into the dark-room and had a look at the negatives, brought out the one I wanted not the one with the "extra" on, and gave it to me. I said I could take it all right. Then she went into the dark-

room again, and brought out the negative with the "extra" on, and I was highly delighted to see a charming female form looking over one of my shoulders. I said I wondered whether this was my mother, and Mr. Seymour said, 'Surely your mother would be older than that.'[9]

'My mother died at the age of forty-one,' I said. Mrs. Buxton said, 'This is a very good one indeed.' I said, 'How many prints can I have?' She said, 'Mrs. McKenzie arranges all those matters. Will you see her?'

At that moment Mr. Hope came in again and showed me a letter he had recently received from Glasgow,

Plate I : Harry Price with the psychic "extra" which appeared on the plate.

where one of his sitters had recognised a relative. I then once more thanked Mr. Hope for the great service he had been to us that morning. Mr. Hope said that he thought the result was very successful and that he was usually at his best early in the morning, and that accounted for a very successful "extra." I said if I happened to be near Crewe I should like to call on him, and he said 'Do, and we will fix up a sitting with you, but let me know a little beforehand.'

---

9. Note that the lower drapery is in front of Price's arm and leg and not <u>behind</u> as a pre-prepared plate would have been.

I took my negative away; shook hands with them both; saw Mrs. McKenzie; thanked her and told her it had been very successful and asked her if I could have a dozen photographs.

She said, 'You are entitled to two,' and so I offered to pay for the other ten, which she said would be 6d. each. I gave her a £1 note, and she went into the office and brought me back the change. We left the college at 11.20 a.m."

[Mr. Seymour is in substantial agreement with everything that Mr. Price has said concerning the part that he played in the sitting.]

[Signed] Harry Price.

The official Report on 'A Case of Fraud with the Crewe Circle' in the May edition of the S.P.R. *Journal* goes on to describe how the unexposed plates were developed that same afternoon and the X-ray markings came up on all of them. Adding that Plate II. taken from the negative brought back from the sitting and ought to have shown

Plate II –*Harry Price*

that part of the design shown missing lower right segment of the image on page 169.

"This plate, now lying before us, is of thinner glass than those received by Hope at the sitting and of slightly different colour. It is one of the two plates substituted by Hope (as described above).

Of the two original plates retained by Hope, one is now in our possession, thus making only one blank in the complete set of eight plates, including the two kept by the Imperial Dry Plate Co., Ltd., which they returned for the purpose of discovering what portion of the design had been retained by the medium."[10]

The report concludes with:

"It can hardly be denied that Mr. William Hope has been found guilty of deliberately substituting his own plates for those of a sitter. The move was as good as *seen* [11] to take place, and the supposition that it did was abundantly confirmed both when the slide was examined, and when the plates were developed."

It was three months before the S.P.R. published this report and not

10. *Journal of SPR* Vol 22 1921-22 May pps 282-3
11. The italics are in the original Report (p283)

once in all this time was any approach made to the British College nor to the medium giving an indication of the suspected fraud.

Sometime before the 'official' Report came out, Harry Price, with the permission of the powers that be within the S.P.R., made the bold step of issuing a pamphlet – *Cold light on Spiritualistic Phenomena,* declaring the "Fraud" he felt had been perpetrated, spicing it with literary 'Hope' quips, and asking the Press "to give it all the publicity they could."[12]

Light magazine responded quickly to the publication of the S.P.R. report and kept their readers fully up to date with the progress of the investigation.

On June 10th just two weeks after the publication of the Report by the S.P.R. they published this:

"The Society for the Study of Supernormal Pictures has under its serious consideration the report published in the current issue of the Journal of the Society for Psychical Research, in which Mr. Harry Price, who is a member of the S.P.R. and closely connected with the conjuring profession, alleges fraud against Mr. William Hope, the Crewe photographic medium. ...

Mr. Price alleges that a dark slide was adroitly changed by Hope, who returned to him during the course of the experiment a dark slide which was not the one which Mr. Price had at the beginning, and which he had marked indelibly on both sides. ....

We are also left to speculate why Mr. Price, on detecting the changing of the dark slide, did not at once tax the medium with the trick and verify the suspicion that two slides were in use, one of them concealed on Mr. Hope's person.

If there is a valid case against Hope, let it be dealt with without compromise, weakness or evasion. But let us have the testimony on both sides. those who are anxious to uphold the truth of psychic photography and those who are equally anxious to discredit it and prove it to be all imposture."

Following this, letters poured in — many in this vein.

Mr. R.A. Bush of Surrey: (*Light,* June 24th)

".....You remark, "If there be a valid case against Hope let it be dealt with without compromise, weakness or evasion." Good; but may not Mr. Harry Price and Mr. James Seymour be the real deceivers?

Upon what ground must we take their word? They were not subject to any test conditions. They came in circumstances under which they should be suspect from the very start. Membership of the S.P.R. is no guarantee of

---

12. *Inter'l Psychic Gazette*, James Lewis (Ed.) writing in May 1933.

honesty nor is aptness for conjuring. The onus of proving *bona fides* is as much upon them as upon Mr. Hope, who has after many tests acquired a reputation for such. Are these gentlemen cleverer than everyone else?

Everybody who knows Mr. Hope knows that it would be the easiest thing in the world to trick him. He takes no precaution, imposes no conditions, receives all visitors openly. There would be nothing clever in tricking him— a novice in legerdemain could do it.

What means are available now for Mr. Hope to defend himself against this particular accusation? Absolutely none. It was a test of no value in the cause of truth."

* * * * *

A thoughtful 'agnostic' who was –"still waiting personal evidence of the fact," writes:

"The investigators appeared to have undertaken the test with the full expectation and desire of proving fraud. They conducted the operation with "*suppressio veri suggestio falsi*"[13] methods to perfection. They constituted themselves prosecution, judge and jury, without giving any loophole for possible defence or explanation. ....

If this is the "impartial" method of the above society, I suggest the formation of another society to investigate their investigations—a guardian to guard the guardians of research."

'Lieutenant Colonel'

* * * * *

Light had already taken the investigation into their own hands.

Declaration Under Oath on June 9th 1922

On the ninth day of June an examination of Mr. Hope was conducted by Mr. H. W. Engholm, in the presence of the Editor of *Light* [D. Gow.], Mr. George E. Wright, the Organising Secretary of the London Spiritualist Alliance and a member of the S.P.R., Miss F. R. Scatcherd, also a member of the S.P.R., and Mr. E. S. W. Isaac, a member of the firm of C.O. Humphreys, solicitor, at this firm's office.

Mr. Hope, after answering some 68 searching questions, finally made the following statutory declaration before a Commissioner for Oaths:

"The allegations against me contained in the said Report ("S.P.R. *Journal*" for May, 1922), are untrue and have no foundation whatever."[14]

Mr. James Seymour, in replying to the question, "Are you quite satisfied in

---

13. "the suppression of truth, the suggestion of what is false." (*Light* June 17th, 22)
14. For the S.P.R. allegation re the substitution see page 176, last paragraph.

every way that this test with Hope was watertight and conclusive," put to him by Mr. H. W. Engholm, on July 6th, answered as follows: "I think it is conclusive and as watertight as the conditions would allow."

To the same question put to Mr. Harry Price on June 28th, by Mr. H. W. Engholm, the following answer was given, "I am satisfied that the test showed that Hope substituted my two plates for others."

These were the answers Hope gave to some of the sixty-eight questions put to him.[15]

"In the Statutory Declaration made by Hope on June 9th before a Commissioner for Oaths the following are the questions and Hope's answers on this point:

Q. Were plates Nos. 1 and 2 your plates?

A. No.

Q. Where did Mr. Price get these two plates from?

A. He got them out of his packet.

Q. In your opinion Mr. Price brought these plates with him?

A. If he did not, I don't know who did.

On the question of the substitution of plates by a change of dark slides, when Mr. H. W. Engholm asked Price, "What kind of dark slide was it Mr. Hope handed to you and which you say you marked indelibly?"

He replied: An ordinary wooden slide.

Q. What was the dark slide like which you say Mr. Hope substituted?

A. Like the one I marked, only without any marks.

The Alleged Marking of Slide.

We have only Price's word that he marked the slide with the thumb-instrument. He, it will be noted, admits that the alleged substituted slide was similar to the marked one in appearance. Did Price mark the first slide after all, or only imagined that he did?

This tiny device, used by conjurors, was intended to allow the wearer to impress 3 marks, as might be made by drawing pin tips, into any surface.

Light comments:

"The S.P.R. Report gives us no proof that he marked it. Even Mr. Seymour could not say Price did so. Had Price, at this juncture, the time to examine the dark slide carefully to ascertain if he had really marked the slide at all?

---

15. *Light*, Critical Examination', August 12th, 1922

Is it possible that he trusted to his thumb-pressure only for the marking, and did not look at the slide (both sides) for fear of rousing Hope's suspicions? If this is so, when Price looked at the slide after it had been loaded in the darkroom he may have been looking at the same slide again on which his attempts to mark has failed.

Again – as Hope may have been looking at him, he may have made only a hasty examination and missed the pinhole marks, if, of course they had been imprinted at all.

In the Statutory Declaration, what does Hope say regarding this question of slides? Our questions and his answers are as follows:

Q How many slides do you keep?

A. I could not tell you; any number. I only used two slides for the Colley camera at the British college.

Q. Can you again bring to your mind whether you had two slides that day?

A. To the best of my recollection I only had one on me; the other one was in my trunk broken.

Q. Did you in the dark room take the slide from Mr. Price and put it in your breast pocket and take out another dark slide?

A. No."[16]

As *Light* began their 'Critical Examination' of the Case they declared:

"We will endeavour to present this experiment step by step and deal with the case in a strictly judicial manner. Nowhere in this case does the question arise as to whether Mr. Hope or Mrs. Buxton are mediums or not. The crux of the evidence rests entirely on the fact that a trick was perpetrated by someone. The plates were changed.

At what period in the history of this experiment was this substitution effected? What opportunities had any of the parties concerned for doing this? – and what motive underlies this substitution? These are the main questions."[17]

The British College Responds to the S.P.R.

Throughout the Spring of 1922, James McKenzie, the Principal of the British College, had been abroad researching suitable mediums to visit the College. On his return at the beginning of June, he was horrified at the charges and replied in no uncertain terms to the report in S.P.R. Journal in the college's new Quarterly Journal *Psychic Science*.

16. *Light* 'Critical Examination' Aug 12th 1922
17. *Light* July 29th, 1922

"As Principal of the B.C.P.S., I have requested that the S.P.R., the Magic Circle, the S.S.S.P. and the B.C.P.S. shall each appoint three independent members to form a Committee of twelve, which will elect its own Chairman, and proceed to examine all the evidence, inspect the plates in question, hear the witnesses and issue a report of its conclusions. The S.S.S.P. has elected its representatives, and the Council of the B.C.P.S. has agreed to act in conjunction with the other Societies.

The question to be settled is: Did Mr. Hope and Mrs. Deane substitute plates by a trick at some moment during, or previous to, the experiments described?"

He then goes on to reinforce the fact that no challenge was made at the time to the mediums nor the "officials of the College" that there had been some underhand dealings – that an exchange of plates had taken place – which would have been the normal thing to do!

Why not?

The conspirators in this obviously had their own plan. They presumably didn't want it "hushed up" by revealing there and then, in private, what they considered had happened.

Did Harry Price want glory, notoriety? Was it to reinforce a name for himself as an 'exposer' of fraudulent mediums? A chance to air his "expertise" to the world? Or perhaps to show that Hope could "be caught out" and to make it as widely known as possible. (See Dr Hall's comment on Price in Chpt 2).

But it seems that someone was playing Price at his own game.

As disclosed in the S.P.R. Report

... "Of the two original plates retained by Hope, one, as we have said, is now in our possession ..."

On March 3rd, just one week after the experiment, a package had been delivered to the S.P.R. offices containing some plates, wrapped in a British College Syllabus for 1921, with the instruction that they be developed. When this was done one was found to be one of the two missing 'marked' plates – complete with the missing quarter of the X-ray design. Nothing of this was revealed to those beyond the "conspiratorial circle" until the statement in the closing paragraphs of the May Report – 11weeks later!

As there was no letter enclosed with the package just a note saying – "From a friend. Fix in the dark." Miss Newton decided as the plates were wrapped in pages of the College's syllabus that the package must be from them and so sent this letter:

20 Hanover square, W1   6th March 1922

Dear Madam

"I received last week a packet containing four undeveloped photographic plates from which the covering letter had apparently been inadvertently omitted, for there was no indication as to who had sent it or why they had been sent here. The packet bore the Notting Hill postmark and the plates were wrapped up in the syllabus of the lectures at your College. Do you happen to know anything of these plates, for we would like to acknowledge receipt of them? I should be much obliged for any information on the matter.

Yours faithfully

I. Newton (Secretary)"

As no-one at the College as yet knew of any photographic work involving the S.P.R., Mrs Ford, the assistant organiser, believing this was a matter of no particular importance, replied briefly as follows the same day:

7th March 1922

"Miss I .Newton

20 Hanover Square W1

Dear Madam

    I cannot think what that packet of plates could refer to. Sometimes our sitters take some of the unused remaining plates away with them to develop at home, but I have not heard of any of them mention about sending to your Society. I am sorry I cannot give you any light on the subject.

Yours truly

(signed) E. Ford"

And there the matter was left.

But on March 31st,, three weeks after the first anonymous packet a second one was delivered to the S.P.R.— This was found to contain a small cardboard box in which there was, a rubber contrivance, five small transparencies on glass, a red celluloid disc with perforations somewhat resembling part of the Imperial Company's X-ray marks, a small portion of a letter, and a typewritten note, which read as follows:

"I would have sent these before but was afraid Hope would miss them— they were found in his room with the plates I sent you before.

Don't write to Madame again as she is getting suspicious."

Immediately below this typing appeared in pencil the words:

"I shan't write again."

The address of the S.P.R. was typed upon the outside wrapper and bore a Paddington post mark.

The original "marked" plate was kept under wraps with established members of the S.P.R. denied access to it for over four months. Even Sir Arthur Conan Doyle – himself a long-standing member of the S.P.R. – had been denied access.

He writes:

"The S.P.R. claims that after this experiment one of the two marked plates had been returned to them, but in so secret a fashion that it could not be explained who had brought it or how it had been obtained.

This was apparently a point against Hope, the charge inferred, though not stated, being that he had left this plate about, after abstracting it from the carrier, and that some enemy had recognised it and brought it to clinch the case against him. So secret were the proceedings of the Society that though I am one of the oldest members of that body I was refused leave to see this mysterious plate. Eventually, however, some of our people did see it, and then an extraordinary state of things revealed itself.

First of all the plate was undoubtedly one of the original set supplied by the Imperial Dry Plate Company.

Secondly, [when received] it was a virgin *unexposed* plate, so that it is *impossible* that *anyone* at Hope's end could have picked it out from any other plates, since the marks were invisible. ...

This plate was sent on March 3rd, just a week after the experiment and three days after Hope and Mrs. Buxton, who knew nothing yet of Price's trap, had returned home to Crewe. ....

Now consider the situation thus created. Since the plate had not been developed it is clear that *neither Hope nor anyone at the College could possibly have known that it was a marked plate*, for there was no publication of the alleged exposure until more than three months after.

Who was there in the whole world who <u>did know</u> that this was a marked plate and one in which the S.P.R. might be expected to take a special interest? Clearly the experimenters of the S.P.R. and their confidants—no one else. But if the marked plate had been abstracted by Hope in the dark room and mixed up there with other plates, how could any friend or emissary of the S.P.R. have picked it out as being the plate that was marked? – It could not have been done.

Therefore, the conclusion seems to be irresistible that this plate was *abstracted from the packet before* the experiment by someone who knew exactly what it was.

If this be so Hope is the victim of a conspiracy and he is a much ill-used man. I see no possible alternative to this conclusion." [19]

---

19. *The Case for Spirit Photography*, Chpt IV (1922)

In commenting on the source of the package he went on to say:

"Wherever it came from it is clear that it did not come from the College, for when a man does a thing secretly and anonymously, he does not enclose literature which will lead to his detection. ....."

Meanwhile at Crewe a supportive message had been received in the form of a psychograph demonstrating the interest Mr. William Walker was still taking in the Crewe Circle.[20] This was received late on Friday evening, July 28th, 1922, and reads:

"Dear Friends of the Circle,

"I would not spend a moment with the Psychical Research Scty, because they are nothing more nor less than fraud hunters and I want you to come to Buxton for a sitting with Mrs. Walker, 3, Palace Rd., about the 8th-9th of Aug. Then the spirit friends can further demonstrate the wonderous powers which to-day are needed more than ever. Peace be with you.

"Yours faithfully,
"W.WALKER."

"Please inform Henry."

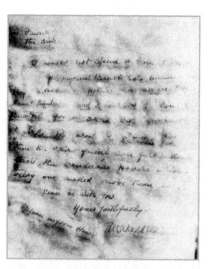

The psychograph is shown left. A portion of one of Wm. Walker's life-time letters is reproduced above, for comparison with it.

"It is perhaps unnecessary to state that the instructions given by Mr. Wm. Walker were carried out to the letter. The results of the short visit of the Crewe Circle to Buxton are best described by quoting an extract from a letter I received from Mr. Henry Walker:

---

20. *The Case for Spirit Photography,* Chpt VIII (1922)

'We (Mrs. Buxton, Mr. Hope and myself) went to Buxton on Wednesday, 9th inst. (August, 1922.-ED.). Two sittings were held, and four exposures made. The first exposure was made on mother, and gives a message from father to Mrs. Buxton and Mr. Hope, dealing again with the S.P.R. test – and *promising a puzzle.*

The second exposure was made on mother, Mrs. Marriott (an old friend of ours) and myself, and shows a very large face of father nearly covering the three of us.'

Henry closes his letter with this supportive reference:

'I fancy father's record alone should be sufficient to satisfy any sensible being. I daresay I can find well over twenty psychic results received from him on different occasions, most of them under reasonable test conditions.'

(Signed) H. Walker."

Here then, is a message from the unseen friends "promising a puzzle" and what a puzzle this case was turning out to be.

Under the tireless persistence of *Light* in mid-August the two "substituted" plates were compared with the original X-ray marked plates and found to be noticeably thinner and with rough cut edges.

Four days later, on Monday morning last (21st August), a meeting was arranged at the British College of Psychic Science, 59 Holland Park W11, when Mr. Eric Dingwall, the Research officer of the S.P.R. produced what had been called the "Mystery Plate" in the presence of Dr. Allerton Cushman, Mr. J. Hewat McKenzie, Mr. Harry Price, Mr. James Seymour, Dr. V.J. Woolley, Dr. Hereward Carrington and Mr. H.W. Engholm. This plate was found by all present to fit exactly into one of the sets of the three X-ray marked plates and thereby completing one sheet of glass and supplying the missing portion of the X-ray design in that set. This left the other sheet of glass incomplete to the extent of one X-ray marked plate, the whereabouts of which was still unknown.

On examination of the 'Mystery' Plate it showed, at one end of the plate, the negative of an extra which appeared to be that of a child's head; very small and surrounded by a cloud. At the opposite end of the plate was a cloudy effect. There was no sign of a sitter on the plate, and it was impossible to decide whether the plate had been exposed or not.

Following this examination, a statement was issued:

"It is obvious from our examination this morning, that Plates I and II are of thinner glass (plainly noticeable by the naked eye) than the negatives showing X-ray marking, and that these plates were substituted by someone at the Price-Seymour-Hope test of February 24th for the two X-ray marked plates selected by Mr. Price, as stated by him in his report published in the S.P.R. Journal for May 1922.

We are convinced that the test with Hope on February 24th does not rule out the possibility that Hope has produced supernormal pictures, or that he is able to produce "extras" by other than normal means."

(Signed)

Allerton F. Cushman;   Harry Price;
Hereward Carrington;   J. Hewat McKenzie;
H.W. Engholm

— August 17th 1922

By now it was obvious to many that the original package must have been tampered with.

However, it was not until <u>late October</u>, when Mr. Mckenzie's demands to see the original packaging were met, was it revealed there was second anonymous packet delivered to the S.P.R. on March 31st. As already disclosed, it was found to contain a small cardboard box in which there was, a rubber contrivance, five small transparencies on glass, a red celluloid disc with perforations somewhat resembling part of the Imperial Company's X-ray marks, a small portion of a pencilled letter, and a typewritten note (see image opposite of the page from the College's Journal).

In reporting this in *Psychic Science* Jan '23, James McKenzie wrote:

"It is quite obvious that whoever sent the packets to the S.P.R. had full information regarding the experiment being conducted with marked plates by Mr. Price, facts which no one at the College had any knowledge of for three months afterwards.

It might be pointed out, ... that Mr. Price was a stranger to them, but brought an introduction, asking for an experiment with the Crewe Circle, from Miss Phillimore, of the L.S.A., of which he is a member. In view of this ignorance of Mr. Price's connection with the S.P.R., it was clearly impossible for anyone at the College to communicate with that body a week after the experiment, as the matter was kept a complete secret from the College.

The only person, therefore, who could have sent the anonymous packets to the S.P.R. had an immediate and first-hand knowledge of the experiment, even to the fact that an ordinary letter of enquiry has been received at the College on March 7th from the S.P.R.

It should be observed here that as the four anonymous plates were sent to the S.P.R. in an *undeveloped* state two days after Mr. Hope left the college and a week after the experiment, it would be something amounting to a miracle for anyone to select four plates from the scores of others lying in the College

Box, label, and contents of second anonymous packet sent to S.P.R.,
March 31st.

1. Box label.   2. Cut portion of a letter.

3. Red celluloid perforated disc.

4. Slightly reduced dimensions of typed note, which reads:

> "I would have sent these before, but was afraid Hope would miss
> them—they were found in his room with the plates I sent to
> you before. Don't write to Madame again as she is getting
> suspicious." Then in pencil the words "I shant write again."

5, 6, 7, 8, 9   Five glass miniatures, exact size.

10. Tubular Rubber sucker with brown paper attachment round the
mouth.

Nos. 5 and 9 miniatures appear as imitation psychic "extras" upon
two of the unexposed plates received in the first anonymous packet of
March 4th.

Contents of the second anonymous package as shown in Psychic Science darkroom, *one of which had the special X-ray marks upon it,* as this marking is *invisible* until *after* development.

The glass <u>transparencies</u> enclosed in the second anonymous packet have been examined by the College Committee, who are all very well acquainted with Mr. Hope's results, and they agree that they are a spurious and bad imitation of the work of the Crewe Circle. Can it be supposed that if Mr. Hope were capable of such fraudulent practices, he would have continued to work at the College after missing such damning apparatus? On the contrary he explicitly denies all knowledge of these matters and has constantly claimed that he has been tricked in this experiment."

Not only was the honour of the medium at stake so was that of the British College for employing Hope in whom they had complete trust.

In an interview with Miss Newton (S.P.R.. Sec) on Monday 23rd October, at which a Mr. Pugh (at Miss N's invitation) and Mr. & Mrs. McKenzie were present, it was revealed what had been in that first anonymous packet delivered on 4th March.

Miss Newton told them that:

"On undoing the outer wrapping of brown paper—an inside wrapping was found, also brown—with a note, "From a friend. Please fix in the dark," in large, printed characters. It did not look to me like an uneducated person's writing. The word "dark" especially had a curious "d". In the outer wrappings the address, again printed and disguised, I noticed the letter "S" in "Square" was reversed.

On the S.P.R. opening the box in the darkroom, four plates were found packed with torn pieces of the college Syllabus for the previous term. On developing all were found to have extras and one also had a portion of the Imperial Plate Co's X-ray design and proved to be one which fitted with plates in the Price experiment. None of the extras, to my thinking, looked like one of Hope's I have seen in the hundreds that pass through my hands. One was of a lady with a Gainsborough feather in her hat, and in which the sloping shoulders and dress could be seen. Another woman's face had curious fancy braid work and large ear ornaments.

There was also a dotted design as if to imitate Imperial Co's trade mark. Some small red marks as if made with a red gelatine subject were noticed on two plates. Some curious X-ray marks from the heads did not resemble any ectoplasmic effects. On one plate it seemed as if a holder had gripped it at the bottom and left a rectangular mark, about one inch and a half each way. One or two plates has a "light" effect at one corner in addition to "extra", and all the effects were in the corners of the plates."[21]

---

21. *Light,* November 4th ,1922

Again, Mr. McKenzie renewed his efforts:

i) to see <u>the box and the wrappings the original plates</u> from the Imperial Co. were in, to examine for signs of previous, perhaps surreptitious opening. (The plates had been with the S.P.R. for 3 weeks before the sitting.)

ii) to know what had happened to the *'sealed' wrapping provided by Mr. Moger.*

We know that: "On the morning fixed for the sitting, Mr. Dingwall, the Research Officer, met Mr. Price and his companion at Holland Park Station, and handed over the sealed packet of plates for use in the experiment."[22]

But it wasn't until November, almost nine months, after the sitting, that the "wrappings" were delivered to Mr. McKenzie and having examined them he took the wrappers to the Imperial Dry Plate Company for investigation. Only then did Mr. McKenzie get some answers.

November 13th 1922

"Mr. J. Hewat McKenzie

"Dear Sir, Further to your call here on Saturday last, the 11th inst, we beg to confirm herewith the conversation we had with you in reference to a portion of a wrapper taken from a box of our "Flashlight Plates" and submitted to us for our opinion. After careful examination of the label attached to the wrapper in question, we are of the opinion that <u>one end of the label has been unstuck so as to leave the "ear" of the brown paper wrapping uncovered. This "ear" also appears to show signs of having been unstuck and refolded.</u>

Yours faithfully

Imperial Dry Plate Company Ltd

" (signed) H.T.G,."

The wrapper from the box of plates used by Harry Price on February 24th.
Note the lower and right edges are torn where the box was cut open in the dark room but it is the top left corner that is of investigation by the company. (See overleaf)

---

22. *Journal of* S.P.R. Vol 22, May 22 pps 274.

Magnification of Label and Wrapper in dispute.
1. Crease (dark line) showing where label was opened. (top left of previous image.)
2. Knife point marks showing at "ear" of brown paper wrapper.

The men who originally packed the box were proud of their work and would never have allowed a "creased" package to leave the works. They further stated that "the labels were all gummed by rollers which made it impossible for them to send out such work. They also stated that they believed they could tell by unsealing the label and wrapper as to whether an adhesive other than their own which is a particular preparation, had been used."

They later confirmed the glue used to reaffix the flap was not theirs.

Someone, it seems, had been into the box while at the S.P.R. office!

When challenged as to what took place at Holland Park Station on that morning in February – Mr. McKenzie tells us.

"Mr. Price now definitely states after careful consideration and presumably after collaboration with Mr. Dingwall, that either he, Mr. Price, or Mr. Dingwall opened the sealed envelope at Holland Park Station and took out the packet of plates. Mr. Price is not quite clear as to whether he examined the seals at the time but thinks he must have done so."

Mr. Dingwall, in the above quoted letter to the college of November 13th says, regarding this point:

'I note that you say about the wrappers. It is possible that I removed the outer wrappers at Holland Park. I do not remember doing so, but then the persons concerned in the case did not take notice of every action of each other. I agree that the statement on page 274 of the report is ambiguous.' "

Why did they not take notice of every action? This was purported to be an "approved" scientific experiment under the aegis of the S.P.R. to expose a medium suspected of fraud. Surely every stage should be recorded – it seems not in this case.

However it seems that by January 1923 they did remember, as in the report published in the S.P.R. Journal for that month it is recorded that:

"When received by the S.P.R. the packet remained in the charge first of the Secretary and then of the Research Officer of the S.P.R., until it was delivered by the Research Officer, exactly as received from Mr. Moger, to Mr. Price on the morning, and very shortly before the sitting of February 24th.

Mr. Dingwall then removed Mr. Moger's postal wrapper and his sealed envelope, and the packet was taken to the British College of Psychic Science and laid before Mr. Hope and Mrs. Buxton in the postal wrapper in which it had been despatched by the Company. This postal wrapper was then removed in their presence, and in the presence of Mr. Seymour who accompanied Mr. Price, and the labelled wrapper was closely scrutinised by both Mr. Hope and Mrs. Buxton."

Mr. McKenzie continues:

"It would be interesting to know from Mr. Dingwall or Mr. Price what purpose was served in sealing the envelope so carefully with six seals if these were not to be examined later and a note made regarding their condition.

By this careless handling Mr. Moger's carefully sealed envelope has been completely spoiled *as evidence on the testimony* of the chief witnesses.

Upon inspection of the grossly damaged wax seals it is found that five of the six are of a bright red colour, and the sixth of a much darker red. When the attention of Mr. Price was called to this on November 10th, he seemed to have no remembrance of this fact and suggested that in all probability the darker seal had been burned when the sealing was done, but this is not so. The wax used is of two entirely different colours.

In a letter from Mr. Moger, dated November 10th, he states that he cannot now remember whether more than one colour of sealing wax was used.

Another point which it is unnecessary to labour but which should be stated is that *the envelope sealed by Mr. Moger had no gum upon its upper flap, and that in spite of six seals, it was only necessary to remove one, the centre and darker one, to enable the envelope to be opened and the parcel of plates extracted.*" (My italics. AH)

When referring to the involvement of Mr Dingwall in all of this Conan Doyle in his book at the time wrote:

It is a curious fact which should be recorded that though the experiment was on February 24th, and though the report of the alleged exposure was not issued till the end of May, we find Mr. Dingwall applying for a sitting with Hope early in May, and writing, when Hope refused to give him one:

"As I understand from your letters that you still refuse to have sittings with the only scientific body in Great Britain investigating this subject, I shall be obliged in my coming report on psychic photography to publish certain facts which may not be of advantage to yourself!"

That letter was on May 2nd. Apparently, it seems, the 'publication' of the "exposure" depended upon whether Mr. Dingwall was piqued or was humoured. If he were sure that the exposure was a genuine one this is a very singular attitude to assume."

James Lewis, Editor of the *International Psychic Gazette* writing eleven years later in his article "The Historic Exposure of William Hope" pointed out:

"Mr. Dingwall's Challenge.

This is rather important to note, especially if it be true—and we had no reason to doubt it— that this S.P.R. Research Officer had previously boasted he, could open any sealed packet of plates without anyone being able to discover that he had done so! Our trustworthy informant, the late Mr. J. Hewat McKenzie, told us he had promptly challenged Mr. Dingwall on the spot to do it, for £50, and Mr. Dingwall declined the challenge! He was also alleged to have been heard expressing considerable animus towards Hope and an intention to "smash" him!"

So was it Eric Dingwall who substituted the plates?

Did Harry Price have an enemy within the ranks?

We shall never know.

To sum up

1. Harry Price set out to prove Hope could be a fraud by having his plates previously marked invisibly and not carrying out the usual, accepted method of signing the plates to ensure no substitution. Perhaps he made a show of giving Mr. Hope the opportunity to switch them for doctored plates by refusing to sign them.

Or did he already know they had been substituted?

2. Price says he attempted to mark the dark slide with a conjuror's pinpricking device but there was no corroborative evidence that he had done so. He found no marks on the slide he was given after the "half turn....". His statement that he had made them was accepted as gospel.

At that time the carriers/slides were made of very hard wood usually Mahogany (Spanish or Honduran) and it is very difficult to impress them with marks, so I'm not surprised he couldn't find anything as he'd barely a moment to try to make the marks, while Hope was presumably watching (in the dim red light). Mr. McKenzie confirmed that Hope had only the one 'working' slide for use at the College and did not have one to substitute. ... After close examination – (admittedly some months later) – no marks could be found on the one which had been used that morning.

3. The charge that Hope had exchanged the slides by putting one in his breast pocket and bringing out another was 'as good as _seen_' –was not confirmed – but accepted. (italics in the original)

Is a jacket 'breast pocket' of a 1920s jacket large enough hold TWO 4x5 inch dark slides half-an-inch thick (1.45cms) and without any "talking or knocking" sounds? or was it an inside pocket?

These illustrations below are of modern dark slides so not in the darker hard wood of the 1920s but the dimensions have not changed.

4. Would Hope have 'exchanged' a slide, as is suggested here, and then asked Price if he wanted to initial the plates?

It was usual for a sitter to mark his plates before loading them into the slide to prevent substitution. But a fraudster might ask someone to sign the plates after he had substituted them – if he had.

5. When developed, the X-ray marks did not come up on the two plates supposedly substituted by Hope, but an "extra" was found on one of them. (This extra was attested to by experienced investigators as a genuine Hope "extra".) The drapery of the "extra" is in front of Price's shoulder and arm so <u>not</u> a pre-prepared plate.

6. The plate Price took away with him was of thinner glass and a different colour from the plates which the Imperial Plate Company had supplied and he was permitted to take it away with him. Some months later the plate with the "extra" was also found to be of thinner glass – but who had substituted it was never established. Under examination the wrapper label of the box showed signs of tampering –at the opposite end from the tear Price made at the College when he removed the wrapper. (See right end of image p.189.)

Left: a 1/4 plate "dark slide"
- (carrier) showing the length
measurement.
Above: the same "dark slide"
- showing its thickness.
(Courtesy of Diane Milner)

7. One of the marked plates, supposedly one that had been substituted by Hope, was returned to the S.P.R. anonymously *one week* after the sitting, undeveloped – almost three months before Hope and anyone at the college even knew that the plates had been marked with X-rays. The marks were *totally invisible* until developed so presumably only the person who knew they were the marked plates could have sent it. Could it have been Price himself having opened the package before passing it to Mr Moger for sealing? or Mr Dingwall while it was in his charge to diffuse Price's success? After all he was The Resarch Officer and supposedly 'top dog'!

8. A second anonymous package was sent to the S.P.R. three weeks later. It contained suspicious articles supposedly from Hope's case at the College. As the letter to Miss Newton was known only to Mrs Ford and her stenographer, only someone who had knowledge of Miss Newton's original inquiry and the reply could have used the phrase 'Don't write to Madame again as she is getting suspicious.' – which had no basis in fact, as no one at the College was suspicious.

8. The outer wrapping sealed by Mr. Moger was removed in the street by Mr Dingwall (as stated in S.P.R. Journal, Jan 23), before the sitting, without examination of the seals.

The seals were not examined but later it was found one was of different coloured wax and with that original seal removed it would have been easy to open the packet, extract the box of plates, and then resealed but with a different wax.

9. The plate company stated that their original sealing of the label on the box of plates had been tampered with. It had been carefully opened and re-glued with a glue different from their own. Meaning someone most probably substituted the plates while still in the S.P.R. offices.

And then there are the rather "questionable" remarks made during the reporting of the experiment.

10. Extract from statement: "In my opinion, at that juncture they came to the conclusion that the packet had not been tampered with, because at that moment Mrs. Buxton asked me whether the packet had been opened. I said, "It is exactly as I got it from the makers, outer wrapper and all." I was careful to say that."

Why did Price think it was necessary to say the underlined phrases?

Did he know something else?

In his book on the 'Case' Conan Doyle wrote:

"...as Mr. Seymour has been very searching in his inquiries about mediums, he will not take it amiss if I ask him what he meant when in his evidence he says: 'They (i.e., Hope and Mrs. Buxton) were thoroughly <u>taken in by the packet and were not suspicious of it</u>.'

How could they possibly be suspicious of a packet which had never been opened? On the other hand, if the speaker knew that the packet had been tampered with it would be a most natural remark to make."

The Two Worlds comment

Early in the controversy the editor, Ernest Oaten, the Editor, made this statement:

"One story is always good until the other is told, but the S.P.R. report is putting too great a strain on our credulity when it says: "It can, we think, hardly be denied that Mr. William Hope has been found guilty of deliberately substituting his own plates for those of a sitter. The move was as good as SEEN to take place."

That sentence – "as good as seen"– is delightfully ambiguous and rests on the impartiality of one witness only, and that the man who had set himself the task of discovering fraud.

After the thousands of experiments conducted by the "Crewe Circle" under varying conditions, some of them under far more stringent tests than any applied in this case, we must confess that we shall require far more evidence of the ability and impartiality of this self- appointed committee before we accept the conclusions which the S.P.R. present to us.

In this case there is no doubt that the plate bearing an extra was NOT one of the plates from the original packet as packed by the makers.

Substitution did take place, whether by the medium or the experimenters, however, is still an open question."

In *Light,* November 4th

"They [the S.P.R.] admit this plate came into their possession on March 4th, a few days after the Holland Park experiment. Two months later in their official report, in which they charge the Crewe Circle with fraud, they bring this plate forward as part of the evidence of fraud against Hope. They made the bold statement that this plate was one of the two original plates retained by Hope. It is now perfectly clear, when they made that statement, they had *no proof* whatever that the *plate in question had even been* <u>into the premises of the B.C.P.S.</u> *There are no independent witnesses brought forward to prove that the original packet sent by the Imp. Dry Plate Co. to Price had not been tampered with.* No one except the officials of the S.P.R., Price and Seymour, together with the Imp. Dry Plate

Co. had any knowledge that special marked plates were used for the test with Hope. But it looks pretty obvious *that the individual who sent the plate to the S.P.R. anonymously knew something about it.* If the mystery surrounding this plate is not cleared up, the S.P.R. cannot, in the eyes of all honest people, be considered to have <u>proved their case against the Crewe Circle.</u> It is essential to all concerned that the present stigma be removed from this most unfortunate experiment."

In a 'Case' worthy of 'Sherlock Holmes', Sir Arthur Conan Doyle writing in November 1922 sums up the case with this:

"Only at this last moment has a new and strange fact been admitted. It is that when the mysterious marked plate was returned it was not alone, but that three other plates not belonging to the marked series, were with it, each of them adorned with psychic photographs. These photographs in no way resembled the results of Hope.

"Even now—I write nearly nine months after the original investigation— we have no assurance that this secret of the S.P.R. has been fully divulged or that they have been frank with the public. It is possible that they have received other anonymous communications which bear upon the case.

As I have shown, these new facts place the Society in a very invidious position and that may be the cause of their hesitations and concealments, but they have to remember that they have made a wanton attack upon a man's honour, and that their own *amour propre* is a small thing compared to the admission of the injustice they have done. "In all attempted explanations let them bear in mind the central fact *that no one but themselves and their associates knew that there was a marked plate in existence until several months after the experiment, and one had been returned to them.*" [23]

Unfortunately after 100 years they cannot – as Conan Doyle requested:

"...come forward honestly, admit the blunders they have committed, apologise to Hope, and remove any slur which they have cast upon one of the most important and consistent psychic manifestations ever known in the history of the movement."

As the year closed, letters and criticisms continued to come in to *Light:*

To the Editor of *Light.*

"Sir,—I see in your current issue a long *ex parte* statement [24] under a heading which seems to imply that it is a judicial summing up. It is customary, however, to take evidence and to hear Counsel on the other side before coming

23. *The Case for Psychic Photography*, Ch IV. 1922
24. Reference to Mr. McKenzie's summing up, *Light,* November 25th 1922

to a conclusion; and I presume that the officials of the S.P.R. have something to say about the facts."

I am, Sir, Yours, etc.,

Oliver Lodge. (November 27th, 1922.)

– and in response to this:

To the Editor of *Light.*

"Sir,—I heartily agree with Sir Oliver Lodge as a matter of general principle, but I would ask him, as a member of the Council of the S.P.R., whether he thinks that principle was applied by the Council before they published the accusation against Hope of deliberate fraud.

Mr. Hope is "only" a medium, presumably fraudulent and unworthy of consideration, perhaps, in the eyes of the S.P.R., but surely before the publication of the article in the S.P.R. "Journal" Mr. and Mrs. McKenzie, at whose institution the photographic test was made, should have been informed, and been given access to all the evidence, and this as a matter of courtesy, of fair play and even of worldly wisdom." —Yours etc.,

C. E. Baddeley (December 2nd 1922)

Following all the tos and fros of the case the S.P.R. issued their opinion in January 1923 and this was followed by publication, (a year later), of a statement from that renowed thinker Rev. Charles Drayton Thomas who maintained at the end of his list of points:[25]

"In the S.P.R. Journal for May 1922, page 283, it was stated that: "It can, we think, hardly be denied that Mr. William Hope has been found guilty of deliberately substituting his own plates for those of a sitter."

On an *ex parte* statement of the case this impression was natural; but now that the other side has been heard and fresh facts have come to light it is inconceivable that any impartial Court would convict him on the evidence."

This trail has taken much close scrutiny to unravel and at the close of it, it is inconclusive. **The case of fraud is not proved,** and two years later in an article about sittings with Mrs. Irvine, Harry Price stated:

"I cannot believe it is all fraud. I feel convinced that Mr. Hope has produced genuine extras." [26]

He, however, still maintained, twenty years later, in his book *Search for Truth* that he had exposed William Hope in a fraud in the sitting on February 24th 1922.

---

25. For his full statement see Appendix 4
26. *Light,* December 20th 1924 pps 758/9

But as Ernest Oaten said – "Substitution did take place, whether by the medium or the experimenters, however, is still an open question."

So many unanswered questions –

so many possiblities of interference

so many egos –

The S.P.R.'s reputation and membership suffered because of their handling of the affair but the Crewe Circle's work went on unabated. In December 1922 Sir Arthur Conan Doyle's book in their defence was ready – as this notice from *Light* shows!

In a brief review they wrote: "This would be a welcome addition to the literature of psychic inquiry, if only because it puts into a compact form for the general reader much information that has hitherto been available only in a scattered way. It gives a reasoned summary of the mediumship of a man who has for years been the centre of much acute controversy, coming lately to a head in the "Price-Hope Case." But for the recent attacks on Mr. William Hope, attacks often ignorant, sometimes malicious, and senseless, it is probable that the book would never have appeared. There is truly some soul of goodness in things evil.

A volume of such cogent evidences of the reality of the phenomenon sometimes known as spirit photography cannot fail to have a very pronounced effect on the public which is too often at present distracted by random and irresponsible statements in the Press."

Meanwhile – The Work goes on

Following the sitting on February 24th 1922, work at the College proceeded as normal and in *Light* on March 11th Mrs. Barbara McKenzie published this:

"The Crewe Circle has just concluded a ten day's visit for Experimental work at the British College of Psychic Science.

In addition to giving many valuable sittings to inquirers a special test sitting was carried out, details of which will be given when the matter is complete. Mr. Hope and Mrs. Buxton are the present focussing points of research or attack – either name will apply – by Psychical Researchers, members of the Magic Circle and conjurers. Their gift is sufficiently developed to stand a good deal of testing but not without much physical expense, as those closely associated with them well know. The human instrument is the most delicate thing imaginable, and in the investigation of psychic science there is practically no other.

"In a recent article in the American S.P.R. Journal Mr. Eric Dingwall says that the task of the psychical researcher has been rendered doubly difficult by the fact Spiritualists, through their hold on mediums are able to withhold from him the means for adequate investigations. ....."

Barbara McKenzie.

It was not to Price's "covert" experiment that she was referring – not knowing it had been a test at all, let alone approved by the S.P.R. It was of a sitting for James Douglas, Editor of the *Sunday Express*.on the previous day. A carefully controlled experiment, with an impartial witness, culminated in a plate showing "a ring two inches in diameter completely covering the body of Mr. Douglas, the sitter.

"The ring seems to be composed of a very thick band of gauzy material bits of which show at the extreme edges of the ring, and within the ring the fabric seems stretched in a single piece and the cross weaving of the gauze is shown on the lapel and parts of the coat of the sitter. At the right-hand side is a piece of gauze seemingly torn out of the thick ring which shows the fabric very clearly. In the middle of the ring half-way across the gauze is torn, and in the middle of ectoplasmic looking material appears the following words in the well-known calligraphy of Archdeacon Colley, the early friend of the mediums, and whom they have good reason to believe supports them from the other side of life. The message is as follows:

'Dear Friends, have nothing to do with Marriott. T. Colley.'[1]

"It was possible to read the writing on the negative immediately the plate was fixed, but on the print it appears as mirror writing. The message was considered singularly appropriate, as Mr. Marriott, who is well known as a prominent antagonist of Spiritualism and of the Crewe Circle, was that week lecturing in London on the subject, and Mr Hope had been particularly anxious to be present, but was dissuaded by friends from exciting himself over the matter."

Was the message intended just for the Crewe Circle though?

Mr. Douglas had had a run-in with Mr. Marriott two months earlier, after issuing an invitation to "any expert in photography to attempt to do the same [as Hope] under similar conditions by a normal process."[2]

Mr. Marriott took up the challenge. In the ensuing experiment at the British College before eminent witnesses an "extra" was produced on one plate and on another – a ring of fairies around Sir Arthur Conan Doyle—a member of the British College as well as the S.P.R..

As Colonel Baddeley wrote later, in the April edition of the S.P.R. Journal:

"Mr. James Douglas was altogether too easy a prey for a skilful conjurer like Mr. Marriott, highly strung, nervous and so flustered that he signed the same plate twice, one signature over the other, and packed and stowed away in an inner pocket his opened packet of plates without being aware that he had done so."

Before this experiment Mr. Douglas agreed to make public the report whatever result was obtained. The College officials had asked him to do this and waited patiently but no reply was received. The Editor of *Psychic Science* felt – "as there was evidently no intention to do this, in the interests of justice, the facts should be made known."[3]

Perhaps Mr. Douglas was too embarrassed at the result to publish!

* * * * *

1. The handwriting verified by an "in-life" letter supplied by Miss Scatcherd.
2. *Journal of S.P.R.* Vol 22 1February "An Experiment in Faking "Spirit" Photographs" pps 219.
3. *Psychic Science* Oct 1922

Basil F. Andrews of Streatham Hill sent a report to *Light*[4] of a sitting he had had on April 1st 2022.

"My wife, a lady friend, and myself sat with Mr. Hope and Mrs. Buxton in a room at the Psychic College in order to obtain, if possible, a spirit photograph of a relative of mine who had passed over about eighteen months before, or some other evidence of the proof of psychic photography.

After the usual little "sitting" beforehand, four exposures were made, and on two of them "extras" were shown. We had of course taken certain precautions to obviate any possibility of fraud, but the results proved to my mind that such was quite impossible in this case, so it would be a waste of your space in Light to enumerate them.

The prints were received by me a few days later, and much to our disappointment we could not recognise either of them, although fairly plain. The interesting part, however, is that within a week both "extras" were identified, in each case by several people.

The "extra" which appeared on the print of my wife and myself was shown to a neighbour (whom my wife had interested in psychic matters) who immediately recognised it as a sister-in-law who had "passed over" during a bombing raid in the war. Several other relations also confirmed this. The other "extra" appeared on the photo of our friend, the head, eyes and nose only being visible, but again was identified at first sight by a neighbour, who stated it was undoubtedly her son. He had died in Africa some years ago. The photo was also recognised by the father.

The precautions taken were as follows: I took my own plates, put them in the slides, signed them, and afterwards took them out, developed them, and carefully examined the "extras." The prints were taken by the College.

Now, as none of us had ever seen either of the originals of the two "extras," and in one case did not even know that such a one had ever existed ... I see that there is no other supposition to go upon, except that the "extras" were genuine."

* * * * *

Shortly before the publication of the S.P.R. Report, in May 1922, a business man who had been Chairman of a large company in Britain, and also, for a while, a J.P. of an important district in the North of England, applied for a sitting with the Crewe Circle at the College of Psychic Science. At this time, he was not a member of the college, and knew very little of the subject, except from reading. He was a complete stranger to the Crewe Circle.

"His desire was to test "truth" for himself, and he gave the very best

---

4. *Light* July 8th 1922

conditions for mediumistic experiment while closely watching the whole photographic process."[5]

He supplied his own plates, having marked them carefully, and expressed himself as perfectly satisfied with the procedure. When the prints were sent to him, he did not recognize the "extra", but it made a profound impression on him, and there remained a feeling that identification would come in time.

Almost a year later he wrote to the college telling them of success in identifying the "extra".

"I happened to show the photograph to one of our old domestics, telling her she might take it to the servants' hall should the rest of the staff care to see it. Imagine my surprise on her telling me the next day that our housekeeper-cook, Mrs. M—, had at once recognized the face as being that of her late husband but when a younger man, and as she first knew him. M— was my butler, and while in my service joined up and lost his life. My

housekeeper fetched from her room a small photo of her husband at a younger period of his life than I had known him, and I saw in it the expected identification which, for the last ten months, had been in my mind. Two others of my old domestics were struck with the resemblance to M— as they had first known him. I have forwarded the small photo to the College to be examined."

He goes on: "There is one striking resemblance between the life and spirit photographs which I think must have impressed me, namely the expression of innate goodness which was so typical of the man himself. Neither his widow nor I would have any objection to your making public use of this letter, and I would like to take this opportunity of expressing my gratification to the College for the consolation I have received through membership, giving me assurance of spiritual existence after death."

The 'businessman' sitter with the "extra" of his erstwhile butler (see inset, top right, for comparison).

Mrs. McKenzie comments:

"It has been frequently known that the "extras" reveal the communicating spirit as younger than when death occurred. Perhaps our spirits are hampered

5. *Psychic Science* July 1923 p 142 'Recognized Psychic Photography'

by the flesh after middle life and, having thrown this off, take on an unexpected youthfulness[6]. The negative and letters are in the possession of the College."

* * * * *

On June 29th that year, three delegates from Belfast, Mr. Skelton, Mr. Gillmour and Mr. Donaldson, travelled over to attend the London Spiritualists' Conference. They broke their journey at Crewe in order to have a sitting with Mr. Hope, who was deeply distressed at the time on account of the attack made upon him in Mr. Price's report.

They had travelled from Belfast with Mrs. Crawford, whose late husband's affairs had been under criticism, though Hope had no means of knowing it. Dr. Crawford who had done so much excellent research work with the Goligher circle had committed suicide in July 1920.

Under good fraud-proof conditions, on their own specially-marked plate, they obtained a message in Dr. Crawford's handwriting.

"Dear Mr. Hope,

Needless to say I am with you where psychic work is concerned, and you can be sure of my sympathy and help. I know all the difficulties and uncertainties connected with the subject. I am keenly interested in your circle and will co-operate with you. Regarding your enemies who would by hook or by crook dispose of the phenomena, leave them alone. I, W. J. Crawford, of Belfast, am here in Crewe on Friday, June 30th.

"W. J. Crawford."

In *The Two Worlds* of July 22nd they write:

"We travelled together to Crewe, Mrs. Crawford then going on to London, whilst we went to see Mr. Hope, arriving about 10.30am. The usual sitting then took place. Mr. Hope asked for the plates, and Mr. Gillmour produced the sealed packet and handed them to him, and they were magnetised in the usual way. We saw that the seals affixed by Mr. Bell were intact during the time Mr. Hope handled the packet. Mr. Donaldson then took charge of the packet, and he and Mr. Hope proceeded to the darkroom to load the slides. Mr. Donaldson alone handled the plates from beginning to end. Four plates were exposed, for the first of which we three were sitters, Mr. Hope lifting the cap. Each of us subsequently sat alone."

Conan Doyle in his book reports:

---

6. This has also occurred, a few years ago.. A medium clairvoyanantly 'saw' a young man she did not recognise until the following day when she saw a photograph of him, aged 30, in a lecture I was giving on the Minnie Harrison Mediumship. It was of course Tom Harrison. It was just one week after his passing, aged 92. The evidence she relayed was totally accurate.. (See *Harrison Connections* by Ann Harrison SNPPBooks, 2014)

"Each word is on its own little patch of ectoplasm, or upon its own pad of cotton-wool, if the critics prefer it, though it would puzzle them, I think, to reproduce the effect which is given in fig.3. (Psychic letter) the plate alongside (fig.4) (Physical letter) shows a reproduction of an actual note of Crawford's which will enable the reader to judge the extreme similarity of the script."

Left: A facsimile of the psychograph received in Crewe on July 30th 1922 from Dr. Crawford.

Below: A copy of his handwriting in a letter to Mr. Oaten for comparison.

* * * * *

Throughout the months of controversy with the S.P.R. Sir Arthur Conan Doyle had thrown his efforts into defending William Hope and the Crewe Circle against this challenge of fraud and had called for support. One of those who rallied to the defence was Mr. Cowell Pugh in Middlesbrough of whom you read in Chapter 11. This is his letter:

"It is a number of years since I first sat with the Crewe Circle, and I have sat with them quite a dozen times since. And on each occasion, I have received convincing proof of the genuineness of their phenomena. I have beside me quite a collection of photographs taken by them, and each photo has a message of its own; some contain extras of friends who have passed on, and others contain messages from interested friends beyond the grave. The extras on practically all my photos have been recognised by relatives and friends.

I enclose a copy of one of these with two extras which have been readily recognised by all my friends as my father and mother, both of whom had passed on before I met the Crewe Circle.

I also enclose copies of original photos for comparison.[7]

My opportunities for testing the genuineness of the Crewe Circle's work have been unique because they have taken over a hundred photos in my house in Middlesbrough. When they have spent a few days here they have lived with us. My wife and I made all the arrangements for their visit and entertained them during their stay. Applications for sittings were made to us and we fixed them up.

In the vast majority of cases the Crewe Circle had never seen the sitters till they arrived at their appointed times. In many cases they never saw them again. Yet their success has been phenomenal. Many have received photos with extras which they recognised at sight. Others have taken them home and had them recognised by friends or other members of their families.

Mr & Mrs Cowell Pugh with the "extras" of his parents as submitted to Sir Arthur Conan Doyle.

The Circle brought no plates with them. Each sitter provided his or her own. My sitting-room was the studio. My bathroom was the developing room. Unused plates were left behind when the Circle went away, and my lad, who has a camera, has been supplied with a stock of plates for use amongst his friends.

To those of us who know the members of the circle so well, some of the statements appearing in the Press have been very amusing. The idea of Mr. Hope beating the conjurers at their own game is too ridiculous for words. Expert photographers who have had experience of Mr. Hope's methods must also have been greatly amused.

Then there is the question of motive. Let me state that the Crewe Circle have never had one penny piece out of their various visits to Middlesboro'. We charged sufficient from each sitter to pay railway expenses only, nothing more. We paid for the railway tickets, that was all. Where on earth was the incentive for these people to leave their homes to come here to deceive us? One's sense of humour must have been neglected if they cannot see that the whole of the charges are too funny for words.

---

7. The photograph mentioned in the text was among the photos Tom had inherited but unfortunately, not the life photos Mr. Pugh mentions as comparisons.

THAT THE PHENOMENA ARE GENUINE I AM CONVINCED.

"What is behind the phenomena is another matter and does not enter into the present question.

"If the scientists care to continue to drag on behind plain common-sense people let them do so. I have scores of good friends who have had that experience which no scientist can take from them, and I prefer to accept their opinions, along with my own experience, rather than listen to those people whose one desire seems to be to bolster up preconceived ideas.

The world would be better for some more people as honest as are the members of the Crewe Circle."

(Signed) William Cowell Pugh
61, St. Paul's Road,
Middlesbrough

* * * * *

In early September William Hope wrote this in *The Two Worlds,* in defence of their circle's mediumship:

"Concerning my experiment with Mr. Harry Price, there has been so much said on both sides that readers are at a loss as to what to believe. Every story has two sides and if *The Two Worlds* will favour me, I would like to place a few facts before its readers.

It must be remembered that Mr. Price, on his own confession, acted as a deceitful friend throughout the whole of the séance. He says that he 'as good as' saw me change the slide for another taken from my breast pocket. His plates had been marked with X-rays, and because these marks did not appear on the plates after development, he concluded the plates had been changed.[8]

It may be as well to show your readers some of the incidents arising from the unreliability of the many of the sitters one meets.

Not very long ago we gave a test to a gentleman under the impression that he would publish the results if successful. I even conducted the test in the lines he laid down. I even allowed him to tie my hands together and I did not enter the darkroom at any time during the test. We obtained a very good result. Upon leaving he shook hands with us all and said he was completely satisfied. We are still awaiting the publication of the facts, but shall probably have to whistle for them, as he had published a great deal against Spiritualism, and probably objects to eat his words.

A little while ago a lady commented upon Major Spencer's test in which he used his own camera, and suggested that Mrs. Buxton might have

8. Which of course they had – but not by him - at this stage not all the facts were known to Hope.)

tampered with the camera whilst the Major was in the dark-room. She conveniently avoids telling us how it would have been possible to have produced the results obtained by any form of tampering with the camera especially under the conditions the Major imposed.

One critic contemptuously said that our results were smudges and complained that some words in the written messages were mis-spelt. A little later he asked for a sitting, and I simply asked him why he did not get the sitting before finding fault with our work. I have his reply before me, saying he was not finding fault with our work, but with that of our friends, (meaning I suppose the spirits). This is a prominent S.P.R. man.

I want to ask your readers, can they blame any medium for refusing to sit with such people, and so put himself to the inconvenience of giving them tests? These folk want psychic phenomena delivered in a motor car and at present it can only be delivered in a wheelbarrow, and vey imperfectly at that. I am an ordinary working man, and I think the straightforward method for Mr. Price if he thought I had changed the slides would have been to have charged me with it there and then when I could have let him examine my pocket and speedily undeceived him. Instead of that he went away in the garb of friendship, and we never heard a word of the case for nearly four months afterwards. Perhaps he hoped I had forgotten the case."

Wm. Hope."

In the same week Harry Price had this published in *Light*:

"The Editor having kindly given me the opportunity of recording my impressions of the examination of the Hope Case, which has been conducted by *Light*, I will gladly avail myself of this offer. The investigation I consider quite fair and impartial, though there are a number of points that require elucidating. The case itself has not been affected one iota by the critical examination or the various criticisms which have been levelled against methods employed to detect the fraud. The case is still "cast iron"; it is still "watertight". And nothing will ever upset the evidence because it is the truth. Consciously or unconsciously William Hope changed my plates on the morning of February 24th. ....

I do not know why this particular Hope case has caused such a commotion. Hope has been exposed before. If my readers will turn to their files of *Light* for 1909 they will read of an experiment with Hope conducted by Sir Oliver Lodge and which proved eminently unsatisfactory. The case is worth reading in full. Again, there is the case of the ex-Indian missionary who had a sitting at Crewe...[9]

---

9. see Rev. Tweedale's letter p209.

I should not be at all surprised to find that the test committee investigating Hope declare that he has the power to produce some type of "extra" supernormally. But I should be astonished to hear that "extras" as good as mine with drapery reaching the full length of the plate can be obtained under scientific test conditions."

In response to statements made by Price in the above letter Fred Barlow wrote:

"Mr. Price admits that Mr. Hope may have the power to produce some type of extra supernormally, but he does not think that such productions would be as good as the one he got. This is amusing! If Mr. Hope can (as I am quite convinced he can) act as a medium for the production of supernormal pictures, why should they not be as good or better, than the one secured by Mr. Price, which I consider a genuine result? ...

When experimenting at Crewe and elsewhere I have invariably marked the plates as I took them from the packet. Sometimes I have loaded my slides beforehand at home with marked plates. Either method is an adequate check on substitution. A little common-sense and the adoption of test conditions are sufficient safeguards. In fact, the best safeguard against unconscious deception is to prevent it from taking place. Mr. Price encouraged it and so got what he asked for...

Hope has been a medium for many years. There in not a single instance, in the whole of his career where he has been detected in deliberate fraud. There are thousands of definite positive instances of his genuineness. All sense of proportion is lost—the 999 genuine cases are overlooked and attention is concentrated on the one doubtful case. The very people who should appreciate the difficulties of mediumship are the first to bend the big drum and cry "Fraud!". Assuming fraud had been definitely proved, the next step should have been to verify whether it was deliberate or unconscious. Instead of careful investigation we are offered haphazard conjectures, and even Mrs. Buxton, against whom there is not the least shadow of a case, is subjected to absurd innuendoes. People claiming to be scientific seem to approach these intricate psychological phenomena in a biased and most unscientific manner, and those who have had the least experience are the most dogmatic in their assertions."—Yours etc.,

Fred Barlow.
"Bryntirion,"
105, Springfield-road,
Moseley, Birmingham.

September 9th, 1922.

* * * * *

In reply to the reference by Mr. Price to the "ex-indian missionary" Rev. Charles Tweedale wrote:

To the Editor of *Light.*

"Sir,—I have known the gentleman described as an ex-Indian missionary for some forty-years. He became a missionary and went out to India, and I lost sight of him for a long time. A few years ago I was surprised to receive a visit from him, and he informed me that he was interested in psychic phenomena, especially psychic photography. He afterwards called on me several times, and we had long talks together. He told me that he was anxious to prove the truth of survival, but I found him full of philosophical arguments, and objections which had no direct bearing on the case.

I soon came to the conclusion that he was far more concerned in endeavouring to refute the modern evidence for survival than he was to prove it, and that his interest did not present a *bona fide* attempt to utilise and assimilate the modern evidence, and this impression was strengthened by his visit. He told me of his experience with Hope, and informed me that although he himself did not recognise any of the extras, yet one of the party did recognise one of the forms as that of a deceased relative or friend. This important point does not transpire in the published account.

I asked him whether he would be satisfied if he had evidence of the obtaining of recognised pictures under good evidential conditions, and he said, "Yes." I then showed him three recognised cases: first that of my father-in-law; of whom there is no photo similar in detail in existence; another of a little girl of whom there was never a photo or drawing made during her mortal life, and another splendid evidential one of a young soldier killed in the war, obtained by his mother, who entered and left Hope's studio without giving her name, and was entirely unknown to him. He started somewhat on seeing them, as though they were unwelcome testimony, but, quickly recovering, he calmly laid the three psychic and the two comparison photos aside in a little heap, saying, "Well! that's that!" There was no acknowledgment of the evidence which a few minutes before he had said would satisfy him.

This still further confirmed the very strong impression conveyed by his previous conversation and general attitude that he was more concerned in attempting to disprove the modern evidence than to utilise it as evidence for survival; and this desire to disprove is still more apparent in the furnishing of the story as evidence against Hope. He seemed to think that the story of his own failure (though he acknowledged that one of the party obtained a recognised picture) discounted all previous successes, many of them obtained under "conditions rendering all fraud or trickery impossible."

Yours, etc., Charles L. Tweedale.
Weston Vicarage,

September 22nd, 1922. Otley, Yorkshire.

In defence of the Crewe Circle, James Coates wrote of a sitting he and Walter Jones, J.P had had at Crewe in March 1921.

"This circle has been the subject of criticism on the one hand and on the other has given undoubted comfort through its mediums to thousands in Great Britain and Ireland during the last twenty years.

Mr. William Hope has been tested more than any other medium photographer in this country— nay, more, he has willingly submitted to be tested by expert photographers: The late Mr. Walker of Buxton, Major Spencer, Dr Lindsay Johnson F.R.P.S. of South Africa, the late Sir William Crookes F.R.S., OM., a leading official of Kodak Ltd. Mr. Fred Barlow, of Birmingham (an ingrained sceptic and investigator), Mr. J.P. Skelton of Belfast and by the writer.

Mr. Hope has been well tested, but as a psychic he cannot command the phenomena—the appearance of extra faces and figures—that come on the plates, and he is not always in good form for the work. Of his co-worker Mrs. Buxton nothing but good can be said about her, and both extend freely to investigators their services within the limits of physical strength and possibilities.

In my opinion the crux of psychic photography is not diamond marked plates, the investigator's camera, or the elimination of the medium photographer's work etc., but a supernormally produced picture of a departed person of whom the psychic did not or could not know. I could give many instances of this veridical proof, meanwhile I refrain.

Another phase is the production of a picture presenting features—such as those prior to death—which the medium photographer could not know, although he might have seen the original in life, or a photograph representing the original of the "extra" taken in the fullness of health.

With the foregoing I can aver that William Hope can get supernormal photographs of the departed, not smudges but clearly defined pictures for recognition by those who knew the originals in life.

Receiving an invitation to attend a conference of various Lancashire Societies in Burnley on Good Friday, 1921, I left London for that purpose, breaking the journey with Walter Jones, Esq. J.P. at the Uplands. Mr. Jones proposed to join me, and we motored to Crewe on Thursday, March 24th, where we might have a sitting. We purchased a packet of medium rapid quarter plates from Mr. Selleck, High Street Stourbridge. Ours was a surprise visit, no intimation that we were coming for a sitting having been sent to the Crewe Circle.

Mr. Jones, entering the darkroom, opened the packet, selected two plates, marked them and put the slide into his pocket. Meanwhile I examined the camera in the "lean-to", which passed for the studio. Mr. Jones posed, handing me the slide: That slide was put into the camera. Mr. Hope timed the exposure. The slide was closed and removed, and passed to me by Mr. Jones. I was then posed. The procedure was followed on the refilling of the slide, and we sat again. I need not go into the details further.

On the marked plate exposed on Mr. Jones was a high light on the plate representing a man, which has not up to the present been recognised. On one exposed on me there was the figure of a woman. On the remaining two plates developed, only Mr. Jones and myself, no extras. I may mention that Mr. Jones developed the four plates, which Mr. Hope did not handle till they were washed.

On my plate the extra or picture of a woman proved to be a clearly defined representation of the late Mrs. Coates, and was easily recognised by those who knew my dear wife in life. Fortunately, Mr. Jones was able to recognise this photograph—as different to the original as water is to wine, or illness to health, but thoroughly evidential. I am not out to convince anyone, I merely state the facts.

Walter Jones Esq., J.P., is in full agreement with the foregoing in so far as it deals with our mutual experience in Crewe on March 24th 1921."

Walter Jones did not publish his notes on that sitting for another ten months (and more than two years after the original sitting) when the identity of the "extra" of the young man was confirmed during a visit by a friend from overseas. (see Chpt 18)

* * * * *

On March 17, 1923, two sisters, one of whom holds a position of responsibility in her own city, visited the College in Holland Park for their first sitting with the Crew Circle.

One of them understood photographic processes and her report shows that the experiment was carried out with care.

They used plates marked for the College by the Imperial Dry Plate Co., and were given an unopened sealed packet before they went to the studio. Bringing "a kindly spirit of goodwill to the occasion, harmony prevailed,"[10] throughout the sitting.

Having received prints of their sitting in early April they wrote:

"You will be interested to know that we have recognized the 'extra' on the photograph as an aunt who passed over quite thirty years ago. An old photograph of her and the position and expression of the face seems to us almost identical with the face on the 'extra'."

10. Quote from Mrs. McKenzie's report *Psychic Science* July 1923 p 143 'Recognized Psychic Photography'.

They sent a copy of their aunt's 'in life' picture for comparison. In sending this the sitter wrote: "It was the strong family likeness in the 'extra' that made my sister feel we ought to know her and sent us to look among the old photographs. At the séance previous to the exposure, Mr. Hope gave us clairvoyantly a very correct description of our father, and this person (the 'extra') is his sister. It is the first time she has manifested to us in any way."

It will be noticed that this is what is called a "moving" result where the "extra" attempts to focus several times before success is achieved. Mrs McKenzie said she thought that the sisters hoped that their father might appear, so that thought does not appear to have influenced the result in the least.

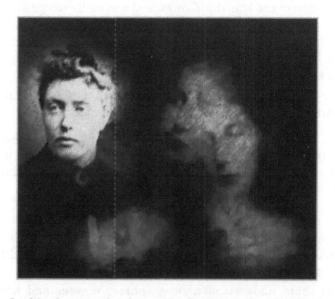

In this photograph taken at the British College in March 1923 the "extra" has made several attempts to show herself. The sitters are not visible but a life-time image of their aunt is inserted top left for comparison.

Remarkable Evidence – Delayed Identification

The three cases of recognised psychic extras in this chapter needed verification involving time and correspondence with family across the world. All show the determination of those who have "gone before" to link with their family and friends and prove the reality of this method of photographic communication.

In *The Two Worlds*, August 31st 1923, under the heading "Photographic Extras." Walter Jones, J.P. writes:

"On March 24th, 1921, Mr. James Coates and I went to Mr. Hope at Crewe to sit for our photographs. No prior engagement of our visit having been made, we were fortunate to find him at home.

We purchased a packet of plates in Stourbridge these were unpacked, marked, put into the camera and developed in the darkroom by the writer, Mr. Hope being present but taking no part in the work.

The photo of Mr. Coates has clear and distinct extra of his wife, Mrs. Jessie Coates,

The plate on which my photo was taken had a perfectly clear extra of a young man with a moustache, but my relatives and I failed to recognise who it was.

Mr Walter Jones and the as then unrecognised "extra".

Two years later, April 10th 1923, my psychic friend, Mrs. Wilson, who had just returned from South Africa, came to stay with us for a short time, and when I submitted the photo and asked if she recognised the extra, she replied 'Yes it is your nephew, Walter Jones of Christchurch, New Zealand, he passed away in 1908 before I went to New Zealand. I never saw him in the flesh, nor have I seen his photograph, but I frequently saw him clairvoyantly when talking to his mother during my stay in Christchurch.'

My brother, Edward, born November 16th 1841, married and left for New Zealand in 1863, passed to the higher life

November 7th 1912. They had ten children all born in Christchurch, of whom Walter Albert (named after me) was the sixth, born April 7th 1872. Translated in 1908, age 36. My brother being engrossed in public work, and a poor correspondent, our correspondence was very limited, and I have never seen or written to any of these nephews until April last when I sent the photo to the youngest, Charles Ernest (born November 1st, 1879), who lives near Christchurch, and asked his opinion.

On Monday, July 30th, 1923, I received a reply as follows: 'I have a photo of my brother Walter and his wife in my bedroom, so that his likeness should be impressed on my mind. I recognise the forehead and hair and the general outline of his face but to make assurance doubly sure I sent your photo to his wife, and now quote her own words: 'It seemed rather strange you should send that photo, I have been thinking of Walter most of the afternoon. I was feeling a bit off-colour, that is when I miss him most. Yes, there is a likeness, not so much when looking straight at it, but hold the picture two feet to your right, and it is very clear.' "

* * * * *

In November 1922 a letter arrived from America in defence of the Crewe Circle.

To the Editor, 'Remarkable Evidence'

"Sir, — May I enter into the defence of Mr. Hope and Mrs. Buxton? I am a long way from the scene of the action and have not until lately had the copies of *Light* dealing with the subject.

An account of David's appearance to an officer friend at the time of his death appeared in the S.P.R. Journal for July '19. In the following November he asked us to go to Crewe and get his psychic photo taken. He said, "Ask Raymond's father," which we did, we ourselves having no idea of who there might be at Crewe who could do such things.

Mr. Hope rather deterred us from sitting, as we had far to go, but on January 13th, 1920, on our way from Scotland, we visited Crewe without arrangement, saw Mr. Hope that evening and sat at eleven the next day in the broad sunlight. We brought our plates from Edinburgh unopened, took part in the religious meeting; David's father entered the dark room with Mr. Hope, took out the two centre plates from the packet which had been hitherto unopened, signed them, and placed them in the carrier. Mr. Hope put the carrier in the camera. Mr. McConnel developed, and the face of our son came out, close beside my own, but larger, and leaning in a peculiar position towards me. The form of the face was unmistakably that of David.

On February 11th, before we saw the prints, David, at a séance with Mrs. Osbourne Leonard told us that it was not what he wanted, but that there was something there which he would show us that he was there. We went home, and the prints had arrived during our absence. We were disappointed; we expected to see a glorified form of David's face but it was the face of a boy. The flying helmet and goggles of the Air Service were on the head, and the wounds which he obtained at death on the face. His father had not seen this, but I who had seen him after death distinctly recognised the marks; it would have been impossible to have done otherwise.

It was suggested that certain childish memories had passed through him as he stood beside me, which might account for the child face. I asked Mrs. Sidgwick if she could send to Mrs. Leonard an investigator to get from David what the memories were. She could send none, but suggested Sir Oliver Lodge's secretary, who kindly went. She did not know the nature of the photograph, nor any family history of place or circumstance. David gave her memories of his Australian life, claimed the photograph, and said the upper lip spoiled it, which it did—the upper lip was cut in the accident.

David said also of this photograph that his little dog was in the picture, and his hand on my shoulder, and that his grandfather—my father—and another man unknown to him were also there. These all were found.

I had a picture of him and his little dog taken just before we left Australia at the age of eleven. There was only one copy of this picture, and it never left my possession, in England. In Australia his old nurse had another copy, and the negative was also left there with the photographer; also the picture of my father had no fellow copy in England. It is like a miniature which I possess, which was copied, but the negative is in Australia.

Sir George Beilby arranged with us to take a test photo with Mr. Hope and Mrs. Buxton. The date was fixed, and the Crewe Circle came to our house, but, unfortunately, Sir George Beilby was that day called away to Scotland by telegram, and we had to have the sitting without him.

We prepared our own darkroom and my husband acted as before, Mr. Hope never touching the plates, which were obtained in Petersfield and were unopened until just before they were placed in the slide. The development took place under Mr. McConnel's hands. One picture was taken in our drawing room at 9pm, without a previous sitting, by flashlight. Mr. Hope said the atmosphere was very psychic, he had felt his arm grasped, and a tortoise-shell pin had been taken from my hair and flung on the floor. There were two plates; David's face appeared on the second, much larger than ours and with a great deal of ectoplasm. This face of his was like a brother of mine, whom I have always thought him to be like, but in which opinion others are not agreed. There is no photograph of this brother in England other than a small one of him in my own room. The face of David is this time that of a man, and there are also in the folds of the ectoplasm faces of his grandfather on his father's side and of a young bishop in a mitre. David says there are three faces on this photo beside his own but we have not been able to find the third face.

The following day at 11 o'clock we sat with the Crewe Circle again and had the usual religious meeting. The result of this sitting was most extraordinary. I had concentrated for a girl to come who had been working "over the border" with David. Her face did not appear, but her brother's head came on my hand. He is not dead, nor had I ever seen him nor a picture of him, but she was devoted to him, and this was evidently a thought form of her mind.

Mr. Hope and Mrs. Buxton on the same day took photos at David's grave and in our garden. Nothing came upon the plates at the grave, but there were two photos taken in the garden, in one of which my husband and I changed places with Mrs. Buxton and her little boy, and on both of these photos there appear two fairies. The fairies appear as Titania and Oberon. There had been a discussion as to whether the girl friend passed over had ever acted. David represented her as doing so. This photo was evidently a confirmation of his statement, as on inquiry, we afterwards found that she had taken the part of Titania in a play at school, which was known to David.

It would have been quite impossible for the Crewe Circle to have obtained the results which we have of the survival of David, in any way which could have been other than truly psychic.

Mr. Hope's simplicity and his simple methods and, may I say, his want of time and of good material lay him open to criticism, because much better results might be obtained by the use of scientific methods at the disposal of most photographers. But at the same time the adverse conditions show his sincerity. Some day we hope ourselves fully to demonstrate to the public the wonderful results which we have had with the Crewe Circle."

Yours etc.   May McConnel

Box 115, Santa Cruz Ave,
Mento Park ,   California.

* * * * *

A further intriguing puzzle case involving Miss Scatcherd and the Crewe Circle, began in October 1922. It was a year later that the puzzle was solved and published in *Psychic Science* in April 1924.

First experiment at Crewe

"The story goes back to October 3, 1922, when Miss F.R. Scatcherd, one of the oldest living friends of the Crewe Circle, journeying south from Liverpool, made a stop at Crewe for the purpose of visiting Mr. Hope and Mrs. Buxton in order to have an experiment. She had with her a packet of the College-marked plates containing four plates, and inviting some of the inmates of the house to sit with her, she carried through the whole experiment herself, carefully marking plates and developing with her own hands. Two plates were exposed with one result (see Fig 1).

Miss Scatcherd retained the other two plates in the box, and later in the day another experiment was attempted, with the idea of getting a written message upon one of the remaining plates. The box with these two was held by Miss Scatcherd, Mrs. Buxton and Mr. Hope between their hands, and then taken to the darkroom by Miss Scatcherd; the plates were signed and developed immediately without any exposure. One result was obtained, fairly clear on one print, but does not reproduce well, in which the same face as appears in Fig. 1 had impressed the plate several times with more or less clearness, showing connecting luminous bands.

Fig 1. At Crewe with Top: Mrs. Buxton's daughter & Mrs. Buxton. Front: Mrs Buxton's sister & Miss Scatcherd.

Miss Scatcherd took the wet plates with her to London and had prints made, when it was seen that the same face appeared in both, and was not recognised by anyone present on the occasion."

Second Experiment in London at a Private House

On Sunday. October 15, 1922, the Crew Circle paid one of their periodical visits to the College. The Price-Hope controversy was at its height, and had seriously affected the psychic forces of both Mr. Hope and Mrs. Buxton. Miss Scatcherd invited them to tea and finding some old friends wanted a sitting, the meeting place was changed from her abode to their house.

The conditions were not very good as one of the sitters was rather unwell, but with a box containing four College-marked plates, intact from the Imperial Plate Co, as before, two exposures were made; a temporary background being rigged up by using a cloak of one of the sitters.

At the first exposure of two plates on four sitters, the result obtained was a head repeated several times with a luminous effect between. Two more plates were marked and exposed upon one sitter, and a similar effect, but clearer, resulted (see Fig 2)

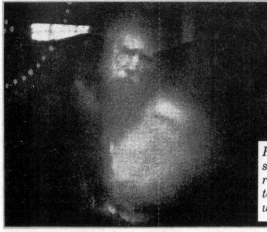

Fig 2. In London, on second set of plates, a head repeated several times, the top one being clearest and was the same as at Crewe.

The plates were taken possession of by Miss Scatcherd, and when printed the same face was found on both, but, to the great disappointment of all the sitters was not recognised. The names of the sitters were not given, but they are well-known public people.

Third Experiment at the College

Miss Scatcherd writes "In view of the controversy regarding psychic photography I had about December, 1922, invited a well-known photographic expert, who had been interested in this matter for some years, having had previous experiences, to take an experiment with the Crewe Circle at the College.

This was accepted, and at the Crewe Circle College visit on January 25, 1923, he came bringing with him another expert to check results. They brought their plates but used Mr. Hope's camera, after making the most careful examination of this and of the dark slides. I usually find that experienced photographers are men of genial temperament, with whom Mr. Hope is at once at home, while the scientific investigator, either by a probably unconscious 'high brow' attitude, or by his hidden thought that he means to find out where the fraud is, makes the psychic feel ill at case, with a corresponding difference in result.

Carrying out the whole experiment with the greatest care one result, a clear single head, was obtained, and the wet plate was taken away by the sitters. A print was sent to me the following day (see Fig. 3). with the information that it was clearly recognised by the chief sitter (to whom the experiment had had been offered) as a friend of thirty years standing; who, in his life time had been associated with a well-known photographic firm, and who had passed over the previous August.

Many others in the firm recognised it as an excellent likeness of Mr. E. Schumann; but to prove the matter thoroughly, a print was sent abroad to the son of the deceased, who is also engaged in photographic work.

After a considerable interval, as some difficulty was found in tracing him, the following clear reply was received:

Fig 3. At the British College, Jan.1923. The "extra" was recognised by a sitter who had been his friend for 30 years.

Left for comparison is an ordinary photograph of Mr. E. Schumann.

This was taken a number of years before his decease, and is evidently a studio portrait, with all characteristic lines removed from the face, and before he was attacked by illness.

Fig 4. Mr E. Schumann

"September 24, 1923.

Dear Mr. ——

"Like a good many more, my dear Dad included, I have never had much faith in so-called 'Spirit Photographs', my belief being that they were faked. The photograph you sent me however, does not give me that impression. It is undoubtedly a photograph of my dear Dad. I know his dear old face too well to be mistaken. How his face came into the picture I don't pretend to know, but if it is indeed a genuine spirit photograph, then I should like to know a little more about the subject. I showed the picture to everyone here who knew my dad, and they all agreed it was his picture. . . .

"Schumann"

An interesting fact was given by the sitter, that the gentleman in question had to go abroad for his health two years before his decease. He spent his last evening with the sitter, saying in parting, "Well, I don't believe in your 'spirits' but if anything happens to me, I will do my best to come back to you if it is at all possible."

He was abroad two years and returned to England, dying immediately on his arrival in August, 1922.

If we assume that the sitter and the son, and many others who knew the deceased gentleman, are right in recognising the extra as a portrait of Mr. Schumann, we see that in fulfilment of his promise to his friend he made two attempts to "get through" within two months of his passing over, two other attempts a fortnight later, and a third effort three months later—producing the latter result in the presence of his own particular friend to whom the promise of return had been made."

The Editor added:

"It was some time after the January experiment that the sitter met Miss Scatcherd again, and showing her the result, she recognised the face as the same which had appeared on two separate occasions and on four different plates, when she was present, at previous experiments. On comparison they were found to be the same; the final one being the clearest and steadiest of all.

Miss Scatcherd had for some months had a desire to meet the photographic expert and whether this and her close association with the Crewe Circle had in any way made it possible for the first and second manifestation we cannot positively verify, but the use of such delicate links of association by those who wish to manifest is well known in other cases.

The whole story is a remarkable one. Those who took part in the experiments knew the right conditions to give, and knew what precautions to take, while not hampering the mediums with destructive thought forces; and this, combined with the determination of the one who had passed over to make himself known to his old friend in a way which could not be called a thought-form in the first two cases at any rate made such a result possible.

From the photographic point of view, that it happened to a photographer, and that the deceased was a photographer, and recognized by many in the photographic world, is interesting, but it is more deeply interesting to the psychic student who, looking all-round the facts, sees in it a vindication of the belief that it is a manifestation of intelligence, and that intelligence, of one who before his passing out had made a definite promise, which he found an opportunity to fulfil in a conclusive manner."

* * * * *

A Family Affair

All the focus throughout these pages has been on 'Billy' Hope, but without the support and dedication of the rest of the Crewe Circle none of this might have happened, in particular that of Mr. and Mrs. Buxton whose home was used for all the sittings and in particular Mrs Buxton who travelled with him throughout the country.

Dora's development had proceeded along with Hope's and her clairvoyance and psychic energy were invaluable during their work, particularly her ability to receive and transmit psychic impressions on to previously unopened and unexposed plates.

Mrs Dora Buxton

Her contribution to the work of the Crewe Circle was acknowledged by the inclusion in 1924 in *Psychic Science* of this portrait taken by an established London photographer, at the request of Mrs Barbara McKenzie for their major article on psychic photography.

In *100 Years of Spirit Photography* Tom Patterson writes that the Buxton's youngest son, Percy Buxton told him: "My mother was not a spirit photographer in her own right, but I can say without hesitation, that she was the finest physical medium I have ever seen and at one time she had, to decide whether to remain a practicing physical medium, or continue her partnership with Hope in the field of spirit photography. My mother chose to remain with Hope and carry on in this good work."

Arthur Buxton married Dora in 1894 and the following year their daughter Ada was born. Described as a wood turner, he moved the family to Crewe around the turn of the century where their son Arthur was born, followed shortly afterwards by a second son Leslie. At this point they moved from Oakley Street (where the Hopes were to live) to Market Street, a short distance away. Their youngest son Percival was born in 1909, and would be the 6 month-old baby referred to by Miss Scatcherd in the 'zigzag' psychograph experiment with Professor Henslow in Chapter 6.

In the census for 1921 Mr Buxton is described as an Employer at the Public Saw Mills and two of his sons are working for him, the younger, Leslie, as a carter — so it is presumably he who had a close attachment to Tommy, the pony, in the photo shown later.

Over the twenty plus years of the Crewe Circle very few photos of the Buxton family made it into the public view, however, I have found these following four occasions.

This first one was published by Mrs. Sylvia Barbanell in her book *When your Animal Dies*.

The terrier, Floss, makes her return. Sitters: Mrs Buxton (rt.) with two of her children and her two sisters.

"Some members of Mrs. Buxton's family met one day for the express purpose of having a psychic photograph taken by Mr. Hope. Mrs. Buxton's father had recently passed on. They hoped that he would succeed in showing himself as an "extra" if they sat in a group.

The medium took the photograph, but instead of the expected relative there appeared on the plate an "extra" of a terrier. The delight of Mrs. Buxton in recognising her "dead" pet Floss somewhat made up for the disappointment of the absence of her father's picture.

A curious thing about the spirit form of the dog is that it appears on the lap of Mrs. Buxton's sister Amy.

Amy, unfortunately, was unable to control her antipathy towards animals. No doubt for a reason beyond her own will, she could not bear to be in the room with them. In consequence whenever she paid Mrs. Buxton a visit, poor Floss had to be removed to another part of the house.

I do not know why Floss appeared on Amy's lap in the photograph. Perhaps the terrier wanted to impress on the sitter that she bore her no ill will for the number of times she caused Floss to be removed from the living-room when she visited the Buxtons' house! At any rate, the psychic picture, which is reproduced in this book, is a clear and distinct likeness of the terrier."

They did eventually get a psychic picture of the father / grandfather as seen in this next one used in Conan Doyle's book of 1922, and he was looking much happy than he had ever done when photographed in life. (compare with the inset in life), *(shown opposite)*.

Early in July 1924 the Buxtons—father, mother and son made a visit, together with Mr. Hope, to Hulham House, a "Retreat" on the south coast of England, – ostensibly a family holiday – but it was a working one. The family had time for relaxation though and used the centre's Gypsy caravan to take a trip to the seashore. There Hope took a family photo of the Buxtons arranged on the steps – not intending it to be a psychic photo but the following *(below)* was the result.

Mrs. Buxton is almost hidden by the cloud of energy which resolves itself into the head of a pony, and in the doorway of the caravan by the pony's head is the face of a young man, the Buxton's middle son, Leslie, who had passed away in the previous year. He had been very attached to the pony, Tommy, who had died some years earlier.

If you examine Mr. Buxton's waistcoat you will see another face. Mr. Buxton's brother had also died that year, and this is presumed to be him. A real family holiday.

In the grounds of this peaceful retreat was a small 'summer house', newly erected for private meditation and named "The Dawn" (*shown right*).

It was suggested that Hope might take some photographs in it and a resident at the Retreat challenged him to use his roll film camera (an Ensignette, No2) which had lain in his case unused for some months. It had in it a new film and having exposed the first, to make sure it was working, he wound on to the second and handed it to Hope. As far as we know this was the first time Hope had used a roll film camera and a later letter from Mr Craven said that Hope was concerned that the steel case of the cameara would prevent the psychic rays from pentrating, he also had doubts about the efficacy of the roll film.[2]

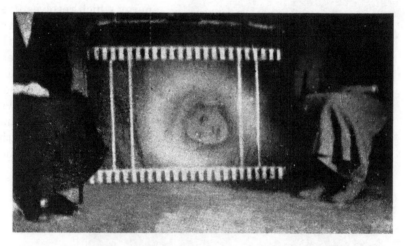

Image captured on 'roll-film' at Hulham House, Summer 1924

The result was a clear psychic extra *(shown above)* which, by those who knew her, bears a likeness to Mrs. Fair, the lady to whose memory the chapel was dedicated. The rest of the film was not used. Mr. Craven, the owner of the camera assisted Hope in removing the film and developing it and later wrote this letter confirming the experiment.

---

2. *Psychic Science:* 'Notes by the Way', July 1933

"To Mr. Hope, of Crewe"   Hulham House,
                                           July 13th, 1924.

"I have pleasure in stating that the camera used was charged in August last and has been lying in my trunk since then. As you noticed when I handed it to you, the Fig. 1 showed at the back; and in showing you how to work the time lever I spoiled No. 1 on the film, consequently the photo taken in "The Dawn" was No. 2.

"I opened the camera myself, and assisted you in the development of the film, and witnessed all that took place."

                                           "(Signed) J. A. Craven."[3]

In F.W. Warrick's book, *Experiments in Psychics,* we find one other impromptu psychic event for the Buxtons. This time it occurred at a family wedding. Taken only as a souvenir of the event they were surprised to find an "extra" in front of Mr. and Mrs. Buxton. It was their son again.

Mr. Buxton had been a powerful influence on the energy during the circle's development but the need to provide for his family prevented him travelling with them all the time. With their combined psychic power it is no wonder that their son could show himself.

The Buxtons' Wedding party with their son showing up from spirit – top left, next to his father.

3. *Psychic Science:* 'Psychic Photograph on a roll film', October 1924 .

Dr. Geley Returns to keep Appointment

Dr. Gustave Geley gave up great popularity and excellent prospects by not returning to his medical practice at Annecy following his military duties in the First World War. Instead, he took on the directorship of the International Metapsychic Institute in Paris.

Stanley de Brath in writing of him says:

"He was a friend that a man can trust in all the contingencies of life — warm-hearted, sincere, cautious in coming to conclusions, and as fearless as he was courteous....

He had faculties that far transcend the powers of the normal senses. He has thus thrown a clear light on many otherwise inexplicable phenomena of clairvoyance, healing, telepathy, and ectoplasmic creations, and has demonstrated quite conclusively that thought is not a mere secretion of the brain—a notion that makes survival a contradiction in terms. He stated at the recent Metapsychic Congress at Warsaw that these faculties are very strong indirect evidence for survival of bodily death. This is the main line of Geley's thought, as given in his book *From the Unconscious to the Conscious*. As an evolutionist he fixes his attention on consciousness rather than on the organic mechanism and complexity of structure by which consciousness is seen to increase from the lowest to the highest forms of terrestrial life."[1]

For the return from that conference in Warsaw Dr. Gustave Geley took the offer of a lift in a private airplane back to Paris. Both Geley and the pilot died when the airplane crashed on July 15th.

He had been due to join Mr. De Brath at the British College of Psychic Science for a sitting with the Crewe Circle on July 24th. Mr. De Brath was at Hulham House near Exmouth in July 1924 when he heard of the sudden death of his friend.

---

1. *Psychic Science,* October 1924 pps 173-77 'Dr. Gustave Geley and His Work' .

De Brath recorded the following:

"A quite unmistakable likeness of our distinguished friend was obtained at an experiment at the British College of Psychic Science on July 24th. This experiment was conducted by Mrs. McKenzie, Miss Scatcherd and Mr. De Brath, by the aid of Mr. Hope and Mrs. Buxton, of Crewe. The experiment and the circumstances that led to it are detailed below.

"The sad news [of his death] was received by me at Exmouth on July 17th. Having an engagement at Hulham House Nursing Home on the same day, I met Miss Harvey (one of the nurses in charge), who speaks under "control" of "Dr. Beale". After some general conversation lasting about twenty minutes, Miss Harvey, speaking as "Dr. Beale" said:

'I have met Dr. Geley, he cannot yet believe he has passed over, but he has friends who will help him. I think if you arrange for the photography next week, as was settled, he may be able to impress his photograph, as his mind was set on those experiments.'

I noted down these words at the time, took the signatures of Mrs. De Brath, Miss Storr and Miss Harvey, as well as my own, and passed the paper through the post without an envelope addressed to myself so as to have the postmark as proof of date.

Thereupon it was arranged between Mrs. McKenzie, the Hon. Secretary of the BCPS and myself that the date settled by Dr Geley for the experiment with Mr. Hope and Mrs. Buxton (Thursday July 24th at the College) should be kept with another medium on Dr Geley's behalf, but we obtained nothing. In the evening I made enquiries through a private automatist who knew nothing of the whole matter:

Q. – I have been to ------- and have got nothing; am rather disappointed. Can you tell me anything?

A. – All was ready and right but your poor friend cannot yet realise that he is here, and he is very distressed by the grief in his home and all his circumstances. We could not get a proper picture ...

Q. – That is sad. Now I want your advice. Mrs. McKenzie has offered me a sitting with Mr. Hope to-morrow at 11am. It would seem from the answer you give that it is useless. . . Shall I take my own camera (which might put Hope out) or shall I let him use his own?

A.– Do not introduce any innovation to-morrow; you go with my promise in mind, and we will do what conditions allow. By then Dr. Geley may be sensible of what has happened or be asleep. You see, dear, his arrival was so sudden and he was in good health.

Such communications as these are generally supressed for fear of being thought superstitious. I think that everything should be disclosed."

Certificate Of Procedure

On Friday July 24th, Mr. De Brath and Miss F.R. Scatcherd came to the College at 11am. Mrs. McKenzie provided one of the packets of four plates, specially marked and sealed for tests, by the Imperial Dry Plate Company, before being packed. This packet was left absolutely intact as it left the works.

Mr. De Brath took the unopened packet which was not for one moment out of his possession till opened by him as described below.

"The packet was laid on the table in the photographic studio, and the experimenters Mrs. McKenzie, Miss Scatcherd, Mr. De Brath, with Mr. Hope and Mrs. Buxton joined hands round it. After Hope's usual procedure of singing, and an invocation from Mrs. McKenzie asking for help for the sake of the grieving friends left behind, Mr. De Brath cut open the packet, taking care not to injure the seals, went with Mr. Hope into the dark room (continuous red light), and without allowing the packet out of his hands, signed each plate as he took it from the wrapper. He placed the first pair of signed plates one by one in the slide and initialled each again when in the slide. He then examined Mr. Hope's camera and lens minutely, retaining the slide himself, after which no one touched the camera till he had himself placed the slide in the camera back. No cloth was used to cover the camera, focussing having been done beforehand, and the slide remained in full view during the exposure, about twelve seconds. The plates were "Imperial Special Rapid" plates supplied by the Company.

After the exposure, Mr. De Brath took the slide into the dark room, opened it himself, and developed the plates together in the same tray. An "extra" appeared on the first plate of the batch. This "extra" was imperfect as a portrait and was accompanied by what seems to be an attempt at writing. The scratches that appeared on the print are not superficial or defects in manipulation but were photographic in the gelatine itself. The second plate was normal.

The second pair of plates was left in the box on a shelf in the dark room which was entered by no one; it has only one door opening into the studio. Mr. De Brath went in, took the second pair of plates from the wrapper, signed them as before and put them into the slide, initialling each as before. They were then treated exactly as the first pair except that Mr. Hope poured on the developer under Mr. De Brath's close supervision.

The third plate of the batch had a very good portrait of Dr. Geley in nearly the same position relative to the sitters as the former one, but slightly more inclined axially (Print no 3). The fourth plate showed no abnormality. All the negatives bear Mr. De Brath's signature and initials."

Certified correct Barbara Mckenzie.

Felicia R. Scatcherd.

Stanley De Brath.

Mrs McKenzie also commented:

"It is noteworthy that during the preliminary seance before exposure, Mrs. Buxton was much distressed in mind, complained of feelings of great fretfulness and impatience, and could barely continue the sitting. This condition seemed relieved after the five sitters had "magnetized" the sealed packet. She mentioned that her head seemed to be particularly affected."

The image of the "extra" is not clear in this reproduction but it evidently bore a clear similarity to the sitters who knew him.

"It is photographically interesting, and, as a matter of analysis very important, to note that both as to position and detail Print No.1 shows an imperfect attempt, improved in Print No. 3. Everyone who knows Dr. Geley can see the fidelity of the portrait.

This remarkable success should also be a complete vindication of Mr. Hope from the charges so cruelly brought against him not long ago. It is perfectly certain that at no time whatever, either before or during development did Mr. Hope or Mrs. Buxton have access to the plates in any way whatsoever."

Stanley De Brath, M.Inst.C.E.

July 25, 1924.

Dr Geley was not unfamiliar with the Crewe Circle as he had sat with them in 1919.

When writing of this earlier sitting, Mr. De Brath said:

"In November, 1919, Dr. Geley visited me in England expressly to experiment with Hope. We went to Crewe for that purpose taking with us two packets of quarter-plates, one panchromatic and one ordinary, bought in London. Once the packets were opened every precaution was used that the medium should not touch the plates in any way. The panchromatic plates were first used. At the first exposure a heavy cloud completely masked both sitters; in the second exposure it partly covered the faces; the third exposure (ordinary plate) showed a message, transparent on the negative, '*Bonjour vous êtes le bienvenu*' across both sitters—Dr Geley and myself—taken in the slide loaded by ourselves; the fourth, from the same slide, contained the portrait of the lady who in previous automatic writing had promised me her photograph " if possible." Mr Hope had certainly never seen this lady nor any photograph of her. Three of these photographs are reproduced in my book *Psychical Research, Science and religion* (p38). All the negatives are quite clear of any double exposure marks. They are also of such a nature, being far too large for any "Nehushtan"[2] device to have been imprinted on the plate, apart from my own certificate that the Medium never had the opportunity of using any such instrument."

The psychic "extra" obtained at Crewe by Mr. De Brath and Dr. Geley, November 1919

The writing below the photograph states:

"I certify that this photograph was taken by Wm. Hope, Nov 1919 on plates bought in London same day, opened by me and signed, not lost sight of during the whole process. Recognised by the lady's brother (non-spiritualist) and 3 intimate friends. She "died" Aug 1913. There's in no similar portrait extant."

S. De Brath. M.Inst C.E.

It was later recorded that – "...the very clear "extra" which appears between the sitters is recognized as a lady who was a professional colleague of Mr. and Mrs. De Brath for seventeen years. It is recognized by both in addition to the persons mentioned [in the caption], and appended certificate. Dr. Geley was much impressed by this result, and by the recognition to which Mr. De Brath bore witness." [3]

* * * * *

---

2. The Nehushtan device is a minute flashlight projector used to place fraudulent images on to photographic plates.
3. Cyril. Permutt *Photographing the Spirit World*, 1983

Two months later in September 1924, Mr. De Brath was back at the College. This time with Sir William Barrett. He writes:

"In September 1924, I prevailed on Sir William Barrett to meet Hope at the British College of Psychic Science and he kept Hope in conversation while I loaded the slides and [later] developed the plates. The result is a portrait of Letty Hyde, as she looked in her last illness. She died Nov 1st 1921. She was a parlour maid in our house, and her portrait was recognised by her father, mother and three brothers and sisters none of whom were Spiritualists. Letty was never photographed after she fell ill. Sir William was convinced by this experiment."

Sir William Barrett told the S.P.R. (see Proceedings xxxiv., for December 1924)[4] that this experiment had convinced him of the fact. He says with regard to the so-called 'spirit' photographs:

"'I have been extremely sceptical of their genuineness, until quite lately. Recently, however, experiments conducted by my friend Mr. De Brath – in one of which he kindly allowed me to take part – appear to afford indubitable evidence of supernormal photography. This conclusion confirms the opinion held by some expert and critical experimenters who have discussed their results with me.'"

Sir Wm. Barrett, Miss Scatcherd with Mr. De Brath
in a sitting at the British College Sept. '24

---

4. *This was the last paper Sir Wm. Barrett wrote for The S.P.R. before his passing in 1925.*

Sir William added: 'We shall never arrive at any knowledge of the conditions requisite for these and other marvellous psychic phenomena until hostile incredulity becomes no longer possible.' "

Writing in 1937 for *The Two Worlds* De Brath states:

"As this experiment came on top of many others, including one which gave me a portrait of a lady-partner with my wife and myself in our school (she died in August 1913), and after many evidential messages given week by week, which I have not detailed, I usually date my complete conviction of survival from September 1924."

* * * * *

In the same article Mr De Brath gives more detail about working with William Hope:[5]

"In October, 1924 I stayed for a week at Hulham House, Exmouth, during which time he visited the house. The proprietors had fitted up a small cycle-store about 8 ft. square as a dark-room, with sink and tap. There was no other furniture in the room, but three plain board shelves, the lowest being wide enough to be used as a table. It was exceptionally well lit through ruby glass covered by ruby fabric. Every movement could be clearly seen. In this friendly environment, Mr. Hope was at the top of his form and good humour.

He asked me to work with him, and I often loaded his slide for him, using the one and only slide that he had for his little wooden camera. I verified its markings that the slide used was always the same. The photographs were taken one after another, each morning without pause: I sometimes developing one plate while he was taking another.

When Hope was developing, I stood at his elbow: he worked in his shirt-sleeves, and there was absolutely nothing suspicious in his movements. The photographs he took for me were always on my own plates, and I took special care that the plate was my own, and that he did not touch it in in any way or at any time till it had been fixed.

On another occasion at Holland Park, I brought my own 5in. by 4in camera and plates. Keeping the packet unopened, I asked Hope casually if he would use my camera. He consented at once. I set up my camera, loaded the slide, and set the shutter. All that Hope did was to touch the spring. My purpose in this experiment was to show that "magnetisation", though it may assist the process, is not essential to a successful experiment."

---

5. 'Supernormal Photography Examined', *Nov 5th 1937*.

Successful Sittings and Diversification

In Sir Arthur Conan Doyle's book *The Case for Spirit Photography* (1922) he included many accounts of psychic photographic proof from 'reputable' people but he was only able to go as far as his publication deadline of December 1922 let him. There were ten more years of work still ahead for the Crewe Circle.

Here are some more beautiful and "watertight" accounts from the years following Price's "exposure" from amongst the many hundreds of photographs that were taken and whose stories we will never know – Mothers reunited with sons, sons and daughters with parents, wives with husbands and families with unknown relatives and friends who had "passed through that veil of death" – as well as several from my husband's family photograph collection.

Psychic Photography in Middlesbrough

I start with some of my husband's family and his in-laws who sat whenever they could during the Crewe Circle's many visits to Middlesbrough, and also those of the Batten family, Mrs Pugh's parents, another staunch Middlesbrough Spiritualist family.

In my researches, I found this letter from the head of the Batten family published during the Price-Hope controversy.

To the Editor of Light.

"Sir,—I have had several sittings with Mr. Hope and Mrs. Buxton, and received results that have proved conclusively—to me—that there has been no trickery, for they can't fake photos or "extras" of persons passed over when there are no photos in existence prior to their passing, and yet the "extras" are true portraits.

One thing, in all the sittings I have had which has struck me as being of importance and which precludes the mediums from entertaining the idea of faking, is that Mr. Hope has always said prior to a sitting, "We do not guarantee any result."

After saying this there is nothing for Mr. Hope or Mrs Buxton to do but trust to the powers at work to get an "extra" on the plate. If they fail no one can object. Therefore, why risk a good name by attempting any fake?

Were I able to get such results as the Crewe Circle, and, if I gave a test sitting for the S.P.R. or any other such body, I should expect the following result.

Medium to Sitter: I suppose you have brought some plates?

Sitter (answers): Yes.

Medium: Do you object to the use of my own plates?

Sitter (emphatically): Yes!

Medium: Why ?

Sitter: Well, it would hardly be fair to us—I don't say you would—but—there is the possibility of you having done something to the plates.

Medium: Then on the same basis of reasoning I am quite justified in not using your plates. But, to show that my efforts are honest and genuine please select someone on whom you can place implicit trust to act as intermediary for us both.

Mr. X. is selected and buys some new plates, being the only person allowed to handle same.

Sitting takes place. Everything in the process of taking and developing the photos is left entirely to Mr. X. in every detail.

Now, if an "extra" appears, I should think everyone ought to be satisfied."

Yours, etc., Wm. S. Batten.

61, St. Paul's-road,

Middlesbrough

You can't fault his thinking in this suggestion.

Here (*left*) we see Mr. and Mrs. Batten (*seated*) with their daughter, Mrs. Pugh and her son John.

Unfortunately, the "extra" has not been identified for us. William Batten's signature is clearly seen, scratched into the emulsion of the plate when loading, before exposure.

There also appears to be a face to the left of Mrs Pugh.

In the photograph *(below left)* it may be noticed that Mr Pugh, has his head down as he became blind. It was probably taken during a visit in 1922. Mr Cowell Pugh passed in 1925, and in the second photograph in 1927 *(below right)* he returned as the "extra" with his head up (and with more hair!) for his widow and son, who had now grown to a man.[1]

After the passing of Mr. Cowell Pugh sittings were often held in the home of Mr. and Mrs. Charles Hudson (later to become my husband's in-laws) at 87 Ayresome Park Road, Middlesbrough.

This one *(left)* was taken that year and immediately developed in the bathroom of the house. Once 'fixed', the glass negative was held up to the gas 'mantle', the only light in the living room, to examine it – a clear image of Mr. Hudson's father. Again, note the signature (Charles Hudson) on the plate.

---

1. Twenty years later Mr. Cowell Pugh made his presence known in the Harrison's 'Saturday Night Club Circle' by writing on the sheet of paper put out for spirit visitors to 'sign in' - "not blind now". The medium for the Circle was Minnie Harrison who had worked for Pugh in the Post Office. (see *Life After Death: Living Proof* by Tom Harrison.)

In 1927 they sat again, this time with Charlie, Mr. Hudson's son by his first wife, Hannah, and it was she who came as the "extra". Clearly recognised.

Twenty years later Hannah materialised at the Harrison's Saturday Night Club Circle when the Hudsons were present as visitors. Mrs Hudson was good physical medium particularly with the trumpet and lent a great deal of power in any sitting.

More sucessful examples found in our collection of photographs are these of Mr. Pidd, a member of the Lyceum in Middlesbrough, who sat with Mrs. Lumsden (Mrs. Hudson's mother) in these next two photos from 1927.

Notice in this first one how sharp the "extra" lady's face is at the right of the picture where Mrs Lumsden is completely obscured. Her daughter Ada had died in childbirth in April of that year and it is believed this was her. The male "extra" is William Lumsden, her husband who had passed 30 years before.

2. Mrs. Lumsden was less than 5-foot tall, as can be seen in the photograph overleaf. Known to all as 'Grannie', having passed in 1930, she materialised frequently in the 1940-50s to chat at the Harrisons' Home circle. (see *Life After Death: Living Proof* by Tom Harrison.)

In this second photograph (*right*) Mrs. Lumsden can be seen clearly on the right and the spirit appears to be linked to Mr. Pidd, but the identity of "extra" is not recorded.

Left: Mr. Jim McKenzie sat with Miss Hanks and his wife and had his grandmother show herself as the "extra". Jim lived next door to Mrs Lumsden, he was a Lyceumist and good friend to all the family.

The same year – judging by the type of card used for printing the photographs – this one (*above*) was taken of the Middlesbrough Church Committee. Here there appear to be three "extras" but only one is really clear and of a different form than is usual with the Hope images probably recognised but not identified on the back of the card.

In this photograph *(left)* used for Mrs. Cowell Pugh's booklet, *The Land of Eternal Summer*, there is the full-length veil (the existence of which Mr. Price was so doubtful) for the young lady and a beautiful "cotton wool" cloud for the gentleman – which by the moustache I would say is her husband, Mr. Cowell Pugh. I have as yet been unable to trace a copy of the booklet but I do have the article about it from the Middlesbrough *"Evening Gazette"* (date unknown).

It is possible that the spirit world could mould the psychic energy into different forms, the veil, the cloud and those with almost no surrounding effect.

* * * * *

In October 1924 *Psychic Science* published an article from a minister of the Free Church, Rev F.C. Spurr. He and his wife had had lost their son. He published the detailed account as a booklet under the title *From the Heart of a Father*.

Rev Spurr writes:

"I had heard a great deal of Mr. Hope and a Mrs. Buxton, of Crewe. Some years ago, he discovered, by the merest accident, that he had a special almost uncanny gift of being able to project upon a sensitive plate an 'extra' which was generally the photograph of some deceased person. He could not account for his gift then: he cannot account for it now. He has simply to accept it and to use it.

I have seen scores of these photographs and they present a delicate and difficult problem. What is it that is photographed? It is something invisible to the naked human eye, but something that the more sensitive film of the plate can catch."

Describing Hope as "a blunt, plain-spoken, straightforward Lancashire man. He received us without asking our names, or anything else concerning our affairs.", Rev. Spurr goes on to tell us how he had the Secretary of the local branch of Psychical Research write to Mr. Hope asking him for an appointment for two strangers, whose identity was completely hidden from him, and had the Ilford company X-ray mark his plates. Having received his plates he made sure that throughout the session at Crewe he was the only one to handle them.

He writes of the Buxtons' house:

"There is no suggestion of mystery about the house in Crewe. It is a small uninspiring dwelling, consisting downstairs of a small parlour, a kitchen, and outhouse, a room under the stairs which serves as a darkroom. The outhouse is the 'studio'. At one end is a cage containing some birds. At the other end are a few household oddments curtained off. The space between the two contains nothing but a couple of chairs and the camera tripod. The Place is marked by primitive simplicity."

Having placed the plates on the table around which they sat —"Hope conducted a short religious service and offered a prayer of touching simplicity. "If it be Thy will, O Father, may we have some manifestation of the Spirit World," was one sentence of the prayer. Then the hands of the entire company were placed over the packet of plates, to 'magnetize' it."

Rev Spurr loaded the plates and signed them in the darkroom before taking them to the camera. Following each exposure, he returned to the darkroom and developed and fixed each plate.

But it wasn't until the twelfth and final plate that they had a result:

"The final picture startled us, for there, clearly and sharply defined, was the spirit photograph of our little Anthony. Had he indeed been present and sat for his photograph? If not, then how was that unmistakeable face impressed upon the plate?

We left Crewe with a feeling that the 'real' things are not the material things that we measure and weigh and see. These clumsy things are illusive. It is the spiritual things that are real. I am bound to add that Mr. Hope took no fee for his work (he never does) although no gift could have been too handsome as a reward for what we received through him that day."

* * * * *

In late 1924 *The Two Worlds* published the next two accounts.

"During August 1924, Mr. Hope visited Shrewsbury at the request of Mrs. Simpson and Mr. and Mrs. Higgins. The visit arose through a message received by Mr. Simpson to the effect that if they could make arrangement for the family of Mr. and Mrs. Higgins to sit for spirit photography on a particular date the guides and relatives of the family would provide evidence of their presence. This sitting took place three weeks before the visit of Mr. Hope.

Mr. Hope brought his own camera. The plates were bought in Shrewsbury by Mr. Higgins, the whole process of loading the carriers and developing the plates was in his hands. Other than the magnetisation of an unopened packet of plates, we are assured that Mr. Hope had no contact with the plates.

An Evidential Spirit Photograph.

Mr. and Mrs. Higgins with other sitters and an "extra" with a strong likeness to their 7-year-old son

Four exposures were made, two with Mr. Hope's camera and two with Mrs. Simpson's, and on three of the plates "extras" were found. Each of these three, however, showed the same face, though in different positions. The "extra" shows a striking likeness of Mr. Higgins' son, Ronnie, who passed to spirit on March 27th 1923, at the age of 7½ years, and for comparative purposes we reproduce a photograph of the child taken some weeks before death. The fact that the same face appeared on three of four plates, though its position was different in each one, is a rather exceptional feature. The sitting took place at the house of Mr. Higgins, 46 Montague-place, Belle Vue, Shrewsbury, and was conducted under conditions which in the opinion of the sitters, places all attempts of trickery out of the question."

* * * * *

"In December '24, Mrs. M. S. Hipwood. of Stourbridge, sent us a copy of a spirit photograph taken at Crewe on June 26th last, Mrs. Hipwood and her daughter, Mrs. Miller, being the sitters. Mrs. Hipwood had previously sat with the Crewe Circle[3]and familiarised herself with the necessary conditions for checking the proceedings, and stated that "every protection was taken to satisfy us and every reasonable person" that the photograph was quite straightforward.

---

3. See Chapter 14, p158

Four plates were exposed: three of them were normal, and the fourth is reproduced left.

The "extras" are Mrs. Hipwood's son, who was killed in France in 1918 whilst serving with the 13th Welsh regiment, while the lady (left) is recognised as Mrs. Hipwood's youngest sister, who passed away three weeks before this photograph was taken. Mrs. Miller confirms that the "extras" have been recognised by those who are not Spiritualists.

The Editor writes: "Quite apart from any question of the procedure in the taking of the photograph, the obtaining of photographs of two relatives who must be unknown to the sitters [i.e. the circle members] at Crewe constitutes a type of evidence which in our opinion, is quite as strong and far more crucial than the mere proceedings of taking the photograph."

* * * * *

In June 1925 *The Two Worlds* received this report of a second sitting by Mrs Simpson.

"It was taken at Shrewsbury in February last, the medium being Mr. Hope, of Crewe. The plates were provided by the sitter, and the whole experiment was very carefully supervised.

The "extra", (*shown right*), is recognised as a friend of the sitter, a Mrs. Sykes, who had been the sitter's teacher, and who died at Manchester some twelve months before. The interesting fact is that in November, 1923, Mrs. Sykes was ill, and during Mrs. Simpson's visit to her she made the promise that if at all possible she would endeavour to appear on a photographic plate after her decease, and Mrs. Simpson is satisfied that this is a fulfiment of the promise then made."

The Two Worlds added "We have compared the psychic extra. with a photograph of Mrs. Sykes taken while in the body, and are satisfied that there is every reason to believe that it is the same person."

A rather interesting fact in connection with Mr. Hope's visit to Shrewsbury was that a Mr. Higgins [see p.240], who is keenly interested in mediumship, persisted in bombarding the medium with questions concerning the how and why of spirit manifestations. A photograph was subsequently taken with Mr. Higgins's camera and plates at his own house, and the psychic result. upon the plate was a huge "query" [?] outlined in light."

* * * * *

Psychic Photography Lecture in Sheffield

Following the passing of William Walker, William Hope had, since 1918, taken up the mantle in spreading the knowledge in the form of illustrated lectures. In October 1925 he was in Norwich and in Sheffield in 1926.

The Two Worlds provided this detailed account of the second of those evenings.

"There was a crowded audience at the Theosophical Hall. St. Paul's Parade, Sheffield on September 23rd, where the Sheffield and District Society for Psychical Research held a meeting, open to visitors, at which Mr William Hope, of Crewe Circle, gave an illustrated lantern lecture on "Psychic Photography.""

The President, Dr Frank Ballard, D.D. who occupied the chair, in introducing the lecturer, said that Mr Hope, who had come again to lecture on this subject, has such an amount of interesting information to give that he would not take up any time himself and kindly played the accompaniment to the hymn, *"Praise the Lord,"* which Mr. Hope had thrown on to the screen and to which the audience sang vigorously.

Mr. Hope in speaking of the photographs which he was about to exhibit, explained that they were of two classes, namely photographs in which the camera was not used, termed "psychographs" or "skotographs," in which the packet of unopened plates was placed on the forehead of his colleague, Mrs. Buxton, and then developed to see if any picture or writing was on them.

He then showed a photo of the first leader of the Crewe Circle, Archdeacon Colley, of Stockton Rectory, who thus obtained a psychograph of 1700 words in 39 seconds which he used as a sermon, and then was shown a photo of the Archdeacon's successor Mr. Walker of Buxton, and "skotograph" of an angelic being holding flowers which he recognised as "Our Lily". ...

A lady, who lost her husband in the war, was photographed, when a message was written from him on the plate.

A portrait of Sir A. Conan Doyle was shown with an "extra" on it of his son. With a lady from Bury the photo showed an "extra" of her grandfather; and a lady from Edinburgh, her father—a photo from life was shown to illustrate the resemblance.

The next was a photo of a lady and Mr. Jeffrey, of the "Magic Circle" taken with his own "Kodak" on which an extra of his wife appeared, and Mr. Hope announced that Mr. Jeffrey made an offer of £100 to any conjuror who could, under similar conditions, produce similar results.

A photo of a gentlemen, Thomas Moffit, of Watford, showed an "extra" of his son killed on March 10th 1915 at Neuve Chapelle.

His next picture was of Sir William Crookes, taken under his own conditions, on which an "extra" of his wife appeared.

Then the photo of a ship's engineer on which his wife appeared, and who then used his own film camera and an "extra" of his little boy appeared.

Then followed a photo of two ladies, who asked him to take a photo of them standing by a grave, on which the "extra" of the mother and the child buried there appeared.

At Mr. Hope's request the hymn "*Never, no never alone*" was thrown on the screen, which the audience sang lustily.

Then followed the photo of a lady who would not believe, but who got an "extra" of "Our Nance," her sister who died 12 years ago.

A photo of a lady and gentleman, of Glasgow, came next, showing an "extra" of a pretty child, who had been killed by falling from an attic window.

A lady from Macclesfield obtained an extra of her mother, and sent a life photo for comparison.

The ladies by a child's grave with the "extra' of the child and its mother.

Mr. Hope then told of a gentleman, formerly a sceptic, seeing his mother's form by the coffin on a bier, and having his photo taken, and on it an "extra" of his mother appeared.

A lady and gentleman from South Wales got an "extra" of their little girl, and for comparison sent a photo of her in life, in Welsh costume. A gentleman from Lancashire said the "extra" was his mother-in-law (Mr. Hope offered him his sympathy).

The next photo was particularly interesting, as the lecturer called on Mr. Lewis Childs, who was present to explain it. Mr. Childs said he had an agreement with a sceptical friend, a Mr. Turton, that when either of them died, the other should endeavour, if it was possible to come on a photo, and

Mr. Turton, dying nine months later, carried out his part of the bargain by appearing as an "extra" on the photo of Mr Childs.

The next was a photo of Mr. Hope's colleague, Mrs. Buxton, and her daughter, on which Mrs. Buxton's father came as an "extra".

Two sisters from Macclesfield got their mother, and sent a life photo for comparison. A Staffordshire soldier and his wife got an "extra" on their photo and sent a life photo for comparison. A lady from Manchester got an "extra" of her boy. A lady and gentleman from Ashton-under-Lyne got an "extra" of the lady's father.

The next was again of local interest, and Mr. Hope called on Mr. Dobson to explain it. He told how he went to Mr. Hope and got an "extra" of his foreman killed eight years before, and how his mother at a séance subsequently told him to look at a certain part of the photo, and he would find her, which he did. A gentleman from Platt Bridge, Wigan got an "extra" of his wife using his own camera. Two ladies from Middlesbrough got an "extra" of their aunt living in America, whom they eventually found had died a fortnight before her "extra" appeared on the photo. The fact that she had passed over was unknown to them.

Mr. Hope told a story about the old woman who complained, on seeing a photo of a cow, that she could not see the other side, which shows how ridiculous are the requirements of some of the critics.

The next photo was particularly interesting. A lady and gentleman from Port Talbot gave Mr. Hope a lift in their motor car, and stopped *en route* to have an open air photo taken, which showed their dead son at the steering wheel.[4]

4. Photograph from the Science Museum Group Collection 2002-5054/13

The following photograph was that of the Rev C.L. Tweedale, Vicar of Weston, and his wife on which was the "extra" of his father-in-law. A photo taken during life was shown for comparison.

A gentleman from Belfast got his mother. ...

A gentleman from Sweden, on getting an extra was made fun of by his doctor, whom he made come to Mr. Hope and be photographed by him. When an "extra" recognised by the doctor appeared on the plate he was convinced.

A photo was shown of Mr. Evan Powell with his guide as an "extra" and then two investigating gentlemen from the *Scientific American* got an "extra" on a photo. A gentleman got an "extra" which proved to be his cook's husband.

A photo was also shown which was taken soon after Dr. Geley was killed, on which he appeared as an "extra".

A lady and gentleman got their son, a clergyman got his father. In a Devonshire chapel the altar was photographed, and a face came on it as an "extra" and on being photographed by another camera the face came again.

A lady and gentleman from the Isle of Wight got their nephew and sent a life photo for comparison. A lady and gentleman from Horwich Lancs., got an "extra" of the lady's mother.

A gentleman came in a great hurry one evening at 6.30, got plates in Nantwich, and the photo showed three "extras" of which his wife and child were two. He had been told at a trumpet séance to come at this time to Mr. Hope.

A lady and gentleman brought a parcel of clothes sent from Australia, and an "extra" came on the photo of the wearer of the clothes in the parcel. The next was Mr. Tomas, the medium, and his guide.

The evening was brought to a close with *"God be with until we meet again"* being thrown on the screen, the audience signified by their vigorous singing their appreciation of Mr. Hope's lecture, which Dr. Ballard put to the audience, and Mr. Walter Appleyard and Mr. C. Cooper supporting it, was carried unanimously.

Mr. Hope made a few remarks on what he considered formed the best condition for obtaining photos with "extras," and said it depended much on the auras of the sitters being in sympathetic accord.

* * * * *

In *The Two Worlds* for March 12th 1926 there was an obituary notice concerning the passing of Mr Robert Telford Jackson of Stretford, who had "done good work in the South Lancashire area." In October of that year they published a spirit photograph (see overleaf) received through the "mediumship of Mr. William Hope of Crewe."

"Mr. Hope was in Manchester and was invited by Mrs Jackson to her house at Lonsdale-road Stretford. A packet of quarter plates had been previously bought from the chemists by the sitters.

One of the observers filled the slides and superintended the focussing, using

Mr. Hope's camera. The exposure having been made by Mr. Hope, the observers themselves developed the plate and saw the extra appear. The plate was then fixed, the identification marks noted, and handed to Mr. Hope for printing. The result shows a very clear representation of Mr Robert Telford Jackson, which has been clearly and readily recognised by all his friends. We have made careful enquiries into the whole of the procedure, and can find no other explanation of the phenomenon but that, by some means or another, our old friend, Jackson was concerned in its production.

* * * * *

Rev Tweedale[5] recorded the following, which occurred in late 1927, when, early one morning, there was a ring at his front door-bell and the Chief Constable of Sunderland[6] was announced. On going down to the dining room into which he had been shown, Tweedale found that he was accompanied by one of his daughters, and he came to break his journey on the way to visit Mr Hope. He proposed motoring on to Crewe and having a sitting with him. They had breakfast at Weston, and about 8.30 set out in their car for Crewe.

"Afterwards, he informed me that he arrived about noon, and at once had a sitting with Hope who was not aware of his coming. The Chief Constable had lost his wife only about ten days previously, she having died of cancer. To his great delight he obtained at this sitting a marvellous spirit photograph of his deceased wife. It was so wonderfully accurate and such a good likeness that he was greatly impressed, but there was apparently one little discrepancy – "one little fly in the ointment", so to speak. That made him hesitate, although the likeness was so perfect; the hair in the spirit photograph was parted on the right side, whereas his wife invariably parted her hair on the left.

As soon as he got a print from the negative he hurried to the nurse, who had nursed his wife through her terrible illness, and said to her, "Nurse, did

---

5. *News from the Next World* p234
6. Error: for Sunderland read Newcastle upon Tyne but initials on photograph confirm identity.

you ever see my wife with her hair parted on the right?"

The nurse at once replied, "Oh yes, sir, didn't you know? I parted her hair on the right for ten days before she died in order to ease her head on the pillow." That settled it, and was one of the most evidential details that could be imagined, and one that completely destroys the theory of telepathy and the subconscious.

On the back of the photograph which is shown here, he has written: "This is a perfect likeness of my wife.-F. J. C."

Tweedale closes with: "It is certainly one of the most evidential spirit photographs ever taken and inspection shows the difference in the arrangement of the hair, and in other details."

Mr. F.W. Warrick[7] tells us that Frederick J. Crawley was "Chief Constable of Newcastle-on-Tyne, who sat many times with Hope and had twenty-three excellent results with him, many recognised Extras.

"Mr. Crawley brought to bear on the subject the training of the detective, for he was formerly a member of the C.I.D. of Scotland Yard, and at one time its representative on the Continent and a detective with experience in photography. He obtained six Extras of his late wife, at different ages, and other recognised Extras— twenty-three extras in all, through Mr. Hope and Mrs. Buxton."[8]

In a letter to the *News-Chronicle*, London, on April 8th, 1931, Crawley wrote: "I have obtained psychic phenomena with Mr. Hope when my own camera and slides were used, and when Mr. Hope at no time entered the dark room."

* * * * *

The year 1929 seems to have been another busy one for the Crewe Circle. In June Rev. Chas. Tweedale posted this in *The Two Worlds* magazine:

"A few experiences connected with the visit of Mr. William Hope to

---

7. *Experiences in Psychics* appends (321)
8. See Appendix 6 for details of Crawley's protocol and results for his Experiences at Crewe.

Bradford on March 25th 1929, may be of interest to readers. Two days before, on March 23rd, my wife and I had retired to rest. The time was about midnight and my wife was asleep and breathing heavily. Suddenly she was entranced in her sleep (being entirely unconscious of what happened), and began to call my name loudly and eagerly, not in her own voice, but in that of Elizabeth Coates, my aunt, who died 20 years ago— the information and inflexion being perfect. In answer to my query as to who was speaking, I received the eager reply "Lizzie, Lizzie!" Then followed loud expressions of delight that she was able to speak with me.

I must here explain that for six years prior to her death she was paralysed, unable to speak or move; enduring with rare patience and fortitude what must have been a living death. It is impossible to describe the note of triumph in her voice as she cried, "I can run and walk now." "I can sing now." I know it filled me with delight, and made me realise what St Paul meant when he said, "O, grave where is thy victory?"

Continuing she said, "When that photographer comes, I am coming on the plate." The communication then ceased.

After Mr. Hope had lectured at the Mechanics Hall, Bradford on Monday 25th March, he accompanied me to Weston, [11 miles] and stayed the night at my vicarage. We were very careful not to tell him about my aunt and her expressed intention to show up on the plate. During supper he suddenly became clairvoyant, and said that he saw the spirit of a woman in the room, and gave a most perfect description of my Aunt Elizabeth, whom he had never seen in the mortal, and whose photograph he has never seen.

On Tuesday, the 26th, he exposed a number of plates under good test conditions. The plates were purchased by me in unbroken boxes. I loaded the slides, signed the plates after insertion, carried the slide to the camera, which was carefully inspected, and developed and fixed the plates after the exposure had been made by Mr. Hope, who was not allowed to place his hand over them or handle them until fixed.

The plate bears a perfect likeness of Elizabeth Coates as she was shortly before her death, clearly recognised by us beyond the possibility of mistake or doubt. As she was never photographed after middle age, and there is no normal picture or photograph in existence showing her as she was towards the close of her life, as the psychic photograph does, this fact makes fraud impossible.[9]...

Another face to show up on the plates was remarkably strong and vigorous. The features being clearer and better defined than my own, which are shown on the same plate. We did not immediately recognise it, but on careful

9. Unfortunately the photograph of 'Lizzie' as the extra is too indistinct on scanning from his book, *News from the Next World* vol II, to warrant including.

comparison with several photographs showed it to be none other than Sir William Crookes. Copies of this psychic photograph were dispatched to relatives and friends of Sir William with the result that it was at once identified by two of his relations, and by the family doctor and the doctor's wife. The psychic photograph being shown suddenly and without explanation to Sir William's grand-daughter, she instantly recognised it, which testimony is again reinforced by that of Sir Oliver Lodge, who knew Sir William for many years, and who in a letter to me says, 'the face above your head might well represent a younger portrait of Crookes.'

Rev. Tweedale with an "extra" recognised as Sir Wm. Crookes

Comparison of the spirit face with that of the portrait by Ludovici, [see inset] which formerly hung in Sir William's dining room, will show the identity to those who did not know him personally.

The obtaining of the recognised spirit picture of Elizabeth Coates, foretold in trance by the deceased herself, and confirmed by the clairvoyant vision of the photographer, the manifestation and recognition of Sir William, constitutes a wonderful convincing and evidential experience, proving conclusively that the dear arise immediately, and not at the Last Day, and that communication with them is as natural and as possible as it was to Christ and the Apostles."

* * * * *

This next account, also in *The Two Worlds,* in August 1929, was sent in by Mr. Barrett of Nottingham:

"A short while ago we had a sitting with Mr. Hope and Mrs. Buxton at Crewe," says Mr. Barratt. We were very successful. The "extra" which appears on the plate I enclose is that of a young doctor with whom I was intimate in Hull. I am not sure of his nationality, but he appeared to have come from Northern Ireland or Scotland. He was about 26 years of age when I knew him, his name being John MacKnight. Together we set out to investigate the terrible disease of cancer, in the hope that we might be successful in formulating a cure.

We carried on investigating for about two years, when he was suddenly called away to visit some friends in Leningrad. He told me, before leaving,

that he would be back in about two months. My subsequent investigation reveals that he was taken ill with fever and died shortly afterwards. His remains were interred in Leningrad. Dr. John MacKnight has been of great help to me in diagnosing where cancer is concerned. The psychic photograph is the only photograph of MacKnight believed to be in existence."

Mr. Barrett with an "extra" of his close friend Dr. John MacKight.

* * * * *

Then in November:

<u>A Psychic Photograph of Tom Tyrrell</u> [10]

"At the end of last month Mr. W. Hope of Crewe paid a visit to Blackburn, and gave a successful lantern lecture before members of the Blackburn Temple.

Subsequent to his visit a number of experiments were tried with individual sitters for psychic photography. The plates used in the experiments were bought privately by the sitters and were handed to Mr Hope in sealed packets. A short service was held round a small table upon which the sealed packets were placed, and the sealed packet was then held between the hands of the

sitters. A hymn and invocation having been rendered, seven sitters in all were photographed, the first being Mrs. Tyrrell. The experiments were conducted under close supervision of the President of the Church, the first sitting taking

---

10. Tom Tyrell of Blackburn, England, a well-known clairvoyant medium earned a passage in *Power of the Spirit* by Maurice Barbanell, in remembrance of his mediumship – "As a young man, I went, while on holiday, to a Spiritualist church in Paignton, and Tom was giving clairvoyance. He specialised in reading memorial cards. His recital included the full name of the communicator, the address where he had lived on earth, complete with the number of the house, the street or road, the district and town.

place in Mrs Tyrrell's home on October 28th. A plate having been exposed by Mr Hope, under close supervision, was taken from the camera and immediately developed in the bathroom, with the result which we reproduce herewith. As several members thought they recognised the photograph from the negative, a print was immediately taken, the development of the other plates being postponed to a later date. His many friends will be delighted to know that this photograph of Mr. Tom Tyrrell has been received under conditions which effectually prevented any duplicity."

* * * * *

This next is an account that was not published until four months after William Hope's passing. There is no indication of when it took place but its author was no stranger to psychic investigations. Major C. H. Mowbray submitted this account to *The Two Worlds* in July 1933 in defence of William Hope's mediumship.

"Penanne"

"A little girl friend of mine passed over, and first came to me through the mediumship of Mrs. Cooper. She also came through Mrs. Barkel, Mrs. Mason, and the Misses Moore.

After I had convinced the child's mother, who had a successful sitting with Mrs. Blanche Cooper, I took her to Mr. Hope, the psychic photographer. Her identity was quite unknown to him,

Left: 'Penanne' returns as an "extra" in a photograph with her mother and Maj. Mowbray as sitters.
(Note the light ring of 'energy' across the faces of the sitters).
Above: Enlargement of the "extra"

and he had no idea that she was coming. I took my own plates, and at no time did Hope touch them, except to place his hand on the unopened packet, in full sunlight, and with my hand on his.

I opened the packet in the presence of Hope in the dark room, selected the plates, signed them, put them in to the dark slide (which I had thoroughly examined) and placed the slide in the camera, which I had also previously examined. Hope made the exposure by drawing the shutter of the slide.

I inverted the slide, and Hope made the exposure again, and I withdrew the slide from the camera. I went to the darkroom with Hope, developed and fixed the plates. One showed an extra of my little friend.

It is undoubtedly her for the following reasons:

1) Both parents say it is she.

2) before passing she had to have an operation, which necessitated the hair on the side of her head being shaved. This is shown in the photograph.

3) She had a slight cast in one eye—also shown in the photograph.

4) She had a slight scar on the top of the head. This too is shown in the photograph.

At no time whatever did Hope touch the plates. I am convinced that not only did he not fraud, but he had no opportunity to fraud. No photograph was in existence showing the child with her shaven head, etc., as I have described. I am supposed to be an expert amateur photographer.

* * * * *

It is not well known that Hope helped and worked with other mediums in the late 1920s-30s.

Lilian Bailey

At some point in the 1920s Lilian Bailey, in a desperate attempt to know she had not "lost" her mother for ever, found some answers in Oliver Lodge's books. She eventually read of 'Billy' Hope and visited a spiritualist church in her home town of Crewe on the off chance tracing him. This she did and made an appointment for a sitting. Once there, instead of receiving an expected photograph, she fell into a trance and woke to find that a man had spoken through her. Though terrified, she was persuaded to have the photograph taken and this man revealed himself as an "extra" on the photograph.

In *"Death is Her Life"* W.F.Neech describes how she eventually did get a photograph of her mother, and later saw her and spoke with her at a Helen Duncan séance, where she pleaded with Lilian to do the work that she was intended for. Gradually overcoming her fears, 'Billy' undertook her development as a trance medium, with the man in her photograph as her Guide.

It took three years before her husband was persuaded to overcome his religious prejudice of contacting the "dead". When Hope took a photograph of them on a plate, which her husband had bought, initialled and loaded into a slide in their own home and then developed, his mind was changed. For there on the plate was a "perfect likeness of his "dead" parents totally different to any they had had taken."

He agreed that Lilian should pursue her work for the spirit world but he would take no part in it. In Neech's book we read:

"Six months later Hope was dead. ...

More than ever determined to perfect the development of her psychic gifts now that the one who had started her on her destined path had joined his "extras" in the Beyond, Lilian reformed the Hope circle in her own home."

She sat for many months and discovered that she had remarkable natural powers of clairvoyance and clairaudience which enabled her both to see and hear the spirit communicators. Especially did she achieve regular contact with Bill Wotton whose job it became to pass on spirit messages, sometimes direct —sometimes through Lilian, to members of the circle and guests, from their loved ones. One day he told her, "The time has come to start our mission."

* * * * *

Bertha Harris

In *Photographing the Spirit World,* Cyril Permutt tells us:

"When Bertha Harris was a girl her father, Arthur Hindle Hughes, a low paid civil servant, augmented his income with photography and Bertha acted as his assistant. To her father's annoyance his photographs were often spoiled and a day's work lost because of the extra images and what he called 'those damned ghosts' that appeared in them. After a while he realised that these extra images only appeared when Bertha was assisting him and she was promptly banned from his photographic sessions."

As Bertha grew up her psychic talents developed. She became a Spiritualist and had been working as a medium for several years when Lady Conan Doyle introduced her to William Hope who was producing psychic photographs with Mrs Buxton. Mrs Buxton became ill and was in hospital for several months in 1930 and during this time Hope made many visits to Bertha's home in Chester where they experimented and together produced many successful psychic photographs.

Mrs Harris' talent for psychic photography has waxed and waned, as all the psychic powers seem to do from time to time, but she has been instrumental in producing psychic photographs when working with several other photographers all of whom were men. She told me that in her experience one of the factors necessary was the presence of a man and a woman working together and that even then there could be no control over the appearance of extra images on the photograph. "

In *Battling Bertha,* Maurice Leonard writes:

"When, at Sir Oliver Lodge's instigation, Bertha teamed up with Billy it seemed as though the whole of the spirit realms were determined to help, for hundreds of photographs were produced.

When she asked Sir Oliver why it was necessary for her to work with a man, he explained it was something to do with an excess of albumen in her body. And she had to be content with this explanation for no better was forthcoming.

All the photographic sessions were held under Sir Oliver's strictest surveillance and the most satisfactory sessions were at a circle in Crewe which consisted of Mr. Hope and his assistant Mrs. Buxton, Bertha and Sir Oliver. The quartet would join bands, sing a few hymns and say a prayer or two. During this Billy and Mrs. Buxton would hold the photographic plates in the camera shutters [slides].

Apparently, the guides got a bit sick of the hymns after a while and suggested that "Lead Kindly Light" might be swapped for "Any Old Iron". They explained that it was not the pious sentiments that produced phenomena but the "raising" of the vibrations from the singing. "

* * * * *

The Final Challenge

William Hope's work continued on into the '30s, including a visit to Nelson in Lancashire in 1931, plus visits to Bradford, and to York in 1930 and '32 as described in Gerald O'Hara's book *Dead Men's Embers* (2006) which included many of the photographs from the York Spiritualist Church's albums of those years. Over 54% bore the statement "recognised". One denoted in November 1930 that the "extra" was his first wife and another, in September 1932, her "own boy". Both very clear, identifiable portraits.

Mr. and Mrs. Lord with an
"extra" of his first wife.

Mrs. Calvert with the
"extra" of her "own boy".

His visit to Nelson in Lancashire in 1931 was reported by Mr. Harry Clark, of 6 Branch Street, Nelson.[1]

"In 1931 I was sitting in a friend's home circle, when the leader of the circle was controlled by a friend, whom I and others present had known for years. He was the late President of the Spiritualist Church at Vernon Street, Nelson (Mr. H. Hargreaves). He was aware of Mr. Hope's pending visit to our church and emphasised that he would do his utmost to appear as an "extra" upon one of the plates.

---

1. *The Two Worlds*, August 31st 1933

Some weeks later Mr. Hope visited Nelson to give a lantern lecture on psychic photography, and also to demonstrate his powers. He was not informed of the above incident and knew nothing of our President's intentions. Test conditions were suggested by Mr. Hope himself. Two witnesses went into the dark room, extracted two plates from the packet, wrote their names on the plates, placed them in the slides, and put them in the camera.

Mr. Hope made two exposures of a group of sitters, and later the same witnesses took charge of the plates and developed them. One turned out unsuccessful, but on the other was an "extra" which appeared directly above my head.

Mr Clark with two sitters and the "extra" reconised as their late President.

While the plate was still wet I held it up to the window, and was astonished to recognise the familiar features of our late President. A print was sent to his wife and family who immediately recognised the "extra" even a little granddaughter exclaiming 'Why, that's grand-dad.'

I am sure that no one could wish for a better test, and although many people have seen this picture of the late President of our Church, it is but one supernormal photograph in the many hundreds of equal value, which Mr. Hope took during his life-time."

The reporter adds: 'The picture loses some of its clearness in the reproduction, but Mr. Clark is convinced, from the original photograph, that there can be 'no mistake' concerning its recognition."

But notice! There may only be an "extra's" face but there is a large faint cloud ring of energy reaching from around the sitters, so not, as many sceptics maintained, impressed by a flashlight.

* * * * *

The Rev. Charles Tweedale had been a friend of Hope's for many years. His wife, Marjorie, was a good trance speaking and writing medium, and after the passing on July 7th 1930 of Sir Arthur Conan Doyle they received news through her trance that he would "try to communicate photographically next week."

That was on the 9th of July, and on the 14th, Rev. Tweedale travelled the 11 miles to Bradford. He writes:

"Monday, July 14th. I went alone to Bradford and sat with that wonderful psychic, Mr. William Hope, of Crewe, under good test conditions. I took a new, unopened packet of plates which I purchased in Bradford as soon as I arrived in the town. Arriving at the house I loaded the slides and signed the plates myself, carefully inspected the camera, lens, slide and background. After loading the slide, I put it in my pocket and proceeded to the camera and thence back to the dark room after the exposure, where I developed the plates myself, and Hope was never allowed to touch them or place his hands over them.

On the first plate (*shown right*) are three faces in cloudy banks of ectoplasm around my head, upon which one face is partly superimposed. They are distinct and clearly recognisable pictures of Sir Arthur, thus fulfilling the forecast of July 9th, and what makes them extraordinarily evidential, each face is shown in a different aspect as though he had walked past looking at me from three different angles!

After the exposure and development of the first pair of plates a remarkable thing happened. Seeing that the faces were in a cloudy band of ectoplasm, and that one was superimposed on my own head, just before the second pair of plates were exposed, I cried aloud *the moment before the exposures were made*: 'Will the manifesting personality please take care not to show up on my face?'

Rev. Tweedale is obsured by "extras" of Conan Doyle (see 'lifetime' inset)

On developing these exposures, I found that one plate bore a face, and, *as requested*, the face showed itself close to, but not touching, my head.

This photograph of Sir Arthur was published in many papers, including *The Dispatch, Bristol Times, Sheffield Daily Telegraph* and *Two Worlds*.

Writing to me under date July 28th, 1930, Lady Doyle says of the photograph showing the three pictures of Sir Arthur, 'We have no doubt whatever about it being my dear husband, and we think it delightful that he should demonstrate his continued activity so quickly from the other side, by sending such proof.'

Writing also to the press she described it as '100 per cent evidential.'

The special correspondent of the *Sheffield Daily Telegraph* personally took a copy of that paper and interviewed Lady Doyle. His account is as follows:

" 'This is my dear, darling husband,' said Lady Doyle to me, when I showed her the spirit photographs published in the *Sheffield Daily Telegraph*. Lady Doyle was pleasantly astonished and radiantly happy because this picture had confirmed her belief in her husband's return. I sat with the famous author's widow in a long room, fragrant with beautiful flowers. Time and again she looked at the photograph of the Rev. Charles L. Tweedale, Vicar of Weston, Otley, and the three extras on it, of Sir Arthur. Then she said with great enthusiasm, "Yes, these are undoubted pictures of my husband. I know Mr. Tweedale and also Mr Hope, and my husband also met them on many occasions. I think the photograph is simply wonderful, and it is the first since he passed over."

Just then the luncheon gong sounded, and I was invited to join the family at the midday meal. I did so, and when I showed Sir Arthur's children – Mr. Dennis, Mr. Adrian and Miss Doyle they displayed great enthusiasm. 'My word, that is father exactly,' they said. 'Isn't it remarkable, mother? We knew he would come through, didn't we? We are convinced that the photograph is true, knowing as we do Mr. Hope and Mr. Tweedale. Surely this picture should do more than anything else to disarm sceptics and prove to them that spiritualism is a vital thing which is bound to change the outlook of the world within a few generations.' " [2]

Conan Doyle continued to communicate through Mrs. Tweedale's mediumship and two years later when Hope visited them in Weston at the end of October 1932 they received more psychic photographs.

The day was dull and gloomy, with snow falling at times when Hope arrived at Weston Vicarage. While he was resting after the journey they chatted and Mrs. Tweedale had casually mentioned the recent press attacks on psychic photography to which Hope had replied he felt "disposed to give up sitting for the public and sit only for friends."

Rev. Tweedale records the occasion thus:

"About 2.30 p.m. we commenced the short service which Mr. Hope invariably holds before photographing. A hymn was sung and prayer offered.

Taking a new and unopened packet of plates purchased an hour before at the local dealers, after carefully inspecting the camera, lens and slide, I loaded the slide myself, and signed each plate through the open shutter [of the slide] to make sure there was no intervening film inserted and no substitution of the plate effected. After loading the slide I carried it out to the camera, and posed for the picture, together with my wife and youngest daughter. I then handed the slide to Mr. Hope, who inserted it into the camera under my vigilant and critical inspection, and made the exposure of the two plates in rapid succession.

---

2. *News from the Next World* vol.1 pps120-1.(Psychic Book Club 1947, 2nd Edit.)

He then handed the slide back to me, and I took it to my dark room and there developed the two plates in his presence, first carefully verifying my signature on each. Exactly the same procedure was gone through with the second pair of plates.

On one of the first pair came, over my head, a splendid likeness of Sir Arthur Conan Doyle (who has been dead for two years), showing him just as he was towards the end of his mortal life. My signature on the plate is seen at the top. On one of the second pair came a marvellous letter, or written message, in Sir Arthur's identical handwriting and signed with his identical signature. The writing appears in a mass of ectoplasm which almost entirely obscures the sitters.

Sitters: Dorothy, Rev. Tweedale, Mrs. Tweedale with Sir Arthur as "extra".. Inset: in life for comparison

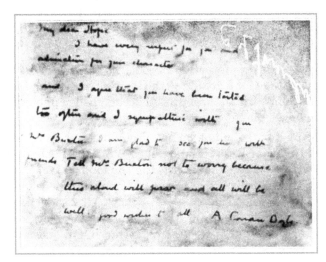

Above: Letter to Hope from Sir Arthur Conan Doyle which obscured the sitters, received on 29th October 1932.

Below: Fragment of a letter from Sir Arthur sent to Rev. Tweedale in life for comparison of the writing.

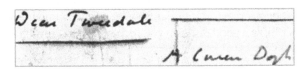

Lady Doyle, writing to me under date December 9th, 1932, recognises the spirit picture, and says of the message, "There is no doubt whatever about it being my husband's own writing on the plate."

The wonderfully evidential nature of this manifestation – apart from the fact of the identity of writing and signature – lies in the further fact that it takes up the conversation which was *casually* introduced by my wife only a few minutes before *and continues it*, showing clearly that Sir Arthur was as actually and really present –and was able *both to see and hear us, and to give a convincing demonstration relating to the conversation...* The message—which covers nearly the whole plate, and through which, in the negative, my face and my collar and waistcoat can be clearly seen—reads as follows:

"*My Dear Hope,*

I have every respect for you and admiration for your character, and I agree that you have been tested too often, and I sympathise with you and Mrs. Buxton. I am glad to see you here with friends. Tell Mrs Buxton not to worry, because this cloud will pass, and all will be well

Good wishes to all. A. Conan Doyle."

My signature on the plate is seen in the right-hand top corner. The message to Mrs. Buxton about 'this cloud' referred to the trouble of a threatened operation, about which she was worrying. As foretold, the 'cloud' did pass, and an operation was found to be unnecessary."

On the following day, before Hope returned to Crewe, Mr. Hirst arrived at the Vicarage for a sitting with Hope, as had been arranged. He brought with him a friend[3] who was an accomplished photographer to assist in the development of any exposed plates.

As instructed by Rev. Tweedale he had brought a new and unopened box of Imperial Special Rapid plates, over the flaps of the cover of which he had firmly pasted a label bearing the following declaration: "We hereby certify that this box of plates has not been opened by us or by anyone else to our knowledge, but is in exactly the same condition as when purchased by us from the dealers," followed by their signatures. After the usual short service with a hymn and a prayer, Rev. Tweedale tells us:

"Hope suddenly said, "It is not often that I see, but I am doing so now."

Turning to Mr. Hirst, he said, "There is an elderly woman near you with hair parted in the middle and taken down the sides of the head and over the ears. Has deep lines at each side of nose. There is something on the top of the head. It might be a cap, but it is difficult to see it. This woman was very religious and read her Bible a good deal. Do you recognise her?" Mr. Hirst said that he did.

---

3. Described by Tweedale in *Light,* 9th June '33 as an "influential gentleman."

Mr. Hirst and his friend now went into my dark room with their packet of plates and Mr. Hope's slide, after thoroughly inspecting the camera, lens and slide. *They did not allow Mr. Hope to go in with them or to take any part in the photographic process.* They loaded the slide with two plates and signed the plates through the shutter so as to prevent any possibility of substitution. They then carried the slide into my dining-room, where a dark grey rug was slung up for a background.

Mr. Hirst sat in a chair before it, and his friend focused him in the camera, then inserted the slide and made the exposure. *Hope was not allowed to touch the slide or camera to make the exposure, or to approach nearer than four feet, where he stood in an attitude of prayer, having nothing in his hands.*

Mr. Hirst's friend then reversed the slide and exposed the other plate, and after this they carried off the slide to my dark room where they developed them both, *Mr. Hope not being allowed to go into the darkroom.* Any fraudulent action on Hope's part was impossible.

One of these plates bore the likeness of the elderly lady described a few minutes previously and which proved to be Mr. Hirst's grandmother, who died six weeks before he was born. This very deeply impressed Mr. Hirst.

A few days *afterwards* Mr. Hirst brought me an old Daguerreotype of his grandmother for comparison. It shows the same face as the spirit extra on the plate, and agrees marvellously with the clairvoyant description given by Hope to Mr. Hirst, whom he had never seen until a few minutes before the picture was taken, and of whom he knew nothing. The old lady has a small cap in the Daguerreotype, but it is so thin and slender on the top of the head that it is not readily seen, exactly as Hope described, and to crown the accuracy of the description, she is shown with *a small Bible in her hands."*

* * * * *

It is not well-known that William Hope was a good clairvoyant as well as a wonderful photographer. Another instance of the accuracy of his clairvoyance was reported to Rev. Tweedale by a Mrs. Gibbs (date unknown) who declared on oath it to be "true in every detail." She told him:

"My daughter and I went from London to Crewe to have a photo taken by Mr. Hope. We bought our own plates, and my daughter signed the plates, examined the camera, and did the whole of the manipulation, developing, fixing and washing.

On one of the plates came a *clearly recognised* extra of my son Harold. While we were sitting at the table, Mr. Hope distinctly saw a young man, tall, about six feet, very good-looking, hair brushed back, very white even teeth, age about twenty-four, dressed in officer's uniform, who had passed over. He was leaning with one elbow on the mantelpiece appearing very pleased with what we were doing. By his side was a beautiful young lady with an abundance of fair hair. The young man asked Hope to tell us that they were now together and very happy.

The girl held up her hand for him to see how thin she had gone. Hope said that she passed out with some wasting disease about twelve months after the young man. She had on a large white apron, on the bib of which was a large red cross. (She was a hospital nurse.) Mr. Hope's description both of my son and the girl was *perfect* and the age correct. They had been great friends, and she died about a year after my son.

Mr. Hope knew only that we came from London, and could by no possibility have had any knowledge of these facts, nor did we tell him who we wanted."

On October 31st the Tweedale family sat for communication – as he says on "the real Communion of Saints". – Conan Doyle again manifested, through Marjorie's trance, and, referring back to the photographs of the 29th, gave the following message:

"*I came to give Hope encouragement, for I do not wish him to give up. Also to convince your friends, for it is a perfect fool-proof picture and message.*"

* * * * *

At the end of November 1932, Fred Barlow and Major Rampling Rose read their paper on "Supernormal Photography" at a Private Meeting of the S.P.R.. In this paper Fred Barlow maintained that he now saw that all the results he had had through the mediumship of William Hope were fraudulent. Though he had no proof.

After the test by Harry Price in '22, Barlow said he had begun to examine the ones he had had with Hope and noticed that after the test – when the college had elected to supply marked plates to all sitters – those at the British College were 'all' of Flashlight type that could have been taken by use of a small flashlight gadget. These produced a rounded face without the 'cotton wool' effect or the 'veiling' around the face.

Hope had put this effect down to the fact that the plates had not been in the possession of the sitter for any length of time but were provided by the College, on arrival, in packs sealed in the factory. The reason given was to avoid substitution beforehand following the Price-Hope Case. It was said that at Crewe, the "drapery" still occurred. Implying that there, "prepared" plates were being used.

Their claim of the use of a flashlight appeared to be backed up by the disclosure later by Mrs. Barbara McKenzie that her husband said he had found suspicious material in Hope's case, and he had mentioned it to Barlow, (Barlow states that was in 1925) but no action had been taken. There was no mention in her statement that there was a miniature flashlight gadget among the items, only a "flashlamp and bulb", nor that one had ever used it at a sitting. No complaints were ever made about the photographs taken, and Mr. McKenzie did not approach Hope about the discovery.

Under the guidance of Major Rampling Rose, an expert in photographic matters and their sittings with Hope they were able to show that, under the cover of the focussing cloth over the camera, small flash-light images *could be* thrown on to the plates by partially withdrawing the shutter before exposing the whole plate, or possibly by Hope carrying the slide into the darkroom ahead of the sitter – and holding it close to himself, shine the light ("concealed in his hand") on it before they developed it.

Barlow stated:

"There is no doubt that the whole fabric of the evidence for the reality of psychic photography is based on the claim that on many occasions sitters who were quite unknown to the mediums have obtained "extras" of dead friends or relatives which could not possibly have been prepared in advance. This claim I myself once made, and if it could be substantiated the supporters of the reality of psychic photography would be in an impregnable position."

"Recognised likenesses have been produced, but in every single case *I have investigated*, where there is no doubt as to the likeness, the "extra" has been an *exact copy* of some existing photograph or painting. The proportion of cases in which the identification of the "extra" is certain is very small—perhaps one in a thousand—but even such a small percentage, or even one in ten thousand, if obtained under conditions precluding fraud, would be sufficient to establish the genuineness of psychic photography. In no instance *that I have investigated*, where such definitely recognised "extras" have been obtained, have I been able completely to satisfy myself that the medium did not have an opportunity of faking the picture beforehand." (Italics are mine. AH.)

He even classed the plates *he* had exposed in a stereographic camera as fraudulent as the extra only appeared on one plate.[4]

Maj. Rampling Rose closed his input by saying:

"I have taken photographs in almost every part of the world, and during the war I had four years' aerial photographic experience.

I mention these facts to emphasise and underline the following statement. *I do not remember ever seeing a single abnormal photograph of all those which have*

---

4. Compare detail in Mr Colledge's report in Chpt 12

passed through my hands that could not be explained by purely natural means. If anyone doubts the fraudulent nature of all the results and can find a reasonable supernormal explanation, I shall be glad to hear it. (italics/underlining are mine A.H.)

It will not be profitable to discuss results that others have obtained, and in any case, it is only by making a series of experiments that a satisfactory conclusion can be arrived at. Photography is still a very mysterious thing to the large majority of people and the ways of faking results are endless, even in the hands of those who have only an elementary knowledge of it."

Barlow, in concluding, covered what he considered were the main points of evidence against Hope.

1. There is the Price experiment which most definitely proved plate substitution.

2. There is the evidence of my friend, a well-known investigator, concerning the very suspicious circumstances he observed at sittings with Hope.

3. There is my considered statement to the effect that every definitely recognised "extra" *I have seen of Hope's* is a copy of a normal photograph, or such as could have been prepared from an ordinary photograph.

4. There is the definite evidence of double exposure on Hope's negatives.

5. There is the evidence showing that Hope's psychographs or photographic messages, in themselves, provide internal evidence of a very suspicious character. (Reference to spelling errors similar to those in Hope's own letters – but could his brain patterns affect the spirit writer of the message as suggested by one correspondent?)

6. There is the evidence of the British Photographic Research Association and their definite conclusion that Hope produces his effects by trickery.[5]

7. There is the fact that in every so-called test sitting *I have conducted, or have heard of,* I know of no instance where Hope has got an "extra" which could not be produced in identical circumstances by normal means.

8. There is the evidence of our own common-sense which rejects these cut-out faces, block markings, magazine illustrations, cotton wool and muslin effects, and which tells us that these things are just as suspicious as they look.

(Agreed, but what of those *indubitably unlike* the above? AH.)

Details of that S.P.R. address were soon leaking out, and very soon, before the publication of it in the Society's *"Proceedings"* in March, letters appeared in the psychic press in defence of Hope and in criticism of Barlow who had championed him for so long. Particularly critical were those members of the S.S.S.P. to whom the *Budget*

---

5. See Extract from the 'British Photographic Research Association' report by Mr. S. De Brath, *page 266.* Full detail in S.P.R. *Proceedings* vol LXI pps121-138 .(IAPSOP)

newsletters had been sent with details of many "infallible" tests. These newsletters had been for 'members only' but as the society was now defunct some felt they could disclose the contents. Unfortunately, very few of these *Budgets* have been preserved for the researchers of today to check the detail.

In early February 1933 Hans Hamilton wrote from France.

"I would like to be permitted to remark that, as corresponding member of the Society for the Study of Supernormal Pictures, and during the period of activity of that Society, I received, in common with all other members, photographic prints of extras obtained with the Medium, William Hope, representing deceased persons totally unknown to the medium and formally recognised by relatives (who had, or their representatives, often brought their own plates and signed them in the dark room).

These prints thus distributed to us, were arranged in the following manner. On the left is the print of the sitter and the "extra" (appearing in close proximity or partially covering the face of the said sitter). On the right is a portrait of the same person taken during life. .... *The extras were not however slavish copies of the portraits, but appeared in a different attitude and often had a rejuvenated appearance. The sitters came sometimes from afar, and sometimes did not give their names.*

Perhaps Mr. Fred Barlow of the British Photographic Research Association would hesitate to proclaim that such photographs as these I have mentioned could have been fraudulently obtained by Hope by his "giving a helping hand," in the dark room, or by "some simple form of flashlight apparatus."

I have in my possession an article by Mr. Fred Barlow in which he says (textually): "With Mr. Hope I have, on a number of occasions, been granted as strict control as that required by Traill Taylor with David Duguid, and under such conditions have secured supernormal results."

We were also informed in those days, by Mr. Fred Barlow, of "extras" obtained in a test experiment with Hope, made by some of Mr. Barlow's friends, *on photographic roll films contained in a film camera.* These experiments were described in the fortnightly Bulletins forwarded to members of the Society for the Study of Supernormal Pictures.

I must apologise for referring to these experiments, in the interest of the truth concerning psychic photography, as these Bulletins were not intended for publication. The Society in question being to all intents and purposes defunct, I have thought it permissible to reveal the fact that Mr. Fred Barlow had every reason to believe in the genuineness of William Hope's mediumistic faculties.

Extras obtained on plates in light-proof packets and never exposed in a camera at all, can hardly have been obtained by the use of "a simple form of flashlight apparatus." Such supernormal effects have often been reported as having been obtained in the presence of William Hope. His "helping hand" would not have been of much use here, if the packet was properly marked for identification after having been bought by the experimenters."

C. J. Hans Hamilton,
Mauzè-sur-le-Mignon, De Sèvres, France.

On March 10th this reply from Mr. Barlow appeared in *Light*:

"In position as the Secretary to the Society of the S.S.S.P., I was responsible for the distribution of the prints to which Mr. Hans Hamilton refers and am fully acquainted with the many cases which at one time I considered incontrovertible.

From the time of the dissolution of the S.S.S.P., I have continued my experiments in spirit photography and on going carefully through the records of experiments with the Crewe Circle, in the light of my present knowledge, *I have yet to come across a case which did not afford a loophole for trickery.*"

Fred Barlow"

So, they "afforded a loophole" but he cannot say that trickery <u>did occur.</u>

In October 1923 a report on a sitting at the British College had appeared in their Journal *Psychic Science*. This appears to show two of those circular images of a face fitting their charge of the "Flashlight" frauds but there is a twist in the tail (tale?).

Mr Schofield's montage of psychic results of the Late Major R.E.E. Spencer.
Left: Result with sitter and exposure in camera
Centre: A normal photograph
Right: Result without exposure in camera – held by Mrs Buxton.

Mr. H.C. Schofield described a sitting he had with Mr. Hope and Mrs. Buxton on 23rd June of that year. Taking his own plates, camera and 3 metal slides – which each held only one plate – he loaded two plates into Hope's slide, having inspected it, and three plates into his own slides. The second of the two plates exposed in Hope's camera gave one extra; two of the plates in the metal slides were exposed by Hope in Schofield's own camera but gave no results; and the fifth, Schofield tells us –"at the same time I asked Mrs. Buxton whether she would also take one of my slides in her hand, and hold it there until the exposure of my plates had been finished."

Upon developing, an "extra" was found on the plate held by Mrs. Buxton. It had never been in the hands of Hope nor in a camera!

Mr. Schofield gave these details of his experience and procedure that day:

1. I am an experienced amateur photographer and have, on two previous occasions, photographed ectoplasmic effects.

2. For the experiment, on the 10th June, I purchased my own plates, and these were used for the experiment.

3. I loaded Hope's double dark slide after examination and my own three single metal slides.

4. I examined the interior of the camera and was satisfied on this point that there was nothing abnormal, either with camera or lens, no shutter was used, the exposures being made by raising the focussing cloth from the front of the lens.

5. I timed the exposure with my own stop-watch, these were twenty-three and thirty-eight seconds respectively.

6. I developed the negatives myself, and did the subsequent operations of fixing and washing.

7. I am satisfied that these results were obtained genuinely, they were satisfactory in every way, so far as an ordinary shrewd observer and enquirer, as I consider myself, could provide for.

The results have been examined by members of the Spencer family, who are all agreed as to the likeness. It is reported that a further psychic "extra" of Major Spencer was obtained by a private sitter with the Crewe Circle at Middlesbrough, in July, on a colour plate, provided by the sitters.

Schofield had met Major Spencer the college a few times before his passing and "since Major Spencer's passing I have been anxious that, if possible, his co-operation might be secured in some photographic experiments being made at the College."

So was it possible for Hope to have used a 'flashlight' to obtain the first image in his camera?

How then is the second identical one accounted for, and could he have known Schofield was hoping for 'help' from Major Spencer?

Or is it possible that the spirit operators had been *experimenting* with a new form of image – perhaps to remove the suggestion of 'cut outs' and to use less 'psychic energy' when at the college?

In February 1933 Mr. Stanley De Brath issued a challenge to Mr. Barlow:

"Sir. We must, of course, assume that Mr. F. P. Barlow is sincerely desirous of a true conclusion. I therefore pass over the assumptions contained in the earlier part of his letter (in last week' s issue of *Light*) and will only ask him how he explains the statement at the head of the right-hand column on page 34 of the issue of *Light* of January 20th.

Mr. Colledge states that he opened *a new box of plates intact as it came from the factory*, never lost sight of the slide which he himself had loaded, and developed the plates himself, one of which had an "extra" upon it.[5]

I have myself tested Mr. Hope for a whole week Hulham House, Exmouth (as well as on other occasions) and can certify that he had no "flash-light" or other apparatus about him at all, but produced some twenty different "extras" on plates of my own, exposed by him in my presence, and developed by myself alone in a very simple dark-room.

I should like to see the official report alluded to by Mr. Barlow.

Stanley De Brath, M.Inst.C.E.

This report was indeed seen and reviewed by him two months later in *Psychic Science* (April 1933); the relevant extract of which is the following:

"It is marked "Confidential," and I shall not violate that restriction as regards the names of the experimenters Drs. X. and Y. But in Dr. X.'s last letter occurs this sentence: "We are at a loss to understand why the results we have obtained have not been communicated to a wider circle."

That I now purpose to do. I quote from the *Report on the Experiments of Oct. 22nd by the Crewe Circle.*

" *Afternoon Sitting.*

A fresh unopened box of quarter plates was used. Two exposures made in Mr. Hope's camera yielded no result. Two exposures in my camera yielded one result.

" A further four exposures were made in my camera under the following conditions : One dark slide was loaded by me directly from the box and handed to Mr. Hope, who placed the same in his left-hand pocket which was on the far side from me, he kept his left hand in this pocket while I proceeded to load the second slide, which I retained all the time. HE THEN PRODUCED THE FIRST SLIDE AGAIN AND I MANAGED TO SUBSTITUTE FOR THIS ANOTHER LOADED SLIDE WHICH I HAD BROUGHT WITH ME.

---

5. *See full Report in Chpt 12*

This and the second slide, which I had retained all the time, were specially treated but yielded no results on exposure, to the obvious disappointment of Mr. Hope, which was rather remarkable, as normally he does not show such disappointment.

The slide which had been in Mr. Hope's pocket, I estimate for about two minutes, was brought by me to the laboratories and developed in the presence of two members of the staff of the Association, and was found to contain one unaltered plate, and one which exhibited images of a large number of superimposed faces, similar to those obtained in the other results during the day. A print of this is appended hereto. The negative is in our possession at the laboratory. [not available. AH.]

Results.– All the results obtained upon exposures during the day were obtained under conditions which gave Mr. Hope every opportunity of faking results in the way described in a previous Report, with the difference that he was prevented from doing the faking except when the slides were in his pocket.

He was purposely permitted to have every opportunity of carrying out any fraudulent practices, if he purposed to do so."

Mr. De Brath adds:

"This "experiment" seems to me to have been conducted on quite wrong lines. Hope should have been requested to turn out his pocket at once. The omission of this renders the whole Report nugatory. It enables the medium to say that he did not use a flash-light, and was tricked. There is no defence possible. To take away a man's character, even a medium's character, on a Report of this kind, which can be quoted as "official" but cannot be produced because it is marked "Confidential," seems to me unfair and wholly alien to judicial procedure.

It amounts to saying: Hope _might_ have used trickery, _therefore_ he did. ... but there is a general tendency among scientists to reject testimony to all phenomena for which they cannot find a theory, or at all events a working hypothesis, but this does not include the hypothesis of survival"

* * * * *

As letters and statements in support of William Hope poured in to the psychic press offices Mr. Barlow came up with this defence:

"I have some fresh evidence to submit to you. On one or two occasions Hope asked me to obtain for him a chemical known as calcium sulphide. A month or so ago on going through some of his old correspondence I was surprised to discover a letter from his private address at Oakley Street, Crewe. Almost without exception Hope's letters were addressed from 144

Market Street, Crewe, the home of Mrs. Buxton. This particular letter, among other things, contained the following request: "Will you paint me a card with that luminous paint. Give it a coat or two, and let me have it this week if you can, or tell me where I can get it, for I cannot get it in Crewe. We are due at the College next week. Let me have the card early, and I will do as much for you some day. Write to me at my address, which is 50 Oakley Street, Crewe." (I have this letter with me here.)

In my enlightened frame of mind, I immediately realised he wanted this sent to Oakley Street, so that Mrs. Buxton would know nothing of it, and that he probably wanted it to prepare a stock of extras for his visit to London. ...."

Is it likely Hope would have been so "unguarded" in his use of words if it was to produce fraudulent images?

Is it not more likely they wanted to know what the effects could be, as Mrs. McKenzie later confirmed – they had been carrying out experiments with the luminous paint at the college at that time.

Mr. H.J. Osborn wrote in his critical report for *The Two Worlds, May 26th 1933,* of the meeting at the Queen's Hall:[6]

"If Hope wanted the chemical for faking at all, surely Mr. Barlow would have been the very last person to whom he would have applied! The chemical was sent, and Mr. Barlow entered on his new course of testing by suspicion. Yet nothing but suspicion, and a very doubtful assumption, emerges. There is not enough [in this allegation] on which to damn a good reputation of over a quarter of a century, and it can only damage that of Mr. Barlow himself."

A short time later, *The Two Worlds* received this from Mr. James Hobbs:[7]

"To smirk [besmirch?] the reputation of a man of such transparent goodness and honesty as William Hope is nothing short of a very serious crime, as it is based on innuendoes and presumed possibilities.

There is nothing strange in the fact that Mrs. Buxton's address, 144 Market Street, Crewe, was used in respect of seances, and Hope's address, 50 Oakley Street, Crewe for private correspondence. I have used both addresses myself.

Hope treated Fred Barlow as a friend, and knew he had been Secretary for the Study of Supernormal Pictures. He knew that Fred Barlow was familiar with that luminous paint and could supply it. Was Barlow already using it in producing fakes, as he has done since? Unless it can be proved that Hope adopted and used Barlow's luminous paint the attack fails completely.

6. *The Two Worlds* May 26th 1933 "Vindication of Wm. Hope" by H.J. Osborn.
7. *The Two Worlds* 23rd June 1933.

I have had splendid results after providing my own plates, used under test conditions, and I have every time seen the result on the negative before it was printed, and, like the Rev. C.L. Tweedale whose *Vindication of Wm. Hope* should be obtained and studied by everyone interested in spirit pictures, I stand as witness of the sincerity, honesty, and usefulness of a man who was blessed of God."

E.. James Hobbs.

Rev. Charles Tweedale also responded in *The Two Worlds* to Mr. Barlow's statement re the luminous paint:[8]

"Mr Barlow, whose letter appeared in a recent issue of *The Two Worlds*, has no proof that Hope ever used calcium sulphide in any way to produce his extras. Mr Barlow's statement that he could have used it is characteristic and is no proof that he did.

Mrs McKenzie testifies that at the College they experimented with Hope and luminous cards and if Hope did request Mr. Barlow to send him calcium suphide and luminous cards as Mr Barlow says they were evidently wanted for these experiments. There is no proof of fraud on Hope's part. The fact that Hope wrote from his home address, 50 Oakley Street, proves no fraudulent intention as Mr Barlow insinuates. I have had dozens of letters from the same address.

Because Mr. Barlow (given plenty of time and working at his leisure) has produced a fraudulent picture of extras, this is not proof that Hope ever did. The result of Mr Barlow's fake is quite unlike Hope's extras.

All Mr Barlow's ridiculous charges are whistled down the wind in view of the fact that—

1) Scored of recognised pictures containing all sorts of evidential detail, were obtained through Hope's mediumship under circumstances making it impossible for Hope to have any knowledge whatsoever of the extras.

2) Scores of recognised extras have been obtained through Hope in cases where *no normal photo, sketch or other representation of the deceased existed.*

3) Many cases have occurred of spirit warning appointments that the deceased would show up on the plate, which warnings have been kept strictly private and withheld from Hope (and in some instances of which the deceased have resided abroad, and no known photo has existed in England). Yet under these conditions recognised extras of the deceased who made the appointment have been obtained both by myself and others.

4) Recognised extras have been obtained through Hope in cases in which Hope did not enter the dark room touch the plate, carry the slide, make the

exposure or develop the plate afterwards, thus making all fraud impossible. Such a case occurred at my vicarage on Oct 30th 1932. A gentleman introduced to Hope only a few minutes before the photography, obtaining the recognised extra of a relative, Hope never approaching nearer than four feet of the camera.

In view of these facts, Mr Barlow's charges against Hope cannot be substantiated. The great majority of those who had the privilege of sitting with that wonderful man, "Honest Hope of Crewe" do not believe them and never will. Hope was a man whose shoe lachet his detractors were not worthy to unloose."

* * * * *

In March 1933 of the many people who responded to the publication of the report, are the following who had known Hope professionally for fifteen years or more.

George Lethem, the then Editor of *Light,* (March 31st 1933) wrote:

"On the strength of assertions contained in Mr Fred Barlow's 'Report on Psychic Photography,' the late William Hope has been branded in certain daily and Sunday newspapers during the week as a trickster and a charlatan. In earlier days as Secretary of the Society for the Study of Supernormal Pictures, Mr Barlow himself vouched unequivocally for the genuineness of Hope's mediumship and for the supernormal character of the photographic "extras" obtained in his own presence.

On reconsideration, he has changed his views; and, in the 'Report' read before the Society for Psychical Research, he gives his reasons for doing so. These reasons are interesting but they do not include definite and conclusive proof of fraud by Hope. In fact they do not include *any proof of fraud.* They are based entirely on suspicion. Mr Barlow shows how, in his opinion, the "extras" obtained by Hope *might* be produced by fraudulent means, and then he argues that, because fraudulent means exist, Hope *must* have used them.

Only those who rule out the possibility of "extras" being obtained honestly will accept such reasoning—and unfortunately, the sensation-mongers on certain sections of the Press are so badly informed that they readily adopt it.

To psychic students, the weakness of Mr. Barlow's reasoning is glaringly obvious. Presumption of fraud such as he puts forward would be allowable only if the evidence of the genuine production of photographic "extras" were lacking or doubtful. Then fraud would be permissible *as a hypothesis.* But as regards Hope's mediumship, evidence is neither lacking nor doubtful. That this is so, is shown conclusively in this issue of *Light* by the testimony of Mrs. Hewat McKenzie and Mr. Stanley De Brath, both of whom, as experts, write of their own fraud-proof experiments with Hope, as well as the experiences of others. To that testimony we could add our own, and doubtless hundreds of our readers are ready to do the same. In short, the evidence that supernormal photographic "extras" have been obtained in Hope's presence is as plentiful and as conclusive as evidence can be. An allegation of fraud against Hope could be justified *only* by the production of direct proof of fraudulent practices; and as already stated, Mr Barlow does not advance such proof.

In this manner, therefore, we unhesitatingly affirm that, whatever be the grounds of Mr. Barlow's suspicions, there is no reason to accept his conclusions, which are based on assumptions entirely contrary to the evidence of perfectly trustworthy witnesses."

Mrs. McKenzie said this in the report of her address in *Light* 31st March '33

"While not attempting to criticise the experiments made by Mr. Barlow and Major Rampling-Rose, one might quote equally cogent ones made by others with Mr. Hope and Mrs. Deane. For instance, I would mention a series of experiments by Mr. Chas. Lyle at the British College of Psychic Science, and known to Mr. Barlow.

Mr. Lyle was an experienced photographer, and always brought his own stereoscopic camera, with plates loaded at home already in the slides, he took the plates away with him at once for development, and sent reports and prints of results to the College. The only contact Mr. Hope and Mrs. Buxton had with these plates was when their hands and Mr Lyle's were placed on the slides in full light in the studio. *Sometimes an "extra" would appear on one plate in Mr. Lyle's camera and not on the other or the "extras" would differ on each; sometimes there would be the same "extra" as on the plate exposed in Mr. Hope's camera, sometimes not.*

If any trickery could have taken place, Mr. Hope must have operated two separate flashlights, as the plates were magnetised and exposed simultaneously.

Similar curious stereoscopic results were noticed in the experiments made by Mr. Traill Taylor in 1903, with the Medium David Duguid, under his own conditions — Duguid sitting a few yards away, but touching neither plates nor camera.

The confirmation or discovery of recognised "extras" through communications from other Mediums should also be remembered. In the case of my own son the "extra" was received at Crewe by Lady Glenconner, whose experiment was quite unknown to us, and only by information, detailed and exactly verified, received through Mrs. Osborne Leonard's mediumship, were we able to gain knowledge of its existence and verify the communication.

Mr. G.L.J.D. Kok, a Dutch investigator reports in *Psychic Science* (July, 1924) a sitting with Mrs Blanche Cooper in which a clear clue was given whereby he was able to find a photograph in Holland which enabled him to recognise an "extra" received by him with the Crewe Circle and another, two years later obtained with his son at Crewe which had many points of resemblance though one had a "cloud" surrounding and the other had not.

Neither were recognised, but the information given at the voice sitting that they were of the same person giving the name and relationship and indicating where the verification could be found, makes a most valuable "case". There must be many other such instances.

Were these other Mediums deceiving or did some "other side" friend who knew the facts lend assistance?

Mr. Barlow suggests that "draped extras" are suspect and probably mean substituted plates. I recall an experiment made by Mrs. St. Clair Stobart with the Crewe Circle at the College. Mrs. Stobart, unknown to anyone, had taken the precaution of asking the Kodak Co. to mark her plates without informing her what the marks were. A clear "draped extra" unrecognised was secured on one plate. Mrs. Stobart took this back to Kodak and asked them to point out their identification marks, of which a record had been kept. These were clearly shown. Some months later, at a sitting with Mrs. Cooper, Mrs. Stobart was given information which enabled her to recognise the "extra" as a relation whom she had never seen, but of whom she managed to secure a photograph for comparison.[9]

.... Mr. Barlow and Major Rampling-Rose protest too much in this lecture, which is largely built up on surmise and suspicion."

<u>James Coates</u> added this in response to the public press disclosure:[10]

"There appeared in *The Daily Express* a long article, being gleanings by a Special Correspondent from a Report in the *Proceedings* of the S.P.R., in which Mr. Fred Barlow attacks the genuineness of the photographic phenomena which took place under the mediumship of the late respected Mr. William Hope.

Mr. Fred Barlow was Secretary of the Society for the Study of Supernormal Pictures for four years and Editor of its Proceedings; afterwards, similarly with the Birmingham and County Society of Psychical Research. During these years he was familiar with thousands of spirit produced, supernormal pictures and never doubted their genuineness or the test conditions under which they were taken, or had a thought of attacking Mr. Wm. Hope, the departed psychic photographer.

---

9. See details of the sitting in Chpt 13
10. *The Two Worlds,* 31st March 1933

....The writer, among many others (Sir William Crookes, O.M., F.R.S., Lady Conan Doyle, etc.) has obtained identifiable pictures of relatives. I have had at four different sittings with Hope identifiable pictures of the late Mrs. Coates, *not one of them being a copy* of a photograph or painting.

As to *marked* plates: in Glasgow, Mr. Shaw, then of the Kodak Company, supplied six dry plates, all marked. No other was used; and in all cases some member of the Committee—including a professional photographer who did not believe in psychic photography—checked the proceedings and development. During this period a large number of identifiable pictures were produced.

As to the battery and bulb secreted in the Medium's hand, as Mr. Barlow ridiculously suggests and described with some wealth of imaginary detail, he never saw any such appliance, but a person *told him about it*, and that person's name he withholds.

To quote all the people of standing who had sittings with Hope and were satisfied as to his genuineness would occupy too much space.

I earnestly refute the accusations of Mr. Barlow and wish to vindicate the late and respected Mr. William Hope as being a genuine *tested* photographic medium and a man of integrity and unusual Christian sweetness. His simplicity – nay, even inefficiency – in matters photographic, was only equalled by his sincerity and impulsive warm-heartedness."

James Coates.

Author of *Photographing the Invisible*.

Honorary President of Glasgow Spiritualist Association.

Stanley De Brath directing his statement to the list Barlow had detailed wrote:[11]

"I feel myself called upon as counsel for the defence, but like a counsel I have no *animus* against the opposing side and am only concerned with evidence of fact.

The most serious charge to be rebutted is that of double exposure as evidenced by the rebates shown in the photographs shown by Mr. Barlow. Among the eight charges of fraud detailed on page 133 [of the S.P.R. Proceedings], this — the fourth — is the only one that is really to the point.

The Price experiment [Point 1] was easily shown to be capable of a quite different interpretation. I was myself on the Committee which examined the evidence.[12]

---

11. *Light*, 31st March 1933
12. see Chapter 16. The packet was shown to have been opened.

The sixth shows nothing but the utter incompetence of the experimenters to conduct any Judicial enquiry, as I have shown in *Light* of March 17th 1933. All the others are supposititious, and not evidence in the scientific sense, though they do give a reasonable doubt of Mr. Hope's honesty.

I shall therefore adduce evidence of fact—that Mr. Hope did produce genuine super normal photographs. [Point 7]

In *Budget* No. 58 of the Society for the Study of Supernormal Pictures, dated Jan. 20th, 1921., Mr. Barlow himself says (p.6): "I have got results with Mr. Hope here in *my* own home under conditions where fraud was absolutely impossible. I have loaded *my* dark slides in Birmingham and taken them to Crewe with my own camera and apparatus, have carried out the whole of the operation myself (even to the taking of the photograph) and have secured supernormal results."

This testimony is to a fact—it is not an opinion. It was given in connection with the "Nehushtan" Flashlight apparatus, which Mr. Barlow now considers explains many of Mr. Hope's photographs.

In *Budget* No. 63, of April 21st, 1921 Dr. Ellis Powell gives the whole detail of an experiment with Hope in which he performed all the photographic work himself, and testifies that Mr. Hope never had possession of the plates, nor of the slide after the plates were in it ...

From first to last there never was a scintilla of opportunity for Mr. Hope to play a trick. He details how he placed the plates in the dark slide himself, and never allowed Mr. Hope to touch them. The experiment resulted in a photograph of Olive R. which was recognised by her mother and brother.

In *Budget* 67 of May 17th, 1921, there is a very fully detailed account of a test experiment (pp. 9 and 10) by fifteen members of the S.S.S.P. which is signed by them all, which certifies (underlined) that "*Mr. Hope did not touch the plate till fixation was complete.*"

The account shows that the observation of Hope was very close. It is signed by Dr. Abraham Wallace, Colonel Baddeley, R.E. Mrs. McKenzie, Major R. E. E. Spencer and Mr. F. Barlow himself with ten other reputable witnesses. There also is testimony to the fact, which no change of opinion can alter.

One of these is from *Budget* No. 86 (p. 10) at which Mr. Barlow was present and states that Mr. Hope "turned out his pocket" before inserting the dark slide in it. Mr. Barlow signs the Report, with two other witnesses.

The S.S.S.P. was a society for the *critical examination of evidence.*"

Mr. De Brath, having included detail of the 1919 sitting by Geley and himself already given in Chapter 20, concluded with:

"I have always maintained that the correct procedure in examining any photographic medium is to be certain that camera, background and all accessories are impeccable, and not to allow the Medium any opportunity of touching the plates in any way."

Mr. Barlow replied to the criticism by saying:

"Our Report was made whilst Mr. Hope was alive with the design of checking deception. Now that he has passed on, there is no object in conducting protracted arguments except in the interests of Truth.

Incidentally, let me say that I had no bitterness against William Hope. I was friendly with him for many years, and he had his good points. Convinced as I now am that he practised trickery, I believe that even in this, in part, he did evil with the idea that good would come out of it. His sitters were deriving more comfort from what he gave them than if they received nothing at all, so he did not disappoint them. That, at all events, is how I regard his attitude."[13]

But let's examine Barlow's claims – note that he does repeatedly say:

"every definitely recognised "extra" *I have seen* of Hope's where there is no doubt as to the likeness, the "extra" has been an <u>exact copy of some existing photograph or painting</u>...."

And again –

"in every single case *I have investigated*, where there is no doubt as to the likeness, the "extra" has been an exact copy of some existing photograph or painting."

"every so-called test sitting *I have conducted, or have heard of*...

"In no instance *that I have investigated*, where such definitely recognised " extras " have been obtained, have I been able completely to satisfy myself that the medium did not have an opportunity of faking the picture beforehand."

Has he now shown himself to be the less than scrupulous investigator everyone took him to be?

In response to the points Mr Barlow puts forward as his evidence of fraud I counter with these records and findings, many already included in these chapters:

1. The 1922 Price-Hope case. – Yes, the plates were substituted, but when and by whom? Certainly not Hope – as one 'marked' plate was returned to the S.P.R. the following week, three months before it was revealed there had been a test case by the S.P.R. It was also proved by the manufacturers the label had been prised open and restuck – note Hope had never touched that label. (See Chpt 16)

13. *Light,* 14th April 1933

2. He does not tell us who this well-known friend was. If Price – he "as good as saw" Hope substitute the slides – not witnessed and not proved. If Higson of the British Photographic Research Association see the report extract and comment by De Brath (p268/9)

3. "..every definitely recognised "extra" I have seen of Hope's is a copy of a normal photograph." Many instances are given in this book of no image in existence or in the country – perhaps he hadn't seen them!

4. "Evidence of double exposure" – This has always been a problem in psychic photography, but not evidence of fraud (see Tweedale Appendix 7)

5. "Hope's psychographs or photographic messages provide internal evidence of a very suspicious character." – The spelling has, occasionally, similar errors to those in Hope's own letters but could his mental patterns have affected the spirit writer of the message?

6. British Photographic Research Association conclusion that Hope produces his effects by trickery. – see Extracts from the 'British Photographic Research Association' report as No 2.

7. In Tests Barlow has conducted "no instance where Hope has got an "extra" which could not be produced in identical circumstances by normal means." – Was he such a poor observant experimeter where others gave testimony of no possible interference?

8. "Our own common-sense which rejects these cut-out faces, block markings, magazine illustrations, cotton wool and muslin effects..." There are too many counter instances to list. However, if we consider that the images may be a thought process of that spirit person, as expressed by William Stead in Appendix11, and more recently by Walter Stinson, a communicator in Stewart Alexander's circle (Feb 15th 1994), when speaking of materialisations:

"... the chemists from this side of life withdraw the Ectoplasm from the medium, but at that stage it is in a very unorganised form. Now 'Christopher'[14] would then press his thoughts, and his thoughts would then mould the Ectoplasm. ...you would then perceive his thought – you would then see exactly what he was thinking. ... so you are not actually seeing him as such – but his thoughts."

– then may not the spirits themselves have chosen how they wanted to appear on the photographs and perhaps used their remembrance of an old portrait etc. (see Crawley p247 & Appendix 6).

Had Barlow forgotten / rejected all he had written just ten years earlier for his chapter in *The Case for Spirit Photography* in 1922 (page 83/4), which must have been approved by Arthur Conan Doyle before publication?

---

14. Christopher is another communicator with the circle.

"With the Crewe Circle I have had so many tests that it is difficult to select the most stringent. As the well-known Price case of alleged fraud bears on the question of the substitution of dark slides, the following case may be of interest. On this occasion the substitution of dark slides was impossible, for the simple reason that no dark slides were used.

Saying nothing to the members of the Circle beforehand, I took with me to Crewe on November 12th, 1921, a loaded box camera containing six specially marked plates of a size smaller than those usually employed in experiments of this nature. All that Hope and Mrs. Buxton did was to arch their hands over this magazine camera whilst one of them flicked the shutter-catch. Photographic readers will realise that it is impossible to tamper with the plates in a box camera, in daylight, without spoiling the lot. To enable the "power" to flow from Mr. Hope on to the plates, the controlling intelligence stipulated that Mr. Hope should be allowed to take hold of my right wrist as I dropped each plate into the developer. Psychic effects were secured on two out of the six plates under conditions which, I am convinced, rendered deception impossible.

I have been told that Mr. Hope must have printed the effects on to the plates by flashlight whilst he had hold of my wrist. If the critic derives any comfort from believing that this actually occurred, he is welcome to his belief.

In another evidential case is that already mentioned by Sir Arthur Conan Doyle of an experiment conducted by two photographic members of the S.S.S.P. and myself at Crewe. In this case the camera and slides employed were brand new and were not examined by the sensitives until after the sitting. The dark slides differed from those usually employed by the sensitives. Neither Mr. Hope nor Mrs. Buxton were in the dark room for loading the slides or for developing the plates. The central face of three supernormal faces secured on this occasion is an undoubted likeness of the father of one of the sitters. The result was absolutely conclusive to my friends and myself. We emphatically declare that under the circumstances, trickery was impossible.

Since the above was written I have been favoured with further excellent personal proof. On October 7th, 1922, I secured at Crewe several fine photographs of my father. The best were secured on plates exposed in a camera brought by one of three friends who accompanied me. He is an experienced and critical photographer and was responsible for the whole of the photographic operations. Reference to Fig. 31 will show that the psychic face has moved and appears in no less than six different places. This face is very similar to the Deane photo (Fig. 30), but by no means absolutely identical." (see overleaf)

So, he did recognise it and it was in a friend's camera! He comments on the Deane "extra" that it was *like the photo inset but 'aged a little in the 12 years'.*

"Fig 31" Recognised faces of his father taken on a friend's camera

"Fig 30' Recognised face of his father by Mrs. Deane. (See inset in life)

Barlow continued in Conan Doyle's book:

"The next chapter contains a series of abbreviated accounts and reports by investigators in every station of life. For the purpose of this book, they are confined to accounts connected with the Crewe Circle. In my capacity of Hon. Secretary to the S.S.S.P. it is my privilege to receive these documents in ever-increasing numbers. I imagine that the most hardened sceptic, occupying a similar position for a few months, would be convinced of the reality of psychic photography by this evidence alone. *Knowing it to be true, I look forward with confidence to that day, not far distant, when all this talk of fake and fraud shall be no more* and when the psychologist and scientist shall combine the investigation of this vital problem."

So what made him vehemently deny validity of all he had written and, apparently, so purposefully tested?

* * * * *

The proposed discussion on the paper went ahead at the Queen's Hall, London in May 1933. *Light* advertised it thus:

"Another interesting coming event is a discussion on Psychic Photography, with special reference to the mediumship of the late Mr. William Hope, to be held at the L.S.A. on Thursday, May 11th, at 8.15 p.m. Mr. Fred Barlow and Major Rampling Rose will explain the reasons for their adverse report on Mr. Hope's work ; and the evidence in favour of genuineness will be advanced by Mrs. Hewat McKenzie, and also by Mr. Stanley De Brath who will show lantern slides of evidence of "extras." Major C. H. Mowbray is to preside, and a very lively and instructive discussion is expected."

From the floor of the Queen's Hall that night in May Mr. H.J. Osborn told everyone of his remarkable experience in defence of Hope's mediumship. He gave "in briefest outline" the history of the fullest test of many in personal experience, and of the result: that of a perfect spirit picture of my wife ("Mrs. Jennie Walker") obtained under tests with Hope, six weeks after her passing. (*see image opposite*)

"Spirit" picture of Jennie Walker

"The plates never left my own possession. Hope never touched either packet or plates. They were bought the same day in Manchester, opened by me in the dark room; the two middle ones signed, the remainder replaced in my coat pocket. The two were loaded by me in the shutter, and I carried these to the camera. I focussed the distance myself, placed the shutter in the camera, turned the shutter after a first exposure, and carried it back to the dark room. There I took out the two plates and developed them myself. Hope did nothing whatever, except to flick away a duster from the lens (the cap of which had long been lost), and to raise the slide of the shutter for the exposure. All this was part of a careful test. It was absolutely "fool-proof" even against that self-foolishness on which Mr. Barlow now relies to account for his turn-about-face.

The first time I showed the picture by lantern, in November 1922, Dr. Abraham Wallace was by my side. He interrupted me and said, "That picture is marvellous. It is not the dear lady as we knew her in her prime; but it is exactly as she was during the last weeks of her illness, when I stood, day by day, at her bedside as her consultant." There was not, and could not have been, any portrait remotely like it."

Two weeks later Mr. Osborn added to this disclosure with a letter on the subject of the Barlow-Rose report in *The Two Worlds*:

"Imbued as the writer was, and is, with warm admiration of Mr. Barlow's services years ago, when he was the Secretary of the Society for the Study of Supernormal Pictures, one could not resist a deep sense of regret in contemplating him in this new roll, amongst the Dingwall-Harry Price type of pseudo psychic researchers. ...

I could discover nothing new or conclusive in the case presented. Moreover, the transparency of the first, and principal exhibit, might be an example in the opposite direction. ...

Mr. Barlow was disappointing. One would have expected much clearer evidence; closer running to earth of alleged suspicious clues; and above all, a fact or two. Instead, was presented a set of theories, weakly bolstered by numerous assumptions, used to besmirch Hope's memory, but never touching the point of truth.

Mr. Barlow committed himself to the broad assertion that Hope had never produced a single spirit picture; asserted that he himself, after hundreds of tests, was now convinced he had never had a real "extra"; that he now knew that he had never really applied his own tests of observation; and although he always thought he was sure Hope never did anything suspicious, now he is convinced he was mistaken; and that, confused by the many possibilities of the dark room, he must have overlooked vital points. It is difficult to imagine anything weaker, as coming from an accomplished photographer and a keen critic; and one fully familiar with Hope's tiny dark room under the cottage stairs.

All this is surprising: the complete antithesis of all one's estimates of Mr. Barlow's wide knowledge, analytical keenness and alert observation."

* * * * *

Other careful investigators were already carrying on the defence. In mid-April Rev. Tweedale gave an address in Bradford on the *"Vindication of William Hope"*.

The Two Worlds reported:

"The Mechanics Institute, Bradford. was crowded on Wednesday April 12th, when. under the auspices of the Yorkshire Psychic Society, a lecture on psychic hotography was delivered by the Rev. Charles L. Tweedale.Mr. Tweedale's lecture was illustrated by lantern slides, and was entirely devoted to the *Vindication of Mr. William Hope.*

"Hope's reputation stands firmly established and the base calumnies of his detractors will have no more effect on his good name than the splashing of water upon a granite rock." said the Rev. Tweedale.

The speaker proceeded to quote some most positive declarations on Mr. Barlow's part, as to the truth and reality of psychic photography. In the light of subsequent experience, Mr. Barlow had altered his views and even professed to know how Hope's pictures were fraudulently produced.

Dismissing the flashlight allegation as "silly", Mr. Tweedale said that it covered the accusers with ridicule. He cited personal experiences, in which Hope touched neither plate nor slide, from loading to development, and yet evidential extras were obtained.

In so far as the charge of substituted plates were concerned, it was proved that the onus of suspicion lay on the experimenters and not on Hope. The phenomena were due to natural and spiritual processes and not the product of fraud. The evidence of results was abundantly sufficient to triumphantly clear Hope's reputation from any imputation of fraud.

The Rev. Charles Tweedale spoke with emphasis and vigour, and the impression made upon his audience was that Mr Barlow had failed to produce sufficient evidence to establish any of his claims. The Address is to be published as a pamphlet (3d.)." [15]

Hans Hamilton wrote again from France:

"Sir, ...A very probable explanation of the appearance of double rebate marks on some of Hope and Deane's photographs is given in the pamphlet recently issued by the Rev. Charles Tweedale. That the psychic image is produced *after the normal exposure on the sitters*, and probably impressed in a fraction of a second, seems to be demonstrated, at least in many cases, by the fact of *the draperies or other part of the psychic image being superimposed on the faces or clothes of the sitters*, partly obscuring them.

As instances of this, I would mention two half-plate photographs sent the members of the Society for the Study of Supernormal Pictures, one representing a large figure of a young woman, upside down, in front of the two sitters; the second representing the two "guides" of Mrs. Deane and her daughter, the psychic draperies being very evidently superposed on the faces of three of the sitters. Both of these photographs were taken by Mr. Fred Barlow in his own house and on his own plates, and the latter one was obtained at a "surprise" sitting (see *Budget* No. 53 of the S.S.S.P.).

Left: Photograph referred to in the letter above; taken at a moment's notice on the suggestion of Mr. Barlow, in his own home, using his camera.[16]
Front row, Mrs. Barlow and Mrs. Deane, psychic photographer.
Top row standing. Miss D., daughter of the psychic, and Mr. Fred Barlow. The psychic portraits were recognised and claimed as the Guides of Mrs. and Miss Deane.[17]

---

15. *Read a copy of it in Appendix 7*
16. *Light,* 29th Jan 1921 'Birmingham Test Photography' in James Coates' series of articles.
17. See Mrs. Deane's letter to Warrick in Appendix 8.

If the psychic images are really *in front of the sitters* they cannot have been impressed on a *previously exposed plate* and the plate then substituted for an unused plate.

C. J. Hans Hamilton.

Mauzè-sur-le-Mignon,

Deux Sevres, France.

On checking the facts ninety years later of the position of first and second exposures, now that photography has become so much part of our lives, I found this statement on a photography website:

"The first exposure or layer of your image serves as the base layer upon which elements of the second frame will blend into. [For] double exposures that show ghostly apparitions, when shooting the second layer, you'll have your subject move out the frame to get that translucent, ghost-like appearance. "[18]

This was confirmed by my niece who is a photographer.

Another letter in defence of Hope came from James Norbury, the Editor of the *Lyceum Banner*:

Overwhelming Testimony

"Sir, Surely the overwhelming testimony of the many hundreds of sitters who have carried out experiments with Hope under all conditions during the many years of his mediumship far outweighs the suggestions of fraud recently made by Mr. Fred Barlow and Major Rampling Rose.

In reference to Mr. Barlow's recent talk upon the genuineness of William Hope's mediumship, the following point, I think, calls for consideration. If Mr. Barlow's Experiments—which he claimed were carried out under the strictest conditions and which, upon analysis, led him to the conclusion that he had received super-normal results—were so carelessly undertaken that it is now possible for him to reverse his judgment, surely this points to the fact that Mr. Barlow is not a reliable witness in the case. We shall do well to remind ourselves that the accounts originally produced by Mr. Barlow outlined, in many cases, his experiments step by step. If his searching analysis of the past is not to be relied upon, what justification have we for accepting his scathing criticisms of the present?"

James Norbury.

Ardwick, Manchester.

* * * * *

---

18. From www.techradar.com

And finally, in July, this letter arrived at *The Two Worlds* office from Canada, from Mr. Jas. P. Skelton who had been present when the Crawford psychograph was captured in 1922. He was now the General Secretary of the Spiritualists' National Union of Canada:

"I read with surprise the attacks made on the mediumship of Mr. Hope by Mr. Barlow, late Secretary of the S.S.S.P. as reported in the recent issues of *The Two Worlds*, and how he can do otherwise than accept the evidence which was secured under the conditions under which Mr. Hope worked, is beyond my comprehension.

I have experimented with him personally for many years, and if there has been any "faking" while the experiments were proceeding, then I did the "faking" (which I don't admit) and not Mr. Hope, as he allowed me to impose any restrictions I considered advisable. What more could any man do to establish the honesty of his work? The same may be said about Mr. Barlow's personal experiments, and if he did nor impose the necessary conditions at the time, then he has no right to speak now. It was up to him to see at the time that everything was above board and not malign him now, when he has passed where he cannot refute the allegations.

But I have no need to accept the conclusions of Mr. Barlow as to the genuineness or other wise of the mediumship of Mr. Hope. The late Dr. W. J. Crawford's "script message" in his own handwriting, with Mr. George Donaldson, Mr. J.W. Gillmour and myself as the sitters, satisfies me entirely that Mr. Hope neither faked nor could do so, even if he tried, as this message was secured under conditions that made "faking" or any other fraudulent practice impossible, also the fact that I obtained a complete likeness of my mother twenty-six days after her passing, is still more proof to me of the honesty of the man.

What is behind all this belated criticism? Is the evidence too strong for the critics who want to destroy the Movement by fair means or foul? Are the Churches trying through Mr. Barlow to discredit the evidence for their own purpose and motive? Surely Mr. Barlow would not allow himself to be made a tool of in this way? I cannot think so.

I have lectured all over Canada and many parts of the States, as well as in the "old country" on Psychic Photography, illustrated by lantern slides (many of which he supplied me), and without doubt this places me in a serious position. I will soon be going on tour of our Western Provinces again, and if Mr. Barlow can explain reasonably and intelligently how the following were secured other than by spirit agency, I will destroy every slide I possess, and admit the fraud when I go West.

1.) How can psychographs be accounted for and how were they produced?

2.) Was the message of Dr. Crawford written on the plate by myself, any of my colleagues in the experiment, Mr. Hope or by Dr. Crawford himself from spirit. How did any of us do it, or who did it?

3.) The message in neat copper-plate writing in three different languages—how was that secured? Was it by the chemicals asked for from Mr. Barlow by Mr. Hope from his home address?

4.) How was the handwriting of Dr. Crawford imitated if there was any fraud?

5.) How was the photograph of my mother obtained? Could this be "faked" by a man who held his mother in such a sacred memory?

No true Spiritualist wants to propagate either fraud or "faked" spirit photographs, and if Mr. Barlow establishes anything in the nature of fraud in the experiments with Mr. Hope, the Movement is entitled to his revelations. It is a serious matter for the cause if Mr. Hope is proved fraudulent, his work having convinced thousands where other forms of mediumship left them cold. But he must give facts, not theories or mere speculations, to unseat our confidence in the genuineness of the mediumship of Mr. Hope.

* * * * *

But William Hope was no longer with them to defend his work in his inimitable way.

MR. HOPE'S LAST COMMENT
One of the last letters written by Mr. Hope from Salford Royal Hospital was addressed to Mr. F. H. Haines, of Bedmond, Watford. " Your article in LIGHT on attacks on Mediums," he wrote, " I consider very good, for no one knows better than the poor old Mediums what they have got to put up with. You did your level best for some of them, then if it does not quite suit them they rush into print and nothing is too bad to say against you."

(Light March 24th 1933)

His Work is Done

William Hope took his transition at 11 o'clock on March 8th, 1933.

Lilian Bailey's biography[1] tells us:

"He had been taken to hospital with internal cancer, and during the two weeks he was there, sank rapidly.

When Mrs. Buxton and Lilian visited him on his last day on earth, screens had been placed round Billy's bed in readiness for the inevitable end. Then came one of the most dramatic and moving moments in Spiritualist history as Hope's guide controlled the dying man and bade farewell to the woman who had partnered the humble carpenter from Crewe in a remarkable mediumship that had convinced thousands. 'We are going to take over his body now,' the guide told Mrs. Buxton, 'because the pain is so great and we wish to spare him any further agony.'

Then he turned to Lilian and said, 'Good-bye till we meet again.'

Those were the last words to come from Hope's lips. He died soon afterwards . . . in trance.

Light announced his passing thus:

"Mr. William Hope, the world-famous psychic photographer, passed to the higher life on the evening of Wednesday, 8th March, after undergoing an operation for cancer in Salford Royal Hospital. His final illness was mercifully brief, lasting for little more than a week.

The news of Mr. Hope's transition will come as a shock and a surprise to the many hundreds of people who have benefited directly by his mediumistic activities and to the many thousands who have benefited indirectly by seeing his photographic "extras", hearing his racy lectures or reading of his work. Quite recently he lectured to a large gathering at the British College of Psychic Science, London.

At meetings all over the country on Sunday, mention was made of Mr. Hope's transition and of the valuable and consoling work accomplished through his photographic gift. At the evening service at the Grotrian Hall, London –where Mrs. Hewat McKenzie was the speaker – the audience stood in silence for a minute as a token of respect."

---

1. *Death is Her Life*, W.F. Neech

Rev. Tweedale gives his account of the closing of William Hope's life:[2]

"Friday, February 24th, 1933. Major Brownlow of York called with a friend. Sometime ago, after calling here, he went to Hope's house and got a splendid photo of his little son, of whom there is no similar photo in existence – one of the most beautiful child faces I have ever seen – which convinced him on the spot. Coming again to-day I advised him to go again and take his friend with him.

Monday, February 27th. By the afternoon post got a letter from Brownlow saying that he went to Crewe on Saturday and arrived just after Hope had been taken away to the hospital for an operation. We were horrified and greatly distressed. We sat at once to see if any advice could be given. Sir Arthur came, and said, "Hope is beyond your control. He has not taken my advice." I asked, "Does he need an operation?" Answer: "No." Question: "Is he going to have one?" Answer: "He has had all he ever will have." Question: "Has he had it?" Answer: "He has had all he will have. I am sorry." Question: "Will he recover?" Answer: "No, he won't."

"You said a short time ago that he would be here in three weeks." "He would have come had you sent for him then." (They had asked us to send for him.)

I at once wrote a letter to Mrs. Hope and Arthur begging them to have no operation, and sent my son down with it to Otley to catch the evening post.

Friday, March 3rd. Got a letter from Arthur Hope saying that he had seen his father in the hospital and found him a little better.

Friday, March 10th. Got the sad news that Hope passed away on Wednesday the 8th, and that the funeral is on Monday, the 13th.

Saturday, March 11th. Shortly before midnight my wife, who had fallen into a deep sleep by my side, suddenly was entranced and began to sing in Hope's low, sweet voice:

> *"Swift to its close ebbs out life's little day;*
> *Earth's joys grow dim, its glories pass away;*
> *Change and decay in all around I see:*
> *O Thou who changest not, abide with me."*

I listened breathless with awe and amazement, wishing that more would come, but, after singing the verse, she continued in deep slumber, and I did not awaken her, or inform her of what had happened until morning, when she was greatly affected and astonished. How splendid that Hope should so return in this way on the third day after death and before he was buried.

Monday, March 13th. Set off early for Crewe, where I arrived at 12.50, and at once walked down to 50 Oakley Street, Hope's private residence, and found

---

2. *News from the Next World* pps225-228

all that was mortal of my old friend looking calm and peaceful in his coffin, but the face drawn and worn with suffering, and oh, how one missed the bright, merry smile.

Madge got a message before I set out, to get three white Madonna lilies, so, as I passed through the town, I purchased them and they were laid on the coffin. Proceeding to the Buxtons' at 144 Market Street I found, on entering, Mrs. Buxton with several others seated round a table and busy making some arrangements.

After a hasty greeting I at once began to tell them about the wonderful singing of Mr. Hope in our room at Weston Vicarage on March 11th, and I sang the verse that Hope sang to me. Astonished, they cried out, "Why, that is the hymn we are talking about now and arranging to sing at the funeral service!" All were much impressed by this incident.

Half an hour after, we all sang that hymn around Mr. Hope's coffin, and then, proceeding to the cemetery, the burial took place. There were very many splendid wreaths of flowers sent from all quarters. After the coffin had been lowered into the grave, Mrs. Hope picked up our three Madonna lilies and, supported by her son, let them drop into the grave on the coffin. These were the only flowers placed on the coffin when in the grave. So passed one of the most wonderfully endowed men that ever lived. The grave was a terribly deep one, so deep I could only dimly discern the plate on the coffin and the flowers at the bottom.

Never did the grave look so terrible or unlovely. Had I not known the glorious evidence for survival, that grave would indeed have appeared to have gotten the victory over the brave smiling spirit of my friend, but knowing what I did of the wonderful evidence he had so often given, and with his own voice still ringing in my ears and sounding from beyond the grave, I could say with St. Paul:

"Thanks be unto God who giveth us the victory,"

The Two Worlds edition of March 17th tells us:

The funeral took place on Monday, March 13th, and following a short service at the house, there was a large gathering at the Crewe Spiritualist Church. The building was insufficient to accommodate the large number assembled. A prayer was offered by Mr. James Norbury, and Mr. G. F. Berry conducted the formal service, Mr. E. W. Oaten adding a few words of appreciation of the life and work of Mr. Hope.

The long procession wended its way to the cemetery, where a crowd of many hundreds had assembled for the brief committal service. There was a wonderful collection of wreaths, and the assembled company included representatives of all the Spiritualists of England. Among the wreaths was a tribute from the combined Spiritualist journals, *Light* and *The Two Worlds*.

* * * * *

Exactly three months after his passing "Billy" made his presence known at a direct voice sitting at the College in London with Mrs. Perriman as the medium.[3]

"Sitters: Dr. H. Coulthard. Mrs. Mckenzie. Mr. S.O. Cox. Lady Currie. Judge McIlwaine. Mrs. McIlwaine. Mr. Herten. Mrs. Macleod. Miss Tom-Gallon. Mrs. De Crespigny. Mr. West[4] . Mr: S. De Brath. Miss Hyde. Colonel N. P. Clarke. Mr. John McIlwaine. Mr. Heron.

Mrs. Hankey (Notes). Mr. Perriman (Gramophone and Musical Box.)

The seance was held in complete darkness. No trumpet was used. Mrs. Perriman was not controlled. Mr. Perriman operated the gramophone at intervals throughout the sitting. After the lights were put out, a gramophone record, "Hallelujah" was played. Mr. Perriman then offered a prayer, and "The Lord's Prayer" was recited by the sitters.

(the sitters' names and comments are shown in italics.)

After a number of communicators and messages passed on this voice was heard:

"Hello ! Billy."

Mr. West. Oh, is that you, Billy?

"I am William. Good evening, Mrs. McKenzie."

Mrs. McKenzie. Do you want me?

"I want to thank you for what you did for me a little while ago ... what you did when you spoke. I have been here before. I know this place."

Oh, you do?

"I am William Hope. I want to say God bless you all. God bless you all for having faith in me. God bless you. I just want you to know that I do thank you. I do thank you from the bottom of my heart for what you did. I knew you had faith and I knew I would take a chance to-night. God bless you all, for I know now, I know the real, and I see the splendour, and I see where a man has a chance to realise the ambition, and I see the help, and I want to tell you something else, Mrs. McKenzie. After this sitting is over, will you and four friends together; I think your husband wants to try to speak in light. Will you please have this little woman here, if you will just gather together. He wants

---

3. *Psychic Science* Oct 1933 page 212   Stenographic notes taken at a Direct Voice sitting with Mrs Perriman at the British College, Thursday, 8th June, R933, at 7.30pm.
4. Mr. West is the same Mr. W.J. West, the authority on photography referred to in Chpts1 & 10.

to try and speak in light. He wants to be the first. Only about four or five of you, and he will try and speak by light.

You mean the others will go, and we six will then stay?

"You know that he was always enterprising. If there was anything new he would have hold of it. He wants to try and speak in light.

Eh, I say, Mrs. McKenzie, will you just send a message to, you know, Mrs. Buxton, and tell her this: If ... shapes at all, ... you know what I mean, with photography, I mean."

Do you think she will get it?

"Tell her to stick by and I will help her to. I am going to try to help her to all I can. God bless you all. I have been here in flesh and now I am here in spirit. And all of you do try to understand. I thank you. Billy Hope, of Crewe."

Hope was here referring to Mrs. McKenzie's address, given just two days after his funeral in which she had made a strong plea for the better protection of mediumship, primarily photographic mediumship.[5]

"She had commenced her lecture by expressing the regret of the meeting at the passing of William Hope, one the of the greatest of the Mediums for psycho-photographic work. She gave a graphic sketch of his career, referring to the long and devoted attention he, as one of the "Crewe Circle" had given to the subject. For some eight or nine years the little group had sat for the development of the gift. Hope had come out of the Salvation Army and carried into Spiritualism a religious fervour that seemed almost fanatical and this was the key to some of those features of his mediumship which so puzzled the uninitiated."

Rev. Tweedale tells us of more of his experiences following Hope's death:[6]

"Four years elapsed before we were to obtain any further physical manifestation of our friend's survival, and we were to again hear the voice of our friend sounding from beyond the grave.

During these years we often wondered how it was that one who had given such unique evidence of survival to others should not have given further objective evidences of his presence to us. The years sped, and it was not until February 28th, 1937, just four years after his passing, that the silence was broken.

For nearly a week previously I had been laid up with 'flu, but as I appeared to be better and the weather was mild, I had arranged to go out on that day.

---

5. *Light,* 24th March 1933, Mrs. H. McKenzie on 'Psychic Photography'
6. *News from the Next World* pps229-231

In the early hours of the morning—about 2.30 a.m.—my wife, who was alone and was occupying the next room owing to my illness, was awakened by a loud rumbling on the floor of her room. She at once turned on an electric lamp standing by the bedside, but could see nothing unusual. The door was locked and bolted, as also was the door of the dressing-room. She put out the light, and immediately the loud rumbling noise was repeated. Before she could flash on the light again, suddenly all the bedclothes were snatched away and thrown completely over the foot of the bed. She scrambled down to the bed's foot, and seizing the bedclothes drew them back again and arranged them in their normal position. Then, rather alarmed, she called out for me. Immediately afterwards the bedclothes were again drawn down and flung over the foot of the bed. Then a white hand appeared in the air between the bed and the wardrobe, turned palm towards her, as though warning her. This remained visible for about half a minute, then a voice, loud, clear and distinct, which she at once recognised as Hope's, said, "Don't be afeared: do as I tell thi." She said, "What do you say?" The voice replied, "Don't be afeared. Do as I tell thi. Tell that mon o' thine not to go out to-day, or he'll be wanted." Then silence. She lay awake for an hour or so, it being still dark, and then got to sleep again. On winding up the blind in the morning she found to her astonishment a totally unexpected and savage winter scene – snow falling heavily, a boisterous gale drifting it from the north, and the whole countryside buried under drifts.

Not a trace of this had been apparent when she retired for the night. The cogency of the warning in the night was obvious. They knew of the blizzard which had come evidently in the night, though she did not. My wife and Dorothy sat at 10 a.m., and Chopin then said that the hand and voice were Hope's. Sir Arthur said that it was absolutely necessary to stay indoors, or serious consequences would ensue. The voice was not only recognised as Hope's, but the words were perfectly characteristic of him; "afeared," "thi," and "mon" being characteristic of the Lancashire dialect, and of Hope's speech, when he relapsed into it.

Again on Saturday, July 31st, at 11.30 p.m., my wife saw William Hope by the bedside here at Weston. She particularly noted the colour of his eyes. He remained visible for some time, but did not speak, as he previously had done on February 28th last; but she got the strong impression that he would be seen at York on the occasion of the visit of a well-known materialising psychic. She, therefore, wrote to Mrs Holdgate of Leeds – who had informed her of an invitation to visit York – and told her of this strong impression, and asked her to take particular notice of the happenings, but not to inform any person of the impression she had received.

The sitting duly took place in York on the evening of August 8th, and Mrs. Holdgate describes what happened:

"'Albert', Mrs. Duncan's control, first said that this sitting was going to be an outstanding one. After one or two forms had appeared for others, he called the name 'Holdgate', and on my replying, said that he was sending a man out to be recognised. Then, wonder of wonders, out walked William Hope, twirling his moustache, with his well-remembered smile, and saying, 'It's Billy.' He then said, without any prompting, 'The Tweedales have had plenty of evidence.'

"This was very wonderful in view of the fact that no one present, save myself, knew of your (Mrs. Tweedale's) impression. I recognised him instantly, and so did several other people who were present."

* * * * *

There was another striking return (date unknown). Paul Miller records in *Faces of the Living Dead*[7] the return of 'Billy' under the pencil of Frank Leah, the artist:

"You may have read Oscar Wilde's famous psychic story, *The Picture of Dorian Gray*, in which the living portrait changes. Now here is the story of a fact — the psychic portrait of a great medium William Hope, the spirit photographer of Crewe, which was transformed as two people watched. One was Frank Leah, the artist; the other was Betty Shaw. This is her story.

She had a sitting with Hope, taking with her a packet of sealed photographic plates. She opened the packet in the dark room, initialled the plates, and loaded the camera. Three photographs were taken, and of the two clear psychic extras which appeared she recognised one.

After Hope "died" Betty Shaw says he returned to her through three mediums. Then she desired to have a picture of her guide, and asked Leah to do it. He was to her what he was to the others — a stranger. Thomas Wyatt, another medium, agreed to sit with them to provide extra power. Then the séance began. Wyatt was in trance. As so often happens, Leah was in pain, not his own, but the pain of another returning to this world.

They were in the dark when Leah said to Betty Shaw: "Over where your face must be, there is the face of a man so well illuminated that I must draw him."

The artist then touched her face and described in detail the face he had seen superimposed on it. He switched on his torch, which gives a dim red light, and drew rapidly. Betty Shaw was anxious to see her guide, and when the features grew on the board she exclaimed: "Why, that's Billy." Leah said sharply: "Don't give me any names."

Betty Shaw had met Hope. Leah had not, but both stood and watched this amazing happening. She describes it:

"As I watched the drawing, without the artist's hand touching it, we both

7. *Faces of the Living Dead*, published by SNPPBooks in print and digital form.

noticed that the features were altering. They took on an expression of extreme suffering."

The portrait took about seven minutes to draw, and when the lights were put on Betty Shaw produced a photograph of Hope that she always carried with her. No one knew this, and she says: "The difference between this photograph and Leah's charcoal portrait is that my photograph is full face and wearing a cap, while the drawing shows him three-quarter view without headgear. The likeness is quite unquestionable."

Portrait by Frank Leah   *Photographic Portrait 1924*

Wyatt's guide said, before the lights were turned on, that the spirit people were pleased with a most successful experiment, and at a later sitting, when Leah asked why he, who knew nothing of Hope, should have been chosen in this unusual fashion to do his portrait, he was given this answer:

"When we looked for means of vindicating this great warrior who has suffered so much persecution in his work for us, even since he came over, we sought the one means of proving his features through a source independent of photography. That's why we chose you. We wanted Billy's features to be given through a pencil — through a medium who had no knowledge whatever of them. By doing so, we have accomplished our object. He has given incontestable proof of his survival."

"Thus does the spirit world regard its warriors, the men and women who lift the load from the heart of the world."

Charles Tweedale writes in closing his chapter on William Hope:

"To return again to the subject of this marvellous man's photography. Thousands of pictures of the departed, very many obtained under absolute test conditions and standing up to the acid test of complete and absolute recognition by relations and friends, were obtained by him.

Some of his experiences had their humorous side, as witness the following: On one occasion a man came to him in a very sceptical mood saying that he would be quite convinced if he could obtain for him the spirit form of his deceased wife upon the plate. He was staggered when the clear likeness of his two deceased wives showed up in the photograph. I could fill a big book with accounts of his work and reproductions of his photographs."

I have hundreds of his pictures and negatives, and obtained many of the results in my own Vicarage under rigid test conditions, precluding even the possibility of fraud. I say, without fear of effective contradiction, that no man ever lived who has given such permanent proof of survival and the spirit world as did Hope of Crewe.

Evidence piled upon evidence, testimony on testimony, photograph on photograph, all proclaim with unswerving persistence and unfaltering iteration this glorious truth."

> "There is no death, what seems so is transition:
> This life of mortal breath
> Is but a suburb of the Life Elysian,
> Whose portal we call death."

This was a man who worked until the last two weeks of his life.

At some point in early February (as already mentioned) Hope had given an illustrated lecture in London. Report shown below from *Light:*

Mr. Hope lectured at the British College of Psychic Science on Wednesday evening last week and showed a large number of lantern-slides, many of which had "extras" which, for various reasons, could not be explained by flash-lamp manipulation or by duplication of normal photographs. Mr. Stanley De Brath presided and there was a good attendance.

– and several people had had sittings with him in Crewe – Among them were these reported in *The Two Worlds:*

Ernst Oaten included this one in his tribute to Hope:

"A photograph (shown right) was taken only a few months ago at Chorley. Mrs. Yates claims that the psychic extra is the image of her father, whom Mr. Hope could not possibly have known, and the inset represents a photograph of the father taken during life."

– and also included this:

"Mrs A Pears, of Rhos-on-sea, sends us a photograph which was one of the last Mr. Hope could have taken, and which we have pleasure in reproducing herewith.

In the early part of February of this year. Mrs Pears and her daughter had been to Coventry to attend the funeral of a relative, and on returning home the daughter expressed a desire to stop at Crewe for a sitting with Mr Hope and Mrs Buxton. This was done, and the photograph was taken under Mrs. Pears careful supervision. She had mentally asked for her grandchild to appear on the plate. The child was born on February 27th 1930 and passed to spirit a few days later. The mother of the child had a serious illness with septic pneumonia and nervous collapse. Despite the opinion of the doctor that she would pass away, the mother made a recovery.

Mrs Pears assures us that not only is the extra a striking likeness of the child, but also shows a remarkable similarity in features to that of the child's mother at a similar age. At a subsequent voice séance, not only was an affirmation of identity given but also the statement that the other extra on the plate was the nurse in present charge of the child."

* * * * *

Several correspondents claimed theirs must have been his last picture but the following was certainly one of the last.

From *The Progressive Thinker* of Chicago came this. In *The Two Worlds* on June 9th 1933, the sitter, Hampton W. Howard wrote this:

"I feel it both my duty and pleasure to record the details of a sitting I obtained with Mr. William Hope less than a month before his passing. Having for the past year been a regular sitter at the "Station Astral" séances in New York city and interested in all activities of Spiritualism in America and abroad, naturally when I stated that I was planning a trip to London, Mr Arthur Ford and Mrs Drouet were desirous for me to have some new experiences as for instance, a sitting with Wm. Hope.

Armed with letters from these two friends for Mrs. De Crespigny, I arrived in London. Mrs. De Crespigny was not only kind enough to give me a personal letter of introduction to Mr. Hope, but also sent him a letter relative to my arrival at Crewe on Thursday evening, February 16th.

Early on Friday morning I presented myself at 144 Market Street. A Mrs. Buxton received me, and informed me that Mrs. De Crespigny's letter had preceded my arrival, but that her home was only the locale of the sittings, and that Mr. Hope's residence was a short distance away. On calling (as directed) at Mr. Hope's home, I was welcomed by his son, aged about thirty, and informed that his father was away visiting his daughter, who was ill, but that he would be back soon. After repeated calls I caught Mr. Hope at home during his lunch hour about 1.30 o'clock.

Mr. Hope is a typical British working-man, rather uneducated, poorly dressed and very kind hearted. I found him most cordial upon making myself known. He said he would be glad to give me a sitting as soon as he had finished his dinner. He then asked me if I had brought my own plates. I had not. He instructed me to buy a package of plates at any chemist's. I went to Russell's, of Crewe, and bought (for about 35cents) a sealed package of plates. I then returned to the Market Street address and waited with Mrs. Buxton and her three year old grandchild for Mr. Hope's arrival.

Mr. Hope, Mrs. Buxton, the three-year-old grandchild and myself went into the front parlour, and sat around a small table. Mr. Hope said, "I do not know what your religion may be." He asked us all to touch hands upon the table, and said we would sing a few hymns. After singing these, Mr. Hope prayed that we might be vouchsafed some manifestation.

During this service I had taken the package of plates from my pocket and placed it on the table. When Mr. Hope commenced to pray he picked up the package of plates, placing one hand under and one hand above them. Then he asked me to place my hands upon his; then Mrs. Buxton placed her hands upon mine, and finally the grandchild placed her hands upon those of her grandmother. It was while we were all in this position that Mr. Hope offered up his supplication. His prayer finished, he asked that I again take the plates in charge. I placed the plates in my pocket. We then left the parlour and went into the kitchen. Mr. Hope then asked me to come with him into what proved to be a very small sort of pantry, better described as a cupboard. This cupboard was illuminated only by a lantern flashlight, the lens being covered by a red cloth.

At this point Mr. Hope asked me to break the seal on the package of plates which I did. He then said, "We work by impressions entirely; do you have any impressions as to which two plates of the six you hold to try first?" I had no strong impression, but after a moment's delay I chose numbers 3 and 4. He then asked me to place the first two plates I held in my hand, to examine the slide or rack into which they were to be fitted. This I did. It was only an empty frame. Into this frame, after examination I placed under Mr. Hope's instructions, plates numbered 3 and 4. Mr. Hope then insisted that I, not he, place the frame containing my plates (which please note had not left my sight) in my pocket, and follow him.

We again entered the kitchen, and passed through it into a sort of conservatory attached to the house. Leaning against the wall was a tripod box camera, which Mr. Hope mentioned as being a gift from Sir William Crookes, the scientist. This camera was the one we used. Upon invitation I made a thorough examination of it. It was an ordinary camera, devoid of any extraneous features.

I next sat on a chair, placed in front of a green curtain, which I personally pulled across a rod, running the width of the greenhouse, having made sure that there was nothing behind it other than the wall of the house and two glass sides of the greenhouse. After being seated I handed Mr. Hope the frame in which were the two plates, signed across the corner by myself while in the darkroom. These plates had not left my sight, except while in my pocket, and, still within my sight, they were placed in the camera.

Mrs. Buxton was then called and stood beside the camera with both hands, held palms down, above it. Mr. Hope then exposed first one plate and then the other. He then withdrew the frame with the plates still in it, and again asked me to place the frame in my pocket. In the darkroom I handed them to Mr. Hope, who in my sight, placed them in a plate of chemicals. After a few minutes' submersion they were taken by me to the kitchen, where Mr. Hope poured faucet water over them.

In a minute or so my own likeness was clear on both plates and on one plate was a very distinct extra. This extra has been recognised. In closing, I wish to state that no photograph of the extra has ever existed in England."

* * * * *

Just eight days after this successful sitting Hope was admitted to hospital and passed to a better place eleven days later.

Rev. Charles Tweedale made up his mind that so wonderful a man should have a memorial in the Church of which he was Vicar. He designed and had 'carried into effect' a handsome engraved brass plate mounted on a solid oak backing.

This was unveiled in Weston Church on December 10th, 1933. The brass plate bore the following inscription:

TO THE GLORY OF GOD, AND IN MEMORY OF

WILLIAM HOPE

OF CREWE

BORN DEC 10TH 1864 : DIED MARCH 8TH 1933
WHO BY HIS WONDERFUL SPIRITUAL GIFTS
BROUGHT CONSOLATION TO THOUSANDS.
DEMONSTRATING HUMAN SURVIVAL
AND "THE LIFE OF THE WORLD TO COME"
TO HIS DAY AND GENERATION.

"TO ANOTHER DISCERNINGS OF SPIRITS" I COR XII 10
"MADE MANIFEST BY LIGHT" EPHES V 13

The service was attended by a large number of people from all over the country, filling the Church. Rev. Tweedale preached the sermon, and felt it a privilege to do so; giving some of the facts of Hope's extraordinary life and adding:

"Only those who have made a close study of his work can realise how wonderful it was and how far-reaching the influence and consolation given through him. Of no man in modern times could it be more appropriately said:

"They rest from their labours and their works do follow them."

* * * * *

Tributes and Observations

<u>Ernest Oaten</u> – Editor of *The Two Worlds* – (March 17th 1933)

"For over twenty-five years Mr. Hope and Mrs. Buxton have been the centre of the Crewe Circle, and over a long period Archdeacon Colley and Mr. Wm. Walker supervised the circle and tabulated the results.

Gradually the fame of Mr. Hope spread, and it is safe to say that influential men and women from all over the world have visited Crewe. In the vast majority of cases they have gone away with the conviction that psychic photography was a fact, and that it is possible to get reproductions on photographic plates of people long since dead. Scores of professors from European Universities have visited him, while journalists, chemists, photographic experts, detectives and professional men of all types have visited Crewe. Of course, in the nature of the case, sceptics have occasionally levelled charges of fraud against Hope, but a serious survey of the whole of the facts, even of these charges, will convinced the unbiassed mind of the amazing lengths to which critics have to go even to establish a suspicion of fraud. In spite of recent attacks made upon Mr Hope's mediumship, we do not hesitate to say that the evidence he has produced on hundreds of occasions is convincing to any fair-minded man.

The most repulsive and detestable practices have often been resorted to in order to lure him into a position which would compromise his reputation.

He has been known for many years as the most successful spirit photographer Spiritualism has produced. Now that he has passed on, he has left behind him a reputation even in the minds of hundreds of sceptics who have sat with him, which will stand unsullied amidst all the attacks.

Even if nothing else had emerged from Mr Hope's mediumship he has done more than any other medium of his type to enable us to determine what are the definite scientific conditions under which psychic photography should be obtained.

He was a lovable type of man but he took strong likes and dislikes. If you won his friendship and his confidence, you could practically conduct your experiment as you liked. He gave you a free hand. If he took a dislike to a sitter, he was adamant in his refusal to do anything to oblige that sitter.

His work will be criticised through the years yet to be, but there are thousands of people in this country who have learned to love and respect William Hope.

Rev Charles Tweedale – in *Vindication of William Hope* (1933)

"I knew Hope intimately for 15 years, during the whole of which time I found him to be an upright, God-fearing, honourable and transparently honest man, and I count it an honour to have known him and to have received him into my house. He had God-given powers which rank him as the equivalent of one of the great prophets of old time, nay caused him to exceed them, in his powers of demonstrating the Spirit World, human survival, and 'the life of the world to come'."

James Lewis – Editor of the *International Psychic Gazette* (1933)

"He was a simple-minded, honest, truthful, inoffensive, richly-gifted medium, whose powers had been tested and proved genuine by hundreds of critical and uncritical observers, from Sir William Crookes down to humble investigators wanting infallible proofs of the survival of their own dear ones, whose portraits they were not likely to mistake."

Stanley De Brath, (Tribute in *Psychic Science,* April 1933)

"We have lost in him one of our very best mediums for supernormal photography, and a very simple-minded and sincere man.

He has comforted scores of bereaved souls with whom he was entirely unacquainted, by portraits of their lost relatives, plainly recognisable from photographs taken in life. He has been vehemently attacked both in England and on the Continent, ignoring the fact that an immense repertory of normal portraits and an extraordinary versatility in extracting information, would have been necessary to support the charge of fraud. My own testimony that he produced portraits without touching the plates, which I have verified on five separate occasions, is also ignored."

And in *The Two Worlds*, Nov 1937 he added:

"It is often asked, 'Why should this medium refuse to experiment with a scientific committee?' I endeavoured to get him to do so.

His answer was that he had given scores of such tests to the S.S.S.P., as I very well knew; that he once consented to have his hands tied and take off the cloth from the camera with his teeth, under promise that if an "extra" appeared the two experimenters would bear witness. The "extra" was there, but they broke their word. Another "scientific" society played a disgraceful attack upon him, surreptitiously substituting another slide for his own, assuming that he must have been fraudulent.

He said to me, "Whatever they see they will deny it; I have given scores of tests and will give no more. There are hundreds of people who know that my work is genuine, and I do not care if scientific blokes believe it or not. The loss is not mine but theirs." Mr. Hope was a trade unionist, a class not especially remarkable for amenability.

I suspect myself that the antagonism to supernormal photography is because it is not explicable by "the subconscious mind"; but whatever the reason – my own careful experiments, added to those by the Society for the Study of Supernormal Pictures, and the very decisive certificate given in Hope's favour to Lady Glenconner by the professional photographer, Mr. Colledge, after supervising in the closest manner the experiments at Glen – make me certain that supernormal photography will have to be admitted as one of the fundamental phenomena on which the new science rests.

<u>Felicia R. Scatcherd</u> – in the "Problems of Psychic Photographs" lecture at the LSA, (*Light*, Feb 3rd 1921)

Miss Scatcherd referred to several cases in which Hope had never come into contact with the plates, or had any opportunity to do so. She also mentioned that Hope himself was as much interested as anyone in the problem as to how the effects were produced, and had often discussed the matter, although, of course, he was satisfied that they were due to spirit agency.

She remained a loyal friend to Hope and the circle throughout the years that she knew him and took many eminent people to sit with him, so sure was she of his gift. (See David Gow's tribute below).

<u>David Gow</u> – (Editor of *Light*, 1914 -1930) "A Genuine Medium", (*Light*, March 17th 1933)

When I first met William Hope many years ago, I was confirmed in the impression I had formed from some previous correspondence with him, that he was a simple honest man.

I came on several instances of identifiable faces obtained with people who were strangers to Hope, notably Mrs. Neilsson, the wife of the Icelandic professor who went to Hope incognito and obtained a singularly clear likeness of her husband which she showed to me. Having known Professor Neilsson in life, I recognised it at once as being a clear and unmistakable portrait. There were many other cases but to me that was one of the most outstanding.

Mrs. Neilsson came from Iceland to visit Hope. She kept her identity secret, and, as she told me, Hope supposed her to be an American visitor.

Of Hope's honesty I have never had any doubt from the beginning; but I noticed that, by his very simplicity and "casualness" he often played into the hands of his critics. During all his career as a Medium, he had become so accustomed to accusation and abuse that he had grown case-hardened. His attitude seemed to be that, knowing himself to be honest, it did not matter how many people thought otherwise.

I found, too, that in his almost cynical indifference, he was given to play tricks on sceptical inquirers by pretending to cheat and then boasting that he had scored over his enemies in that way. Miss Felicia Scatcherd, who had studied his mediumship and was always his friend and champion, once told me of the scolding she gave him when she discovered this little eccentricity. Knowing of other cases in which Mediums, after being browbeaten and watched suspiciously by unbelievers, had reacted to the treatment by resorting to the very trickery of which they were accused, I was not exactly surprised. To pretend to cheat as a method of getting even with one's accusers is obviously a very unwise thing, even if, human nature being what it is, it is rather to be expected.

Mr. Hope, in my view, was a genuine Medium, but of a type of mentality which might easily lead to the opposite conclusion on the part of an unsympathetic observer. I know that he regarded his mediumship as a mission; that he never made a trade of it and was quite oblivious of its scientific implications. He was essentially good-hearted, and I bid him farewell not entirely with regret, for he has gone to a world in which his true nature will be better understood."

Sir Arthur Conan Doyle – In *A Case for Spirit Photography*,(1922)

It has been said that Hope is suspiciously restless and fussy in the dark room. This, so far as my own observation goes, is correct. It may be that he is nervously anxious for success, or it may be that he is not in a normal condition—for he usually holds a service and occasionally goes into apparent trance immediately before the experiment.

He is impatient of tests and restrictions. Mediums are touchy people more delicately organised in many cases than any other human type. They may occasionally show an irrational annoyance and resentment against any action which implies personal suspicion. And yet, though he certainly prefers to be left to his own methods, unrestrained save by ordinary observation, it is a fact that he has in the past consented to a great number of tests and has come out of them remarkably well.

I have heard him say, "What have I to gain from tests? I am put to a deal of trouble, I do what I am asked to do, I get the result, and then I hear no more about it except that perhaps I have convinced the person. Or perhaps, even if I have done all he asks in his own way, he still says he is unconvinced."

Mr J. W. West – previously Gen. Manager for Scotland of Kodak Ltd. in a letter to F.W. Warrick in August 1930 expressed this:

I have pleasure in giving you a written testimony of my initial experiences with Mr. Wm. Hope, the Crewe Psychic Photographer. It was in my official capacity in June, 1914, that I was approached in Glasgow by folk who termed themselves "The Glasgow Association of Spiritualists." I was informed that they were to be visited by Mr. W. Hope and Mrs. Buxton, of Crewe, who were alleged to be able to obtain through some extraordinary psychic gift, pure spirit photographs of disembodied entities, and as they knew little or nothing technically about photography, they desired me to enlist the services of an expert to ensure reason able satisfaction to them that they were not being hoaxed. I agreed to place my services at their disposal and was privileged to attend the various séances in company with two photographers whom I had selected—the one a well-known professional, at whose studios the first experiment was made—the other a professional attached to the leading Glasgow newspaper.

The camera Mr. Hope used was an old-fashioned Lancaster's "Le Merveilleux" with which I was well acquainted. In putting him under strict test conditions he was in no instance allowed to handle the actual plates, either for the purpose of loading the slides, taking out, or developing. Various makes of plates were used, all of which were supplied by the manufacturers through me only. Each plate was initialled in the presence of a second and third party before exposure. Our own developer was used.

In the circumstances we were satisfied that no supernormal result could obtain; but to our amazement, on the first negative of a group of twelve sitters, a. large head appeared as if superimposed over the sitters, which was at once recognised as a Mr. Jas. Robertson, a previous President of the Glasgow Association of Spiritualists, who had passed away three years previously.

Other identifiable results were obtained of which Hope could not have been cognizant, as the relatives informed us that in most cases no such photographs of those obtained were in existence: moreover we were assured that neither Mr. Hope nor Mrs. Buxton had been in Scotland before this date.

I have had innumerable sittings since with Hope, including some at the College of Psychic Science, at all of which "Extras" have been obtained, mostly identifiable.

The conclusion I subsequently arrived at was, that Hope was not sufficiently well acquainted with photography to enable him to produce results of this nature, even if he desired so to do.

It was impossible to detect anything in the nature of fraud on the part of Hope and his co-worker Mrs. Buxton, and my knowledge of them since my first experience with them in 1914 has afforded me ample justification to regard them as honourable people.

<u>James Norbury</u> – Editor of the *Lyceum Banner*, (April 10th 1933)
<u>A Tribute:</u>
William Hope – The Modern Troubadour of God

> Alone with Thee amid the mystic shadows,
> The solemn hush of Nature newly born;
> Alone with Thee, in breathless adoration.
> In the calm dew and freshness of the morn.

There exists a strange kinship between Francis of Assisi and William Hope of Crewe. Each can be said by common desire to have been wedded to My Lady Poverty. Each met the storms and battles of life with a song of praise on their lips, and each surrendered himself entirely to one dominating purpose that coloured the texture of his life.

When we turn to medievalism we shall find that the rich little poor man, the singer of songs whose simple beauties are a highlight in an age of darkness, was undoubtedly the transforming factor of the religion of his day. Through his ministry men and women who had become disillusioned about life, who had lost their vision, who had seen the darkness of a closing era folding in upon them, found a new inspiration and discovered the way of the courageous life once more. The same can be said of William Hope.

To him people of all lands and climes have come to rediscover a faith in themselves and the certainty of first and last things. With his passing, not only Crewe, but the world has lost one of its greatest men, and no matter how much Spiritualism may grow and blossom forth into the universal religion it is destined to become, the Crewe circle and their labours will be unforgotten, for they are without doubt, one of the corner stones of the new vision of life which Spiritualism presents to mankind.

Speaking of him at the moment when we were bidding his mortal remains farewell, Ernest W. Oaten, a man who had stood by him when the storm waves were beating in upon his reputation, said:

'William Hope was one of God's simplest souls, but he was more than this; he was also one of His greatest servants. He was essentially a man of the people, simple, rugged, and direct. In treading the thorny path along which every public medium must walk he was as one who sits on the top of a wall for every fool and ignoramus to throw stones at. And yet he never bore malice. I do not think he had any ill-will to anyone.

Peers considered it a privilege to be in his company. Scientists laughed at his simplicity but admired his sincerity. All who knew him intimately learned to love and respect him. He has brought comfort to thousands and I know of no man in the world who can fill his place.'

In these few words Ernest Oaten has done more than pay a tribute to a great man, he has re-created that man's character for all time.

I well remember my first contact of Billy Hope. It is one of the high lights in my psychic adventures. There was something so tremendously humorous about the whole atmosphere of that first sitting. I do not know quite what I expected when I arrived at Crewe but I certainly did not expect a funny little man, in a dirty old cap, with a face wreathed in smiles, and a welcome in every word, to open the door to me at 144, Market St.

In that first contact. I felt I was in the presence of one whose essential nobility strangely contrasted with my own unworthiness. There was no fuss about the whole business. I had taken my own plates, I watched every stage of the proceedings, and I obtained an extra. I gained much more, however, than a psychic extra for in that first hour's association with Billy Hope one glimpsed a faith so sublime, a surety in the guiding hand of God so certain, that one's own halting acceptance gained new re-assurance, a vitality that was stronger than anything one could build into one's philosophy of life from reading tomes or burning the midnight oil for years.

Of his passing I need say little. That he suffered more deeply than even his most intimate friends realised is a fact that we now fully appreciate. But in those last hours as the twilight of life in this world closed in upon him, as he wandered in the shadows that lie along the last valley, he was still his cheerful self. Whereas some might hope for a hereafter, Billy knew. What a host of friends must have gathered to welcome him as he awakened in that new dawn time. Friends who had walked a little way ahead, yet whose memories of earthly associations with him must have linked them in bonds of affection that naught can destroy.

As we walked along to the graveside the thought flashed through my mind how terribly unlike Billy Hope this strange, yet dignified, procession was. He would have like all the flowers, for his was a soul that revelled in simple things, in the beauty of springtime, in the merry tinkle of childish laughter, but all the fuss that we were making would have seemed to him to be a huge joke. Somehow, I felt he was there, laughing at us all, cracking his little jokes at our expense, for I cannot imagine Billy Hope without thinking of that hilarity which always marked our meetings.

And so, over the centuries, there stretches the bonds of a great kinship; the brown habit of a Franciscan monk, wandering along the lanes of Umbria, pouring out his soul in divine melodies; the old home-spun clothes, the rough tweed cap, the strains of evangelical hymns, the rugged face, wreathed in smiles, of the modern troubadour as he too wandered the length and breadth of England, proving triumphantly there are no dead to the multitudes who came to him, seeking facts to prove the survival of man after bodily death. He wandered so much in the shadowy places of life, he was often unjustly and bitterly attacked by those who not only did not seek to understand him, but who failed entirely to appreciate his nature. ...

As I lay down my pen, I realise how inadequate any words of mine are to tell this story. At the best I am but a poor Journalist, one used to dealing in sensations and evolving fictions, but here I meet one whose essential simplicity cannot entirely be captured by my subtleties. Of him we can say best with Homer, "He was a friend to man and lived in a house by the side of the road."

* * * * *

"I am quite convinced that the death of William Hope in 1933, brought to an end a most astonishing mediumship in spirit photography. 2,500 spirit photographs in the short space of 24 years is indeed a record which so far has not been repeated."

Major Tom Patterson, '100 years of Spirit Photography'.

Appendix 1

TIME LINE FOR WILLIAM HOPE, FROM CENSUS AND **BMD** RECORDS.

1864 Birth - Dec 10th Moorside, Worsley (Father Thomas, Mother Jane).

1881 Thomas now married to Alice. Wm. (aged 16) an apprentice plumber.

1886 William age 21, married Mary Atherton.

1888 Daughter Jane born in Man/c area.

1889 Son Harold born Moorside Man/c.

1886-89 Interested in photography – discovered spirit photography.

1891 Living in Wharton Bridge, Winsford - working as a painter. Age 24.

1896 Daughter Annie born in Winsford, Ches.

1899 Daughter Florence born in Swinton Man/c.

1901 William now named as John on the census, a photographer, in Over Winsford – (A Better part of town.) Age 34.

1903 Family moves to Crewe.

1905 Meets up with Buxtons in Crewe. Form the circle for development.

1908 Jane dies. Archdeacon Colley calls, spt photos/ psychographs develop.

1909 Son Arthur born in Crewe.

1909 Circle does experiments for Oliver Lodge. Assertion of Fraud by Lodge – disproved.

1910 Harold dies, registered in Nantwich, age 22.

1911 Living in Crewe. Name - William again. Age 44.

1912 Archdeacon Colley dies. Anonymity of circle mediums dropped.

1914 Circle starts to travel to give sittings.

1921 Bush controversy (sitting in 1920) Consensus - Psychic 'Extra' not the same as the photo he had supplied to Hope but a genuine spirit 'extra'.

1921 Same address in Crewe. Shown as Photographer (on own account).

1922 Price controversy (February) – Plates substituted before arrival in College.

1924 Daughter Florence marries Harry Latham.

1932 Fred Barlow with Maj.Rampling Rose (October/November) Challenge of Fraud with mini Flashlight – No proof given – all supposition, vigorously defended by many.

1933 Wm. Hope died in Salford Hospital of cancer, March 8th, registered by Son-in-law (age given as 64). He was 68.

Extract from Census of 1891

Extract from Census of 1901

Extract from Census of 1911

CENSUS OF ENGLAND AND WALES, 1911.

Before writing on this Schedule please read the Examples and the Instructions given on the other side of the paper, as well as the headings of the Columns. The entries should be written in ink.

The contents of the Schedule will be treated as confidential. Strict care will be taken that no information is disclosed with regard to individual persons. The returns are not to be used for proof of age, or for any other purpose than the preparation of Statistical Tables.

Number of Schedule 219

NAME AND SURNAME	RELATIONSHIP to Head of Family.	AGE (last Birthday) and SEX.		PARTICULARS as to MARRIAGE.					PROFESSION or OCCUPATION of Persons aged ten years and upwards.				BIRTHPLACE of every person.	NATIONALITY of every Person born in a Foreign Country.	INFIRMITY.
		Ages of Males	Ages of Females	Write "Single," "Married," "Widower," or "Widow"	Completed years the present Marriage has lasted	Total Children Born Alive	Children still Living	Children who have Died	Personal Occupation	Industry or Service	Whether Employer, Worker, or Own account	Whether Working at Home			
1 William Styles	Head	44		married	20	5	3	2	Photographer				Lancashire Bolton	British	
2 Mary Styles	Wife		43	married	25	5	3	2					Lancashire Bolton	British	
3 Maggie Styles	Daughter		19	single					Dressmaker				Lancashire Colne	British	
4 Florence Styles	Daughter		13	single					scholar	390			Lancashire Colne	British	
5 Arthur Styles	Son	9		short									Bacup Lancashire	British	
6															
7															
8															
9															
10															
11															
12															
13															
14															
15															

(To be filled up by the Enumerator.)

	Total	Persons
	Males	Females	
	2	3	5

I declare that this Schedule is correctly filled up in completion, or in charge, of this dwelling)

Signature William Styles

Postal Address 80 Oakley St Barnes Bridge S.W.

Appendix 2

Paget 'Colour' Process described by William Walker.

Light, January 1915. from a report on the lecture by William Walker at the L.S.A on January 14th 1915.

During the evening he included many of the instances already recorded in these chapters and he also exhibited a few slides to show the effects of natural colours when photographed by the Paget method of obtaining direct colour photography. (A.H.)

"He informed his hearers that the psychic flowers obtained led him to inquire of the spirit friends whether it would be possible for them to give him spirit flowers in natural colours, with the result that they expressed their willingness to try. On the day fixed for the experiment a journey was made to Crewe for the purpose of holding a séance.

The plates employed in the process, and which were known as panchromatic plates, were, Mr. Walker said, affected more or less by all colours, and consequently he had to place them in his plate-sheaths in the dark, with a taking screen in contact with and in front of each plate. This he did on the evening previous to the visit to Crewe, in his own dark-room at Buxton.

He took his own quarter-plate camera with him, and it was the one used when the plates were exposed. To cut out the extra violet rays a specially prepared yellow screen had to be used in front of the lens, so that the light would have to pass through (a) the yellow glass screen, (b) the lens, and (c) the taking screen to reach and affect the sensitive plate. It was important to keep this in mind, because no matter how the sensitive plate was affected by psychic power it would not otherwise produce the requisite chromatic effect upon the developed negative to give transparencies capable of showing natural colours when seen through the viewing screen.

Mr. Walker stated that Mrs. Buxton, Mrs. Walker, and himself were the sitters for the first plate. After the sitters had been focussed, he went to the camera, inserted a plate-sheath, withdrew the plate cover, and then returned to his seat. Mr. Hope pressed the india-rubber ball to open the lens, and thus expose the plate. Mr. Walker then left his seat and, returning to the camera, closed the slide, took it out, and placed it in his coat pocket. Mrs. Buxton sat alone for the second plate, when the same proceedings as for number one plate were carried out. The slide was, as before, taken out of the camera by the lecturer, and he and Mr Hope proceeded to the dark-room to develop—in darkness—and fix the two plates.

Slides were here put on the screen to show that both the plates had been successful and that for the first time—so far as is known—the natural colours of flowers and of the human form had been obtained by <u>spirit</u> photography. The lecturer pointed out that the psychic results varied very much in size whereas the size of the sitters remained the same, which could only convey the idea that on the second plate the spirit form was either shown purposely reduced or had retired farther from the camera, yet on both plates the results were shown to be in front of the sitters, so much so that on the first plate two of the sitters were quite obliterated and only a small portion of the third sitter could be seen.

The puzzle in this case was that one had to take into consideration not only the question of form but the chromatic action of colours as well—as, on the plates to be so reproduced, form and colour could only have been given by the direct rays from the form and by the colours passing through (a) the yellow glass screen in front of the lens, (b) the lens, and (c) the taking screen. It was an important point for consideration that the spirit form and flowers shown were actually present in those dark active rays beyond the violet, which Sheel began to consider so far back as 1777, when he also laid a primitive foundation for modern photography by his philosophical study of the action of light on silver. The lecturer said he had expected to obtain more direct colour spirit photographs, but the war had upset the conditions of the circle."

* * * * *

Copy of page of psychic colour photos Note: Experiments were carried out with Mrs Deane in 1922 and colour photographs published in the Christmas edition of 'Light', (Dec 23rd 1922, facing p809 & notes on p811.) (available on IAPSOP.com.)

Appendix 3

PSYCHIC PHOTOGRAPHY: THE METHODS OF THE UNSEEN OPERATORS.

Light, January 22, 1921   Rev. Chas. L. Tweedale

A careful investigation and examination of existing psychic photographs makes it clear, as I have previously pointed out in my book, *Man's Survival After Death,* page 430, et seq., and more fully in the 3rd edition now in the press, that the spiritual beings—the excarnate intelligences—engaged in the production of these psychic pictures are not confined to one method, but like mortals—incarnate intelligences—can use several methods for the production of a picture or portrait. The methods employed appear to lie under the following three heads.

1.—Direct Portraiture.

The observed phenomena of materialisation show conclusively that the discarnate, or excarnate, spirit can clothe itself with grosser matter in varying degrees of solidity extending from the mist-like atmo-plasma, through the dough-like pachy-plasma, up to an absolute solidity similar to that of human flesh. Evidently the assuming of sufficient solidity to reflect enough light to be recordable by lens and sensitive plate is a matter of degree, and well within the scope of the observed phenomena. Obviously, this method is possible, and I believe that some of the results are obtained in this way, and are to all intents and purposes direct portraits. The pictures obtained by Schrenck-Notzing and Mme. Bisson, of the husband of the latter and of another of the Bisson family, both deceased, seem to be instances of the employment of this method, with a partial materialisation. The degree of materialisation, however, may range from invisibility and intangibility to normal human sight and touch-up through the normal visible etherialisation, to the solid materialisation, such as that exhibited by Katie King, and photographed by Sir William Crookes. These objective figures, when invisible to normal vision, are often visible to, and their objectivity evidenced by, external clairvoyant vision. Prolonged experience and observation of the clairvoyance frequently manifested by my wife have convinced me that clairvoyance must be classed under two heads: (1) External clairvoyance; (2) Internal clairvoyance. In External Clairvoyance the impression-gained is that the figure seen is wholly external to the observer. The figure is seen to move about naturally and often heard to speak, the lips of the figure being seen to move at the same time. Sometimes the figure is seen to touch or point to things in the room, and the whole impression gained is that the figure is an independent objective personality. Moreover, on shutting the eyes or covering them with the band or other opaque object, the figure ceases to be visible like any other material object in the room, but is again seen when the eyes are opened, or the hand or opaque screen withdrawn, proving conclusively that the figure is external to the eye of the observer.

I have often been present when my wife has had this experience. Internal clairvoyance differs from the above in being apparently not a direct objective view, but the result of an image cast upon the retina of the eye, probably from some kind of screen or transparency materialised within the eye. In this kind of clairvoyance the vision persists and the figure continues to be seen, sometimes for quite a long period, when the eyelids are closed or when the eyes are covered with the hand, or other opaque objects, showing clearly that in this case the vision is internal to the eye and not a direct objective view, but produced by intermediate means. I have often witnessed this experience in the case of my wife.

2. —Direct Picture Photography.

Just as one might place an oil painting or other picture of tile relative or friend of a sitter close by his side, and then photograph both sitter and picture, so it is possible for the excarnate spirit operators to construct, or depict, a representation, or picture, of a relative or other person, or of some symbol, and place it near the sitter so as to be photographed with him. This method may also be evidenced by external clairvoyance, and the photographic image of the psychic picture may be produced by the same lens, and by the same exposure, as the image of the sitter.

3. —Psychic Screen or Transparency

Shortly after Miss Estelle Stead had obtained psychic photographs of her father at Crewe in October, 1915, she sent me copies. These showed the face of the late W.T. Stead, one about life size, on the right-hand side of Miss Stead, the other, much larger, and half covering her body. I at once carefully examined them with a lens and made two discoveries. Firstly, that the larger picture of Mr. Stead was an exact duplicate of the smaller one. Both pictures showed the face of Mr. Stead surrounded with a fibrous ring of whiteness, looking so exactly like a ring of cottonwool that I at once dubbed it "the cotton-wool effect." Not only was the exact similarity to be seen in the features, but every fibre of the "wool" was exactly reproduced in the larger picture. It was at once perfectly evident that both pictures of Mr. Stead's face

1. See page 102 for illustrations.

had been produced, from some sort of film or plate, in the case of the smaller picture apparently used in close contact, and in that of the larger used at some distance (as in an enlarging camera).

On carefully examining the larger picture with the lens I was astonished to note a distinct screen effect exactly like that seen in a magazine print from a photo process block. At first, I thought it might be due to a striated grain in the thin card on which the photo was printed, but examination of the other side of the card, and also of other parts of the photo surface, showed me that this was not the case.

I must confess that in 1915 this seemed a very suspicious case, but beyond mentioning it to a few intimate friends I did not set forth the facts publicly until March 9th, 1918, when I drew attention to them in an article published in *Light* for that date. There I say: "One shows a face near the sitter's head, the other exactly the same face, but enlarged so as to cover half the sitter's body. Every fibre of the 'wool' is exactly duplicated in the larger picture, and every mark and blotch on the face is enlarged and reproduced also. In this larger picture the 'screen' effect is seen perfectly all across the face of the 'extra'. The conclusion that the ordinary photographer would come to would be that both 'extras' had been introduced from a carefully-prepared plate."

In conclusion I said: "Psychic photography is a fact, but its phenomena are varied."

On December 20th, 1915, two months after Miss Stead obtained the photographs of her father, I had the privilege of taking spontaneously, and at a moment's notice, the photograph of an apparition which my wife saw clairvoyantly. Full details were published shortly after both in the newspapers and in nearly all the psychic publications, and we made an affidavit of the facts before a Commissioner.

These two cases of Miss Stead and my Weston photo illustrate perfectly the *psychic transparency* method employed by excarnate spirit intelligences for the production of these pictures.

This consists in <u>the materialisation of a kind of film which is apparently transparent,</u> and acts exactly as a transparent positive would do in printing in or introducing a negative effect on to the photographic plate. The principle employed is apparently exactly the same as that used in producing internal clairvoyance (*vide antea*). This film, or transparency, is not only used in the production of psycho-graphs in the interior of unopened boxes of plates held between the psychic's hands, but is also employed within the camera, or slide, **being apparently easily materialised there under the favourable conditions of darkness**. It is generally placed close to the surface of the plate and so produces a negative of normal size. In other cases it is probably used in much the same way as it would be in an enlarging camera, i.e. at some distance from the plate, and so produces an enlarged picture. The Stead case shows this double use of the psychic transparency beautifully. This transparency is often similar in size and shape to the negative photo plate, having definitely square corners and straight sides, just like an ordinary film or plate.

Shortly after the taking of the Weston photo in 1915, I noticed on the negative two straight lines down (the side and along the bottom, about three-eighths and five-sixteenths inch from the edge of the negative. These lines meet at the bottom of the plate in a sharp definite rectangle. An enlargement of the negative shows these lines very clearly and sharply. At first, when concentrating on the "extra" one did not attend to them much, but afterwards one puzzled over them a good deal, and finally concluded that they were some sort of reflection from the side and top of the box-shaped hand camera in which the photo was taken, though I had never seen similar effects on other plates exposed in it. This was in 1916. This sharp rectangle and two straight lines represent the corner and edges of the psychic screen or transparency used by the spirit or excarnate intelligence to produce the picture on the plate. The transparency has not registered perfectly with the negative plate, and so has shown the side and corner. Furthermore, in this case, it has not been applied or held steadily, but has moved downward during the exposure about a thirty-second of an inch in the enlarged negative, the result being a somewhat misty image of the bearded man. This shift of the transparency is perfectly seen as a distinct double line or edge in the enlarged negative. I have another example of this in one of Hope's, in which the extras are rather "flou" or cloudy. Examination with a lens reveals the edges of the psychic transparency in double or triple lines, showing that the psychic transparency has oscillated or wavered, so to speak, during the application, thus producing the double and triple lines of the edge,   and consequent haziness of the image of the extras. This, by the way, is good proof that these "extras" or not the result of "faking" – as a fraudulent operator would be more careful than to get three-eighths of an inch wrong in his register and to allow his transparency to wave about, even if he got the chance to practise such a fraud, which he does not under the conditions in which these pictures are often obtained. Even if he did get the chance it would not explain recognition of the extras, especially when no photo or picture of the recognised person has ever been taken during the earth life. Mr. Fred Barlow; who has had the privilege of examining a large number of Mr. Hope's negatives, informs me that the edges of the psychic transparency are observable on quite a number of them. Of course, in cases where the transparency is accurately applied, or is larger than the plate, its use cannot be detected. (Underlining in this case is mine. A.H.)

In some cases when the "cotton wool effect" is introduced, this ring of nebulous whiteness probably forms the edge of the transparency, and here again, may conceal its use.

All three methods are evidently the result of materialisation phenomena in varying degree. In No. 1 it is materialisation of the face, form, and raiment; in No. 2 the materialisation of the picture or model; in No. 3 the materialisation of the transparency.

Stereoscopic Camera Experiments.

Premising that in Baron Von Schrenck-Notzing's materialisation photographs the employment of stereoscopic and other cameras, some placed within the cabinet, have proved, photographically, the three dimensional nature of the materialisations witnessed by him and his colleagues, it is now necessary to refer to other experiments with the stereoscopic camera. As far back as 1893 Mr. Traill Taylor, experimenting with David Duguid, used a stereoscopic camera. He says (*British Journal of Photography*, March 17th, 1893), speaking of the conditions he imposed: "I proposed to set a watch on my own camera in the guise of a duplicate one of the same focus—in other words, I would use a binocular stereoscopic camera." This he did, and he records that "whatever was produced on one half of the stereoscopic plates was produced on the other."

He found, however, that the image of the "extra" was flat and not stereoscopic, and that it varied slightly in position on the two halves of the plate. From this he argued that the images of the extra had not only not been produced simultaneously with those of the sitters, but also had not been produced by the lens at all (i.e from an object exterior to the camera).

Mr. Fred Barlow, experimenting with Mrs. Deane, has on several occasions, when using an ordinary camera and an additional stereoscopic camera simultaneously, found repeatedly that an extra was produced in the single camera, but none in either half of the stereoscopic camera.

In December last Mr. Charles Lyle, an expert photographer, using a stereoscopic camera at the same time as Mr. Hope used his single camera, found in the first set of simultaneous exposures that an extra was obtained only in Mr. Hope's camera over which he held his hand when he made the exposure. On the second set of exposures Mr. Hope exposed the stereoscopic plate, holding his hand over that camera, and Mr. Lyle exposed Hope's camera plate. This time no result appeared in Hope's camera, but an "extra" was found on one half of the stereoscopic camera. This case is reported by Mrs. Hewat McKenzie. The above three cases are illustrations of the employment of the psychic transparency, apparently materialised, within the camera or slide, and formed from material drawn from the psychic, producing a picture entirely independent of the lens, and which is not directly objective. This, kind of psychic photograph may be produced in some cases simultaneously with that of the sitter, being printed through the transparency by the light passing in at the lens when the normal exposure is made. In other cases it may be an independent psychic exposure using other sources of luminosity. In any case it is best **not to speak of these transparency effects as the result of a "double exposure",** as this, term conveys a false idea to the general public. A far better term is "*independent psychic impression*", which I suggest be used in preference.

Appendix 4

Concerning The "Price-Hope" Case.

S.P.R. Journal Jan '24   Rev. C. Drayton Thomas (pps 191-199)

"In April of this year [re 1923] one of our Members, the Rev. C. Drayton Thomas, sent us a detailed criticism of the report of Mr. H. Price's experiment with the Crewe Circle as printed in the Journal for May 1922 (p. 171), and further discussed by the Hon. Officers of the Society in the Journal for January 1923 (p. 4). In this criticism Mr. Thomas gave reasons why in his opinion the evidence put forward in Mr. Price's report should not be regarded as affording proof that any member of the Crewe Circle had been guilty of fraud on the occasion in question.

Mr. Thomas's statement was examined by the Research Committee of the Society, who discussed it with him at some length, and eventually invited him to make an abstract of his arguments to be printed in the Journal, the original statement being too long for this purpose.

This abstract, as sent to us by Mr. Thomas, we now print."

Statement by the Rev. C. Drayton Thomas.

The following is an abstract of the report upon this case prepared by a Member of the Society for consideration by the Research Committee.

The report itself being considered too lengthy for inclusion in the Journal, the Committee suggested that an abstract should be placed before our readers.

1. The main questions are:

(a) Whether the packet which Price handed to Hope contained the plates marked by the Imperial Plate Company.

(b) Whether the plates exposed in the camera by Hope came out of the said packet.

2. As to (a) : In the first place the neglect to take proper precautions for the continuous security of the packet from the time it left the control of the Imperial Plate Co. till the time of the seance ; and secondly, the omission, when the coverings were opened, to notice whether the seals were effective and intact, weaken the evidence as to the identity of the plates so much that the point is not proved in the judicial sense.

3. As to (b): Mr. Price alleges that the slide containing plates taken from the said packet was changed by Mr. Hope for another slide containing other plates. He says that he marked the slide into which the plates were put, that he noticed a suspicious movement on Hope's part which suggested the substitution of another slide, that this suspicion was confirmed when he failed to find on the slide which Hope gave to him the second time the marks made on the original slide, and that suspicion was converted to certainty when the development showed that the plates were not those which had been in the packet. This appears to be the meaning of his various statements.

He has not said in his published evidence that he observed the results of his attempt to mark he slide; and the presumption, that the performance then was equal to the demonstration before the S.P.R. Annual Meeting in January 1923 is weakened by the consideration that, to elude Hope's observation and hearing, he must have acted more covertly and silently than at the meeting. He certainly did not take the precaution of inventing some excuse to show the marks to Seymour and thus obtain corroborative testimony. It is possible, therefore, that, when he received back from Hope what purported to be the same slide, he found no marks on it because his apparatus had failed to work properly.

4. A subsidiary question touching the respective theories of both sides concerning (a) and (b) relates to the source of the two anonymous parcels sent to the S.P.R. The same person apparently sent both (see letter accompanying the second parcel). The sender's object was to prejudice Hope's case.

To have obtained possession of the plate forming one of the Imperial Co.'s original set, which plate was in parcel No. l, the sender must have been either somebody attached to the British College for Psychic Science who bore ill will to Hope, as the letter and papers enclosed in the parcels imply, or somebody connected with the experiment. There is no evidence that Hope had an enemy at the College, and nothing to show that such an enemy, had there been one, could have found out at so early a stage of the proceedings that the S.P.R. was concerned in this experiment. If the sender was an enemy, he was extraordinarily fortunate in selecting this particular undeveloped plate when rummaging through Hope's stock. If he were one of the experimenters, he must have had access to the packet and obtained the plate before the seance, taking advantage of the laxity of the custody.

5. There were two glass positives in the second parcel representing a Chinese Magician, which are at least as likely to have been in the possession of somebody connected with the Magic Circle as to have been found among Hope's stock. There is no evidence to connect them with any "extra" ever obtained by Hope.

6. The red celluloid disc contained in parcel No. 2 was apparently intended to suggest a device for imitating the stencil dots used for the X-ray outline of the Imperial Plate Co.'s trademark, the figure of a crowned lion. Whether it was made by Hope, or by someone else who wished to convey "the impression" that Hope had so made it, is the point at issue. The correspondence between the pattern of these dots on the red disc and two sections of the crowned lion is too close to be due to coincidence.

One of these sections is the hind leg, as on the plate enclosed in anonymous parcel No. 1, which belonged to the original set prepared for Mr. Price. Nobody could have known what was on this plate who had not seen it after its development, and because it was not developed until it reached the S.P.R. only a person in touch with the S.P.R. could have obtained the knowledge; and Hope is thus absolved from the suspicion of making those dots on the disc which correspond with the lion's hind leg. (My underlining.AH.)

Other dots on this red disc represent the crowned head of the lion. An examination of the complete set of plates shows this to have been the section of the figure which was borne by the plate still missing, that is to say, one of the plates *said to have* been given by Mr. Price to Mr. Hope for the experiment and for which other plates were substituted either then or at an earlier stage (see paragraphs 2 and 3 above). *Whoever had* the plate with the hind leg doubtless had also the plate marked with the crowned head; the same person must have copied from both plates to make the pattern which is on the red disc, *and this person cannot have been Hope.*

(To follow this argument in detail the reader requires the photographic illustrations, and the text, embodied in the report of which this is an abstract.)

7. Finally, there is the mistaken remark in parcel No. 2 about Madam getting suspicious, which may more plausibly be attributed to one of the experimenters than to anyone connected with the College.

8. The general circumstances, therefore, and the internal evidence furnished by the contents of the parcels are favourable to the theory of *their source having been the Magic Circle rather than the College.*

9. In the S.P.R. Journal for May 1922, page 283, it was stated that:

"It can, we think, hardly be denied that Mr. William Hope has been found guilty of deliberately substituting his own plates for those of a sitter."

On an *ex parte* statement of the case this impression was natural; but now that the other side has been heard and fresh facts have come to light it is inconceivable that any impartial Court would convict him on the evidence.

(Underlining is mine. A.H.)

Appendix 5

SUPERNORMAL PHOTOGRAPHY (EXTRACT)

Psychic Science January 1925

In July 1922 the British College were all poised to publish in their quarterly journal 'Psychic Science' a detailed article on Psychic Photography. It was particularly based on the mediumship of William Hope and Mrs. Ada Deane, both of whom were regularly giving sittings at the College. As the news broke of the sitting with Price & Seymour this was put on hold until January 1925. (author not given.)
This is an excerpt from that original article.

".....The fact that Mrs. Deane is not able, as a rule, to obtain psychic "extras" on any photographic plates but such as have been in her possession for some days, and that this limitation operated in respect of the Cenotaph plates, makes it impossible to claim for such a result any public recognition from those ignorant of psychic possibilities. Anyone, however, who may recognize any of the faces, and be able to establish a comparison, should if possible supply Miss Stead with this evidence as an answer to the critics. Sceptics and opponents argue from this present disability of Mrs. Deane that therefore she must have necessarily prepared the plates beforehand, and that the result is achieved by double exposure, or by the method adopted in "fake" photographs published by the *Daily Sketch*. But it is only ignorance which thus speaks. Those who have studied these matters longest have time and again taken far more careful precautions against such methods than anything so far suggested by the *Daily Sketch*, and yet have been completely baffled by the results.

It is noticeable in other cases than Mrs. Deane's that in the early days of the development of the gift, the psychic invariably requires that plates shall have been in her environment, and sometimes even upon her person for some days prior to the experiment. Here we discern a law at work to which we must bow, until strengthening of the psychic force makes it possible to use the plates handed direct to the medium by the sitter as is the case with the Crewe Circle. These photographers, with longer experience than Mrs. Deane, ask, however, that if possible, the sitter shall keep the plates for some time in his environment, and in the early days of their development I understand that Mrs. Buxton often carried the plates on which outstanding successes were secured. Archdeacon Colley, their early friend and adviser, made a great point of this condition.

What is the law at work? Apparently that psychic force of a delicate semi-physical order drawn from the medium, is used to produce the physical effect upon the negative which we call an "extra", and which as far as ordinary photographic knowledge reaches, could only be produced by light rays reaching the plate. There are apparently subtle rays of the spectrum unknown to us, but affinitized to this force, which can be used by those who produce this phenomenon; rays which can sometimes reach the sensitive plate, without such ever leaving the unopened packet; or when the plate has been exposed in an apparently dark room. The operation in the majority of cases to-day seems to be independent of the camera lens. This is a hard saying for photographers and others, but we can but state what the facts show. Some fluidic aetheric substance from the body of the medium amenable to psychic control, a substance which is also, under certain conditions, self-luminous, seems to operate upon the sensitive plate, and between the plate and the medium whilst the former is in his possession, a polarity of some sort is set up—it is within his circle of "power" or "influence". When the moment comes to meet a sitter who wishes for a psychic photograph, this plate is ready for use and can be acted upon quickly.

..... I have heard Mr. Hope say that he has noticed during a visit of the Circle to a new locality for work, that if his first sitter be of a cold unresponsive nature, <u>he feels shut off and chilled, so that the psychic operations are retarded, not only for that occasion but for several experiments following</u>. So little do we know of this strange power.   (Underlining is mine. A.H.)

We note in the case of all past and present photographic mediums, how large is the proportion of unrecognized "extras", as compared with the twenty to twenty-five per cent, of recognitions. Each result, whether recognized or not, is a remarkable phenomenon, but it can only be regarded as such if the conditions be considered satisfactory and the medium a person of integrity.

It will be seen from the article in this issue by Miss Stead that on occasions, with sitters providing the right elements, Mrs. Deane has been able to produce results with plates she has not previously had in her possession, and it is also known to the College that on one occasion, at least, a packet substituted for one of Mrs. Deane's, unknown at the time to her, when subsequently exposed under the most careful supervision of an expert photographer, showed an excellent "psychic extra".

It was at the College that Mrs. Deane obtained the remarkable Cushman "extra" on a plate that remained after two other experiments carried out that day. No one knew that Dr. Cushman, of Washington, was to visit the College; his very name was unknown till he arrived, and yet on the negative appeared an "extra", which he and his wife, who accompanied him, and many members of his family claimed as a life-like picture, clear and unmistakeable, of a dear daughter lost three months previously. ......

Evidence for Psychic Photography

The following classification of psychic photographic results from "The Veil Lifted" may be a useful reminder to experimenters of what may happen during the exercise of this rather rare gift. Spirit photographs, (says the author, Mr. Glendinning, a very practical student,) may be:

1. Portraits of psychic entities not seen by the normal vision, i.e., portraits of deceased persons, recognized or unrecognized by the sitter.

2. Pictures of objects not seen or thought of by the sitters or by the medium or operator, such as flowers, words, symbols and lights. (Many of Mrs. Irving's results are of this class.)

3. Pictures which have the appearance of being copied from statues, paintings or drawings. Sometimes these are busts or heads only. The flatness in some photographs of this class is supposed by persons who have not investigated the subject to be a proof that the photographs are produced in a fraudulent manner.

(I have one before me now, taken by Mrs. Deane at the opening of the Stead Bureau and Library on its removal to Smith Square, in which this flat, cut out appearance is particularly noticeable; sometimes these are most crudely produced, showing even ragged cut edges which would condemn any trickster. I have also one by the Crewe Circle in which a complete locket with the photograph it contains was produced as an "extra". The portrait in the locket had been shown to the medium just before the plate was exposed and then returned to the pocket of the sitter. On development the result was as stated.)

4. Pictures of what are called materialized forms visible to normal sight.
(We do not class these as psychic photographs to-day.)

5. Pictures of the "wraith" or "double" of a person still in the body.

(Examples of this are known to me in connection with the medium Wyllie, with the Crewe Circle and Mrs. Deane).

6. Portraits on plates which developers have failed to bring into view, but that can be seen and described by clairvoyants and by mediums when in trance, and whose descriptions agree though made independently.

(This also we must exclude as non-evidential to the bulk of persons who experiment.)

7. Portraits that cannot be classed as photographs, as they have not been taken by the agency of the camera, or by exposing the prepared plate previous to development of image.

(This is a well-known phase with the Crewe Circle and many examples are extant. The box of unopened plates is usually held upon the forehead of Mrs. Buxton or between the hands of all the members of the Circle and the plates are then developed immediately without exposure. A result under such circumstances is surely the highwater mark of psychic photography, although independent of the lens.)

In the Editorial Notes of the same edition of 'PsychicScience' was this piece concerning the Cenotaph photo of 1924.

In the case of the last "Cenotaph" pictures it is, therefore, to our thinking, a great mistake to assess the value of this photograph on the basis of any individual recognition of features, and to lose sight of the far more important aspect of the picture as a symbol of the immortality of youthful lives. Why should we suppose that out of the millions of those cut off by death there should be any individual recognition intended? The demonstration is one of world-wide import, a message to the race at large, and the faces typical of British youth; symbols only of a larger hope to those that remain in the valley of tribulation and perplexity. Identification in such a case is bound to be difficult, and even if claimed, could always be disputed, for none of the faces is large enough nor sufficiently sharp in outline to establish the assurance of personal identity. All are types that may be paralleled closely among English boys of this century.

But in other ways it is open to the man of science to assure himself of the bona-fides of the published picture, or at least to realize the difficulties that lie in the way of the denial of honesty in the production of this picture. If, for example, a plate bear infallible marks of normal exposure as well as those of a super-normal image, then the imposing of any sort of imprint by mechanical means to represent the faces of the boys killed in the war will be found on examination to be blended with the image of the ordinary picture obtained by exposure of the plate through the lens. Mixed with the faces we should see marks of natural objects. In the dark clear spaces around the faces, the vignettes in the cloud, such objects would be even more clearly visible—bits of the facade of the Government buildings, bare branches of the trees in Whitehall, etc. But the curious thing is that nothing of the sort is present except outside the periphery of the cloud and a little within its edges.

Therefore, in some way the part of the plate devoted to the representation of the "cloud of witness" has been protected from normal exposure and contains no image of any sort. This raises a mechanical problem which must be solved satisfactorily by the hostile critic before he can expect his criticism to receive the respectful attention of the fair-minded. It cannot be dismissed and must be met. And in reply to other criticisms we would say that all experience goes to show that the handling of the packet of plates employed and their saturation by the psychic emanation or "magnetism" of the medium appear to be a condition precedent of success in most cases though not in all. To this we have absolutely no right to object, since, as already pointed out, we are in entire ignorance of the nature of the preparations needed on the part of the unseen artist who obviously is dependent upon psychic forces and material gathered from the medium. We can assume, however, that before these can be effectively controlled, they must first be co-ordinated, and for this a close and prolonged contact may be essential in many cases. "Extras" have, however, been obtained on absolutely fresh plates in sufficient numbers to allay reasonable suspicion.

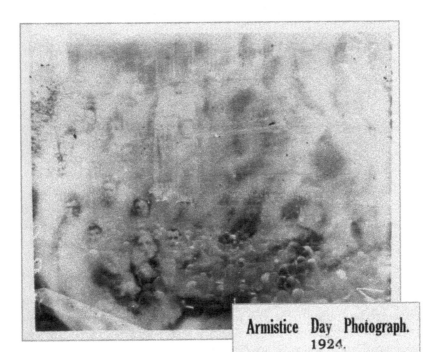

This copy of the 1924 Cenotaph photograph mentioned above is from the Harrison collection, together with the official notice, (shown right.)

Armistice Day Photograph.
1924.

Photograph with Psychic "Extras" taken by Miss Vi Deane from Richmond Terrace, in Whitehall, during 'The Silence," on November 11th, 1924.

The wrappings of the box containing the plate used were slit open on the morning of the 11th by Miss Scatcherd and Miss Stead, who carefully examined the camera and dark-slide. The plate was taken from the box by Mrs. Deane and placed in the dark-slide in the presence of Miss Stead and Miss Scatcherd. It was then initialled and the slide taken charge of by them until they handed it over to Miss Deane a few minutes before "The Silence" and watched whilst she fixed it in the Camera. Miss Scatcherd stood close beside her during the exposure of the plate which was *exposed for the full two minutes* of " The Silence." The plate was then taken charge of by Miss Scatcherd until it was developed by Mrs. Deane, in the dark-room of the Borderland Library, in the presence of Miss Scatcherd and Miss Stead.

(This photograph is copyright.)

Appendix 6

EXPERIMENTS WITH THE CREWE CIRCLE
Light March 1928

Frederick James Crawley, Chief Constable of Newcastle-on-Tyne

"I have during the past five years carried out nearly thirty tests with Mr. W. Hope and Mrs. Buxton, known as the Crewe Circle, in whose presence what are commonly known as "psychic extras" are precipitated on to a sensitized plate. I pronounce them genuine. I have borne in mind the report of the Magic Circle. I do not consider, however, that conjurers, photographic experts, scientists, pseudo and otherwise, are required to test the process, and I assert not only that the phenomena are provable by ordinary deductive common sense, but that if fraud supervenes it must be carried out by the experimenters. Take the procedure at ordinary experiments.

We can dismiss Mrs. Buxton, since she does not enter the dark room nor touch the slide or camera. Cutting out preliminaries, the experimenter finds himself in the dark room with an unopened packet of plates which he has bought elsewhere. Mr. Hope is also there. The experimenter has previously examined the dark room, slide and camera. A friend can remain by the camera after inspection, if one is present. The experimenter cuts open the packet of plates, inserts two in the slide, signs same, returns the remaining plates to his pocket, then proceeds to the camera and inserts the loaded slide therein. After exposure, he returns to the dark room, unloads and takes charge of the plates, reloads and repeats the process till all the plates are used, then finally returns to the dark room and develops the plates, Hope being present all the time. It should be stated that the process is designated as a psychic one and Hope's presence is a factor therein. It therefore follows that in proportion as Hope is kept aloof, so are the phenomena weakened till the line of non-success is reached. To counter this, Hope's hands can, whilst maintaining all safeguards, be directed to the loaded slide in the dark room and he can also be given the slide to carry to the camera.

Now if the foregoing conditions are observed, which they customarily are, it is impossible for fraud to be practised, as I will proceed to demonstrate. The substitution of plates is out of the question if the experimenter retains possession throughout. It is equally out of the question if he hands them to Hope after loading, since the developer produces the signatures, thus proving that they are the identical plates which the experimenter inserted. The slide itself may be marked, but that is superfluous test indications, and it is unnecessary to stress that the plates could not be changed without the operation being perceived, since this and all other contentions of handling are irrelevant. As to the image being impregnated in acid on the cardboard in the slide, this is refutable by the identical image being bound to appear in some degree on other plates laid against the same cardboard face. I say nothing of identifications at this stage. As to the image being in the camera or on the back cloth, the same image would be bound to appear on each plate exposed.

If this statement fails to convince, I affirm that I have obtained psychic phenomena with the Crewe Circle when my own camera and slide were used, and again in Hope's apparatus when he has at no time entered the dark room. I have also had what purported to be an attempt at a psychograph on a plate which had not been in the camera or slide and was developed by myself alone in the dark room. Altogether I have had through this circle twenty-three psychic effects analysed as follows:

(a) Six extras of my late wife; she had already been photographed by Hope, but she is presented in the "extras" from 20 years of age up to the age of her passing at 49; Hope first met her aged 44; there is also in one a peculiarity of hair parting of which the sitters and Hope were unaware which was later confirmed as her last style of parting

(b) Two extras of one friend, both had previously sat with Hope.(sic)

(c) An extra subsequently identified by friends as being that of a soldier.

(d) An extra identified by J. Briggs, my fellow experimenter, as being that of James McDougall, of Bamborough, Northumberland, who passed 35 years ago; I myself carefully carried out the identification tests in respect to this extra, placing same amongst other psychic extras without comment; it was immediately recognised by all to whom it was shown, viz. McDougall's three sons and the wife and niece of the aforementioned J. Briggs.

(e) Three psychic effects which cannot be termed "extras."

(f) Nine unidentified extras; I am satisfied that some of these latter are intended to be representations of certain of my deceased relatives, but prefer that they should be classed as unidentified, being aware of one's proneness to weave familiar features into such.

I have made enquiries in certain localities and entered into correspondence with persons of repute, with the result that I declare that the *bona-fides* of the Crewe Circle can be testified to in all parts of the country, particularly in the Sheffield area. I hold the names of other competent experimenters who have obtained phenomena in their own cameras and slides. I also hold the names of others who have obtained "extras" identified beyond all doubt as being those of persons of whom the Crewe Circle had no knowledge whatever; these are equally as convincing as the classic one obtained by my friend, the Rev. Charles Tweedale. I advance the contention that it is only necessary to establish the identity of one such extra, carrying sufficient detail of features, to establish both survival and the honesty of the mediums. I deal with the sub-conscious hypothesis later. The supernormality of the phenomena is easily provable, but the identification of extras with those who have gone before is more difficult, merely because it is logical to conceive that the characteristics of the timeworn earth features being absent, spirit operators are thus given a prodigious task to present recognisable facsimiles.

I am certain, therefore, that James Coates in *Photographing the Invisible* is correct in asserting that a photograph of a deceased person is of value to such operators, although I have never carried one. I know this also by my association with the experiments of my late friend, Major Spencer, of Walbottle Hall, Northumberland, most "extras" obtained in his presence, without medium, being near facsimiles of existing photos and wood-cuts of such structures as Nelson's column, gargoyles, etc. Some may regard this as affording support to certain experiments of persons in the flesh who have in some measure revealed their spirit nature, by being able by strong concentration, to precipitate a shadow on to a sensitized plate when in an auric milieu.

I counter this reasoning by directing attention to the amazing psychographs obtained in Spencer's home, and also those quoted in *The Case for Spirit Photography* by Sir Arthur Conan Doyle as occurring through the Crewe Circle; these psychographs prove the enlightened activity of discarnate minds which I challenge any psychologist, no matter how eminent, to refute. Further, the casual operation of the sub-consciousness in the direction of psychic "extras" pre-supposes that it has nothing better to do than construct, retain and impress such images whilst on the other hand, our psychological friends are ever ready to tell us that its activities are legion, but always in other directions as revealed through hypnosis and different forms of automatism. This is a paradox; they cannot have it both ways. Excepting that harmony appears to be necessary in order that the right psychic atmosphere should prevail, there is also ground for thinking that many of the phenomena occurring with the Crewe Circle is not mental, nor the photographing of etherializations, but is produced by transfer or transparency with a radiant generated through the Aura, as contended by Spencer as the result of the experiments in his own home.

Hope dislikes tests. He has every reason to. I am satisfied that they produce real inhibition of power. Moreover, his point of view is that he has been before the public for more than twenty years, he has been testified to by scores of competent observers, and he declines to be treated as a possible charlatan. He rightly declares that the crux of the experiments lies in the results and not in the process. It would, therefore, not surprise me if in time he provided his own plates and kept sitters out of the dark room. He lives in a most humble way and receives no monetary compensation for his humiliations, consequently he is disposed to confine himself to rendering service to simple trusting souls. This man can prove survival and in exchange for such proof, a gift of a five or ten pound note might well be made a condition.

Appendix 7

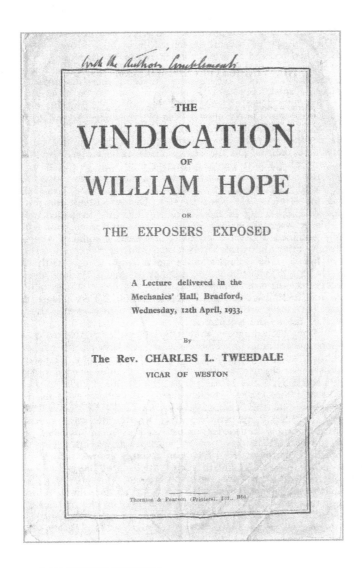

As the typeset of the pamphlet was too small and indistinct to be read easily I have taken the liberty of converting them into a darker form with Photoshop and enlarging them to a full page, for ease of reading. This is the only change to this important pamphlet.

THE VINDICATION OF WILLIAM HOPE.

In November, 1932, Mr. Fred Barlow and Major Rampling-Rose read a paper at a private meeting of the Society for Psychical Research in which they allege that all Mr. William Hope's psychic photographs have been produced by fraudulent means. This allegation against Hope is a falsehood, and an atrocious calumny. The method of these two detractors of Hope is simple. They allege in several instances how Mr. Hope *might* have frauded, and then proceed to argue that therefore he *did* fraud. This comes out all through the paper, and characterizes the report of the Photographic Research Association, which they quote. Anything more dishonest, illogical, un-English, or unjust, could not be conceived, and so far from their paper containing " definite proof of fraud," as they allege, it contains no proof of fraud whatsoever, but merely shows lack of knowledge and of sympathetic understanding in a difficult investigation.

Before dealing with the accusations against Hope we will consider one or two subsidiary points and the **charge made against Mrs. Deane.**

Those who allege that she has frauded may well be asked to face the testimony of Sir Arthur Keith, the anthropologist, also of Dr. Cushman, who secretly and unknown to anyone in England, came from the U.S.A. He went to Mrs. Deane without appointment or introduction and found her in the act of leaving, but persuaded her to stay and take his photograph, which she did there and then, and the doctor immediately obtained a psychic photo of his dead daughter, Agnes, unlike in detail to any other, but more realistic and *a better likeness than any other obtained in life* !! The accusers make no attempt to deal with this case. It is a hot cinder which they make no attempt to handle. Barlow says that one clearly recognised extra is sufficient to prove Psychic Photography. Well, here is one and there are hundred of others. Again Barlow alleges that Mrs. Deane's psychic extras are the fraudulent result of her having the plates in her possession before the experiment.

Now, it fortunately happens that long before Barlow turned against the people whose good name he is now seeking to destroy, he had written a defence of them and of the subject of Psychic Photography. This defence is in the form of a chapter entitled " Evidential and Scientific Aspects of Psychic Photography," and forms part of Sir Arthur Conan Doyle's " The Case for Spirit Photography," which should be read by everyone interested in this subject. In this chapter Barlow says :—" On several occasions members of the S.S.S.P. (of which Society Mr. Barlow was secretary) have, without Mrs. Deane's knowledge, substituted a fresh unopened packet of plates for the packet she has had with her, without interfering with the success of the experiment ! !" This convincingly proves that the previous possession of the plates was *not* the explanation as he alleges.

On another occasion Mr. Barlow obtained, through Mrs. Deane, a Psychic photograph of his father. He wrote to me describing his experience and stating that he was thoroughly satisfied that it was his father, and in his " Evidential and Scientific Aspects " he says : " With Mrs. Deane, in my own home, we secured an excellent picture of my father—a likeness which could not have been produced from any existing photograph. . . . Whatever may have happened on other occasions *nothing can shake my firm conviction* that I have secured genuine psychic photographic effects."

In the face of these declarations what reliance can be placed *now* on Mr. Barlow's present attack on Mrs. Deane, and his statement that all recognised pictures could be copied from existing photos.

Again, he says that when using a stereoscopic camera or two cameras simultaneously, extras or psychic effects are not obtained on more than

3

one plate, and this, he says, shows that the results are not objective. This statement is false and not in accordance with recorded facts.

Mr. Trail Taylor, the well-known photographic expert, relates in the British Journal of Photography for March 17th, 1893 (of which he was the Editor), how he got psychic extras on *both* plates in his stereoscopic camera, with Mr. David Duguid. While on November 5th, 1921, at the British College of Psychic Science, Mr. Robinson, of Brisbane, exposed a plate in his own camera, and Mr. Hope another in his camera at the same time, psychic extras coming on each. Another case of psychic extras being found on both plates of a stereoscopic camera was reported in the Transactions of the British College for April, 1923.

In the occasional occurrence of **reproductions of magazine and newspaper pictures** on Mrs. Deane's plates, or of "screen" effects, Barlow and Rampling-Rose profess to find conclusive evidence of fraud, but even if it did constitute such evidence, it would not do away with the Cushman case of recognition, together with many others. Anyone who has the intelligence and ability to tackle this problem knows full well that the occasional appearance of such magazine pictures is *no proof at all* that the psychic has frauded. Exactly the same remark applies in those cases in which the extra is like a normal photograph of the deceased. We will refute Barlow on this point out of his own mouth. In his article on " The Evidential and Scientific Aspects of Phychic Photography," published in 1922, he says :—" One of the members of the S.S.S.P. (of which Society Mr. Barlow was Secretary) Mr. Hobbs, of Purley, a keen business man, travelled to Crewe with his wife. They and the Crewe Circle were perfect strangers to each other. Mrs. Hobbs was wearing a locket containing a photograph of their son, who had been killed in the war. This was tucked away out of sight under her blouse. To their great delight they obtained a picture of their boy. Trickery was *impossible*. Even supposing Mr. Hope had seen the locket there was no time to produce a fraudulent result and foist it upon the alert sitters. Yet the psychic picture is an exact duplicate of the photograph in the locket. Even the rim of the locket can be seen. This sort of thing has occurred time and again."

" Sometimes the psychic pictures are *fac simile* copies of magazine covers *which no fraudulent medium would ever think of producing*."

" Whether it agrees with his pet theories or not the serious student is bound to realize that sooner or later other minds are at work distinct from, and often superior in intelligence to, that of either medium or sitter. Those intelligences claim to be the spirits of the so-called dead. They substantiate the claims by giving practical proof that they are whom they purport to be."

From the above quotations it will be seen how strongly Mr. Barlow repudiates any suggestion of fraud on the part of Mrs. Deane (such as he has now made) in the matter of the occasional occurrence of these magazine pictures and " screen " effects. As I have pointed out elsewhere, these results simply show (like the appearance of flowers and other objects) that the spirit operators can copy objects, just as we can and, like us, are not restricted to one particular phase of photography. At the same time, it must be noted that many of the psychic extras, while clearly recognisable, are slightly different in pose to any known normal photo, proving conclusively that they are not copies.

Coming now to the main issue in Barlow's and Rampling-Rose's pamphlet, **"The Attack on William Hope."** In the first place. Barlow alleges that substitution of a plate was found against Hope during the experiments of Price and the S.P.R. in 1922. This statement is a falsehood, and one stands amazed at the effrontery of this charge in view of the facts. No proof of fraud or substitution on the part of Hope was found, but it was proved that grave suspicion attached to those who made the charge.

4

It was shown during the investigation that the packet of plates used by the experimenters had been in the possession of the officials of the S.P.R. for three weeks before the experiment, and was accessible to several persons who were hostile to Hope's claims and had said that the opening and closing of sealed packets was a thing easily accomplished. It was also conclusively proved by an independent committee of investigation that the packet of plates had been opened prior to the experiment with Mr. Hope, as proved by the examination of the wrapper made by the Imperial Dry Plate Co. (Ilford). This fact at once destroys Price's case. It was also revealed that one of the specially marked plates had been extracted, as proved by the fact that this plate, together with three others of a different make, and bearing extras when developed, totally unlike Hope's results, were mysteriously returned through the London post (Notting Hill postmark) three days after the experiment, and four months before the attack was made known to Hope. Price has also confessed that when Hope requested him to sign the plates in proof that neither plates nor slide had been substituted or changed, *he refused*. These facts smash Price's case and transform Hope from the accused into the accuser, and point to a conspiracy against Hope which casts a grave suspicion upon all concerned in making the experiment and issuing the libellous pamphlet against him, and show him to have been **a much injured and maligned man**, and the subject of a base conspiracy ; and that the plates, so far from being substituted by Hope, had been tampered with, and others substituted by the conspirators. This is a matter of history and the facts are on record, and yet Barlow has the effrontery to say in the S.P.R. pamphlet just issued that Price proved that Hope substituted a plate on this occasion. The statement is a falsehood and the facts point to the very reverse. With reference to the extra obtained on the plate by Mr. Price, Barlow says in " Evidential and Scientific Aspects," " I am convinced that the effect obtained on this occasion was a genuine psychic result. Price maintains that no genuine psychic photograph has ever been taken. Yet, on December 13th, 1923, and February 28th, 1924, Price, using his own camera, slides and plates in a test of psychic photography, held with Mrs. Irvine, the plates never leaving his possession, as he testified, obtained the picture of a hand, also star-shaped patches of cloud on the plate, when developed by him, the said hand and star having previously been seen clairvoyantly and described by Mrs. Irvine. He signed two statements testifying to these facts.

Now let us turn to **the considered opinion of Barlow** in favour of psychic photography, set forth in " The Evidential and Scientific Aspects," published in Sir Arthur Conan Doyle's " Case for Spirit Photography. He there says : " When conditions are imposed similar to those usually obtaining with the Crewe Circle (Hope) the difficulty of producing a fraudulent result is enormously increased. Where suitable precautions are employed, and where the sitter has a thorough knowledge of photography, plus an acquaintance with trick methods, even the *possibility* of deception without detection can for all practical purposes be ruled out of court. Under these special conditions investigators of repute have on many occasions secured successful results."

Again, " The evidence for the truth of psychic photography is overwhelming."

Again, " Knowing it to be true, I look forward with confidence to that day, not far distant, when all this talk of fake and fraud shall be no more."

Again, " I do not see how we can possibly get away from the fact that many of these photographic effects are produced by discarnate intelligences."

Again, " A very little first-hand investigation will satisfy any unprejudiced individual as to the reality of psychic photography."

5

Equally damning to his present attitude is Barlow's article in " Light " for November 9th, 1918, in which he says : " An apology is due to the Crewe friends for the very suggestion of fraud, so far as they are concerned. To know them is to esteem them," " I declare after mature consideration that in many of the tests trickery was impossible."

Here are seven most positive declarations on Barlow's part, as to the truth and reality of psychic photography, and I shall produce others.

We will now examine the specific charges of Messrs. Barlow and Rampling-Rose. The main one is that all Hope's psychic extras have been produced, either by the substitution of a prepared plate with the spirit form or " extra " already printed on it, or by the projection of the " extra " on to the plate by means of a flash-light projector, containing a small positive film so as to print a negative on the plate.

Let us take the **flashlight allegation** first. This charge is at once so silly that one wonders how any man of intelligence dare bring it forward in the Hope case. It covers the accusers with ridicule. I have personally loaded Hope's slides with scores of plates from new packets broken open by me in the dark room immediately before loading the slide. Hope was not even allowed to touch the plates, or to put his hands over them ; and I have also taken the precaution of examining Hope's hands on many occasions. He has never used such a projector or " switch " in all the scores of plates I have loaded into his slides. He could not have even attempted to do it without *instant* detection by me or by others in the dark room.

I am an old photographer and mechanician whose experience goes back to the wet plate days, and not to be taken in by any such childish device as Barlow and Rampling-Rose describe. I know many people who have loaded Hope's slides, some of them expert photographers and they likewise have never seen Hope use any such device, and they scoff at the suggestion of such use under their keen and critical gaze. The silliness of this flashlight projector theory as the explanation of Hope's results becomes still more apparent when I state that I have frequently loaded Hope's slides when *alone* in the dark room from my own new packet of plates, not allowing Hope to enter, and these slides I have myself *carried to and from the camera,* not allowing Hope to touch them. In some cases I have, in addition to this, and to a thorough inspection of camera, slide and lens, *inserted the slide in the camera myself and withdrawn it, Hope doing nothing but make the exposure, thus not allowing Hope to touch either plate or slide from loading to development,* and yet I have got evidential results in flat disproof of Barlow's statement that there is always some kind of control by the medium. Other experimenters, among whom is Dr. Ellis Powell, give similar testimony. Powell describes in S.S.S.P. Budget, No. 63, how he loaded the slides, carried the slides, and did all the photographic process, and yet got the picture of a girl, Olive R——, recognised by her brother and mother.

In the 58th Budget of the Society Barlow says : "I have got results with Hope here in my own house, under conditions where fraud was absolutely impossible. I have loaded my dark slides in Birmingham and taken them to Crewe with my own camera and apparatus, and have carried out the whole operation myself, even to the taking of the photograph, and have secured supernormal results."

Fifteen members of the S.S.S.P. sign an account in Budget 67 saying that Hope did not touch the plate until it was fixed, yet they got results.

As for the allegation that the flashlight is used in Hope's coat pocket, Barlow himself records in the S.S.S.P. Budget No. 86, that on one occasion in his presence Hope turned out his pocket before putting the slide into it, and Barlow signed this report, while in his article in " Light " he says : " I know of no means whereby he could possibly have printed an image on the plate while the slide was in his pocket, without being immediately detected."

6

As for the further allegation that this flashlight is used during the loading of the plates, or what is still more silly and impossible, during their exposure in the camera, made generally in full daylight and often with half a dozen people standing around him—it is an insult to the intelligence of his readers to suggest such nonsense. We are asked to believe that Hope, in *broad daylight*, with people standing around him and all eyes closely fixed upon him, could open the shutter of a slide under the focussing cloth and print an " extra " on with a flashlight without being detected, and that he could do this not once but thousands of times during the course of 27 years and never be caught in the act once. Could absurdity further go?

Let us now see what Mr. Barlow himself says about this suggestion in " Evidential and Scientific Aspects " :—" I have been told that Hope printed the effects on to the plates by a flashlight while he had hold of my wrist. If the critic derives any comfort from believing that such actually occurred he is welcome to his belief."

He plainly sees the absurdity of the charge he now makes.

With regard to **the charge of substitution of plates,** This is equally false, unproven and absurd. I have shown that on a former occasion of such a charge being made, it was proved that the onus of suspicion lay on the experimenters and not on Hope.

Let us see **what Barlow himself has to say against this matter of substitution,** in " Evidential and Scientific Aspects " :—" On this occasion the substitution of dark slides was impossible for the simple reason that no dark slide was used. Saying nothing to the members of the Crewe Circle beforehand, I took with me to Crewe, on November 12th, 1921, a loaded box-camera containing 6 marked plates. All that Hope and Mrs. Buxton did was to arch their hands over this magazine camera whilst one of them flicked the shutter catch. Photographic readers will realize that it is impossible to tamper with the plates in a box-camera in daylight without spoiling the lot. The control stipulated that Hope should be allowed to hold my right wrist as I dropped each plate into the developer. Psychic effects were obtained on two out of the six plates under conditions which I am convinced rendered deception impossible."

Again, he says : " Two photographic members of the S.S.S.P. and myself went to Crewe. The camera and slides were brand new and not examined by Hope before the sitting. Neither Hope nor Mrs. Buxton were in the dark-room for loading the slides or developing the plates. The central face of the three supernormal faces secured on this occasion is an undoubted likeness of the father of one of the sitters. This result was absolutely conclusive to my friends and myself. **We emphatically declare that under the circumstances trickery was impossible."**

These quotations refute Barlow out of his own mouth. In further testimony let me say that I personally knew a Bradford minister who, taking his own box-camera, which was never opened, went to Crewe and obtained the face of a deceased relative. Hope did nothing but release the catch of the shutter, and the resulting photograph was developed at the minister's home in Bradford.

There are many cases on record of the obtaining of these extras in box-cameras through Hope's mediumship, the said cameras never having been opened and Hope never having seen or touched the plates. I personally witnessed one of these in 1931, when a lady asked Hope to touch off the trigger of her box-camera, which she produced on the spur of the moment. He made two exposures and the plates were developed at a local chemist's, and two extras were obtained. I can also give my own box-camera experience. In 1915 my wife suddenly saw the apparition of a man clairvoyantly, while we were seated in the breakfast room at Weston Vicarage. I rushed for my box-camera and took a photo of the place where

7

she saw the figure, and obtained a clear photo of the man looking exactly as she previously described him. This case is my own and entirely independent of Hope, whom I did not then know. We all swore to the truth of this before a Commissioner for Oaths in due legal form.

There are scores of similar instances which show the utter absurdity and impossibility of the theory of plate substitution or flash-light effects as the explanation of William Hope's spirit pictures.

The foregoing refutations of the flashlight and plate substitution theories are sufficient to satisfy any reasonable man, but there is another consideration which finally blows them to atoms.

Flashlight projection of recognised faces, or plates substituted and bearing such recognised faces (and there are many hundreds of recognitions on record) means the previous preparation of a small positive and its insertion in the flash-lamp, or the careful preparation of the plate to be substituted. In the very many hundreds of recognised spirit pictures produced through Hope's mediumship, how could these pictures be produced in the many hundreds of cases in which Hope *had never seen or heard of the deceased?* Such procuring is impossible. How could this small positive be made and inserted in the flash-lamp or switch, or the prepared plate be produced to meet the cases of recognised pictures obtained for strangers introduced to Hope *at a few minutes notice?* How could the small flashlight positive or prepared plate be prepared or produced in the many cases of recognised extras, of which I have many examples in which *there never has been any photo, painting, or sketch made of the deceased during mortal life?* The thing is impossible, and no one whose judgment is of any value would seriously advance such an allegation.

We now come to **recognition of the extras,** or spirit forms on the plate—this is of vital importance. Let us quote Barlow's statement in his " Evidential and Scientific Aspects." He there says : " Apart from any question of test conditions there are certain results which in themselves afford definite proof of genuineness. I refer to the recognised likenesses obtained by sitters who are unknown to the medium, and who have secured results which *could not possibly have been prepared in advance. One such case would be sufficent to establish the reality of psychic photography.* It is no exaggeration to say that this has actually been done on scores of occasions, and in consequence *the evidence for the truth of psychic photography is overwhelming.* This question of recognised likenesses is a point which *the critic tries to evade.* The reader can judge of the value of this evidence from the illustrations in this book, which are typical of *hundreds* of similar results." Note how strongly he supports and says that one recognition would be sufficient to prove the case. Now he says that these likenesses are copied or prepared from photographs already in existence, or could have been so prepared or copied, and asks us to believe on this flimsy assumption that Hope was a fraud. Those who have studied the subject carefully and thoroughly know it to be no evidence of fraud at all. Rampling-Rose, in a letter to the Press, makes the absurd statement that " Not the slightest scientific value can be placed on the claim that Hope produced hundreds of recognised pictures." Science is not needed for the ordinary recognition of relatives and friends. Nothing more is required than ordinary common sense and honesty such as is used in daily life. Many hundreds of people cannot *all* be mistaken.

Both wish to delude us with the absurd nonsense that Hope has been able to get the photos of many hundreds of people whom he never saw or heard of (many of whom lived all their lives in distant foreign countries) and often at a few minutes notice. All sensible and honest men know this to be impossible, and Barlow himself says that the recognised picture of his father could not have been so prepared. We now come to psychic photographs showing messages in the hand-writing of deceased persons, and Barlow's statement that these messages are the fraudulent work of Hope. This statement is also false.

To refer again to Barlow's own words. In " Evidential and Scientific Aspects," he says :—" There can be no doubt about the genuineness of the handwriting." He then shows Major Spencer's photo-microscopic enlargement of the normal and psychic signatures of Archdeacon Colley, and shows them to be microscopically identical. On this head his charge against Hope that the messages are composed of cut-out pieces of letters surrounded by cotton wool is not proven. He himself fakes a result along these lines then coolly asks his readers to believe that Hope's results are also faked. This " *suggestio falsi* " marks the whole of the paper. The result " *might* " be done in such and such a way, they " *could* " have been done in such and such a way, therefore they *have* been done in that way. This sort of thing is very convenient, but will deceive no one whose opinion is of any consequence.

On October 29th, 1932, we got a written message from Sir Arthur Conan Doyle through Hope. The message takes up the conversation (casually introduced by my wife) a few minutes prior to the photograph being taken, making Barlow's theory of the previous preparation of a " paste and scissors " letter impossible and absurd. The psychic message is in Sir Arthur's identical handwriting and bears his identical signature, both recognised by Lady Doyle, who says, " There is no doubt whatever about it being my husband's own writing on the plate."

The plate was loaded from a new box just purchased, and opened by me immediately before loading and duly signed, the slide carried by me to the camera and back to the darkroom, where I developed it in the presence of Hope and my daughter. He was never allowed to touch or put his hands over the plate until fixed. It does not show paste and scissors effect such as Barlow describes. All Barlow's absurd theories fail to explain away this experience. Again he makes the allegation that some of Hope's psychographs which he has seen, contain errors in spelling similar to Hope's, and that all the " copper-plate " psychographs are faked by Hope. All the psychographs which I have do *not* contain errors of spelling, and comparison of Hope's own handwriting in numerous letters show total dissimilarity to the copper-plate psychographs. If Barlow's psychographs do show these errors of spelling this does not prove fraud on Hope's part. Let him remember what he says in " Evidential and Scientific Aspects " :—" Occasionally in these psychographs the mentality of the medium or sitter will get in the way, with very curious results. Throughout all these phenomena, however, there is every indication that other influences are at work. These influences claim to be discarnate souls."

We now return to the vital point of **Recognition**. This is the real test of genuineness of Hope's mediumship and the reality of psychic photography. Barlow saw this long ago, and he says in " Evidential and Scientific Aspects " :—" One such case would be sufficient to establish the reality of psychic photography. This has occurred on scores of occasions," and goes on to say that if objectors saw the evidences of this recognition which have been sent to him, " the most hardened sceptic would be convinced of the reality of psychic photography by this evidence alone." Now he has the hardihood to allege that the percentage of certainly recognised " extras " is only small, " perhaps one in a thousand." This statement is so utterly false and untrue as to be farcical, and is in flat contradiction to his former statement and to the testimony of many hundreds of sitters. I have personally seen several recognitions obtained *in one afternoon*—some of people who lived and died abroad—under conditions making all fraud, deception or mistake impossible. I have seen events foreshadowed on the photo plates which duly came to pass. It is no exaggeration to say that many hundreds of such recognised " extras "—photos of the departed dead—have been obtained through William Hope's psychic powers, the sitters coming from every quarter of the globe.

We now turn to Barlow's charge that substitution of a plate is proved by the appearance of **"the double margin"** or " double rebate " seen on a few of Hope's negatives. He alleges that this is proof positive that Hope substituted plates. This is another falsehood, and this charge is not proven by him or his colleague.

Now, with reference to the instances of this double margin, let me first remark that they are few in number, and in any case do not touch *the hundreds of cases of recognised extras obtained on plates which do not show any trace of double margin*. This double margin in some cases is seen all round the plate when one image of the rebate has been displaced both vertically and horizontally with reference to the other image of the rebate. This gives a narrow double line all round, the lines of the two images interlocking. In the second class of cases the doubling occurs only at the top and bottom of the plate, the lines down each side being single. Here the displacement has only been vertical.

I have just examined 22 negatives bearing recognised extras taken in my vicarage by William Hope, not one of which shows any trace of this double margin.

In his " Evidential and Scientific Aspects," speaking of this double margin, which has sometimes been called " the psychic transparency," he bears this testimony :—" These particular markings can be seen over the negative obtained by Mr. Harry Price. I am convinced that the effect obtained on that occasion has a genuine psychic result. The possibility of this is freely admitted by Mr. Price."

That the effects on these occasional " double margin " negatives are genuine psychic results and not the result of any fraud on Hope's part. I am certain, from my own experience, and this I will now proceed to show.

In the first place, I have two of the long veil negatives, which Barlow alleges all show double margins, one showing a recognised extra of whom it was *impossible* for Hope to have any knowledge whatsoever, in which the veil extends in a *definite narrow stream*, from the mass of ectoplasmic light around the face of the extra situated above my head, down to a point exactly over my heart and there stops clearly and definitely, as though it were issuing from my heart. It would be *impossible* at a few minutes' notice to make and arrange a faked transparency or a prepared plate, on two occasions at long intervals, so that the end of the thin veil stream should issue exactly from my heart. On one occasion there was a group of five sitters moving about up to the last moment, which makes matters infinitely more difficult for the faker and more impossible of accomplishment.

Secondly, I have a set of three negatives taken immediately one after the other, showing the same recognised extra on each plate. On the first plate the face is much larger than on the other two, and looking to the right, and a long thin band of ectoplasm comes down to my heart. On the second plate the face is much smaller and looks to the left. On the third plate the extra is in a different position and again looking in a different direction—this time it is *joined by the spirit form of his fiancée*, both *recognised.* Now, the first plate shows the double margin at the ends (top and bottom), and *not* at the sides, but the second, taken a few seconds afterwards as quickly as the slide could be reversed, and the third taken a few minutes after that, shows not a trace of double margin, but does show the same man joined by his fiancée, *both as they were* 70 *years before,* and of whom Hope could by no possibility have any knowledge whatsoever. If a prepared plate and double margin was needed for the first picture of the man, how is it that one was not used for the second, and for the third picture when he was joined by his fiancée, who, according to Barlow's theory should have been honoured by an extra fine specially prepared double margined substituted plate. **These three negatives blow all Barlow's silly substitution theories sky-high,** and show that genuine psychic pictures *can* be got on a double margin negative. Now these accusers of William Hope allege that he made no attempt to refute their accusations. The charge was not publicly made against him until his body lay in the grave, but when at my Vicarage in October, four months before his death, he bitterly and indignantly denied these charges, but as touching the " double margin " he could only vehemently deny the accusation that it was the result of fraud on his part. He could not explain it, for the very good reason that he did not himself know how it was produced, or what caused it. When this base charge of fraud was made against an honest and wonderful man, as this phenomenon of the " double margin " was the most important item in the charge, I determined to investigate it. I found it to be a very pretty problem, but one which negatives taken at my vicarage by Mr. Hope, combined with much careful experimentation, have at last enabled me to solve in a manner which proves beyond a shadow of doubt that they are true psychic effects and *not* the result of fraud.

In the first place, as the result of a careful magnification and examination of very many of Hope's negatives, I find that in the majority of cases the psychic extra or image obtained, when there is also a sitter, is *in front of the sitter,* and in many cases is therefore *superimposed upon the image of the sitter.* This fact at once in these cases disposes of the previously prepared plate and the alleged substitution of the same.

Proceeding, it is well known that psychic extras can at times be obtained without the aid of a lens or camera, by holding the slide in the hands, or pressed to the forehead. I have two such negatives, one obtained by being held against my wife's forehead by Hope. The other held between her hands, backed by my hands, my daughter's, and finally Hope's hands outside.

In the first case I loaded and signed the plate *alone* in the darkroom and carried it into my dining room where, in broad daylight and under our critical gaze, Hope applied the slide to my wife's forehead for about half a minute. Then he handed the slide to me, and I took it and developed it, Hope not being present during loading or developing. This plate has a psychograph on it and shows a *single* image of the rebate.

Again, on September 3rd, 1931, I and my wife loaded the slide, she signing the plate. Hope did not enter the dark room, or carry the slide. In my dining room we held the slide between my wife's hands, backed by my hands, my daughter's, and finally Hope's hands outside the lot. On developing this plate myself in presence of Hope and my daughter, Hope not being allowed to *touch the plate or slide,* the words, " Press on, we love you," in the bold large writing of one Spirit Communicator, S——, appeared across the plate. His actual writing *Hope had never seen.* This negative shows the clear *single* rebate.

Another, obtained on August 3rd, 1930, plate loaded by myself and signed, Hope not allowed to touch it, either in loading or developing, bears the words, " My Song," in the writing of our Spirit Communicator, S——, which Hope had never seen and of whom he had never heard. On this occasion we all sat round the table with the plate placed in the centre. After a little while all saw a zig-zag flash of fire descend from the ceiling and strike the slide. On developing the plate, which was done by me, the words appeared across it. The remarkable and evidential thing about this, which makes any theory of fraud on Hope's part untenable, is the fact that our Spirit Communicator, S——, had been dictating a song in Italian to my wife and daughter for several weeks previous, a verse each week. This fact was entirely private, and it was impossible that Hope should have any knowledge of it. In addition to this, Hope had never seen S——'s actual writing. This negative bears a clear single edge, like the other two.

The slide in each case was not placed in the camera, nor was the plate exposed at all. These three cases are similar to the many on record which have been obtained by holding the slide between the hands, or upon the centre plates of sealed unopened packets held in the hands.

Sir Arthur Conan Doyle relates a very striking instance of this kind of result obtained on a plate held between the hands and through Hope's mediumship, which showed a brooch belonging to his sister, with her portrait in the centre, or which Hope could have no possible knowledge.

It is thus clearly established, both by my own experience and that of other observers that extras and psychic effects can be obtained on virgin plates which have never been normally exposed. I have also shown that the double margin effect may, and does, manifest itself entirely independently of the possibility of any fraud or deception on Hope's part. What, therefore, is the explanation of this phenomenon? In order to carry this investigation further I obtained a quarter plate Lancaster Instantograph camera exactly similar in size and construction to the ¼-plate Lancaster Instantograph used by William Hope for the last 27 years, and I commenced a series of experiments with a view to solving the mystery. I found that these small quarter-plate slides when loaded with glass plates of a suitable thickness (plates and divisional cards vary in thickness) on some occasions the slides gripped the plates just enough to prevent them moving about inside the slide as the result of ordinary carrying from dark room to camera, but on the slide being placed vertically in the camera and given a slight jerk or shock, such as is caused by closing the shutter of the slide with a jerk, the carefully marked plate would in some cases drop vertically nearly 1/16 inch, in other cases not only drop vertically, but start aside horizontally to nearly the same extent.

This fact, which I have proved and tested many times by actual experiment, at once gave the clue to the mystery. What happens is this :—The exposure being made on the sitters impresses the image of the sitters and one image of the rebate upon the plate. Now sometimes the image of the extra is impressed after the shutter has been closed, thus giving another and second image of the rebate. (That this can happen and an image be impressed in a closed slide is proved by the cases cited.) When this happens to coincide with those comparatively rare cases in which the plates have been gripped slightly in the slide and so held up, the closing of the shutter with a jerk has caused the plate to drop vertically, or to start aside horizontally in the slide. The result is that the impression of the extra causes another image of the rebate either at the ends if the movement has been vertical only, or at ends and sides if vertical and horizontal, and thus a double margin is formed.

In the great majority of cases, however, no trace of double margin is to be seen, the image of the rebate being single, clear, and distinct, all round the plate, the images of sitter and extra being formed in immediate succession.

12

In these cases (the vast majority) the plate has simply lain normally in the slide after being inserted in the camera and has not moved when the images of either extra or sitter were imprinted. The imprinting of the extra would seem in the majority of cases to be made towards the end of the exposure (or in double margin cases, before the slide is withdrawn from the camera), as is it frequently superimposed on that of the sitter. It will therefore be seen that **the phenomena are due to natural and spiritual processes and are not the product of fraud.** The evidence of results obtained beyond the possibility of Hope's knowledge are abundantly sufficient to triumphantly clear Hope from any such charge. On many occasions we have been told in the privacy of our home circle by our spirit Communicator, S—— and others, that when Hope next came to us or if I would go to meet him at a certain place, he would come upon the plate. The information has always carefully been withheld from Hope, but S—— has never once failed to make his appearance on the plate, and often *in a different pose* to previous occasions.

On another occasion, another gentleman, B——, whom we never knew in his mortal life, manifested at the same time as S——, and said he wished to come. I asked him not to come. He made no reply to this. No word of this was conveyed to Hope, but on sitting with him ten days afterwards a woman appeared with S—— on the plate whom B—— informed us was his first wife, giving also the cause of her death and the street in which her surviving sister resided. We had never heard of such a person, but on investigating in the South of England, found the sister, who confirmed all the details given, recognised the extra of the woman, confirmed it by a gathering of her family, and afterwards sent me the proof in a large photo of her sister, taken abroad, differing slightly in pose, but identical with the extra shown on our plate!! On this occasion I loaded the slide myself from a new and previously unopened box of plates purchased only half an hour before. I signed the plate, carried the slide to and from the camera, and developed and fixed the plate myself, Hope merely making the exposure in broad daylight and never being allowed to touch the plate, or put his hands over it in the darkroom. In this and many other instances Hope could, by no conceivable means, have any knowledge or information which would enable him to produce the result fraudulently and they, together with the many hundreds of recognised extras obtained through his mediumship, triumphantly vindicate his powers to all reasonable and honest-minded men. I knew Hope intimately for 15 years, during the whole of which time I found him to be an upright, God-fearing, honourable and transparently honest man, and I count it an honour to have known him and to have received him into my house. He had God-given powers which rank him as the equivalent of one of the great prophets of old time, nay, caused him to exceed them, in his powers of demonstrating the Spirit World, human survival, and " the life of the world to come."

The more his work is examined the more it will be treasured and its surpassing value realised.

Hope's reputation stands firmly established and the base calumnies of his detractors will have no more effect on his good name than the splashings of filthy water have upon a granite rock.

NOTE.—The image of the extra imprinted within the closed slide is formed by psychic light shining, or operating, in the space between the closed shutter and the plate; and not by the said light passing through the closed shutter.

Appendix 8

F.W.WARRICK'S RESPONSE TO THE BARLOW-ROSE 'EXPOSURE'

Light, 9th June 1933 and Experiments in Psychics 1939

In Light, 9th June 1933 Mr Warrick wrote at length on the Barlow - Rose Exposure of William Hope, and in response Mrs Ada Deane wrote to him about her concerns over Mr Barlow's reversal of the acceptance of the sittings she had had with him 12 years before.

He writes:

"However much we may differ from the conclusion drawn by Mr. Barlow concerning the late William Hope (and if he lives to see his error I am sure he will deeply regret his judgment) we must all be grateful to him for his contribution to the knowledge of psychic photography. ...

That any psychic photographs are genuine is most difficult of belief and only those who are, as experimenters, familiar with psychic phenomena can believe – yea know, as scientists know facts, that some at least are genuinely produced. The proofs of the supernormality of "extras", contained in the conditions under which they have appeared, among others the photographs of the Rev. C.H. Spurgeon and the late Sir Arthur Conan Doyle obtained by Dr. Glen Hamilton, the recognitions (the Cushman photo) would suffice in other branches of science but the human element and the possibility of fraud and semblance of it in other "extras" blind those without sufficient experience of the possibilities of psychics to the evidence which would otherwise jump to their eyes. ...

With the assistance of my friend Mr. F. McC. Stephenson, 440 of my own marked plates treated by the Crewe Circle either by camera or for skotographs. A large majority of these plates were sent to me in London to be developed and were developed in my premises by a professional photographer. A new fact to which I attach great importance is that several of these plates, which were certainly not touched by anyone at Crewe (one of them had not left my slide, had been used in my own camera and had not been in the dark-room at Crewe) bear a mass of finger marks and other marks of a brown colour as if put on by a stiff brush on the surface of the sensitive side of the plates. It is curious that on one occasion, while Mrs. Buxton (the Crewe Circle had not been informed of these marks) was holding a wrapped-up plate to her forehead, she said: "I seem to feel something like brushes working." The lines (a great quantity) on one of these plates are decidedly not finger marks and give so clear an impression of a curious complicated humorous design that a commercial artist had no difficulty in representing the humour of it. ...

These and thousands of other facts reported in psychic literature testify to the presence at psychic happenings of an invisible intelligent power.

Sir Oliver Lodge writes: "My testimony and that of others; to the reality of the spiritual world is based upon direct experience of fact, and not upon theory. Test the facts by whatever way you choose, they can only be accounted for by the interaction of intelligences other than our own."...

To sum up: I maintain that fraud could not cover a hundredth part of the phenomena of psychic photography.

* * * * *

Mrs Deane's letter to Mr Warrick. He writes:

"In October, 1920, Mr. Barlow arranged that Mrs. Deane and one of her daughters should pay him a visit for two days at his home in Birmingham for test sittings for photographic Extras. How satisfied Mr. Barlow was with the results of these experiments can be learnt from a perusal of the account he contributed to Coates' *Photographing the Invisible* (second edition pp. 254-259) where the large Extra obtained is illustrated.

On this occasion he obtained what he then considered (*The Case for Spirit Photography*, p. 8|) to be an excellent Extra of his own father. Mr. Barlow now thinks he was mistaken. How many chances are there in a million that firstly any face so like his own father should appear of all those possible, and secondly on a plate provided by Mr. Barlow, and thirdly in his own home?"

Concerning this visit to Mr. Barlow, Mrs. Deane wrote to Warrick on July 21st, 1933:

" Dear Mr. Warrick—In accordance with your request I am putting in the form of a letter a short account of the visit I paid to Mr. Fred Barlow with one of my children in October, 1920, when I stayed at his house two days. Mr. Barlow had invited me in order that he might investigate my production of supernormal photographs. At that date I had been taking photographs for three months only and knew little of photography. Before July, 1920, 1 had taken one or two photographs only by means of a camera I bought for 9d. It was a sorry day for me when I discovered this photographic power. My life has lost all its ease and serenity. Before that I was respected and happy in my work, though poor; and to-day I am poor and look back on twelve years of worry and trouble and am a cock-shy for any newspaper "penny-a-liner". I cannot understand Mr. Barlow saying now that every Extra face which has appeared on plates used by me has been put there by me fraudulently. In those days I was unsuspicious and not resentful of enquiry nor fearful of accusations. I had no knowledge then of the length the sceptic will go in his treatment of an unfortunate medium, as I am called. I put no obstacle in Mr. Barlow's way but was willing to accommodate myself to his every wish.

Mr. Barlow knows that during this visit he frequently used his own camera and his own plates which had not been in my keeping nor handled by me at all, doing the developing himself, and that he was perfectly satisfied with the genuineness of the Extras which appeared on his own plates. These experiments should be sufficient to convince anyone that it was impossible for me to have produced the effects by trickery. In addition, however, I would call your particular attention to the following incident which Mr. Barlow published and no one can explain away. Mr. Barlow said he would like to have a group photograph of himself and his wife with myself and daughter before we left. He had a half-plate camera (I possessed no half-plate camera. slide or plate) and a half-plate and without any thought of an Extra but simply to obtain a souvenir group photograph, Mr. Barlow took a photograph of the four of us by means of his half-plate camera, making the exposure himself from his seat by means of a thread. Two large Extras appeared upon this plate, one above me which I recognised as my guide[1]. Now it is a curious fact, and Mr. Barlow has published it, that I strongly pressed upon Mr. Barlow to allow me to be seated otherwise than he had placed me, but Mr. Barlow would not permit the change; yet my guide came above me in the picture. Surely this half-plate picture, taken on the spur of the moment and in Mr. Barlow's own house, cannot be questioned.

Once again, Mr. Warrick, I assure you I have never consciously deceived sitters;

I admit that many of the results obtained through me (in a way I have not the least inkling of) have every appearance of having been produced by trickery but I do no more understand how or why than you do.

I forgot to mention that one of the Extras which came during this visit was recognised by Mr. Barlow as his father. This Extra was shown to Mr. Barlow's young son who was asked whether he recognised the face. The child did recognise it without the least hesitation as that of his grandfather who had died.

Yours truly, (Signed) A. E. Deane."

"None who remember the tests to which she (Mrs. Deane) has submitted in her short Career — the tests in the College of Psychic Science by noted photographers, tests made by Mr. Fred Barlow in his own home; the

---

1. See this photograph on page281 and overleaf

photograph of Barlow's father; the Knight and Cushman photographs, — can for a moment doubt the genuineness of her mediumship. No photographer can tell how these photographs are produced, and yet they come."

(James Coates, Light, 1924, p. 771.)

A reproduction of the group photograph alluded to in Mrs. Deane's letter is to be seen on p. 259 of Coates' *Photographing the Invisible* (2nd edition)[2] and this is what Mr. Barlow wrote thereon : "This is a beautiful psychic picture and wonderful evidence. In this instance no séance was held immediately before the photograph was taken and the whole of the procedure only occupied a few minutes. It was taken on my own suggestion and, as already mentioned, only my apparatus was used and the whole of the operations (as regards the normal part of the picture) was carried out entirely by myself. Even had deception been attempted it could not possibly have succeeded, and the result itself rules out trickery."

F.W. Warrick

Group photograph alluded to opposite and above.

Vi's (daughter) guide also appeared on another occasion.
Copy from Tom Patterson's book

---

2. See here and p283

Appendix 9

SPIRIT PHOTOGRAPHY FROM THE OTHER SIDE

Light, May 7th 1921

Given by Edgar Baynes through the [trance] mediumship of Miss Violet Burton at the Stead Bureau.

"You do not take enough conscious thought of us. You know when there is any medium who is good at photography, all the boys here know it, and there is no room where you are taking pictures that is not full of us.

When I went to be photographed with Mother, I was very lucky because I had made friends with the medium's great Guide. Mr. Hope's Indian guide is very advanced, and he told me that if I wanted to get my face right on the plate, to be there very early to magnetise the little greenhouse where the photographs are taken. Some of the chaps who had helped me to build a hospital came to help and I made them promise not to try and get on the plate, too. It was very difficult. There is one of the plates where I do not appear at all, and that is the one I was most sure of. I remembered myself just as I was in the South African War. And I thought it would have been very good, but I do not come out at all. I find it was the fault of Mr. Hope and the lady who helps him. Mother was in the exact sequence, but he should have had incense to burn to clear the atmosphere.

When we are going to be photographed we materialise in thought. We remember what we were like on earth, and we concentrate with all our minds on this thought picture. As I was I thinking of what I looked like I saw part of your atmosphere had been projected round me, and that isolates us who wish to appear from other spirits who may be there. It protects the thought form you have made of yourself from being broken up by others. Thought is the one great power by which you can make yourself sufficiently material to be received or impressed on a sensitive plate, but you have no power of keeping out other spirits, if they choose to come. But if those who are taking the photograph will do something like this – keep the room well aired, make magnetic passes all-round the camera, then have something burnt that would make a special atmosphere (such as 'dead' flowers). Then make those who are going to sit concentrate on the positive love they bear to those they want to appear on the photograph. Thoughts of love are emanations of force, and Mr. Hope gets help from the thoughts of those who are present, and that, added to the thought force of those wanting to be photographed, nearly always produces a great success. We, in Spirit life, need to keep our psychic self together by concentrated thought.

If we want to show ourselves, and we do love to come on the plate, and you had a room given up to this, and were to say a prayer of love for all the world in it, and then a prayer for Divine power, opportunity would be given, to us. Pray to God to let your boy come, and then remind the boy, strongly, of the fact that you love him and want him to come. Then you would have a firm, strong feeling in your mind of your son, he would be trying hard to remember what he looked like when you saw him last, and then you would get a good result. The love you are giving out is the same force as the material we are trying to use, and you give us added power."

Appendix 10

WILLIAM CROOKE EXPLAINS HOW SPIRIT PHOTOGRAPHS ARE PRODUCED.
(with reference to screen marks),

The Two Worlds, April 16th 1937

Mr. W.J. West, who is certainly an authority on photography, and has given much time to experiments in psychic photography, revealed to an interested audience at Sheffield some interesting communications on the subject which he has received from William Crooke.

Mr. West said: "Through the mediumship of Mrs. Perriman on July 28th, 1932, I was conversing with the late William Crooke, Photographer Royal, of Edinburgh. I knew Crooke well, and here I thought is an excellent opportunity to obtain some reliable and perhaps technical information from a man who had passed on, and who, though sceptical of psychical phenomena, was an expert in normal photography. He had reached the top of his profession and had by command, photographed all the crowned heads in Europe.

I said to him, "Now you have passed from darkness into the light, have you been able to ascertain how the 'spirit-photographs' I have shown you from time to time are produced?"

His reply was: "Well, West, you may rule out one fact. The psychic image is in no way an objective one to be seen by the camera lens. The camera has nothing to do with the result. Nevertheless, a lens is used in a similar manner to the crystalline lens in the human eye-which permits the image to be focussed on the retina, which is that portion of the eye directly concerned in the translation of the undulations of light-waves into what you call, or know as, vision.

"We, in the spirit-world, in our demonstrations to the people of earth, assemble where suitable conditions are to be found for experiment. The medium is impressed as to how we desire the plate handled for the purpose of magnetising it, to make it sensitive to the cosmic rays *necessary* to obtain the desired result, and which are used *immediately before development.*

"Let us assume a seance is to be held and a manifestation is to take place. We select the person, object, manuscript or message that is to be produced, and our operator, looking intently at the object, transfers it *by reflection* through 'waves of impression' to the photographic plate, which has been made supersensitive in parts by our own chemists and subject to chemical action. In a similar manner the artist looks at his subject and projects it on to his canvas through his own optic lenses, but develops it with his brushes and colours.

"I now am a spirit-artist, and can look at your brother, or any of the controls about me, and 'throw' their image on to the photographic plate. This image would appear if developed *within a certain time.* I say this because these 'waves of impression' *do not affect the sensitive plate for an indefinite period.* Bear this in mind. If I find you require further evidence I will, with permission, come to you again."

West comments: The above, to me, was a most wonderful piece of evidence. It was something Doyle, Professor Coates and myself had been waiting years for. It was the more remarkable knowing the imperious and autocratic type of man Crooke was—and to think that he should be sent to explain."

Three months after through the same medium, and again by "direct voice", *Professor Henry Sidgwick* replied as follows to a similar question:

"You must understand that we, working under instructions from the more advanced 'spheres of spirit,' do not rely upon or require chemical aid, as you understand it. "Given the right instrument we are able to utilise rays, vibrations and gaseous matter unknown to you on the earth plane. These, mixed with the material conditions you provide, enable us to manifest in this way. It is difficult to explain more intelligently to you, as it cannot be put into language that you would understand. We use astral conditions in conjunction with your own."

West adds these comments: Among Hope's results, as well as some by John Myers, microscopic examination revealed what is known in the lithographic world as "screen markings" on the faces of some "extras." They had the same appearance as if they had been reproduced from "process blocks" and were the source of considerable controversy.

These markings lent colour to the inference that the results had been produced by fraudulent means, and that the photographs were obvious copies from "news cuttings" or prints in connection with which "blocks" had been used, and that they had been superimposed on the normal photograph by double exposure. Under the most severe test conditions this was proven "not to be the case," and we were left in ignorance as to their appearance until Doyle came to our assistance and brought Crooke with him at another "direct-voice" seance at West Hampstead, October 10th, 1932.

Doyle introduced the visitor who said:

"Good evening! It's Crooke. I am pleased to be able to speak to you, and I want you to mention this matter. Get it into the papers, as my opinion as regards photography is of interest to the world at general. Tell them from me, in respect to this screen business, that the screen is extra to whatever the operator throws on the plate and is part of the process. As the ectoplasm comes away you get a thin film left by the plasma *for a time* over the faces of the 'extras,' *not over the sitters*, and if developed before the process is complete you get this protective screen effect. I defy any photographer living to prove with the aid of the microscope that this screen effect that this is the work of block artists. It can be very easily explained away if they will only use a little common sense.

"The greatest trouble possible is centred around those who think they know everything about photography. They don't. When you get the dots and lines through ectoplasm the screen effect on the plate is as though it were projected like wireless in television, and is accomplished with the aid of the ether we get through the medium.

"If you had no medium, you would have no picture—-in the same way as you would have no milk without a cow, milk bottle and a milkman.

The medium must be present or your results would be absolutely nil. I have already explained to West that the camera has nothing to do with it. I am just in my element in putting such things right, but don't forget it is quite impossible to do these things without the contact of a medium. And now William Crooke wishes you good night!"

Through the mediumship of Miss Geraldine Cummins, in January, 1934, that distinguished scholar, F. W. H. Myers, further confirmed the foregoing by automatic writing to the Editor of *Psychic News*.

He said, "Now I perceive that the stranger is interested in photography." Then he wrote: "May I explain that when a discarnate being endeavours to communicate his likeness it is the image of his etheric body that is impressed on the ectoplasm which exudes from the medium: But in certain cases the discarnate being will endeavour to convey the old likeness of himself when he was on earth, *by means of direct thought.*"

You will have now perceived that veridical confirmation has been forthcoming from our unseen friends as to the method adopted by them in the production of psychic photographs and that such method seems incontestable by the similitude of the disclosures, the difference in time between the dates on which they were uttered, and the varying types of mediumship utilised to convey what must be to the scientific researcher valuable information. We are grateful for the knowledge acquired so far but we have still much to learn."

* * * * *

An added comment on the subject is this excerpt from *Miracles in Modern Life.*

MR HOPE'S PSYCHIC PHOTOGRPAHY.

"Note.- With regard to the charge of faked psychic photographs so frequently put forward the following statement made to me by Mr. McCully of Glasgow is interesting.

Mr. Hope had been in Glasgow .and had taken many psychic photographs to the satisfaction of the sitters. Mr. Peter Galloway, at that time President of the Glasgow Association of Spiritualists, showed these photographs to Mr. McCully and asked his opinion of them. Mr. McCully who, from his profession, has a special knowledge of photographs examined them and answered that he was satisfied with the photographs as being psychic photographs with one exception. One of the photographs had a streaked appearance, and he thought it might have been taken from some illustration. Mr. Galloway was considerably distressed, for to cast suspicion on one photograph was to cast suspicion on all. Meanwhile Mr. Galloway passed into the unseen world and remarkable psychic photographs were taken at his grave.

Some time afterwards Mr. McCully took a series of psychic photographs, through the help of a medium, at a gentleman's house near Glasgow. To his astonishment one of his psychic photographs had the same streaky appearance as the photograph he had formerly objected to in Mr. Hope's collection. But in this case Mr. McCully himself was the photographer, and the photograph was undoubtedly a psychic photograph.

The sequel is significant enough. That very night a séance was being held in Glasgow, and Mr. Galloway got through this message:

"To-day, I have given McCully something to think about!"

(*"Miracles in Modern Life"* by Rev. J. Lamond)

Appendix 11

Light, May 12th 1933 – by automatic writing from W.T. Stead.

"As so much is being written about Psychic Photography just now," writes Miss E.W. Stead, *"it may interest your readers to have the impressions and explanations of one who is viewing it from the "Other Side". The enclosed description of what happens was given by my father (W.T. Stead) in writing through the Mrs Hester Dowden. It is taken from a chapter on Psychic Photography to be included in a new book of messages given by him. This book is a sequel to "The Blue Island" which will, I hope, be published within the next few months."*

"Psychic photography is a most important branch of mediumship, more. important than clairvoyance, although clairvoyance is linked up very closely with it. In the chapter on Clairvoyance I have tried to explain what seeing with the Inward Eye is. The Psychic Photographer has to use this as much and even more than the clairvoyant for he has to see the image, in most cases unconsciously, and further to impress that image on the ectoplasm with the help of the control.

I wish to interpolate the remark that the existence of the Inward Eye has been doubted. None but the Easterns recognise its power. We from our side know that, seated deep in the personality of every living human being there is a third eye that knows, but that cannot be used except under certain circumstances and by certain persons. This third eye, the Eye of the Soul, is the vehicle by which all knowledge travels from us to you—and by the Eye I mean the mirror that reflects the unknown.

I will try to explain what happens in Psychic Photography as I see it from my side. It is a much more subtle matter than materialisation. It is supremely difficult to make a good psychic photograph. I have said that the Medium must see with the Inward Eye, although unconsciously. The psychic photographer imagines himself in a normal condition, but the fact is he is in very much the same condition as the automatic writer. He cannot use his inward eye well because images from the normal sight blur his vision.

The many so-called failures in Psychic Photography can be explained in different ways, but roughly speaking they come under three headings:

1. Photographs due to the fact that another sitter has left a strong emotional impression behind;

2. Photographs of spirits who are anxious to use the Medium, who have pressed in without invitation;

3. Photographs which are connected with the Medium himself friends or relatives, who are possibly nearer to the earth than the desired communicator and can show themselves more easily.

I want you to understand that there are different forms of psychic photography. You must not imagine that all are produced by the same process. In some cases where the communicator is accustomed to sittings, and not depressed by the earth atmosphere, he himself is the operator. But in the majority of cases he cannot act himself and the Medium's control must act for him: that is, he must collect the ectoplasm and with it produce a portrait of the communicator. It is a most difficult task.

Imagine a fluid gelatinous mass which is alive, and which must be moulded into shape to form the likeness of a spirit not in its own atmosphere whose shape seems vapoury and transparent. It is almost as impossible as moulding a portrait from flowing water, although ectoplasm as it appears in photographic Mediums has more of the substance of thick cream than water, thick cream possessed of so much vitality that it is an ever-moving mass.

If the communicator operates, the portrait is produced by him in this way. He must press his face into this substance, and when that is done you almost invariably get the impression of a mask. You must understand that when this living mass is floating on the atmosphere, being supersensitive, it may catch up the thought of the Medium or sitter, and then the control who has to handled it can no longer mould the portrait, because thought, being a living thing and entering the living ectoplasm, has left its impress there, and the control cannot impress his idea on it. A psychic portrait is the expression of an idea. Without the vision of the face of the communicator, the control could not do his work. It is the impression of his subject that is photographed, not the communicator's face as others may see it.

You will perhaps improve matters as time goes on with regard to this subject, but you never can be sure of your result. I have no hesitation in saying that it is the most difficult form of mediumship. In all other cases the guide can act as control, but here the very fragile nature of the material he has to handle makes his results very uncertain.

For Psychic Photography, as it is produced when a mass-thought influences, as in the Cenotaph photographs nothing is accomplished by the communicators. The pictures are all executed by controls on our side. These are sent specially on such occasions, well equipped for their work. They have an easier task than the control who is working for an individual portrait, for thought being concentrated from thousands of minds it is easy to record it.

You must not call these portraits "moulds". There is an idea that our controls make masks as a sculptor would and press these into the ectoplasm. "Mould" is not the word. The control has the idea of the face in his mind. He has let this idea sink into himself so that he can reproduce it in the ectoplasm without a sitter on our side. All the Cenotaph portraits are the ideas the controls have formed of individual faces.

This will go far to prove that psychic photographs are never portraits of the actual face of a discarnate human being. They are photographs of a thought in the control's mind, or they can be impressions of the actual faces passed through a sheet of ectoplasm which gives them the appearance of masks.

Mediums for Psychic Photography emit ectoplasm, not in rolling clouds as for materialisation, but as a thin grey mist which varies in character in the same Medium from day to day. On one occasion he or she may send it out in large masses, while at other times it puffs itself out. Little clouds of it lie about the room. It is unevenly distributed. This explains the difficulty, or one of the many difficulties that lie in the path of the control who must shape his portraits from it. If the Medium does not give out the material generously, the control may have to collect it from different parts of the room, and the exposure may be over before his work is half done and then the result is a failure."   W.T. STEAD.

W.T. Stead
(illustration from the cover of
'Communication with the Next World' - 1937 ed.)

Milton Keynes UK
Ingram Content Group UK Ltd.
UKHW021424210923
429112UK00013B/706